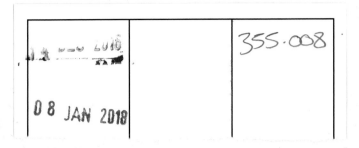

ONE OF THE BOYS

Homosexuality in the Military during World War II

PAUL JACKSON

Second Edition

McGill-Queen's University Press

Montreal & Kingston · London · Ithaca

© McGill-Queen's University Press 2010
ISBN 978-0-7735-3714-9

Legal deposit first quarter 2010
Bibliothèque nationale du Québec

Printed in Canada on acid-free paper that is 100% ancient
forest free (100% post-consumer recycled), processed chlorine free.
First edition published 2004

This book was first published with the help of a grant from the Canadian
Federation for the Humanities and Social Sciences, through the Aid to Scholarly
Publications Programme, using funds provided by the Social Sciences and
Humanities Research Council of Canada.

McGill-Queen's University Press acknowledges the support of the Canada
Council for the Arts for our publishing program. We also acknowledge the
financial support of the Government of Canada through the Book Publishing
Industry Development Program (BPIDP) for our publishing activities.

National Library of Canada Cataloguing in Publication

Jackson, Paul, 1955-
    One of the boys : homosexuality in the military during World War II /
    Paul Jackson. 2 ed.

    Includes bibliographical references and index.
    ISBN 978-0-7735-3714-9

    1. Canada – Armed Forces – History – World War, 1939-1945. 2. Canada –
    Armed Forces – Gays – History – 20th century. 3. Canada – Armed Forces –
    Gays – Government policy – History – 20th century. 4. Gay men – Canada –
    History – 20th century. I. Title.

D768.15.J32 2010   355'.086'64097109044   C2004-902206-7

This book was typeset by Dynagram inc. in 10/13 Sabon.

Dedicated to my parents,
Norm and Joan Jackson

CONTENTS

ACKNOWLEDGMENTS

The following bodies provided financial assistance for this work: School of Graduate Studies, Queen's University; the Social Sciences and Humanities Research Council of Canada; and the Ministry of Training, Colleges and Universities of Ontario. I also relied on loans and gifts from my parents, Norm and Joan Jackson, my sister Lynda Jackson Kennedy, and Rick Hirtle. I am forever thankful for their kindness and support.

At the National Archives, Paul Marsden and Andrew Horrall made the work possible by helping to find lost microfilm reels and then making them available to me as conveniently as possible. I was fortunate to work with Alena Dufault, unfailingly efficient, helpful and intelligent, at the Access to Information and Privacy Department. Also, I warmly thank all of the veterans who took time to help me understand their war. Those experiences were enriching both academically and personally.

I was fortunate to have Karen Dubinsky and Allan English as co-supervisors of the doctoral thesis upon which this book is based. Both influenced the final text by asking tough questions of the work in progress from their distinct fields of expertise and then patiently waiting as I muddled my way to answers. The thesis then benefited from the insights of Jeff Keshen, Marc Epprecht, Elsbeth Heaman, and Sarah Hill. Eric Darier looked over the revised manuscript before Judith Turnbull edited it, with real insight, for McGill-Queen's University Press. Steven Maynard introduced me to the works of Grant Macdonald at the Marine Museum of the Great Lakes. I'm grateful. Finally, Joan McGilvray offered uncommon insights in helping to get my preface to this edition to print. It's always humbling and helpful to find out that your editor knows what you're trying to say better than you do.

PREFACE TO THE
SECOND EDITION

I spent five years at the turn of this century researching and writing *One of the Boys,* a history of homosexuality in the Canadian military during the Second World War. Library and Archives Canada in Ottawa (at that time the National Archives and referred to in the notes as NA) houses the majority of the records upon which I relied. Of equal importance were dozens of interviews, often open-ended conversations that lasted for years, with veterans of the war. In this preface, I want to reflect upon the significance of this work in light of events that have overtaken the world since 11 September 2001. I will discuss how my interactions with NA personnel may be understood in terms of continuities and discontinuities in the history of sexuality and then consider how sexuality and gender are central to the promotion of Canada's current war in Afghanistan in ways that are continuous with the Second World War. For instance, the simplistic heterocentric world imagined by promoters of the war such as Don Cherry masks layers of unknowns that should call into question the war in Afghanistan as well as Canada's fundamental orientation in the world. Conscientious Canadians need to reconsider their relationship with figures and symbols of authority.

In looking at the relationship Canadians have with authority, the most immediate example is Canada's place in the American empire.[1] Increasingly, as historian Chalmers Johnson demonstrates, that empire relies on military force to assert control over resistant populations.[2] Spending more on the military than all other countries combined, as America does, is logical if the goal is to remain outside what has historically been identified as "the balance of power." Some critics of Canada's war in Afghanistan, such as Janice Gross Stein and Eugene Lang, have argued against this policy on the grounds that the Canadian Forces (CF) could be deployed more advantageously in other conflicts in ways that complement American needs.[3] That strategy would leave the United States free to concentrate on the big prizes, like the oil fields of central Asia, allotting Canada the role of a proxy state, subduing local resistant populations, with Haiti serving as a recent model. Canadians and Americans uneasy with that scenario have questioned the idea of the American empire from a number of perspectives – humanitarian, environmental, ecological, ideological, and economic, to name a few.[4] Critics who reject the idea that Canada's appropriate entry point into world affairs is as part of the American empire must trade the comfort of subservience to unaccountable power for the challenge of imagining and implementing alternative models. Meeting the challenge is not going to be easy; fortunately many people have contributed new visions of global politics and economics.[5]

These reflections are particularly relevant for people who feel frustrated and helpless in the face of power that is hidden from view.[6] How does one act morally when it is unclear who is determining the overall strategy and for what purpose? How might decent people transcend the daily compromises that keep them bound to the interests of reclusive, unethical powers? In the introduction to the first edition, I comment on the possibilities created by the attacks of 9/11. A vein had been opened in the centre of the empire and a vast majority wanted it sutured quickly. Now, as increasing numbers reject "the war on terror" as a permanent feature of life, as Afghan and Iraqi peoples confront fundamentalist oppressors, local warlords, and their imperial sponsors, others question the cogency of the official conspiracy theory regarding the 9/11 terrorist attacks, proposed by the American administration and supported by the mainstream media. In this preface, I want to look at how my experiences researching sexuality and gender in Canadian history provide insights into Canada's entry into the "global war on terror."

Back in 1998, the first few months of research for this book were not promising. As there was no mention of homosexuality in any of the finding aids for Military Record Group 24, there was little to do but survey files dealing with Medical Services, policing, and administration in the hope that some research methodology would suggest itself. The Army's Routine Orders periodically listed a serviceman convicted of "conduct to the prejudice of good order and military discipline" or an officer charged with "scandalous behaviour unbecoming an officer." Curiously, those charges sometimes omitted the particulars: they left unstated the conduct or behaviour that was prejudicial and unbecoming. At D-History at the Department of National Defence (DND), I found the naval equivalent of these charges in a ledger that listed the particulars in a big round hand and left no doubt that these courts referred to homosexual incidents. I also found the Army and Naval Service Acts that described these moral (sexual) offences. At the same time, a veteran described to me his own experience on a court-martial board. After several months, a methodology was becoming apparent: I would access the courts to determine who was charged, why they had been charged, and what, precisely, was considered so scandalous and prejudicial about their behaviour ... But it wasn't that easy.[7]

The morality that grounded these offences had been successfully challenged since the Second World War. In a historical moment of lucidity in the mid-1960s, a number of homosexual people refused to accept the notion that they were immoral or perverted. They decided to claim and proclaim their distinctness. Thus the ethics of gay liberation was established. However, we need to understand the ethics of discretion that was being displaced. Before the gay liberation movement, it was the moral obligation of homosexual people to be discreet. As the court-martial and police records make clear, allowing your homosexuality to be known could expose all those within your social circle to potential ruin. Discretion was not necessarily motivated by crass self-preservation; it was also a matter of social conscience. With gay liberation, the logic was reversed; now everyone needed to expose themselves voluntarily in order that the greatest number might be protected. Such actions could never stop discrimination but they could change the form discrimination would take. A minority would now be able to openly protect itself. Both ethical models are based on solidarity – everyone must be either in or out of the closet. The documents that I needed to access were created within the regime that made the closet an ethical necessity. I was intending to bring them out of the dark corners of the archival closets in order to make them serve the new ethical order. Merely doing this research challenged the system under which they had been created and archived. So looking at how the documents became available for analysis is as much a part of history as the analysis of the documents.[8]

The documents in which I had immersed myself – personnel files, courts martial, police records – supplemented by the oral histories I was generating outside the archives suggested to me that actual military service was unlike the impression of it left by public and official histories. There exists a whiggish assumption that the level of discrimination acknowledged in the present must have been greater in the past. And it was certainly devastating for those whose exposure served to reinforce the invisible walls of patriarchy. But you can see through an invisible wall if you open your eyes, and many people were living with their eyes opened. A perverse game was afoot in which everyone was expected to acknowledge the possibility of homosexuality but deny its existence. The police and psychiatrists were solicited to prove that homosexuality existed but, paradoxically, their work had the effect of making it invisible: they accused, you denied. By exposing homosexuality, the authorities made it disappear. What was surprising in my research was the number of people who understood the game and protected the victims.

The more immersed I became in the documents, the more I came to empathize with the victims of both official and unofficial policing. The veterans I was interviewing made me aware of the effects of persecution, allowing me to see the archival sources in another dimension. Exposure during that period could have devastating consequences that could last a lifetime. Many of those veterans wanted me to expose the system while protecting their identities. Their attitude reflected the fact that they straddled the two opposing ethics governing homosexuality: the closet versus disclosure. If the state had been the source of the greatest intimidation during the war, what would happen to a little historian more than half a century later in the NA? How would the national and DND archives respond to the challenge of a researcher interested in the regulation of homosexuality in the military? Was there anyone left to protect the image? What strategies might be deployed?

I was finding in my research that the significance of homosexuality varied according to the context. Among the ranks, as servicemen became valuable comrades within platoons, squadrons, and crews, their homosexuality was increasingly accepted, overlooked, or ignored, as long as they remained discreet. Meanwhile, the institution increasingly tried to purge itself of homosexuality through policies, regulations, and policing. It occurred to me that that those who created the official and public histories had continued that work throughout the Cold War. In fact, they had succeeded where the military had failed, clearing history of homosexuality much more effectively than psychiatrists and police had cleared the actual wartime forces. And so, while I was becoming used to records that demonstrated a quiet complicity in the actual, inevitable existence of deviance in the conscripted wartime forces, I was increasingly out of step with the written history. The more the records spoke to me, the less most military and nationalist historians wanted to hear about it. This development was predictable, but did not make the experience any more enjoyable. The records that I was opening up were wounds that had never healed over: not for the individuals, not for society, and not for me. The records and interviews suggested to me that intimidation was the most powerful tactic employed by the regulators to maintain hetero-centric hegemony. A number of people made common cause with the police in combating sexual deviance. People were frightened of the consequences of exposure: public humiliation, social ostracism, and financial ruin. So when had society changed so much that my work was now being welcomed in military and archival circles?[9] Well, it hadn't.[10]

When I had finally put together a list of references to courts martial that had clearly been based on homosexual offences, I presented it to an Access to Information and Privacy (ATIP) officer with a request to see the proceedings of the courts to which they referred. He, an adept of military history, perused my list with an air of authority and handed it back to me. "Court martial records are closed," he said curtly, definitively, and – perhaps my projection – delightedly. I did not know at the time that he was simply wrong. I don't know if he did. Given the months that I had spent searching for things that did not want to be found, I was thoroughly disheartened. I might have simply given up. Instead, I submitted a formal request, which in archival language means that you intend to be taken seriously. With the intervention of the information commissioner, and after more than a year's wait, the NA, DND, and ATIP discovered and made available almost four hundred unindexed microfilm reels of WWII courts martial.[11]

One afternoon in the NA cafeteria, at the table next to mine, an employee who specialized in the archival holdings relating to the Second World War was making quite public his disgust with changes to regulations that now permitted "queers" to serve in the CF. The uninformed discussion continued for some time among the very people upon whose guidance researchers like me relied. I sensed that a senior employee was vaguely uncomfortable; he left, commenting on the refreshingly open discussions that always animated that particular lunchtime grouping. The consensus formed among the group seemed to be that here we had the courage to speak our minds. The impression I formed was that I was being baited; my research, whose subject they were well aware of, was on track by this time so I could no longer be dismissed as a passing curiosity. Instead, I was being offered the position of gay activist demanding equal rights. Leaving the archives' public spaces and returning to my files, I felt a historical continuity: an identity with the subjects of the avalanche of files that I was accessing. During the war, queer people were derided as innate "liars," "phonies," or "three-dollar bills." In one sense the observation was accurate: under the circumstances, anyone who had ever felt a homosexual urge denied it. Consequently, homosexuality was mendacity; heterosexuality was truth.[12] In the archives, the defenders of the military's honour were claiming courage: the courage to speak their minds openly and plainly, the courage to name a pervert a pervert.

While I was indeed a pervert, my options were limited. Did I really want to enter into an antagonistic relationship, on their terms, with the people who held the keys to the archives? Could I avoid it? More importantly, I found the debate they were offering boring.[13]

I came to understand that members of the NA staff who identified with Canada's military tradition had a special reverence for the records that preserved that heritage. They proudly spoke a language of patriarchal nationalism whose nuances were understood by the civilians and historians they advised. I sensed that my work, rooted in other academic traditions, was a potential threat both to Canada's military history and to the self-image and professional status of those who had constructed their identities in relation to it. One way to deal with my presence was to define me as unequivocally gay. The "gays in the military" debate offered me up to the traditionalists as a target: clearly different, I was imagined to be asserting the right to serve alongside the noble men who had long protected the nation. This kept the history intact and had the added advantage of making me plead my normalcy, which they could then deny or accept according to their patriarchal or liberal proclivities. The cafeteria encounter fit into this strategy. However, it was not a debate that I was interested in - it was not so much a question of being proud to be gay as that I didn't see what was so special about "straight" people.

While I was waiting to see if I would ever be allowed access to the courts martial, I devised a scheme to access the records of servicemen who had committed suicide during the war. While recent research had established homosexuality as a causal factor in suicides (something every gay person knew full well), some psychiatrists during the Second World War had already made the connection. Since privacy regulations protect personal information for only twenty years after one's death, I was able to argue that, in these cases, the subjects' files were in the public domain. I presented a list of over a hundred servicemen whose suicides had been documented during the war and asked to see their personnel files. The files gave me an extraordinary view into the intimate lives of individuals and the military. Since access to the files was restricted, I spent months locked in a corner of the ATIP office. An ATIP officer, who was equally a military scholar, tried to place my work within *his* discipline. Since he sat near the desk I had been temporarily assigned, he would periodically suggest standard military texts for me to read, arguing that the debates in Canadian military history were already established. If I aspired to join the field, then I would be valued according to my ability to contribute to the issues that concerned military historians. Once my diversionary research into gender and sexuality was completed, I would have to join the adults (where I could be promptly ignored.) One day, perhaps in a bad mood, he blurted out in passing: "So, have you proved everyone in the military was gay yet?"

While the perspective demonstrated by the response in the cafeteria to my work positioned me alone as the sexually marked researcher in the field, this new tactic suggested another fear: not only had homosexuals served in the Second World War, but the way individuals had been labelled previously was open to change. While the cafeteria baiting was aggressive in tone, part of fighting off the possibility of gays penetrating the military service, this approach was uneasy, with more than a hint of loathing. (To his credit, he was openly engaging me in a discussion on the significance of my research.)

In fact, the question was not off the mark. As I became more intimate with the records, I came to focus on how everyone was implicated in the creation of sexual categories. The categories themselves were in flux and it was not clear who would evade being stigmatized and who would not, who would choose the role of moral watchdog and why. The meaning of any sexual behaviour was indeterminate until the context was fully considered. To belatedly answer my ATIP colleague, everyone was gay in the same sense that everyone was straight: the meaning of homosexual, homoaffectional, and homosocial behaviours depended on the confluence of a number of factors. Within this constellation of power relations, everyone understood when an utterance could be devastating and how to keep out of trouble. Sometimes, however, fate intervened and then you experienced firsthand how power maintained itself.

The personnel I refer to here were experts on the military holdings in the NA. However neither they, nor the archivists, nor the researchers, nor the historians could offer me any advice as I began my research. One officer from the Royal Military College who had been publishing operational histories for more than three decades based on extensive research in RG 24 told me flatly and unequivocally, "You won't find anything." As it turns out, there was an enormous cache of documentary evidence relating to gender and sexual practices within the military. There were tens of thousands of court-martial proceedings that could be mined by social historians for insights into class, racial, ethnic, conjugal, sexual, and gender conflicts. Many documents within the personnel files and throughout RG 24 hint at the potential richness of the court-martial proceedings. Why had those records sat undisturbed in a damp warehouse of a federal records centre, on the edge of irreparable deterioration? References to these proceedings have never piqued the interest of military historians. Largely interested in operational, technical, and administrative issues, the social aspects of military life have never been their priority. It is therefore not surprising that when, in the recent "global war on terror," Canada was propelled into Afghanistan as a result of the aggressive insistence of the officer class of the DND, in particular General Rick Hillier, the social, historical, economic, political, and cultural lives of Afghans played absolutely no part in the determination.[14] Many Canadians now consider themselves experts in the field, reflecting what was once said derisively about Americans – that war was how they learned about world geography.

So military historians claim records that speak primarily to Canadian social and cultural issues but have not developed the competencies required to exploit them, while social historians, defining themselves apart from the military and militarist traditions, have bypassed RG 24 altogether. This attitude is most unfortunate in relation to study of war years, when a million men and women fall into a social black hole called the military and then, six years later, once again become subjects of research. But the social history of the military, and especially the courts martial, tells us about the strains on the family, the state's management of conjugal and interpersonal relations, and interethnic and interracial tensions in the society at large. Canadian historians, in their research methodologies, can be victims of their own identities. It is tragic that the Afghans now pay for the narrow view of the officer class of the DND and the relative impotence of those whose expertise lies in the humanities. In their powerful study of the effects of the invasion and ongoing occupation on the lives of the peoples of Afghanistan, Sonali Kolhatkar and James Ingalls teach us how truly ignorant we in North America remain about our governments' military undertakings in central Asia.[15] Our bloated defence budgets could be more fruitfully redirected to support re-invigorated departments of foreign affairs and international development or new departments conceived to address the crises that threaten the planet.

But this gets ahead of the story. When the courts martial records finally arrived, there were almost four hundred unindexed microfilm reels. The only way to proceed was to search them for the courts that concerned me. It took about a year of ten-hour days to search the reels for the courts that involved homosexuality. At first, I hunted through the endless courts looking for the rare one that dealt with homosexual offences. However, along the way, I was seduced by the richness of the files. Courts that ostensibly dealt with "absence without leave" or desertion offences revealed much about the conditions of service in the different theatres of war. Why would a soldier decide to absent himself from service at a given moment? What provoked servicemen to disobey orders, malinger, etc? Eventually, I began to see not only that any court could be about sexuality and gender but also that the courts on sexuality were about every aspect of military service. Circumstances forced that methodology upon me. But I was lucky, because it offered me a broader vision.

As the archival records opened up to me, I also broadened the pool of servicemen and women that I interviewed. Veterans unmarked by sexual deviance, when they understood that I had insights into their wartime experience, shared intimate details of their lives. I asked an elderly neighbour if I could harvest the crab apples from his front yard to make jelly. When I returned with a jar of the final product a week later, we began a discussion about his naval service that furnished me with more insights than official naval histories could provide. He spoke about his contempt for the petty hierarchical structure of the RCN and, eventually, even his reactions to the homosexual relationships that he witnessed on board a corvette and a destroyer. He, and others like him, helped me as much as those who had been marked. So who were the historians protecting by writing these experiences out of the past?

Experiences like these informed this book by showing me how much difference there had been in the military between the official policies defended by the authorities and the actual lived experiences of people of all ranks. Policies governing sexuality were marked largely by hypocrisy, with all ranks living their personal lives in a world safe from the impossible standards of the policy book. Sometimes fate intervened and the inhuman part of humanity took control. But people lived their lives in one world while the decisions that would ultimately place those lives in the balance took place in another.

It took extraordinary energy and courage on the part of people marked unfavourably on the basis of their sexuality to force the established order to retreat from its hetero-centric assumptions. As I have tried to argue, established authorities do not easily give up their source of social and political power. And that power resonates throughout many levels of society. Today, we need to question more than ever established policies that are driving our planet to destruction, a number of species to extinction, and populations to despair. We must pull reclusive power out of the closet and force it to account for itself. As political scientist James Laxer has shown, Prime Minister Stephen Harper and other 'leaders' throughout Canada have cynically abdicated their responsibility to justify their war in Afghanistan, choosing instead to attack those who question the aggression. Having exercised the awful responsibility of invading and occupying Afghanistan, the authorities then hide behind the very servicemen and women whom they have ordered into battle: one must support the war because to do otherwise would imperil Canadians who have been sent into battle. One of the ironies of this position is that regulations exclude military personnel from the nation's political discourse – soldiers' public statements are severely restricted by CF regulations. The government thus lays responsibility for the war at the feet of the most politically impotent group in Canada. This circular argument – you must support the war because the troops are fighting it – could be used to defend any act of aggression. If Mackenzie King had placed Canadian soldiers under Hitler's command during the Second World War, then support for them would have been equally justified on this argument. While the decision to go to war is extraordinary and should be based on the most comprehensive vision possible, separate sectors of Canadian society understand the war through the narrow parameters of their fields of interest. Together, they seem to have built a weak consensus. However, the whole is much less than the parts and there is nothing at the centre.

A perverted view of manliness is at the heart of Canada's undeclared war against Afghanistan. Instead of responding to demands for an accounting of the government's actions, Prime Minister Harper berates as cowards those who would withdraw the CF and leave Afghanistan to Afghans.[16] In setting up a straw man, arguing that those who criticize the war are trying to run away from the fight, Harper is running away from his own responsibility to explain the mission.[17] In that context, we see political, economic, cultural, and media personalities praising a renewed branding of Canada as a manly nation.[18] This manliness – for the word means nothing until we fix its parameters – is expressed by force rather than reflection, intimidation instead of dialogue, excess over restraint, canon over compassion, and bravado in the place of caution. In practice, it is manipulative, deceitful, and muddled. As we will see, it is at odds with a model of manliness understood by earlier generations of Canadians that could be retooled and de-gendered in response to today's challenges.

While hockey can be understood and analyzed from a number of perspectives, it, like every other sport or discipline, is self-contained. There are many styles of play and types of players, but all must compete within a framework in which there will be a winner and a loser. When Don Cherry speaks of Canadian soldiers serving in Afghanistan, he places them in the context of *Hockey Night in Canada*. Hockey games, however, do not include recreational skaters who may or may not be playing for the opposing team. While the rulebook tells us when a team scores a goal in hockey, it's far from clear what would be the hockey equivalent of killing Afghan civilians or torturing prisoners.[19] Opposing teams are not allowed to escape in mid-game to a neighbouring rink, only to return with the puck when the adversaries' guard is down. A moment's reflection is enough to put the very notion of an analogy aside. However, members of the military who are prepared to accept the analogy are Cherry-picked to appear on the nationwide program. On 11 November 2006, Coaches' Corner read a letter from Steve Keegan of the Royal Canadian Regiment, who assured the Canadian hockey public through Cherry: "It's the second period and we're winning games, although it's not over yet."[20] American Lt.-Col. Bert Gees told the Canadian troops who were taking over from his Task Force Gun Devil, "When the enemy rears its ugly head, I expect you to kill and capture them and defeat them. ... The change today is similar to a line change in hockey. It's still the same team going down the ice ready to score, just a different capability out there."[21]

There is evidence that Cherry does indeed understand the war through his career as a hockey coach, in which he was known to be fiercely protective and supportive of his players. I suspect that quality made Cherry an outstanding coach of the Boston Bruins. However Cherry never needed to justify hockey itself. The question of the morality of playing the Montreal Canadiens, I hope, never arose. Cherry's orientation towards the war is simple and understandable within a hockey paradigm: "What gets me is, whether you feel the mission is right or wrong, to put it down only puts our troops down [and] encourages the enemy ..."[22] Having established this general framework, Cherry then spends much time emotionally reporting the deaths of Canadian soldiers, with little discussion of the circumstances and no discussion of Afghans. (Mainstream journalists offer little more.) In the background, "The Maple Leaf Forever" sounds a farewell for the young men who have died. I am torn between, on the one hand, sadness in the face of such needless loss and the suffering that I know their loved ones are facing and, on the other, disgust that Cherry is playing an implicitly anti-French Canadian anthem in the background. As for Afghans, they are buried under Cherry's nationalist agenda. French Canadian supporters of the war are playing a similar game in Quebec, although in this case without the support of Quebec nationalists, who largely ignore the difficult questions of their relationship to international power structures raised by the war.[23]

While in Cherry's universe the morality of the war is no more at issue than the morality of hockey, he seems aware that some justification is necessary. So he periodically grounds his support for the troops/mission: "Do they want us there?" he asks General Rick Hillier. Hillier, normally blusterous, responds with a qualified, "Yes." Having thereby exhausted geopolitics, Cherry returns to what he does best. As the camera slowly pans a photograph of soldiers, Cherry muses:

Aren't these beautiful guys? It's the Princess Pats, what else? They all look like hockey players, don't they? ... Look at these guys – great looking guys. Look at these guys, doesn't that bring a lump to your –. We've got some more pictures – *beautiful looking guys!* I mean: I just can't believe it! Do they not look like hockey players? Look like my Bruins, eh? Look at them! Do you think they're ready to go? ... Beautiful people, I'll tell you, beautiful people.[24]

Imagine that his audience knows that a number of the soldiers presented are queer. In that case, it would be difficult not to read sexuality into Cherry's obsession with the physical beauty of the male soldiers. Alternatively, imagine that Cherry had focused on the couple of women who appeared in the photograph, surrounded by a sea of men. Replace the masculine pronouns with feminine equivalents: "Aren't these beautiful girls? ... Do you think they're ready to go?" In either case, Cherry becomes a lecherous old pervert and Coaches' Corner is pulled from the airwaves. Cherry can only get away with his comments because they are presumed to be asexual. His public *needs* them to be asexual. Why?

Cherry's presentation of the soldiers (and hockey players) serves to exclude homosexuality. Albeit implicitly, he defies anyone to call him queer. Only by slandering all of the male members of the Princess Pats as heterosexual, and ignoring the women, is he able to talk effusively about their masculine beauty without the least possibility that it can be read as sexual. It is not merely his emotional love of the troops but equally his love of their physical manliness that he asserts.[25] In Canada, the Cherry phenomenon reveals the continuing relationship among patriotism, sexuality, and masculinity.[26] In response to his support for the troops, the CF have honoured Cherry with the Medallion for Distinguished Service, the Canadian Legion has made him a Dominion Command Honorary Life Member, and the public has voted him the seventh Greatest Canadian in a poll sponsored by the CBC.[27] It is naïve to minimize the influence that Cherry has in Canadian society. His primary service is to make homosexuality and politics disappear from public discourse, offering Canadian men and women the simple world they long for. In this world, the doubts that cloud every action evaporate in the light of certainty.

Cherry's tribute to fallen soldiers – honouring them *because* they have fallen – has precedence in Canadian history. The European public, in the aftermath of the Great War, valued the deepest reflections upon the apparent meaninglessness of the soldiers' suffering: Germany's Erich Maria Remarque and Britain's Siegfried Sassoon and Wilfred Owen all framed their work in a critique of the imperialist war.[28] The English eventually valued the anti-war poetry of Owen over the patriotic verse of Rupert Brooke, who (like Cherry) had never experienced battle. Nazi Germany was forced to ban Remarque's popular anti-war prose.[29] Meanwhile, Canadians also looked for ways to make sense of the fact that their brothers, husbands, and sons had died or been maimed by the war. Historian Jonathan Vance shows how they came to honour death itself, in terms of a great Christ-like sacrifice for the nation. This is the position that Cherry has rediscovered. Through scholarship, Vance essentially does for Canadian history what Cherry does for the present. The question that frames *Death So Noble* is "How did Canadians console themselves?" rather than the more disturbing, "How were the war critics silenced?" Nevertheless, Vance reminds us that Canadian cities and towns are full of monuments to those who fell in the Great War – and not to those who questioned it.[30] Veterans who return from central Asia deeply critical of the war speak an entirely different language. Winter Soldiers confront both Americans and Canadians with some of the real consequences of this war.[31]

I want to return to the nineteenth-century concept of manliness. James Fenimore Cooper, among others, argued that manliness was the building block of the American republic.[32] Those responsible for the government in a democracy – the electors – have the responsibility of demanding accountability from those they elect. This requires a mix of qualities that have as much to do with moral and intellectual courage as physical courage. Responsible men need an independence of spirit and judgment and the courage to resist being cowed by power.[33] That this understanding of manliness was both classed and gendered should not blind us to the fact that all people are capable, then as now, of manliness. In Canadian history, Frère Untel is a notable model. His enormous influence on Quebec society resulted from his confidence in his own questions and his refusal to allow Church authorities to quiet him. In the process, he defended the right of nuns in the Catholic Church to insist, as he did, that authorities stand accountable. Untel drew his strength from the religious conviction that Christ lived within him.[34] Doctor Stockmann of Henrik Ibsen's *An Enemy of the People* offers a literary model of the "manliness" I have in mind.[35] As Ibsen shows, a democracy in which electors are frightened and silenced by the confluence of social pressure, self-interest, and the intimidation of authorities is meaningless.

The questions relating to Canada's role in the "global war on terror" that began with the invasion of Afghanistan were not answered before the invasion and have not been answered since. While never responding to demands from the Canadian public for information, the Liberal cabinet accepted a role in the invasion and in the subsequent United Nations' sanctioned occupation. Law professor Michael Mandel, in a general exposition of American and Canadian hypocrisy regarding justifications for aggression, shows us why the first invasion was illegal under international law.[36] Subsequently, international relations scholars Janice Stein and Eugene Lang have made apparent the decision-making process that led to Canada's involvement in the global war on terror." We know that foreign affairs minister John Manley successfully persuaded the cabinet to blindly support the United States, putting Canada at odds with the United Nations (UN).[37] While the UN as constituted is far from achieving its founding purpose of protecting humanity from aggression, it would have at least stopped the disastrous wars in Afghanistan and Iraq.[38] Canada invaded Afghanistan without UN authorization and Canadians must insist that their government demonstrate that the cause was morally just, since only a moral justification can mitigate a criminal action.[39] Did the Chrétien cabinet have a leg to stand on?

Manley, along with Chrétien's government, seems to have accepted in good faith the Bush administration's *casus belli*. As represented by Stein and Lang, the principle followed is that if the United States is at war, Canada is at war. On this perspective, the two countries are so deeply integrated that the very notion that "Canada" would not reflexively defer to the American government's will struck Manley as preposterous.[40] However, in the twenty-first century supporting America's empire requires explaining away two hundred years of American empire building and war making. Canadians and Americans insensitive to the enormous price paid by Amerindian peoples who were in the way of these two continental empires may have difficulty acknowledging the underside of world domination. But, irrespective of one's appreciation for colonial history,[41] a number of questions need to be asked in the present and about the present.

Academic accounts of Canada's entry into the "war on terror" reveal the duplicitous nature of all levels of state and government in Canada: politicians deceiving the Canadian public about Canada's participation in the war in Iraq, senior officers concealing information from their ministers, the abdication of responsibility at the DFAIT, and an embarrassing obsession over the sensibilities of American officials.[42] If Canadian public servants, elected and appointed, have not been honest with the public they are supposed to be serving, can we at least trust the American authorities to whom they defer? As it happens, the most lucid response to the terrorist attacks came from the Taliban of Afghanistan, who argued that they would indeed extradite Osama Bin Laden or anyone else as soon as the United States tabled evidence of a crime.[43] The validity of this request somehow eluded Canadians. Eight years later, as Canada digs into Afghanistan under Barack Obama's 'leadership,' no evidence has yet been tabled.[44] The justifications now focus on the general undesirability of the Taliban. Canadians defer to their officials, who defer to the Americans, who have clearly lied and obfuscated the events of 9/11 and the subsequent wars. Ideally, Canadians would hold their government to, at a minimum, the intellectual and legal standards required by the Taliban.

In light of the actual consequences, perhaps the cruellest justification for the invasion of Afghanistan was the claim that NATO armies would liberate Afghan women from the misogynistic Taliban. In keeping with the gendered representation of Canadian soldiers described above, we have been encouraged to accept the invasion of Afghanistan as a chivalrous humanitarian intervention. In fact, as Kolhatkar and Ingalls painstakingly demonstrate, the goals of the Revolutionary Association of the Women of Afghanistan (RAWA), as well as other progressive elements of Afghan society, have been undermined by American interventions in Afghan affairs since before the Soviet invasion of 1979. And since the invasion of 2001, the struggles of Afghan women against fundamentalism and militarism have been complicated by American designs on their country. All perceptive Afghans are aware that Zalmay Khalilzad, the American special envoy, exercised the real power in occupied Afghanistan. Khalilzad was a founding member of the neo-conservative think tank Project for the New American Century, whose goal has been to preclude the emergence of any competitor to American dominance in the post-Cold War world. In keeping with that goal, he oversaw the installation of proven despotic and cruel warlords – who should have been tried for war crimes and crimes against humanity according to the progressive elements of Afghan society – in positions of authority. Afghans watched as the dreams for which they had fought under unimaginable conditions turned to nightmares with the NATO invasion and the imposition of American-picked bullies. If NATO's goal had seriously been the liberation of the women of Afghanistan, then RAWA, not the extremely misogynistic warlords of the Northern Alliance, would have been its natural ally. Are Canadians more comfortable with the spectre of helpless Afghan women being liberated by chivalrous, male, hockey-playing soldiers than they are with an alliance with well-organized, determined, feminists?[45]

Clearly, the invasion and occupation have been sold to Canadians with no serious public discussion of its goals or the options available to achieve them. Equally disturbing is the fact that the attacks of 9/11 that precipitated the "global war on terror," under which Afghan women and men are suffering are far from understood. The official conspiracy theory, quickly promoted by the Bush administration and subsequently supported by the 9/11 Commission and the National Institute of Science and Technology report, has been thoroughly discredited in peer-reviewed publications and by experts in every relevant field. Theologian David Ray Griffin has consolidated much of the empirical evidence that the official reports have simply ignored or misrepresented. Experts in all relevant fields have rejected the official conspiracy theory.[46] The evidence is clearly sufficient to warrant an independent commission of enquiry with subpoena powers (as opposed to governmental bodies controlled by the White House) to determine precisely what happened on 9/11. This is particularly relevant as President Obama frames Afghanistan as the "good war" that was the just response to 9/11. If North Americans are not able to understand how power is exercised in their own societies, then there is little likelihood that they can fathom, let alone support, the aspirations of Afghan women and men. A number of conscientious Americans see an enquiry into 9/11 as a way to pierce the ominous grid of power that is choking the life out of their society. Canadians who see their government deferring to the United States – a foreign power over which they have no control – have even more reason to insist on clear answers about the events that led to Canada's participation in the current war.

This deference to American power (the colonial mindset) is suggested by a fact that exists in omission only. For sixteen years, the CF have had no official restriction on homosexuals. During that same period, the American military has operated under its infamous Don't Ask, Don't Tell, Don't Pursue, Don't Harass policy. While countless CF officers have been posted in the American military and Canadian soldiers have fought under American leadership, the incompatibility of the two policies has never been tested. A survey of the Servicemembers Legal Defense Network, whose purpose is to document every event relating to the policy, reveals no instance of a Canadian officer or soldier allowing his or her homosexuality to be known in such a way as to embarrass either country's military.[47] I suspect that this "non fact" tells us a great deal about the pressures that keep all of us bound by power.[48]

Don't Ask, Don't Tell is the guiding principle of our entire world. Asking and telling, however, are very much in demand. People often remember disclosure as a moment of truth. When people "come out" as gay, they often need personal courage and integrity to confront (sometimes debilitating) anxiety. Disclosure of one's sexuality is often experienced as involving huge risks, a situation that can sometimes lead to suicide as the only "safe" option. Alternatively, the act of coming out can be euphoric in the sense of momentarily breaking free from invisible shackles that keep one subservient to power. While it takes energy to remain "out," the affirmation of a sexual identity should not be the end point of self-actualization.[49] The same sense of liberation from oppressive power has been reported by people who allow themselves to question the events of 9/11 that led Canada into Afghanistan and, although not officially recognized, Iraq.[50] In a lucid analysis of the destruction of the World Trade Center (supported by over 800 professional architects and engineers), architect Richard Gage speaks of how listening to the conclusions of the "reluctant" researcher David Ray Griffin, in 2006, "changed [his] life radically."[51] In relation to his finding that unreacted nanothermite, a powerful explosive, was present in samples of the rubble from the World Trade Centre, the Danish chemist Niels Harrit was asked by a journalist, "Why should we believe you?" He replied, lucidly, "You should not believe in me, you should believe yourself."[52] Frère Untel encouraged Quebecers to have the same confidence in their questions at the dawn of the Quiet Revolution.

In the introduction to *One of the Boys*, I referred to the possibilities that were opened up by the events of 9/11 and to the aggressive homophobia that was the result instead. Since then, Canadians have allowed their country to move in a militaristic direction, led by American imperial interests that are increasingly working against the will and judgment of the majority of the populations of both countries. Neither the causes for the war nor its effects on the Afghan and Canadian populations have been seriously discussed in the media or in the House of Commons. The sex/gender/sexuality system and the concurrent unwarranted deference to authority that frame my analysis of the Second World War era are still functioning today, with devastating consequences.

NOTES

1 How should we understand the American empire? See William Robinson, *Promoting Polyarchy: Globalization, US Intervention, and Hegemony* (New York: Cambridge University Press, 1996), Michel Chossudovsky, *The Globalization of Poverty and the New World Order* (Pincourt: Global Research, Centre for

Research on Globalization, 2005), Noam Chomsky, *Hegemony or Survival* (New York: Metropolitan Books, 2003) and *Failed States: the Abuse of Power and the Assault on Democracy* (New York: Metropolitan Books, 2006), Walden Bello, *Dilemmas of Domination: the Unmaking of the American Empire* (New York: Metropolitan Books, 2005), and William Blum, *Killing Hope: U.S. Military and CIA Interventions since World War II* (Montreal: Black Rose Books, 1998). How should we understand Canada's relationship to it? Greg Albo is most clearheaded, "Canada and World Order after the Wreckage," *Canadian Dimension*, May/June 2006. Also see Linda McQuaig, *Holding the Bully's Coat: Canada and the U.S. Empire* (Toronto: Doubleday, 2007), Ricardo Grinspun and Yasmine Shamsie (eds.), *Whose Canada?: Continental Integration, Fortress North America, and the Corporate Agenda,* (Montreal: McGill-Queen's University Press, 2007) and Stephen Clarkson, *Uncle Sam and Us: Globalization Neo-conservatism, and the Canadian State* (Toronto: University of Toronto Press, 2002). The historical continuity in Canadian foreign policy is noted by Robert Bothwell, "Back to the Future: Canada and Empires," *International Journal* 59, no. 2, (Spring 2004).

2 Chalmers Johnson, *The Sorrows of Empire: Militarism, Secrecy and the End of the Republic* (New York: Metropolitan Books, 2004) and *Nemesis: The Last Days of the American Empire* (New York: Metropolitan Books, 2007).

3 Janice Gross Stein and Eugene Lang, *The Unexpected War: Canada in Kandahar* (Toronto: Viking Canada, 2007) note that Paul Wolfowitz told Bill Graham that the United States "valued Canadian military contributions in places the United States wouldn't go, especially in Africa." Stein and Lang argue that the ties between the two countries "can stretch to accommodate differences, partnership, and a smart division of labour" (265). While that is doubtless true, it is the fundamental orientation of the American partner that I, along with the critics I cite, call into question.

4 Linda McQuaig, *It's the Crude, Dude: War, Big Oil, and the Fight for the Planet* (Toronto: Doubleday Canada, 2004). Michael Byers, *Intent for a Nation: What Is Canada For? A Relentlessly Optimistic Manifesto for Canada's Role in the World* (Vancouver, Toronto: Douglas & McIntyre, 2007). Omar Aktouf, *La stratégie de l'autruche: Post-mondialisation, management et rationalité économique* (Montréal: écosociété, 2002) offers a profound critique of the global economy as economists and politicians encourage us to keep our heads in the sand.

5 Herman Daly's most recent elaboration of his ecological economic vision was presented to the Sustainable Development Commission in the United Kingdom in April 2008, "A Steady-State Economy: A Failed Growth Economy and a Steady-State Economy Are Not the Same Thing; They Are the Very Different

Alternatives We Face," http://www.sd-commission.org.uk/publications/
downloads/Herman_Daly_thinkpiece.pdf. The journal *Multinational Monitor*
devoted its March/April 2009 issue (30, no. 2) to the organizing principles behind a transformed economy, including the cautionary and subsidiary principles,
green chemistry and a carbon-free future. The Organic Consumers Association advocates for people to "buy local, organic, and fair made:" http://
www.organicconsumers.org/aboutus.cfm. The Forest Stewardship Council has
developed a sophisticated process for the certification of forest products, protecting social, environmental, and workers' interests: http://www.fsccanada.org/.
These are a sample of initiatives that demonstrate a motivated and informed
North American public. (Websites accessed 7 August 2009.)

6 Linda McQuaig, *The Cult of Impotence: Selling the Myth of Powerlessness in
the Global Economy* (Toronto: Viking, 1998).

7 There was a small literature regarding military justice in Canada. In the wake of
the Somalia Affair, Chris Madsen had surveyed military law as described in the
title of *Another Kind of Justice: Canadian Military Law from Confederation to
Somalia* (Vancouver: UBC Press, 1999). Robert Tooley, "Appearance or Reality?
Variations in Infantry Courts Martial: 1st Canadian Infantry Division, 1940–
1945," *Canadian Defence Quarterly* 22, nos. 2 and 3 (1992). I was apparently
the first person to access the actual courts since they had been microfilmed four
decades earlier.

8 Dana Rosenfeld nicely explains this transformation in *The Changing of the
Guard: Lesbian and Gay Elders, Identity, and Social Change* (Philadelphia:
Temple University Press, 2003).

9 Remember that I was researching a conscripted Army, Navy, and Air Force,
whereas the postwar forces and the military historians and archivists were self-
selected. The wartime forces were largely representative of Canadian, male society.

10 J.L. Granatstein signalled the alarm against social historians who neglected
Canada's national and military history in his polemics *Who Killed Canadian His-
tory and What Can We Do about It?* (Lethbridge, Alta: University of Lethbridge
Press, 2000) and *Who Killed the Canadian Military?* (Toronto: HarperFlamingo
Canada, 2004.) Since my approach applied the insights of social historians to the
military, it would seem to be in a category outside his critical framework.

11 Historian Steven Maynard discussed similar experiences while doing archival
research into homosexuality in " "The Burning, Wilful Evidence': Lesbian/Gay
History and Archival Research." *Archivaria* 33 (Winter 1991–92): 195–301.

12 Of course, this made claims to heterosexuality equally dubious. So, it would be
unclear where 'truth' was located.

13 This experience raises questions about the possibility of 'liberation' in an unen-
lightened world. David Halperin discusses his own experiences as a liberated gay

man still vulnerable to the oppressions within an academe unaffected by his "coming-out" as gay in *Saint Foucault: Towards a Gay Hagiography* (New York: Oxford University Press, 1995.) Eve Kosofsky Sedgwick brilliantly and concisely outlines the problematic in *The Epistemology of the Closet* (Berkeley: University of California Press, 1990), 67–90.

14 Janice Gross Stein and Eugene Lang in *The Unexpected War* make clear the distinction between the civilian and military arms of the DND. It was the military wing that took control, with its eyes locked on the will of the Pentagon. Also see James Laxer, *Mission of Folly: Canada and Afghanistan* (Toronto: Between the Lines Press, 2008).

15 Sonali Kolhatkar and James Ingalls, *Bleeding Afghanistan: Washington, Warlords, and the Propaganda of Silence* (New York, Toronto: Seven Stories Press, 2006).

16 Stein and Lang, *The Unexpected War,* 230–45.

17 James Laxer, in *Mission of Folly,* reports the Harper government's two "threadbare" justifications for the war: "unless Canada and its allies prevail there, the terrorists will regroup to carry out lethal attacks against targets in Western countries, including Canada. ... The second argument is that the struggle is about the creation of a democracy in Afghanistan," 5.

18 Laxer reports how Ottawa sent a warship to Belfast to commemorate the achievement of peace in Northern Ireland in June 2007, with the *Globe and Mail* headline reading, "Warship's Arrival Signals Canada's New International Muscle," *Mission of Folly,* 57.

19 On torture of Afghan prisoners, see Byers, *Intent for a Nation,* 27–39.

20 CBC, Hockey Night in Canada, Coaches Corner, 11 November 2006. First battalion RCR, Charles Company, Section 32.

21 Laxer, *Mission of Folly,* 41.

22 Ibid., 57.

23 Ibid., 50–1.

24 CBC, Coaches' Corner, 11 November 2006, emphasis in original.

25 Eve Kosofsky Sedgwick, in *Between Men: English Literature and Male Homosocial Desire* (New York: Arno Press, 1980), theorizes that sex and love can exist between men in Western culture but not at the same time: either sex or love are permissible within limits. Cherry flirts with the border when he focuses on the physical attributes of the male soldiers.

26 Meanwhile, Dahr Jamail and Helen Benedict, among others, document the culture of sexual assault within the American military. Dahr Jamail, "Culture of Unpunished Sexual Assaults in the Military," 1 May 12009, http://original.antiwar.com/jamail/2009/04/30/culture-of-unpunished-sexual-assault-in-ilitary/ (accessed 7 August 2009). Helen Benedict, "The Plight of Women Soldiers," 9 May 2009, *The Nation,* http://www.thenation.com/doc/20090518/benedict

(accessed 7 August, 2009). Johnson, *The Sorrows of Empire*, 92–3, 105–6.
Soldiers committing sexual assaults against civilians in occupied nations
(by agreement with national governments or by invasion) are protected by the
American military from prosecution by local authorities: Chalmers Johnson
"Three Good Reasons to Liquidate Our Empire and Ten Steps to Take to Do
So," http://www.commondreams.org/view/2009/07/30-11. The sexual humiliation of Muslims, by both male and female service members at all levels
of command, is now well documented: Meron Benvenista, ed., *Abu Ghraib:
The Politics of Torture* (Berkley California: North Atlantic Books, 2004).
(Websites accessed 7 August 2009.) For testimonies from service members addressing issues of sexuality and gender in the wars in Iraq and Afghanistan,
see http://ivaw.org/wintersoldier/testimony/Divide+To+Conquer%3A+Gender+
and+Sexuality+in+the+Military, accessed 8 August 2009.

27 http://en.wikipedia.org/wiki/Don_Cherry_(ice_hockey) accessed 4 August 2009.

28 In *The Regeneration Trilogy*, author Pat Barker explores the response of Sassoon
to the war. She separates psychology, sexuality, and politics and focuses on the
social forces that act upon a man of conscience to pressure him to accept an
immoral war, (London: Viking, 1996).

29 Ian Kershaw, *Hitler 1889–1936: Hubris* (London: the Penguin Press, 1998), 482.

30 Jonathan Vance, *Death So Noble: Memory, Meaning, and the First World War*
(Vancouver: UBC Press, 1997).

31 People interested in the troops' experience of the 'war on terror' might begin
by listening to Winter Soldiers: http://www.livevideo.com/video/embedLink/
F7791AA15724466EA04EEFF0D82F1144/530489/winter-soldier-iraq-
afghani.aspx. See especially Iraq Veterans against the War: http://ivaw.org/
wintersoldier. Websites accessed August 9, 2009.

32 James Fenimore Cooper, *The American Democrat*, (Baltimore, Maryland:
Penguin Books, 1969).

33 David Reisman, in *The Lonely Crowd: A Study in the Changing American
Character* (New Haven: Yale University Press, 1950), described this quality as
"inner-directed" as opposed to "outer-directed," which tends to defer to others
and marks the post Second World War era.

34 Jean-Paul Desbiens *Les Insolences du Frère Untel* (Montréal: Éditions de
l'homme, 2000) provides annotations exploring the issues behind the publication and Desbiens' challenges in confronting Church authorities as a result of his
utterances. To understand the story from the point of view of an authority he
challenged, see Micheline Lachance, *Paul-Émile Leger* (Montréal: Éditions de
l'homme, 2000).

35 Henrik Ibsen, *Ghosts: An Enemy of the People, A Doll's House, John Gabriel
Borkman* (New York: The Modern Library, 1941).

36 Michael Mandel, *How America Gets Away with Murder, Illegal Wars, Collateral Damage, and Crimes against Humanity* (London: Pluto Press, 2004).

37 Stein and Lang, in *The Unexpected War*, demonstrate the failures at many levels of government and state to seek information and inform parliament. The blind deference to the will of the American administration and military is well documented throughout.

38 Not surprisingly since its foundation, along with the Bretton Woods organizations, was primarily informed by the American intention to control the empires forfeited by European nations (allies or adversaries) as a result the war. See George Monbiot, *The Age of Consent: A Manifesto for a New World Order* (London: Flamingo, 2003) for a creative response to the global inequalities set in motion at Bretton Woods.

39 This is nicely argued by Bernard Chazelle, "How to Argue against Torture," in relation to torture, Counterpunch, 22 July 2009, http://www.counterpunch.org/chazelle07222009.html (accessed 7 August 2009)

40 Stein and Lang, *The Unexpected War*, 6.

41 A sample: J. R. Miller, ed., *Sweet Promises: A Reader on Indian-White Relations in Canada* (Toronto: University of Toronto Press, 1991); Geoffrey York, *People of the Pines: The Warriors and the Legacy of Oka* (Toronto: Little, Brown and Company, Canada Limited, 1992); Jim Mochoruk, *Formidable Heritage: Manitoba's North and the Cost of Development, 1870–1930* (Winnipeg: University of Manitoba Press, 2004).

42 See especially Stein and Lang, *The Unexpected War*.

43 Milan Rai, *War Plan Iraq: Ten Reasons against War with Iraq* (London: Verso, 2002), chapter 3, "The Smoking Gun: The Taliban Had Agreed to Extradite bin Laden." Also see, Kolhatkar and Ingalls, *Bleeding Afghanistan*, 50.

44 The Federal Bureau of Investigation (FBI) cites bin Laden's involvement in the 7 August 1998, bombings of the United States Embassies in Dar es Salaam, Tanzania, and Nairobi, Kenya, but there is no mention of 9/11: http://www.fbi.gov/wanted/terrorists/terbinladen.htm. David Ray Griffin reports that the FBI claims to have no evidence connecting bin Laden to 9/11: Boston University, "9/11: Time for a Second Look," 11 April 2009.

45 Kolhatkar and Ingalls, *Bleeding Afghanistan*, especially chapters 4 and 5, relate to the destruction of civil society and the struggles of women.

46 See David Ray Griffin, *The New Pearl Harbor: Disturbing Questions about the Bush Administration and 9/11* (Northampton, Mass.: Olive Branch Press, 2004) and *The New Pearl Harbor Revisited: 9/11, the Cover-up and the Exposé* (Northampton, Mass.: Olive Branch Press, 2008). Niels Harit et al. "Active Thermitic Material Discovered in Dust from the 9/11 World Trade Center Catastrophe," in *The Open Chemical Physics Journal*, 2009, vol. 2. There are

several websites dedicated to making available recent scholarship and discussion of the events of 9/11. See, for instance, Scholars for 9/11 Truth and Justice at http://stj911.org/.

47 Servicemembers Legal Defense Network, http://www.sldn.org/ (accessed 7 August 2009). A survey of this organization's in-depth coverage of the issue since 1993 revealed no such events. Also see Palm Center at the University of California (formerly Center for the Study of Sexual Minorities in the Military) http://www.palmcenter.org/ (accessed 7 August 2009).

48 The idea of being *bound* by power is explored by David Miller in Jeffery Klaehn, "Unspinning Social Inequality: An Interview with David Miller," in Klaehn, *Bound by Power: Intended Consequences* (Montreal: Black Rose Books, 2005)

49 Soeren Kierkegaard, *The Sickness unto Death* (Princeton: Princeton University Press, 1974). Kierkegaard understands despair as a normal process in life. There is no resting place, where one has achieved 'happiness' or 'satisfaction,' but a process of confronting and transcending despair, a certainty in life.

50 Stein and Lang, *The Unexpected War*, 73–7.

51 Richard Gage, AIA, Architect, "9/11: Blueprint for Truth – The Architecture of Destruction," available at http://www.ae911truth.org/.

52 http://www.youtube.com/watch?v=jze33vzCpwo&feature=related (accessed 7 August 2009)

ONE OF THE BOYS

INTRODUCTION

In this book, I explore the significance of homosexuality among men in the Canadian forces during the Second World War. Homosexuality was a significant issue in military life at both the social and administrative levels. Many readers will be accustomed to more recent debates framed around the propriety of granting lesbians and gay men equal access to various privileges and responsibilities of citizenship, such as marriage, adoption, social benefits, and the right to serve in the military. One effect of political action over recent decades has been to consolidate the binary categories of homosexual and heterosexual. Gays and lesbians have positioned themselves, and been positioned by their opponents, as an identifiable minority that stands outside the heterosexual majority that already enjoys particular privileges of citizenship. I ask the reader to be ready to submit all assumptions about the 'nature' and significance of sexual types to the scrutiny of historical analysis.

There are important differences between the era of the Second World War and early twenty-first–century Canada. The gay liberation movement has led to legitimate public images of gay men and lesbian women, protected by the Charter and protective of their rights. While not everyone is convinced that homosexuality is socially or morally acceptable, a book such as this can, evidently, be published today. Sixty years ago in Canada, it would have been unimaginable. At that time, support for queer people was limited to the private sphere. In 1943, for example, the idea of holding a Gay Pride Day in Toronto, with the expectation of attracting a third of the population of the city, would have been considered absurd.

Tracking certain changes in language can help to uncover the way Canadians conceptualized homosexuality at mid-century. When discussing the war period, I employ the words most commonly used at that time to denote those involved in male same-sex love, 'homosexual' and 'queer.' 'Gay' was used rarely. Although other historians have documented its use in gay sub-cultures from the turn of the previous century, it never appears in the documentary evidence and Canadian veterans interviewed for this work advised that they did not use it during the war.[1]

In contemporary records, homosexual sometimes appears as "homosex-ualist," "homo sexual," or simply "homo." Its frequent use may jar those readers who consider it an outdated psychiatric category of oppression. Many gay and lesbian historians and activists once avoided it in order to distance their subjects from the imputation of pathology. However, in the military's records, homosexual was commonly used by legal, medical, and administrative authorities. It was also used by homosexual men themselves. And while the term was certainly co-opted by the medical profession in its (largely) postwar campaign to pathologize queer people, it originated with a homosexual man in 1869 whose interest was in challenging anti-homosexual legal codes. Likewise, it was employed by the first modern homosexual-rights movement, centred in pre-Nazi Germany. I use it here most frequently when discussing the activities of military authorities. Not only was it the term most frequently used by them, but it was a word with layers of historical meanings, as it is today.[2]

Gays and lesbians who feel that homosexual is a regressive label may find 'queer' more attractive. On the other hand, veterans, gay or straight, may see that alternative as abusive and crass. Queer, though, was adopted during the 1990s in part as a replacement for the more cumbersome gay, lesbian, bisexual, and transgendered. Theorists proposed it as an indetermi-nate signifier, meant to identify any deviation from orthodoxy. For in-stance, historian David Halperin defined queer as "*whatever* is at odds with the normal, the legitimate, the dominant. *There is nothing in particu-lar to which it necessarily refers*. It is an identity without an essence. Queer, then, demarcates not a positivity but a positionality vis-à-vis the norma-tive."[3] At the same time, in adopting it, homosexuals were reclaiming a word that had been used to disparage them. Just as many Blacks defiantly use 'nigger' to demonstrate their power over racism, homosexuals have ap-propriated and subdued the label queer. But academics and activists have far less control over language than they might like. Gay was adopted by a previous generation of homosexuals who wanted to define themselves pub-licly on their own terms and with their own term. Today, gay is often used in popular culture to mean weak, useless, pathetic, and inferior, as in "That's so gay." Meanwhile, queer has settled into a more comfortable existence in everyday speech. More and more, it means gay or lesbian.

Non-white homosexuals in North America, however, have increasingly re-jected it. For them, queer has been culturally constructed as white. They point, for instance, to the television series *Queer as Folk*, in which non-white homosexual men are rare and women a marginal presence. Not sur-prisingly, queer reflects the self-images of those who have the economic, po-litical, and cultural means to define the term.

Curiously, during the war, queer carried the indeterminacy sought by modern theorists. In the first instance, it referred to anything unusual or odd. In its most positive usage, queer people were eccentric, unwilling to conform to social pressures and orthodoxies; queer people were free spirits. In its more putative form, queers were homosexual. However, it was not possible to entirely extract the positive essence of the word from its use in designating 'sexual perverts.' Certainly, it had the power to sting when used to reduce a man to his sexual deviance, but its vagueness meant that the sexuality of any eccentric was suspect. The word queer did much cultural work. Never, for instance, was its primary function to slur homosexuals, as can be inferred from its widespread usage in the popular press. Just as ac-tivists in the 1990s co-opted queer in defiance of their enemies, some Cana-dian queers used it in reference to themselves during wartime. They were not blinded by self-hatred, but were more typically self-assured men who accepted that their sexual desires were socially problematic. The word should be read in the following pages with the understanding that it was not a rallying cry for political activism, but was instead employed with a sense of irony and a keen awareness of which way the wind was blowing.

The signifier queer has been helpful in organizing the material in this book. Its linguistic indeterminacy corresponded to a wartime cultural real-ity. In the general population, few men were thought to be 'true homosexu-als.' To label a man homosexual was a serious charge. Like the fallen woman who had become marked by sex, often through licentiousness or prostitution, the man labelled homosexual found that his options had be-come limited in society. Curiously, a number of words that originally re-ferred to prostitutes came to be applied to effeminate or queer men – "queen, punk, gay, faggot, fairy, and fruit."[4]

There were two paths to the label of homosexual, one through gender in-version and the other through moral laxity. Those who took the former route, commonly known as fairies, were most visible. Their original sin was against masculinity, but when compounded with sexual deviation, they were often seen as freaks of nature. On the other hand, masculine men who in-dulged in homosexual relations were thought to suffer from a lack of moral fibre. Homosexuality signalled the degeneracy of those who had succumbed to vice. Unlike women, men were allowed much scope in enjoying hetero-sexual pleasures, but they were no longer classed among decent society once they were marked as homosexual. The sexual landscape of mid-century Canada differed from our own by the more lax application of the homosex-ual label, which was, in turn, a far more serious charge. Precisely because being marked as homosexual was so serious, a measure of queer behaviour could be overlooked before a man was deemed to have fallen.

In all three branches of the Canadian military, contradictory anti-homo-sexual policies made queer men vulnerable to discipline and punishment. Medical policy required the immediate discharge of homosexuals as "mili-tary misfits." Under military law, servicemen were court-martialled and im-prisoned for homosexual indecency. As the war progressed, more extensive policing and surveillance techniques meant that queer men were increas-ingly likely to be discovered and prosecuted. Since the regulations govern-ing homosexual activity were promulgated poorly and enforced erratically, many men were unaware of them until they were caught. However, all knew that homosexuality was a serious offence against morality and mas-culinity. But why was it considered such a heinous offence? What was same-sex sexual behaviour thought to imply about the men who engaged in it? What effect were such men thought to have on their comrades?

While the military subscribed to the proposition that queer men were simply failed men, many gay veterans came to see their own acceptance of their homoerotic desires as part of their personal growth. At the same time, they could be personally devastated should their homosexuality become public knowledge. In the course of my research, I have contacted veterans whose wartime ordeals of courts martial, imprisonment, and ignominious discharges still had the power to evoke such anxiety and depression that they chose not to revisit them. This work documents an important aspect of Canadian military society that has received almost no scholarly attention. Its purpose is not simply to fill in a historiographical blank, but also to illu-minate the dynamics of such omissions. Why were such deep scars left on some of those unfortunate enough to be publicly marked as queer? How did other men deal with their own homosexual desires? Were all men equally frightened of the homosexual label?

It is perfectly understandable that men who were traumatized by being publicly marked, punished, and humiliated because of their sexual deviance would choose to bury that ordeal as deeply as possible. However, that re-sponse hands victory over to those responsible for the oppressive treatment, thereby unwittingly perpetuating it. When bullies are not confronted, they continue to prey on their victims – sometimes they continue anyway. The

Canadian military persecution of homosexual servicemen during the Second World War was part of a widespread campaign to bring reality in line with ideology. The conceit that communities of real men do not include homosexuals can be maintained only when homosexuals are forced out or silenced within. Many tactics were employed to give the masculine world the desired appearance. The silence of victims, too humiliated to affirm that they also existed and performed their work every bit as well as their unmarked comrades, is exactly the result that the courts martial would have applauded. Thus, the public has been able to remain comfortable in its belief that queers did not exist among the real men who saved the world from fascism.[5]

The men who were exposed as queer during the war did not have other traits in common. Many were popular with their comrades, some were not. They varied, too, in their effectiveness as soldiers and officers. In fact, knowing that a man was queer tells us nothing about him otherwise. The one challenge that all queer men faced was that they had to cope with proscribed desires. Studying those myriad coping strategies offers us insight into the behaviour of men under stress. However, what it tells us about homosexuality is that it was not, in fact, an indicator of other character traits. While many people during wartime believed that homosexuality was a significant gauge of a man's character and abilities, the empirical evidence does not support that presumption. Military records also reveal that a great many soldiers and officers were well aware that their queer comrades were not limited by their homoerotic interests. Nevertheless, the ideological insistence that queer men were a menace was strong enough to overwhelm the facts. This ideology held at the official level. Privately, at all levels of the military hierarchy, most servicemen and -women were more sensible.

Anti-homosexual policies were devised, in part, to protect the non-queer military population. (This remains the case in the American forces in the twenty-first century.) However, evidence from the Canadian military during wartime suggests that the run of servicemen and -women were more tolerant than was the institution of sexual diversity within their ranks. Nevertheless, the military supported those who feared or condemned homosexuality. By promoting anti-homosexual policies, the state actively endorsed the attitudes of the least aware and the least compassionate elements within the military. It is not surprising that what is today known as homophobia became central to both the Canadian and American military cultures since the Second World War.

There is much that our present world can learn from the study of Canada's male military society during wartime. In North American society today, there are large and conspicuous urban gay communities that provide a

full range of services to queer citizens, mostly gay men. The sports and asso-
ciational clubs that exist in the mainstream culture have their counterparts
in the gay community. In effect, two parallel cultures exist. Whereas racial
and ethnic communities often track their success by their integration into
the mainstream culture, gay and lesbian progress is marked by its separation
from it. However, from my perspective, the division of the population into
hetero- and homosexual camps represents both a success and a failure. The
existence of gay hockey organizations, for example, reminds me that many
queer men who want to play hockey are not welcome – and therefore not
comfortable – in straight leagues. (Conversely, many straight men are more
comfortable in gay hockey leagues.) In this culture, people are pressured to
choose not just a hockey team, but a sexual team. A large number of people
on both sides of the great sexual divide believe that sexual orientation is a
crucial determinant of one's character. Consequently, sexual orientation has
become significant even in areas where it could as easily be considered irrelevant.

During the Second World War, the infantrymen came to symbolize manhood. Many men who had been jobless, transient, and unwanted were cat-
apulted into the role of saviours of the nation as a result of their real
sacrifices. The common, selfless, courageous soldier provided North American culture with what journalist Susan Faludi calls the "template for postwar manhood." For many men and women, today's military continues to
represent a bastion of masculinity, along with the most combative sports –
hockey, football and boxing. These social institutions are emblematic of a
particular ideal of manhood: aggressive, fearless, passionate, indomitable.
All resist the incursion of homosexuals. Unlike the military, however, sports
teams cannot control the sexual orientation of their members through legislation. But since less visible social practices are much more effective than
legislation at controlling behaviour, sports teams have no trouble projecting
images of exclusive heterosexuality. The men who define manhood in our
culture, we are meant to infer, are naturally heterosexual. Either overlooked or hidden in this formulation are the efforts made to ensure that
queer men are either actively excluded or invisible to the world at large.
The panoply of legal, physical, and psychological techniques for intimidat-
ing, coercing, and frightening all men to comply overtly with heterosexist
norms allows the icons of masculinity in our culture to remain nominally
straight. The few gay men who have dared to come out in the world of professional sport have found the experience daunting.[6]

How are 'real men' served by deluding themselves into believing their
community is uniformly straight? Who are the men in this community?

First, not all men see their gender as the principal determining factor in their personality. Those who do can model themselves upon various ideals of masculinity. However, the huge popularity of aggressive team sports in North American culture suggests that a large number of men and women accept that particular model of manhood. The military has traditionally filled a similar role for many men and remains the ultimate expression of masculinity. For the heroes of these pursuits to remain male icons, it is necessary that they continue to exclude women and queers. As United States Marine General Robert Barrow explained in defending his objection to women in the forces, "When you get right down to it, you have to protect the manliness of war." For those who identify themselves firmly as men, the courage, strength, and grit they honour must be expressed by men. When women are excluded, courage becomes male courage, strength is read as male strength and grit is male grit. However, were men not vigilant, queers could slip onto the field or the rink, and the excellence with which men want to identify could become queer excellence. That anatomical men might feminize and demoralize the military or the sports team represents a double insult to many men and women. The groundwork against this contingency is laid in childhood by taunts of fairy, queer, and fag in all-male environments. For homosexual men who enter sports or the military, coercive factors keep them silent. Such coercion is as effective in the Canadian military, which officially accepts homosexuals, as in the American military, which does not. Ironically, insecure queer men can become complicit in the process that keeps them invisible. When their success among real men confirms the status they seek, it is not in their interest to impugn either themselves or the institution as queer. Whatever their actual sexual desires, real men make sure that they win by not allowing women and queers to play. Likewise, by jettisoning homosexuals from the record of the Second World War, military men have been able to tell their favourite war stories.[7]

For instance, *Esprit de Corps* magazine became the most vocal critic of the 1992 lifting of restrictions on homosexual servicepeople in the Canadian military. Its publisher, Scott Taylor, positioned himself as the champion of the hard-working, self-sacrificing, and always male straight soldier. Meanwhile, the magazine's editorials appealed to the basest homophobia in the troops through inflammatory rhetoric and irrational argumentation:

Despite their whining to the contrary, homosexuals are free to do pretty much whatever anybody else can do. They are free to speak their minds and associate with whomever they wish, unless its [*sic*] your ten year old son in the back of a van. We won't get into that. The fact that society has never wanted to hear what they

had to say as homosexuals (or care to know what they do) is a reflection of our revulsion for what they are, not who they are. Svend Robinson can carry on in his in-
imitable way as a gay MP, but he would be well-advised not to wear a leather G-
string to the House of Commons. The difference is his responsibility to the social
conditions we have collectively agreed to abide by. Homosexuals like to present
themselves as everyday lads and lassies with different tastes in entertainment, but
the distinction is crucial, not incidental.

While in recent years the category of soldier has come to include women
and racial minorities in the text of *Esprit de Corps*,[8] the magazine's reaction to the modern Canadian military's official acceptance of sexual diversity in its ranks highlights a current tension in the armed forces in
particular and in society in general. Unlike the American armed forces,
which effectively defied the elected government that tried to end restrictions
against homosexuals, the Canadian military has been forced to adapt to the
political will of Parliament and the principles of the Charter of Rights and
Freedoms. In Canada, Parliament's control of the military has been well established in the modern era, from the imposition of unification, integration,
and bilingualism over the intense protests of high-ranking officers in the
1960s to the lifting of restrictions on women and gays and lesbians in recent years. But the military's commitment to social equality must be questioned. The difficulties faced by women and the continuing invisibility of
homosexuals in all ranks suggest that an official policy, unsupported by
many officers, may have limited power in challenging entrenched beliefs
concerning the 'natural' gendered order.

The Allied defeat of the fascist powers in the Second World War strengthened the liberal ideology upon which claims to equal rights are based. It
was difficult to argue against the United Nations' Universal Declaration of
Human Rights and, later, the Canadian Charter of Rights and Freedoms in
the shadow of Nazi atrocities. Ironically, then, the success of the Canadian
military forces laid the groundwork for their transformation, and the subsequent changes have been challenged most aggressively by those who look
upon the war as the golden years of the Canadian armed forces.[9]

The flaw in the presumption that bravery, courage, and strength are
somehow functions of heterosexuality has been exposed in the course of
America's war on terrorism. The terrorist attacks on the World Trade Center and Pentagon on 11 September 2001 deeply disrupted the psyche of
North American culture. In the weeks following the attacks, the repeatedly
televised images of three planes destroying American symbols of affluence
and power instilled a sense of fear and vulnerability in the population at

large. But, at the same time, Americans were inspired by the report that a fourth plane had been hijacked from the hijackers and forced to crash in a Pennsylvania field rather than into the White House. A few brave Americans had defied the attackers and thwarted their intention. That Mark Bingham, widely assumed to have been central in overpowering the highjackers, was an openly gay man was largely buried by the mainstream press. That fact might have had the potential to cause a significant shift in attitude. In fusing the categories of hero and gay man at a moment when an insecure population needed evidence of American might, Bingham's actions could have had a lasting, significant impact. Tall, strong, dynamic, and fearless in the face of danger, Bingham is a perfect candidate for hero status. In life, he refused to allow his homosexuality to be elided from his whole personality. In death, he demands to be taken as gay, as masculine, and as heroic.[10]

Meanwhile, on 11 October 2001, the Associated Press released a photograph of an officer aboard the USS *Enterprise* next to a bomb destined to be dropped on Taliban forces in Afghanistan and inscribed with the phrase "HIGH JACK THIS FAGS." In fact, the Taliban regime was more opposed to homosexuality than was the American military. However, by naming them "fags," the marine intended to smear his enemies as unmanly on all fronts. Such anti-gay references are common in both the American and Canadian military cultures. A significant strain of military self-imagery continues to define 'real soldiers' as 'real men' and as heterosexual, but the marine's anti-gay slur seems petty in the face of Mark Bingham's real heroics, demonstrating that the category of fag, as understood by the marine, is clearly inadequate in organizing actual experience.[11]

Social categories, such as the marine's fag and Bingham's gay, are not historically static, but evolve continuously. Categories are always limited and limiting. They require constant reinforcement for their currency to be maintained in the general population. We had no evidence that the hated Taliban were indeed fags and are certain that Bingham was a self-proclaimed gay man, but with the Associated Press's cooperation with the American military the marine's bias has overshadowed Bingham's heroics. By complaining about the homophobic graffito, gays and lesbians surfaced publicly, not through the heroics of Bingham, but as tiresome critics of military men going about the manly business of saving North American society from terrorism.

Historians have identified the late nineteenth century as a watershed in the history of sexuality. British sociologist Mary McIntosh first described "the homosexual" as filling a social role unique to the modern world. Foucault expanded on that notion, describing how nineteenth-century legal and medical authorities assumed power over sexual categories through the process of defining them. By prosecuting homosexual acts and describing a type of person disposed to commit them, these new regulatory regimes facilitated the emergence of a minority that came to define itself in sexual terms. Prior to this, the homosexual did not have a coherent sexual identity. As many scholars have argued, sexuality can be conceived in countless ways, the gender of the object of desire being only one possibility. Nevertheless, in the twenty-first century, sexual orientation has become a master category of identity.[12]

Many historians feel that this account of the emergence of modern gay communities gives too central a position to the regulators. Regardless of what the experts were theorizing and whom the courts were prosecuting, homosexual communities created themselves in the course of modern industrialization and urbanization. Historians John D'Emilio and Estelle Freedman see the medical model of homosexuality gaining influence in American society at the same time that same-sex practices were becoming more widespread in the late nineteenth century. Historian George Chauncey argues that the gay life that arose in New York at the turn of the century was self-generated and self-sustaining. Others have traced a gay urban subculture to seventeenth-century London. These studies highlight the centrality of the cross-gendered male homosexual. The high visibility of 'fairies' in the decades prior to the Second World War has led historians to see gender, rather than sexuality, as the primary category of identity. Men who acted like women were the signifiers of homosexuality, while those who projected a masculine image and were the active partners in sex could be seen, and could see themselves, as normal, whether they were having sexual relations with a man or a woman. By contrast, since the middle of the twentieth century, sexuality has become increasingly significant as a category of identity relative to gender. But while the category of the homosexual was growing, it could not share its masculinity with the straight world. As sexuality came more and more to define gender, gay men – now more commonly identified – were kicked out of the masculine camp. The increasing insistence on the heterosexuality of men who represent the core of masculinity underscores this change.[13]

This shift in the relative importance of sexuality over the last century has altered the equilibrium of the sex-gender system in Western societies. A number of scholars have identified the conceptual links among biological sex (male or female), gender (masculine or feminine), and sexuality (heterosexual or homosexual). These three binary options organize our thinking about who we are and how we interpret the behaviour of others: men are masculine and they sexually desire women who are feminine. Though impossibly unstable, this system has nevertheless had enormous persuasive force in Western thought. When gender is the most important factor in the triangle, then it is seen as normal for the masculine to desire the feminine; the anatomical sex of the person who represents the feminine is of secondary importance. But when sexuality is privileged, then the sex (male or female) of the partner determines the normality of the encounter; who is on top is of secondary importance. Not only does historical research confirm the shift in the importance of sexuality at the social level, but early researchers of sexuality also tended to define sexual deviance according to gender. For the sexologist Karl Ulrichs, a homosexual was a female soul in a male body, or vice versa. Such formulations kept gender categories intact at the expense of biological sex and sexual orientation.[14]

Chauncey argues that the homosexual was not an effect of the regulatory regimes, and British historian John Marshall suggests that the increased policing of same-sex activities between men in the late nineteenth century was concerned, not with sexual orientation, but with morality. While ultimately, after the Second World War, a homosexual minority developed largely as a result of the policing of sexuality, the earlier targets of this campaign were more readily understood as men who had violated moral laws. Thus, the scandals in the late nineteenth and early twentieth centuries uncovered men who had not governed their sexual lives honourably. Oscar Wilde, the most notorious of the transgressors, was not portrayed primarily as an instance of the homosexual species, but as an example of the depths to which an immoral man could sink. Homosexuality fell within a range of extra-marital, therefore immoral, behaviours.[15]

Not surprisingly, during the Second World War in the Canada military, there was no simple, consistent way that homosexuality could be understood. Any one homosexual action could be interpreted in different ways, depending on who was judging whom. Homosexuality was commonly perceived by authorities as a moral offence. Older officers could forgive such transgressions when committed by young recruits, but were less likely to do so when their peers were the offenders. When homosexual encounters were seen as a moral offence, the active partner was generally deemed the most culpable, since it was his sexual pleasure (it was commonly assumed) that was being gratified. However, when judged through the lens of gender, the active partner (the one who inserted his penis in anal intercourse or received oral satisfaction) was less guilty. The true homosexual increasingly came to be seen by military authorities as not responsible for his actions, and therefore as less guilty. However, this also made him even less welcome in the military family. But when men judged each other, he could be welcomed on the basis of other traits. True homosexuals could be defined in terms of their effeminacy (gender) or the strength of their degenerate desire (sexuality). Throughout the course of the war, the military became increasingly concerned with identifying true homosexuals and was particularly uncertain on this terrain. It had been easier to find a man guilty of an act of gross indecency than it now was to determine whether he belonged to a human subspecies based on his sexual nature.

Of course, as they lived their lives, officers and soldiers were largely unaware of the historical processes within which they were acting. People do not stop to notice whether they are interpreting gender through sexuality or sexuality through gender. Seeing a homosexual act as a moral outrage, a deliciously forbidden sin, a crime against masculinity or against the domestic order follows upon the way that sight itself has been fashioned. People learn to see, to assign meaning to events, within their historical periods. The homosexual acts discussed in these pages were subject to a variety of meanings within the framework of mid-twentieth-century Canada, a time of intellectual, social, and economic change. Visitors from other historical moments would have been confounded by the Canadian responses to sex between soldiers. In Japan, the Samurai tradition included intense homoerotic bonds between soldiers and their protégés. New Guinea warriors accepted sexual relations between men and boys as a rite of passage to manhood and warrior status. Likewise, young recruits in the Spartan army during the classical period were led by older mentors who had recently passed through military training; such relationships were presumed to be sexual. Anthropologist Barry Adam describes how the "people of Siwa oasis in the Libyan desert maintained a military caste from ancient times into the twentieth century that functioned as a bachelor society bonded together through sexual relationships." Soldiers from these diverse cultures, confronted with the regulation of homosexuality in the Canadian Army during the Second World War, would have concluded that the authorities were discharging exactly the wrong men.[16]

These cultures differ from that of mid-twentieth-century Canada in significant ways. The variety of male bonds that underpinned warrior societies were different from those of a modern urban, industrial nation. Social and sexual roles in warrior societies were arranged around the fact of ongoing warfare, whereas the Second World War was an interruption of social norms in Canada. Periodic intense national participation in global wars has had significant impact on social, domestic, and political arrangements in Canada. Some interests have used these crises to push their agendas, others have been threatened by the upheavals caused by war. Wars have offered an opportunity for some men to secure their standing in society by distinguishing themselves as part of a warrior brotherhood as a result of their actions. The state has been central in acknowledging and promoting the heroic sacrifices of men who support the country's war efforts. The state has also been instrumental in ensuring that sexuality was contained within the heterosexual family, the primary social unit in Canadian history. The family has been a flexible entity that has adapted to various economic and social challenges. A variety of state policies have supported expectations that young people marry and raise families. Industrialization and urbanization altered the family structure throughout the first half of Canadian history as Canada transformed itself from an agrarian to an industrial society. The economic crisis of the Great Depression both destabilized and strengthened the family. Likewise, the world wars had ambiguous consequences.[17]

From an economic perspective, the Second World War allowed both men and women to save money to help them start families at the end of the crisis. The state contributed greatly to this postwar domestic reconstruction of Canada. Meanwhile, the authority of the patriarchal family was directly challenged by the war. The state stepped in as the surrogate head of families that had been broken apart by military service. As the war progressed, the services imposed stricter regulations on soldiers who wanted to marry. Before granting permission, commanding officers were required to ensure that the soldier was financially prepared for marriage and that his fiancée was of a good moral character. The forces were concerned that marriage might adversely affect a soldier's willingness to engage in dangerous combat. They were equally vigilant against abuse of the dependant's allowance, since some couples may have chosen to marry simply to gain access to financial benefits. Commanding officers could use their authority to prevent bigamous or interracial marriages, and some French Canadian officers in Britain sought to prevent marriages of francophone soldiers to British women. Meanwhile, many young soldier fathers were forced to choose between military and domestic responsibilities. Thousands of soldiers court-martialled for desertion argued defiantly that their family responsibilities outweighed the army's claim to their military service. Farming communities sometimes shielded young deserters from Royal Canadian Mounted Police (RCMP) officers assigned to recover them for the military. Young French Canadian women urged their fiancés to resist the anglophone military oppressors and save themselves for the more important business of populating Quebec. Thus, many people chose to resist the national assault on the integrity and independence of the family. The fact remained, however, that countless families were torn apart when sons and fathers were sent to fight, and often die, in Europe. In the minds of soldiers fighting in distant lands, family could take on a special significance – a touchstone in a frightening world. While actual families were under great stress as a result of the war, the family as an ideal took on special significance.[18]

While the bonds of family were both strengthened and weakened as a result of military necessity, individuals found themselves in extraordinary circumstances that presented previously unknown sexual possibilities. During six years of war, governed by uncertainty about the near and distant future, young people on both sides of the Atlantic lived for the moment. Passion was momentarily freed of the social structures (notably the family itself) that would otherwise have channelled it into domestic life. Wartime England provided Canadian soldiers with a fertile environment for sexual experimentation of all kinds. The mood can be understood through one story, recounted to me by a Canadian airman from Vancouver with whom I corresponded by mail. His story is representative of countless others:

One eve I was in Harrogate waiting for a bus back to the airport. A guy not much older than me stood beside me and with his fingers in his pocket scratched me as near as he could to my balls, then said, "Let's go for a walk." I was really scared that someone would have seen this happen, but went with him. Behind a railway overpass we stopped. He stood behind me and reached around to my dick. I opened and let him go at it. Then a guy and a girl came walking by!! Of course I hid the erection ... but the girl said, "Never mind ... That's OK."

The unusual had become commonplace in wartime England, and the abnormal normal. Heterosexual and homosexual behaviours of all kinds flourished in the war environment, at all levels of society. However, not all transgressions were viewed equally. Only 1 per cent of all court-martial charges laid for sexual indecency between servicepeople during the war related to heterosexual encounters – the rape of servicewomen by servicemen. Ninety-nine per cent of the military courts martial dealing with sexual infractions among servicepeople concerned sex between servicemen, almost always consensual.[19]

While both the psychic and physical environments were conducive to homosexual experimentation, individual men interpreted their own forbidden acts in cultural terms. Since most men could see no attractive cultural narrative within which to conceptualize their homosexual desires and actions, it was sometimes easiest to deny them to oneself and others. Denial was itself a variation on a compelling and tragic narrative that associated homosexuality with death. A cultural narrative is not a fiction; rather it is a set of meanings readily available to order life experiences. For instance, Oscar Wilde's conviction for gross indecency led to his cultural death by way of the destruction of his literary works and the closing of his plays in London, to his social and civil death in that he was imprisoned, and, finally, to his actual death as a result of the physical and emotional strain resulting from his fall from grace. This association of homosexuality with death is widespread in Canada's wartime records. Some men committed suicide when they could no longer bear the psychic burden of ostracism for their sexual deviance. Sometimes suicides followed convictions for homosexuality; other times servicemen found the public knowledge that they were queer too much to bear. Death or disfigurement could also result more immediately from the physical attacks of compatriots who tried to make homosexuality disappear from their view. Terms of imprisonment led to the temporary military death of men convicted by courts martial of same-sex love, and dishonourable discharges ensured that certain civic freedoms would be extinguished. Psychiatrists tried to kill the sexual desire of man for man. This psychic intrusion could have disastrous consequences for men who had only recently admitted such needs into their own consciousness.[20]

Although some queer men were casualties of the military's anti-homosexual policies and practices, a far greater number escaped victimization. For many of them, the war was a time of sexual self-discovery, an education into the fact that they were far from alone in their homosexual desires. Queer men had to become acquainted with how much room they had to manoeuvre in pursuing their sexual interests and living their private lives. While even the most judicious could fall prey to military police practices, those who understood the forces allied against them had a greater chance of evading discovery. Identifying one's allies and enemies within the forces was crucial to survival. On paper, military police, psychiatrists, and commanding officers held the power to victimize queers, but many of those in authority could also be gay men in search of their own sexual satisfaction. The wise recruit or officer gauged each situation according to his insights into human nature and military politics. While homosexuality had no ideological leg to stand on, not all men judged it negatively. Many straight soldiers and officers saw that homosexual practices met the needs of their comrades. Turning a blind eye was a form of compassion. Those who believe that racism, sexism, and anti-homosexual attitudes were all-pervasive in the war years need to account for the fact that many people managed to see past culturally limiting stereotypes.

The current debate over the effect of gays in the military is complicated by assumptions about the nature of various forms of relationships; both homosocial and homosexual relations are narrowly defined. I do not intend here to engage fully in the policy debate, but offer the following comments as a historian who has researched the bonds that formed between and among men during the war. First of all, the proposition that homosexual bonds are too intimate and would therefore be a threat to the smooth functioning of a unit must be questioned. Homosexual relations can be either emotionally significant or simply functional. Many disputants in the debate, both gay and straight, accept the notion that sexual relations entail a transcendent, spiritual connection that bonds the partners. However, for many people, sex can be just fun. In fact, sexual relations often include more than two people and do not require that the participants even know each other's names. Any one person may sometimes use sex strictly for pleasure or physical release and, in other contexts, use it as an opportunity for interpersonal intimacy. More importantly, forbidding homosexual relations does not put an end to profound friendships among soldiers. Evidence from the war teaches us that a great many men formed exceptionally close bonds with their comrades in the course of their service. These bonds were formed between queer men and straight men, between straight men, and between homosexuals. It is not only ahistorical, but naive, to assume that sexual orientation was the main axis of interpersonal relations.

Our understanding of the past is shaped by the access we have to its records and our ability to read them intelligently. Historiographic practices affect the way that social categories are constructed and understood. A brief example will illustrate that process. The Marine Museum of the Great Lakes (MMGL) in Kingston, Ontario, holds the Lieutenant Grant Macdonald artwork collection. Macdonald, a Kingston native who served with the Royal Canadian Navy, was one of the most talented of Canada's official war artists during the Second World War. In the chapters that follow, I will explore how several Canadian war artists, including Macdonald, conceptualized homosexuality within military settings in their wartime art. Grant Macdonald's queer sensibilities and flamboyant personality did not go unnoticed by those charged with public education. As the three Macdonald pieces reproduced on these pages attest, he explored homosexual and homoerotic themes in his artwork. In the early 1990s Maurice Smith, then curator of the MMGL, tried to arrange for a display of Macdonald's artwork at the Canadian War Museum (CWM) in Ottawa. The idea for the proposed exhibition was accepted and then denied. Surprised by the refusal of a public institution to allow Canadians access to Macdonald's work in the context of his

Self-portrait, 1943. RCN official war artist Lieutenant
Grant Macdonald portrays himself with pencils ready.
Courtesy of the Marine Museum of the Great Lakes at
Kingston.

commission as official war artist, Smith asked for a justification. The director at the time told him, simply, "You know." The CWM would provide no
further explanation.

Similarly, military historians have either elided homosexuality from the
field of study or treated it in cursory or degrading terms. Few historians
have attempted to bring gay and military history together. Allan Bérubé
published the first study of homosexuality in the American military during
the Second World War, *Coming Out under Fire: The History of Gay Men
and Women during the Second World War.*[19] There were, of course, differences between the American and Canadian militaries. As well, there are
several interpretative differences between Bérubé's study and this one.

Grant Macdonald, *Return of the Liberty Boat*, 1944. The "Liberty Boat" ferried sailors from ship to shore. These sailors are probably returning from an exhausting shore leave. The two sailors in the foreground are at ease in each other's arms, and their physical intimacy is not at all threatening to their buddies. Courtesy of the Marine Museum of the Great Lakes at Kingston.

Canadians Asleep on Invasion, 1944. Lieutenant Macdonald's art drew upon the real world. Unstaged photographs show that soldiers and sailors were often at ease, even intimate, with each other's bodies. If the sexual element of a relationship was either sublimated, hidden, or, in some circumstances, accepted, then lovers could fit into their units seamlessly. Someone thought this tender moment worth documenting. Courtesy of the National Archives of Canada/PA131439.

First, while in a few instances Bérubé discusses homosexual behaviour as situational, he otherwise sees the subjects of his work as coherently gay and lesbian actors. Likewise, the American military authorities register few doubts about who should be included in the category. Bérubé's study describes a more or less uniform campaign against an identifiable minority. He does not question the sexuality of the officers and service police who implemented the anti-homosexual policies. This difference in approach may be, in part, a function of the sources employed. Court-martial proceedings, police reports, and psychiatric assessments, on which this study depends, are perhaps more equivocal and variable than the published psychiatric papers, newspaper articles, and military reports that Bérubé accessed. Also, in researching this project, I sought contributors who might offer a variety of perspectives. Some men were referred to me by friends retired from the Canadian military. I approached others in gay establishments and asked them to contribute. A small few answered my advertisements for help in my research. Since most of these methods yielded gay men who had a strong sense of their sexual identity, I also interviewed veterans who had lived married lives or whose homosexuality had been a closely guarded secret. While Bérubé's book focuses primarily on gay men and lesbian women, this study questions more explicitly the relationship between homosexual desire and sexual identity and politics.

Second, research into the Canadian forces suggests that military law was the central feature in the regulation of homosexuality. The court martial was the military's most potent tool in punishing and deterring homosexuality. Bérubé's sole example of the power of the court martial dates from 1922, and he does not discuss the frequency or relative importance of courts martial during wartime. By contrast, the various administrative and judicial options are of central importance in this study of the Canadian experience.

Third, Bérubé does not discuss the regulation of homosexuality among officers as opposed to the ranks in the American military. In fact, almost without exception, he presents soldiers and sailors as the victims of the American military's censure of homosexuality. In contrast, I found that rank was an important factor in the management of homosexuality in all of the Canadian services.

Fourth, Bérubé's study has more to say on the subject of female homosexuality. The Canadian military's wartime files are almost silent on the issue. Although a careful search was made of the program and policy papers for the women's forces, no hint could be found that would suggest a path of research. Women were not court-martialled for homosexuality. I combed the rare instances in which Canadian Women's Army Corps (CWAC) servicewomen were prosecuted for other offences, searching for suggestions of sexual improprieties in the social arrangements of CWACs. Although women were court-martialled for fighting – at times staging major public brawls – no mention of lesbianism entered the record. CWACs' personnel files, accessed when court records engendered suspicions of homosexuality or in cases of suicide, were also silent on the subject. I found no investigations into lesbianism in the forces such as Bérubé discusses in relation to the American military. Psychiatrists scoffed at the idea of including servicewomen in their investigations into homosexuality. Finally, as a gay man, I found it more difficult to find lesbian than gay male veterans of the Second World War. The *Canadian Legion Magazine* would not allow the word "sexuality" to be printed in one of my calls for contributors to this study. As a result, most of the women repondents were unprepared and unwilling to discuss homosexuality.

During wartime Canada, the social categories of man and woman were challenged by changes in the activities that actual men and women were called upon to perform. In the case of the United States, historian Leisa Meyer has explored the resistance of legislators in particular, and society in general, to tampering with legislation that protected the category of soldier as male, despite the fact that women were performing the same work as some male soldiers. As a category of citizenship, soldier incorporated the notion of actually fighting the enemy, a task assigned in fact to only a percentage male soldiers (although all male soldiers were liable for combat duty). Nevertheless, all male soldiers were subsumed under that category. Historian Robert Dean has examined the benefits that accrued to men who parlayed their war service into political success after the Second World War. The category of the warrior hero has ordered American assumptions about some soldiers' claims to power and privilege in society.[22]

I hope to contribute to the wartime literature by examining the category of homosexual as represented by different interests in the Canadian military during the Second World War. The category was constructed by military officials as anti-social, immoral, and effete. Whatever inflection was put on the formulation, homosexuals were *officially* seen as universally inimical to military interests. However, in their actual practices, officers at all levels of command understood the limitations of that construct. Queer men themselves expressed their homosexual desires for the benefit of their emotional and physical well-being. Notwithstanding considerable evidence that the official rhetoric was inadequate to describe the reality of queer men's lives, the category of queer could not be politically or socially challenged in the context of the deep-seated historical antipathy to homosexuality. While the three categories of women, soldier, and men were all under pressure because of their dependence on each other for definition and as a result of the inclusion of women in the forces, homosexuals remained outside of all socially sanctioned categories. Sixty years later, a refurbished gay and lesbian category is challenging the integrity of all three classifications, militarily, politically, and socially.

The regulators and the regulated are studied separately in the following chapters. Chapters 1–3 focus on the military disciplinary regimes: policing, law, and psychiatry. Chapters 4–6 discuss the military experience from the point of view of queer servicemen and their comrades. The sources for this history do not break down neatly into those dealing with military authorities and those concerning queer servicemen. Police records, court-martial proceedings, and psychiatric reports often both shed light on the practices of queer men and articulate the institutional response to homosexual behaviour.

Likewise, in describing their experiences in environments requiring constant vigilance, gay veterans offer insights into actual military practices. Interviews with straight-identified veterans were helpful in that they conveyed the assumptions and mood of the war years.

Throughout this study, I make use of images created during the war. While most of my research time was spent reading and analysing documents and talking with veterans of the war, I also examined wartime documentaries, photographs, posters, and artwork. Photographs chronicle the look and feel of the time; they can also capture something of the relationships between soldiers, sailors, or airmen, particularly if they are candid shots. However, there is value in noticing how servicemen deliberately posed for the camera to document their relationships. The artwork reproduced in these pages helps us to understand how several of Canada's official war artists related to the male body and to the bonds they saw forming between men. Their imaginary life was rooted in the material world and helps us to understand the documentary evidence.

Chapter 1 is based on a wide range of sources and provides a road map to help the reader manoeuvre through the sectors of the state most concerned with queer servicemen. When were servicemen most in danger of being caught and punished for their sexuality? While I outline policies, the reader should not assume that they were applied evenly. The chapter's title, "In Search of a Policy," refers both to the military's attempt to articulate a policy regarding homosexual servicemen and to the problem of uncovering the de facto policies that evolved in different areas of the three services. These 'policies' were not always the result of deliberate attempts to discover homosexuals; often they were adaptations of techniques that were introduced for other purposes. The state apparatus for policing Canadians expanded and was mobilized against queer behaviour. The chapter ends with a suggestion of how the policy that actually governed homosexuality in the military might have been articulated at the time.

Chapter 2, "Military Law and Queer Servicemen," explores the place of military law in the management of homosexuality. Only courts martial could publicly burden a serviceman with the label of homosexual; administrative discharges buried the reason in the medical records of the unfortunate. The genesis of the legal codes and their application to homosexual offences is outlined in this chapter. The dynamics of court proceedings, from the taking of a summary of evidence to the holding of a trial, are discussed, including the composition and responsibilities of a court-martial board. The class bias of courts is explored at some length; in all services, officers tended to judge their peers differently than they judged other ranks. Chapter 2 also explores which men came to be court-martialled and which did not. In addition to their con-

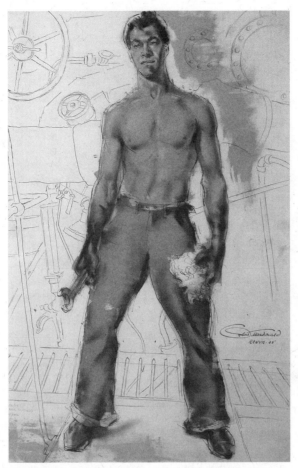

The Damage Is Not Serious, 1945. Grant Macdonald foregrounds the male body of this engine-room artificer (E.R.A.) against the more crude line drawings of the mechanical equipment that he maintains. Another navy artist might have focused on the equipment at the expense of the body. Macdonald's sailor is handsome, with a hint of playfulness in his determined face and body, "braced against the movement of the ship." Macdonald plays with masculinity in his artwork. The E.R.A. holds his steel wrench (hard, masculine) firmly in his right hand. In his left hand ('left-handed' was a synonym for homosexual during the war years), he holds a rag that he would have used to mop up the ever-present oil. While both of his forearms are black from the oil, Macdonald makes the rag white and delicate, almost dainty. Upon seeing the painting, a contemporary artist of Macdonald's commented, "What fluffiness in the waste!" (*Fresh Water: A Journal of Great Lakes Marine History* 6, no. 1 [1991]: 15–17). Courtesy of the Marine Museum of the Great Lakes at Kingston.

The Bath, 1944. Flight Lieutenant Eric Ardwinckle of the
RCAF painted *The Bath* in 1944. In each of the services, official
war artists explored the naked male body, which was on
display frequently under the conditions of war. Source:
AN19710261-1188, © Canadian War Museum.

cern with prosecuting homosexual acts, the courts targeted the desire of men
for men. However, by providing a forum for detailed discussions of instances
of sex between men, the courts could make such behaviour appear commonplace. To counteract this possibility, the rhetoric denouncing such immoral
and disgraceful behaviour was proportionately inflamed. The military
thereby distanced itself from the evidence documenting that homosexuality
was commonplace in the organization.

    Psychiatrists, meanwhile, positioned themselves as the conscience of law,
arguing that the police and legal campaigns against homosexual men were
pernicious and inhuman. Chapter 3, "Military Psychiatry," tests the psychi-

atrists' self-representation as humane and insightful. The official diagnosis of the homosexual as a "psychopathic personality with abnormal sexual behaviour," as well as its context within military psychiatry, is analysed in detail. In fact, this construct represented the most moralistic of medicine's many theories regarding the aetiology of homosexuality. A brief sketch of the various theoretical models to account for homosexuality available to doctors at mid-century is presented. This, in turn, informs the subsequent discussion of psychiatrists' case studies of servicemen referred because of homosexual behaviour. Individual medical officers displayed a wide range of attitudes towards their queer patients, from enjoying sexual relations with them to recommending their discharge from the service. In general, they were reluctant to diagnose men who had sex with men as homosexual.

The influence of psychiatry within the military must not be exaggerated. Those who determined policies regarding the disposition of homosexual servicemen did not seek the advice of Medical Services in the first instance, and doctors had to insist that their expertise was valuable. While some men facing public humiliation for homosexuality received some support from doctors, others were deeply disturbed by the insistence of these 'experts' that they were sick.

Chapters 4 and 5, "Queer Servicemen in Canada" and "Queer Servicemen Overseas," consider the issue of homosexuality from the point of view of servicemen who had sexual and romantic relations with other men. Just as being publicly marked as homosexual was a disturbing prospect, privately acknowledge one's own uncomfortable sexual desires was often avoided. Denying or minimizing one's own queerness, at different levels of consciousness, was the easiest way to protect one's masculine identity. Chapter 4 focuses on experiences in Canada, following recruits through enlistment to basic and advanced training to postings at North American bases. Chapter 5 accompanies the services overseas. The army's role in garrisoning Great Britain presented many Canadian servicemen with previously unavailable opportunities for social and sexual risk-taking. The emergency transformed Britain both psychologically and demographically, and Canadian servicemen were part of the new world wrought by war. Far removed from their Canadian neighbourhoods, in a foreign land where opportunities abounded to think the unthinkable, men of all ranks explored their homosexual interests, often for the first time. On the Continent, during the long campaigns in Italy and northwest Europe, social constraints were further disrupted. Combat put men in situations even further removed from the ordered Canadian society they had left far behind. Still, homosexual soldiers responded to the new opportunities in ways that were consistent with their social and cultural education in Canada.

Chapter 6, "Esprit de Corps, Cohesion, and Morale," considers the effect of homosexually active men on unit cohesion. An extensive military literature is devoted to the study of cohesion, often framed around a discussion of the effects of social differences on the morale of military units. Canada's wartime military effort necessitated a wide range of personnel performing many functions. Homosexuality and homosexuals were present in all types of units, from entertainment to combat. However, homosexuality was expressed differently depending on the expectations of the unit. The masculine core of the army, the infantry units, was less forgiving of overt homosexual expression. Queer men in these units were expected to hide their desires from public view. As the war progressed, however, and soldiers in cohesive units came to know and accept each other well, there could be less need for sexual camouflage. In the navy, long periods of confinement with shipmates meant that secrets were less easily contained. In these instances, the homosexual desires of some men could be accepted among a range of other idiosyncrasies. The closer the soldiers got to combat, dependability became a more important factor in judging men. A queer comrade whose loyalty and trustworthiness had been acknowledged was an asset. The queerness of good men was commonly overlooked rather than accepted by the other men. In the eyes of the authorities, though, homosexuality remained one of the most serious offences. In prosecuting good men for their sexual peculiarity, the military often sowed dissent and threatened esprit de corps.

Chapter One

IN SEARCH OF A POLICY

In this chapter, I offer an overview of the military's response to the presence of homosexually active men in its ranks during the Second World War. I review attempts to devise policies and institute procedures in the air force, army, and navy. However, the actual treatment of men engaged in homosexual activity, gleaned from military records and interviews, reveals that the policy-makers were never in step with the de facto management of queer servicemen. There was also a considerable distance between the category of homosexual and the actual queer men who belonged to units throughout the forces. Officers and soldiers had practical experience in dealing with the reality of homosexual comrades from the beginning of the war, and for the most part, they maintained control of their units' secrets. Anti-homosexual directives were rarely followed at the personal level. However, their existence meant that queer men were always vulnerable at the institutional level. As a result, I present two separate searches: the military's sporadic quest for policies to manage homosexual servicemen and my own investigation into how such men were actually handled at all levels of the military establishment.

This material could be presented in many ways. It would be easy to portray the Department of National Defence, using its own records, as virulently anti-homosexual in its policies and their application. It would also be possible to show that many servicemen and women were offended by their queer comrades. While this approach would be accurate, it would nonetheless be limited and misleading. As one probes more deeply into a wider range of sources, it becomes evident that the significance of a soldier's homosexuality varied greatly throughout the forces. Officers and men did not usually reduce a comrade to his homosexuality, and a soldier's sexual bent was often not recognized (if it ever was) until after he had been judged and accepted according to other factors. However, it would be inaccurate to infer, on the basis of such evidence, that homosexuality was irrelevant in the Canadian military. A more productive approach is to notice when, why, and how homosexuality became an important issue, both for the military in general and for individual servicepeople.

The instances when homosexuality did come to the fore allow us to examine the processes by which people actively defined themselves and others according to their sexuality. Within the ranks, queer behaviour, both in the abstract and the flesh, was a common subject of discussion. At the institutional level, relationships were established – between police, court-martial boards, padres, psychiatrists, censors, personnel and administrative officers on the one hand and servicemen on the other – in which sexual lives were actively, publicly discussed and constituted within a framework overwhelmingly antagonistic to homosexuality. In the aggregate of these countless encounters, the military contributed to the emergence of a historically novel form of identity and citizenship based on the social acceptability of the gender of the object of one's sexual desires. These encounters saw the creation of two sexualities, one of which placed itself socially, morally, judicially, and medically superior to a 'perverted' other. Thus, heterosexuals defined themselves as socially superior in the process of naming and disciplining homosexuals. The war provided a great number of opportunities for such an exercise of sexual differentiation and, as a result, accelerated and put a martial inflection on the creation of a sexual minority, a group of people defined and self-defined primarily, or significantly, on the basis of the gender of their sexual partners.

The ties that bound men together in romantic and sexual relations were largely private. Even in those cases where an entire unit was aware of an affair, it was commonly fashioned as a secret held by a number of people. It is likely that only a small percentage of homosexual affairs ever explicitly came under public scrutiny and discipline. Still, when men jumped at opportunities, created within the context of their military service, to forge sexual and romantic affairs with other men, they challenged the moral order. Likewise, the huge increase in the number of extramarital sexual encounters, undeniable in the face of venereal disease epidemics at home and abroad, alerted many to the threat posed by the social upheaval resulting from war. Many servicepeople found themselves reflecting on how to live their sexual lives. Wartime memoirs describe individuals according to their sexual behaviour, usually framed in terms of moral choices – adulterous, faithful, innocent, promiscuous, romantic, or chaste. Sexuality, the way people fashioned their sexual lives, was not a taken-for-granted category during the war, and even the 'normal' sexual life was increasingly difficult to define.[1]

Not surprisingly, those who believed that Canadian society was disintegrating as a result of the war effort fought to hold it together. The war was a time not only of great change but also of reaction. The military was central to both trends. At all levels of command, officers faced challenges in their private lives at the same time that they were called upon to stop the social fabric from unravelling. In many cases, separating one's private and public lives was the only practical response. Officers, while enjoying or fretting over their own transgressions privately, could pass judgment on soldiers who had broken moral rules. Often, the pressure to impose moral standards on their men originated in higher echelons in the military that were answerable to civilian and political forces. The laws, orders, and regulations dealing with all sexual offences were grounded in a received morality that protected the integrity of the family at the expense of other forms of sexual and domestic arrangements.

Officers became involved in the sexual lives of their men when soldiers became fathers in England, complained that their wives in Canada were unfaithful, asked for permission to marry, or were caught having homosexual relations. Officers and soldiers knew what was expected of them, regardless of how they chose to live their lives in the circumstances of war. Many officers may have honestly believed that they were protecting Canadian society by standing guard against sexual perversion. In recent years, gays and lesbians have positioned themselves as a minority deserving the protection of the state. But at mid-century, it was against such people that the state and society believed they needed protection. There was no contradiction between Canada fighting for freedom and military authorities containing vice. Most queer men lived within the unofficial rules, remaining as discreet as required by circumstances, but some homosexual men challenged attempts to change or demean their desires, arguing that they were perfectly healthy and happy in their sexual lives. These men could draw the greatest wrath of those who claimed the power to define moral standards.[2]

TALKING SEX

Who, during the Second World War, was able to say what about homosexuality? Knowing the way that homosexuality was discussed helps us to understand its place at various levels in the Canadian military. From shower rooms to board rooms to hotel rooms, allusions to homosexuality employed utterly different languages. It was discussed in private between lovers in tender and practical terms. Sometimes those utterances were overheard by third parties and made their way into the public record via courts martial, shorn of their fondness or passion. Censorship operations also transformed intimate correspondence into a public concern; witty or affectionate phrases became coldly cast as the stuff of police investigations. Homosexuality was discussed explicitly in courtrooms and psychiatric interviews in efforts to dissect sexual actions and statements and thereby reveal their deeper meanings. Medical Services had to devise ways to publicly teach queer servicemen about the hazards of anal intercourse while not suggesting that servicemen were actually engaging in such behaviour. High-ranking officers debated, in abstract terms, policies to govern the disposition of queer servicemen. Meanwhile, homosexuality was explicitly invoked constantly by soldiers, sailors, and airmen in the course of their duties. Their most expressive language had a built-in bias against homosexual activity.

Soldiers were regularly court-martialled for using insubordinate or threatening language towards their superior officers. The most vigorous invectives commonly alluded to homosexuality. Actual charges laid against soldiers included the following epithets directed at superiors: "god damned cocksucker," "two-bit cocksucker," "kiss my fucking ass," "I'll fuck you, you savage," "Where is that cocksucking major?", "Go fuck yourself, I can go through you Provost cocksuckers like a dose of salt," "I will not do it until 1:30 and you can tell the Sergeant-Major to kiss my ass," "You are a yellow, cock-sucking bastard," "You bloody, Fucking English Bastard ... Come and take a suck at this if you want to," "What about my fucking pass, you cocksucker," and "You are a cocksucker, nothing but a prick. You know what you are to me, nothing but a punk" ('punk' was the younger partner in a homosexual relationship). These insults not only impugned the adversary as queer, but often set up an imaginary sexual relationship in which he was cast as the submissive partner. "Kiss my ass," "I'll fuck you," and "Suck my cock" all established an explicitly sexual relationship based on an unequal balance of power and pleasure. However, when angry soldiers intended to cast themselves as abused by their superiors or the institution, the expletives used positioned them in the passive role: "I have been fucked around in this army long enough." Men described themselves as being fucked, screwed, buggered, or, most commonly during the war, browned off. To be browned off was literally to have been anally penetrated, but the expression was frequently used in its figurative sense by soldiers defending themselves against any number of charges. For instance, one soldier charged with being absent without leave from the army while in England said that he had gone to see his English girlfriend, who was having his baby. He claimed he had been receiving reports about his wife's immoral behaviour back in Canada. Casting himself to the court as the aggrieved party, he said, "After laying around here for three months and getting reports from home I was pretty 'browned off.'" Sometimes, soldiers depicted their opponents as being both active and passive, as long as they were labelled queer – "I have never had a break since I joined this outfit and you and all those cocksucking buggers can go to hell." Sex between men was widely invoked every day throughout the ranks in a passionate language that was largely their own.[3]

Actual homosexual relations among men were also continually referred to among the ranks. Queer veterans of the war remember the constant talk about homosexuality within their units: "You kidded around all the time ... about sex and about cornholing: 'Take it up the ass like a man. C'mon here, stoop over' and 'Ah, fuck off.' And that's all it was, it was just talk." In his memoir of his war service, Robert Collins speculates that this aggressive jesting may have enforced a cautious silence on his queer comrades. Recalling his training at the Manning Depot in Brandon, Manitoba, he writes: "But if there were gays among us, our merciless banter about 'queers,' 'fruits,' and 'You guys been playing drop-the-soap in the shower?' kept them permanently in the closet. Although eagerly joining in the ribald jeers, I wasn't quite sure what a homosexual *was*." While such taunts were undoubtedly heard most clearly by queer men, they kept the idea of homosexual relations constantly, and anxiously, in view. To step into homosexual relations meant to step outside of the group that ridiculed them. However, this barrack-room teasing could present opportunities at the same time that it outlawed homosexuality. Signalman Edward remembers the uncertainty that could accompany some jesting. In his unit, men joked about shaking their penis after urinating: to shake it more than three times meant that one was masturbating. He remembers the kidding that grew out of this axiom: "And of course somebody would shake it five or six times and say, 'Ya sure, I'm playing with it. Do you want play with it? C'mon, c'mon, here. It's all yours. Do it! – I'm just joking.' And of course, he was joking – but was he?"[4]

It was also not uncommon for soldiers within a unit to discuss actual homosexual relations among their comrades. However, the higher up the military echelon one climbed, the less proper it became to speculate about the homosexual interests of one's colleagues. Moreover, the greater privacy afforded to ranking officers meant that their illicit sexual relations were more easily hidden. Commander Herb Little was the director of naval intelligence during the war. He describes in retrospect the attitude that was expected of any right-thinking person at the time:

My recollection of those times, fifty years ago, is that queers, as they were generally known by, were just something for which you had no tolerance at all ... I have no hesitation in saying that even the slightest breath that any person was engaged with the same sex, you simply wrote that person off ... I think I'm speaking of the attitudes of everybody that I knew at that time, that it was just a NO NO with very large capitals. It didn't occupy any of your time, a fleeting moment would be enough to say, "Not me, I'm not interested ... I don't want to have anything to do with it. I don't want to talk about it."[5]

In speaking for himself and his associates, Commander Little is eloquently articulating the prescribed reaction of the officer class. The documentary evidence fully supports his claim that such an attitude was unquestionably expected of all people, especially officers, who were responsible for representing and defending accepted social values and instilling discipline and self-control in the ranks. Men were expected to control their anti-social passions, of which homosexuality was the most ignominious. His remarks do not address how people, including officers, actually thought and behaved. Nevertheless, they thoroughly ground the bureaucratic machinery under consideration in this chapter. When forced to address the issue of homosexuality in an official capacity, ambitious officers routinely expressed moral indignation. Privately – when tolerance need not be committed to paper – they could be more practical.

ALLOCATING MANPOWER

The Canadian armed forces developed an increasing sophistication in the allocation of personnel as the war progressed, but there are no indications that personnel selection officers (SPOs) and army examiners methodically, or incidentally, restricted homosexual soldiers from the services. Historian Larry Hannant, however, has documented the extensive screening procedures that each of the services instituted during the war, based on the first use of fingerprinting in the Canadian military. He reports that, by March 1942, the RCMP had investigated 104,000 Royal Canadian Air Force (RCAF) personnel for subversive and criminal histories. The RCMP also cooperated with army districts in investigating the civilian lives of some recruits for subversive tendencies. Whether homosexual men and women were affected by those inquiries is not known. Contrary to procedures in the American army, recruits were never asked if they were homosexual. For the first two years of the war, recruits who passed the medical examination were then channelled into basic training. The test of a recruit's ability to cope in the military was the degree to which he was coping.[6]

In September 1941 the Directorate of Personnel Selection (DPS) was established, based on a British innovation, with the purpose of guiding "personnel into the positions for which they were best suited" and advising commanding officers, with the support of Medical Services, "in the handling of personality problems which arise and which may adversely affect training, discipline, morale, efficiency and advancement." While the personnel officers did influence the disposition of servicemen and women, commanding officers were resistant to their intrusions and used them primarily to divest themselves of problem cases. Nevertheless, DPS increased from an initial staff of 43 officers in 1941 to 870 in 1945, in both Canada and the United Kingdom. SPOs were drawn from civilian life and were "mostly men who were not physically fit for other military duties." Through personal interviews, they recorded information about each recruit, ranging from "height, physical fitness, weight, and appearance, to his family background and childhood experiences, through his educational and occupational development, to his attitude towards others and his motivation towards army service."

In November 1942 the Royal Canadian Army Medical Corps (RCAMC) developed a classification system of psychiatric disorders that identified homosexuals as psychopathic and a threat to the military. This was the first mention of homosexuals as a class requiring special attention. Throughout 1943 the RCAMC worked closely with the Directorate of Personnel to develop the PULHEMS system of personnel classification. PULHEMS stood for physique, upper body functions, lower body functions, hearing, eyesight, mental capacity, and emotional stability. Recruits were graded on a scale from 1 to 5 in each category. A grade of 5 signified an inability to serve in any capacity, either in Canada or abroad. Homosexuals were to be graded S5 and discharged as unfit for military service. However, only medical officers would have been aware of those diagnostic categories, and there was no consensus among them over how to identify a homosexual. In practice, very few men were so classified.[7]

In their interviews, SPOs asked potential recruits about their social lives, sometimes referring men of questionable stability to medical officers for further examination. They were typically more deferential towards recruits of higher social standing. Themselves middle class and university educated, they tended to be impressed by cultured, learned men. For instance, after interviewing one middle-aged man who would become a ranking officer in the DPS and whose homosexuality was an open secret in the military, an SPO officer wrote: "Very stable; keen insight into human nature; fine appearance; excellent physique, much younger than his age; high social intelligence; enviable civilian record of achievement. Well known in Canadian

and American Academic circles." It was not unusual for SPOs and psychiatrists to record, as a result of their interviews, such simple facts as "he has
never been interested in girls nor had any sexual intercourse" or "No interest in sports and women." In fact, it is unlikely that they were aware that
homosexuals were to be excluded from the service. One SPO who was himself gay was surprised to discover, more than fifty years after the war, that
homosexual soldiers had been court-martialled and discharged. He himself
had carried on a sexual relationship with one of his superior officers. While
they were reasonably discreet, all of his colleagues in the department were
aware that the senior officer was homosexual. Under such circumstances, it
is not surprising that most personnel and medical officers ignored evidence
suggesting homosexuality. After 1942 the administrative procedures dealing with homosexuality were not commonly known or applied.[8]

Homosexuals in the ranks could represent a challenge in personnel management, but if a particular officer or the men in his unit were uncomfortable with queers in their midst, others could be more accommodating. For
instance, one sergeant from 24 Field Ambulance Company described, years
after his service, the casual manner in which such cases were handled:
"When we were in Camp Borden, there was a chap transferred from an infantry regiment to our unit and the story that came with it is that he'd been
caught sucking somebody's cock and the regimental officers – the commander of the regiment – had spoken to our commanding officer and they
quietly arranged that he be transferred to us." This type of transfer, in
which a soldier's sexual orientation was never cited, probably represents
the most widespread management technique to handle the homosexual
'problem' throughout the war. Although impossible to prove statistically,
since no paper trail was left to connect the transfer to homosexuality, various references support the speculation that queer soldiers unwelcome in
one unit were commonly transferred to another. After one private's trial for
a homosexual offence in 1943, for example, his commanding officer wrote
on his personnel form: "I do not wish this soldier returned to this unit."
The confirming officer recommended "that this soldier be transferred to
another unit on completion of his sentence."[9]

Some commanding officers, however, chose to contain evidence of homosexuality within their units. Precisely because homosexuality was a scandalous charge, making such evidence public could be seen as harmful to a unit's
morale and potentially disastrous to the reputations of otherwise respected
men. In his wartime memoir, Squadron Leader Laddie Lucas describes his
experience with homosexuals under his command. Until the fall of Sicily,
Malta held out in the face of an intense Axis bombing campaign and siege.

RAF fighter squadrons, greatly outnumbered by German fighters and bombers, defended the island. Like many RAF units, 249 Squadron contained many Canadians, and nowhere in the war were greater demands made on fighter pilots.[10] At the height of the battle, Squadron Leader Lucas was told by a trusted colleague "that during the quiet of the previous night at the villa, he had chanced to find a member of my squadron in bed with the officer of another. Somewhat taken aback he had at once withdrawn." Lucas was assured that the two officers had not been drunk but had been discovered having unequivocal homosexual relations. While he wished that his informant had not brought the matter to his attention, he understood that "something had to be done quickly." The two men concerned "had each had an exemplary record in a relatively long run on the Island. They had been successful in the air and brave with it. They were both very well liked and each was now nearing the end of his time on Malta. They were assets to their squadrons." Lucas knew that the "proper, conventional course" of action was to inform the commanding officer of the other man's squadron and then "report the matter to our respective Station Commanders and let them get on with it." He felt certain that, "after weeks of slogging it out with the enemy," the two men would be "dispatched on the next aircraft to the Middle East to await their fate." However, he was concerned about the effect such an outcome would have on his unit: "I thought about the repercussions. No. 249 Squadron, in all its pride, would be stunned. So would the other unit involved. With such a bunch of boisterous, virile heterosexuals (with precious few chances to satisfy their thinly disguised desires), the effect – even if only temporarily – would be cataclysmic. My squadron would suffer and so would its counterpart." Instead, Lucas decided to enter into the confidence of the two queer men. He asked his informant never to mention the incident again and then interviewed the accused. When they gave him "their word that nothing of the sort would ever be repeated while they were on Malta," he allowed the matter to drop. Lucas clearly outlines the priorities that determined his course of action: "By the time I had weighed it all up, I was in no doubt whatever that, wrong though it was according to Service law, my job was to deal with the thing myself and face the music if I had to. What I cared about, on reflection, was my Squadron, its name and its continuing contribution to the battle. I also thought about the individuals concerned, and the effect on the careers of two first-class fighting patriots." Although neither man denied the charge, each "spontaneously volunteered the information that he was not a practising homosexual." The issue resolved, Lucas "shook hands with each and never allowed the incident to cause subsequent awkwardness" between them.

Lucas's account contains many of the contradictions that shaped responses to homosexuality in the military. On the one hand, he outlines his personal attitude to the issue. He writes that the news that two flying officers had been having homosexual relations "did not at first concern me as much as it should. Brought up in a British public school, Oxbridge and Fleet Street environment, the sexual deviations of man (or woman) had always seemed to me to be fairly commonplace fare." On the other hand, he was aware of the grave consequences that would follow upon a public disclosure of the episode. In the end, all of the parties agreed to deny the incident. The queer men assured Lucas that they were not homosexual. Lucas agreed to accept that assurance and to ignore the incident in his future dealings with them. The informant, who had felt compelled to report the matter, agreed to protect the secret. Finally, all of the men involved agreed, not to accept homosexuality in their presence, but to deny its existence.

CENSORING HOMOSEXUALITY

In the game of sex, it was the responsibility of queer men to not upset others. However, wartime conditions complicated that challenge. As the fighter pilots discovered to their distress, privacy was a precious commodity in most military units. Privacy was also violated at the level of interpersonal communications. Censorship operations set the boundaries for what homosexual servicepeople were able to write to each other during the war. Canadian censorship regulations were in place from the beginning of the war and developed according to the particular needs of the services and the RCMP. During the Second World War, censorship was defined by the Canadian state as "the policy of restricting the public expression of ideas, opinions, conceptions and impulses, which have or are believed to have the capacity to undermine the governing authority or the social and moral order which that authority considers itself bound to protect." The reference to "impulses" that were inimical to the "moral order" was a ready-made formula to combat homosexuality. Beyond the concern with public utterances, the chief postal censor oversaw the inspection of a wide range of private correspondence. In 1942 he asked the RCMP and the three branches of the military to itemize the information, culled from this censorship, that they would like to see. The RCAF asked for, among other things, "any information which suggests the presence in the RCAF, or establishes the identity, of inimical elements." The RCMP identified "instances where there is a definite breach of the Law, cases where there is a suspicion and cases where a

'sixth sense' indicates that something is not right." The director of naval intelligence offered a long list of references to be flagged for the navy, none of
which could reasonably be considered to relate to the sexuality of sailors,
but he also noted: "As you know, for the past five months an Officer from
our General Intelligence Section has been calling at your Office daily in order to look over the accumulated censorable mail matter. This system seems
to have worked fairly well in as much as the Naval Service receives such
material as it requires while the remainder is passed without further incon-
venience." The navy, like the other services, creatively used the new tools of
state surveillance in its interests.[11]

RCMP Commissioner Wood's appeal to the "sixth sense" of censors alerts
us to the way that vague censorship regulations came to be applied in practice. Apart from the censorship of public mail undertaken by the post office
department, each of the services censored the outgoing mail written by servicemen. In the field, officers read the letters written by their men, while in
Canada the navy checked servicepeople's mail entering and leaving the
country. The actual censorship was handled primarily by personnel of the
Women's Royal Canadian Naval Service (WRCNS – better known as the
Wrens) stationed in Nova Scotia. Each woman had a list of personnel for
whom she was responsible, so that, over time, she might come to know the
characters that animated the correspondence. One Wren remembers her experience as a wartime censor in Halifax:

We read everything that came from outside the country ... There wasn't too much
to watch for: any details of weather, any ship movements and any unusual comments in the letters ... The first thing was one of the girls coming to me and she
said, "[Margaret], here's a man writing to another man!" And she said, "It's a love
letter!" And she was totally surprised and I said, "Well, I think you'd better discuss
it with the officer in charge." Which is how the whole subject came to our attention ... And the officer said, "If you find any letters of that sort, please bring them
to our attention as a matter of security."

In the social context of mid-century Canada, it was inevitable that regulations that directed censors to watch for dangerous, threatening, and unusual comments should lead to the search for expressions of love between
members of the same sex. Under prewar conditions, same-sex professions
of love had been necessarily guarded and private. The Wren's surprise at
finding such correspondence reveals how effective homosexuals had been
at evading notice. Although she may not have known that homosexuality

was a criminal offence punishable at that time by up to life imprisonment, she could not help but know that it was unusual, even shocking. Similarly, her superior officer immediately saw another opportunity for the work of censorship.[12]

With the enormous amount of mail that was inspected, some expressions of same-sex love were inevitably uncovered. Servicemen and women came to understand that their correspondence could be seen by censors as well as by their commanding officers. Many sailors tried to avoid the problem by posting letters ashore rather than handing them to the ship censor as required by regulations. Similarly, air force and army personnel sought to retain control over their private lives by signing letters with their first names only and posting them in public mailboxes. Such violations could result in minor punishments. Commander Little, director of naval intelligence, requested that the addressees of such correspondence be contacted in order to ascertain the identity of the authors. Many servicemen effactually spoke to the military and civilian censors in the body of their correspondence, thus giving them some control over a world that was constantly spying on them. The following entries seem to anticipate, and perhaps pre-empt, the reprimands that injudicious statements could provoke: "I expect this letter will be read by the censor and I hope he digests this next paragraph thoroughly" and "If I do get raked over the coals for this paragraph it will be worth it." Attempting to fool the censors by signing love letters with a name of the opposite sex was not usually practical, since a unit's censorship officer was aware of the gender of his or her personnel and censors knew the gender of the military units whose mail they were surveying.[13]

As a result of these circumstances, gay men who wanted to communicate fondly to a lover had limited options. The safest alternative was to bring the unit censor into one's confidence and allow him to stamp the letter, indicating that it had passed inspection. Good superior officers often knew and respected the private aspects of their men's lives. However, such correspondence could still be checked by censors, who audited the work of unit officers. Some servicemen tried to communicate their passion either in code or in terms that might not alert the censors to the reality of the love expressed. This was a limited strategy, for the correspondent might also fail to understand the intended meaning. Imagine the anguish of a sailor who tried to communicate with his lover in a German prisoner of war (POW) camp but knew that the letter passed through the hands of the navy censors. Such letters were pulled by all of the services and forwarded to military police for investigation. In one such example, Commander Little wrote to the security intelligence officer in 1944: "Enclosed is a letter from Stoker 2/c [name and serial number of sailor], H.M.C.S. 'Discovery' written to a prisoner of war. It is noted that rather endearing phrases are used and although the letter itself is not conclusive, it is suggested that some sort of watch be kept on this rating [sailor]. Please return the letter to Naval Service Headquarters when it has served its purpose." Such intrusions into sailors' intimate lives were unfortunate twice over: not only was the author now subject to surveillance and possible court-martial proceedings, but a captured Canadian sailor, being held as a prisoner of war in Germany, was denied the comfort of his lover's correspondence. Nevertheless, Commander Little's directive reflects a righteous intolerance of 'immorality.'[14]

The incursion of censorship work into the field of homosexual regulation represents a kind of soft policing. The men and women who uncovered evidence of homosexual love while reading servicepeople's correspondence knew intuitively that something was wrong and needed to ask their superiors for direction in handling such material. Those censors who were themselves queer would most likely have allowed the letters to pass, perhaps deriving some voyeuristic pleasure from the narratives. One of the officers in charge of the censors noted above, for example, was lesbian, as were various other women at the base. But while soft policing was grounded in society's prevailing anti-homosexual biases, military police were explicitly trained regarding the crime of homosexuality. Each of the services, in conjunction with the others and with a variety of civil and state organizations, developed expertise in that field over the course of the war.

MILITARY POLICE

At the outbreak of war, the comparatively small RCAF did not include a provost branch; discipline was the responsibility of the commanding officers at RCAF stations. A provost service was established in October 1939 "to maintain satisfactory standards of dress, deportment and discipline at RCAF Stations and Units and to ensure that Air Force personnel while off-duty or on leave conducted themselves in a manner such as not to bring discredit to the Service." The newly appointed provost marshal chose seven assistants from the ranks of civil, RCMP, and provincial police departments (most were veterans of the First World War) to represent him in the region of the country "with which they were most familiar." His organization, which would become the Directorate of Provost and Security Services (DPSS), sought to fill its ranks with men who were "not less than 5'10" in height and of good physique, not less than 31 years of age, and preferably with some police experience." In all, approximately 20 per cent of the

3,145 service police engaged by October 1944 had civil police experience
from before the war. This heritage forged a link between the RCAF police
and the country's established forces. Indeed, it was felt that the "Service Police were to assist but not to replace the civil police in dealing with Service
personnel" and that they "shouldered a burden beyond the capacity of the
civil police to handle."[15]

In 1942 the provost service was reorganized as a result of two develop-
ments. First, in the fall of 1942, the security guard section of the RCAF police was abolished and absorbed into the service police force. Until that
time, guards had outnumbered service police in the RCAF, as it was felt that
protecting bases and equipment from sabotage was the highest priority.
With the entry of the United States into the war and the cooperation of the
Federal Bureau of Investigation (FBI) in guarding against any organized attempt at sabotage in North America, the RCMP concluded that such a
threat was minimal and that police "protection was primarily needed
against the possibility of attempted sabotage from internal sources, i.e.,
from personnel already enlisted or who would enlist in the RCAF for such a
purpose." Second, in November 1942, an investigation section was established within DPSS, since the RCMP and other civil police forces were "incapable of dealing with all of the very numerous investigations requested by
the Air Force." An investigative officer was appointed in each command,
and eventually all RCAF stations had at least one investigator. These investigators attended a six-week training course at the School of Specialized Investigation in Ottawa, where they studied a wide range of police work,
including the definition of "indecent assault on a male" and the protocols
for the investigation of that crime.[16]

This expertise in criminal investigation techniques, combined with the increased focus on RCAF personnel as opposed to outside threats, is reflected
in the incidence of charges laid against RCAF personnel in Canada. Figure 1
(see Appendix 1) uses data from two sources to show the results of this increase in the policing of homosexual RCAF personnel in 1944. While this
data represents only a fraction of the total homosexual charges laid against
RCAF men, it can be reliably used to represent the trend in policing. At
war's end, the RCAF calculated similar graphs for minor and major thefts,
compassionate investigations, impersonations of officers, and so on, and
found almost identical tendencies. Characteristically, the RCAF did not include a review of homosexual offences. However, the DPSS assessment of
the results is likely correct in regard to the policing of homosexuality: "The
reason for the steady upward climb of all investigations to the peak reached
in 1944 is not apparent but there seems little doubt but that this was prob-

ably due to the increased scope of the Service Police ... In other words it is the belief that the conditions in question always existed but were unreported, and that there was not a crime wave as the figures, on the surface, indicate."[17]

As with the air force, the RCMP was also the backbone of the Canadian Provost Corps of the army. The minister of justice, Ernest Lapointe, rejected the offers of mounted policemen to join the forces when Canada declared war, arguing that they would be needed to maintain order and security at the home front. He did, however, sanction the formation of Number 1 Company, Canadian Provost Corps, comprised entirely of members of the RCMP, to "carry the cap badge and an armband bearing the name of the Force" with the Canadian forces to Europe. As the war progressed, eighteen more companies were formed, drawing on the personnel of the first to fill the most important staff positions. Because of its increased duties on the home front, the RCMP stopped sending reinforcements in 1942. Nevertheless, its influence on the subsequent training, administration, and activities of the Canadian Provost Corps was well established. The provost corps was also able to draw upon a large number of recruits who had experience in civil police work. For instance, the historian of the Hamilton Police Force reports that "in 1944, when the force's strength stood at 150, it saw thirty-five men and thirty-four sons and daughters enlist. This impressive level of wartime patriotism derived partly from a strong *esprit de corps* and partly from the militarism that had always been inherent in the force." Within the Canadian Provost Corps, the special investigation section did work similar to that of the officers of the same name in the RCAF.[18]

Special investigators gathered evidence against servicemen that formed the basis of court martial proceedings. The court martial was the most severe weapon in the military's regulatory arsenal. The number of homosexual charges laid against army personnel in both Canada and Europe (Figure 2,) shows the same trend as the data for the RCAF. The increase in personnel dedicated to policing and the institution of specialized investigators dedicated to the eradication of 'vice' within the forces meant that by 1944 more homosexually active men were being discovered. This heightened policing of homosexuality affected the civil as well as the martial courts. Figure 3 shows that 1944 marked the high point from 1933 to 1951 (inclusive) in the number of charges laid for homosexual crimes in Carleton County, Ontario. All of the increase in civil prosecutions resulted from the added surveillance of military personnel; 62 per cent of the charges laid in 1944 and 1945 were against servicemen who had been uncovered in sexual

relations with other servicemen (one was a pilot with the Royal New
Zealand Air Force, the others Canadian soldiers and airmen). Assuming
this finding is consistent with other civil courts across the country, it follows that the war years were the best of times and the worst of times for
homosexual men. While the social upheavals resulting from the war effort
forced them into all-male environments with a variety of sexual possibilities, the state was only a step behind, using the increased powers of pursuit
and punishment available to it under wartime conditions. As Figure 4 indicates, the war marked a slight increase in the level of policing of homosexuality as a percentage of all police work in Carleton County. Including the
data from the RCN (Figure 5), the total number of charges laid against servicemen in all theatres (discovered to date) is presented in Figure 6. The apparent increase in the level of homosexuality suggested by these graphs was
cause for concern for some authorities. In response to the suggestion that
the air force might be "a breeding place for crime," the chief investigation
officer of the RCAF argued, in defence of the decency of the service, that
"one who is addicted to indecent practices whilst a member of the Air
Force was similarly addicted before enlistment."[19]

The increase in both civil and martial courts was in part a result of the
close communication between various police forces. In all commands, the
assistant provost marshals "were required to maintain contact with inspec-
tors of RCMP, Chiefs of Police, Naval and Military A.P.M.'s, Commanding
Officers of RCAF stations and units, Immigration Officers, hotel propri-
etors, theatre managers and managers of [t]averns, restaurants, etc." It was
at the lower levels of policing that the more practical cooperation occurred.
Cases that had been pursued by the special investigators in the army and air
force could be passed to their colleagues in the civil forces for prosecution.
This was especially true when the increase in the number of prosecutions in
the military drained the capacities of men required to sit on courts and perform duties as defending and prosecuting officers. In 1944 the army asked
the provinces to take over the prosecution of crimes that were not uniquely
military. While the civil courts were not always interested in trying the military's cases as well as their own, cases that had already been investigated
and for which the evidence was prepared could be passed from special investigators in the military to detectives on city forces. Thus, throughout
1944 Constable Herman Boehmer of the Ottawa City Police laid eleven
charges against soldiers and airmen for having sexual relations with each
other over a period of months on military bases.[20]

Pursuing suspected cases of homosexuality was time-consuming for special investigators. While it was preferable to offer evidence that an actual

sexual act had been witnessed, military offences were worded vaguely enough to allow for the prosecution of even the appearance of homosexual activity. Queer men knew that it was wise to find a safe location for sexual relations, and they were usually a step ahead of the authorities in the game of sex. The frustration of that predicament is sometimes evident in the records. Major Moorehouse, an RCAF medical officer, remarked in January 1945, "[A particular airman] is well known to this examiner. My first contact with him was at #1 B&G School Jarvis in 1940. At that time it was realized there must be a homosexual on the station somewhere and after considerable investigation [he] was regarded with considerable suspicion, although there was never any clear cut evidence. In those early days of disorganisation and expansion efforts were made to have him discharged without any success." Military police often investigated suspects who had been accidentally discovered by indignant third parties, entrapped by phobic comrades, uncovered by hotel detectives, or caught in the web of censorship operations. In the absence of a willing witness, special investigators were ruthless in gathering evidence that would result in a conviction. Other military authorities sometimes harshly criticized the police for their overzealous and inhumane tactics.[21]

In many cases, the only witnesses to the acts in question were the partners or comrades of the suspects. In such cases, police were able to use the threat of prosecution to secure the necessary proof. They were especially ruthless in eliciting confessions from the sexual partners of officers. There were no cases of officers being accused of having sexual relations with other officers, however, in any of the services. In part, this was a result of class privilege: officers had greater access to private spaces outside of the gaze of comrades and military police. On the other hand, other ranks were accessible to the investigators, who could harass them to get the necessary evidence. In other words, police could get to officers only through the other ranks, not through the officers themselves. The results of this policing, the courts martial themselves, may lead researchers to believe that the real crime was not homosexuality per se, but the abuse of office. This is in part true, but a more practical explanation for the intense policing of officer/ other rank sexual liaisons is the ability of the police to gather evidence to prove such relationships. The fact that not one of the soldiers who acknowledged having had sexual relations with an officer was himself charged or censured administratively in any apparent way confirms the material benefit to soldiers of cooperating with the police. In some cases, they voiced in court their resentment at being harassed by the special investigators and forced to testify. Some of the men pressed into testifying did not apparently have sexual relations with the officers being prosecuted, but had merely been propositioned by them. Many impressed upon the court the fact that they had not been at all disturbed by these overtures. Such testimony may have been motivated by a sense of masculine pride, since many saw it as an expression of manliness to publicly scoff the solicitations of queers. Others presented themselves as neither judgmental of, nor receptive to, the advances of homosexual officers.[22]

Once the special investigators began to probe the life of a suspected homosexual, their commitment to gaining a conviction was impressive. The case of Lieutenant W is instructive in understanding the investigators' tactics and diligence. Lieutenant W was a highly efficient, thirty-one-year-old administrative officer working at the Exhibition Barracks (the Horse Palace) in Toronto in 1943. His administrative skills were in demand and his superior officers were adamant in their insistence on his value to the district. Among the soldiers that he supervised, it was well known that he was homosexual and that his offers of dinner, movies, or sporting ventures would end up in his private room at the Central YMCA on College Street. Many accepted his proposals. Lieutenant W developed continuing sexual relationships with some of the soldiers, especially those of his own age. Since he was in charge of scheduling the orderlies who worked twenty-four-hour shifts at the Medical Station, he was able to assign his favourites to private sleeping quarters, where he could join them after midnight. At four o'clock one morning in January 1944, he and a medical orderly were awakened by a private seeking attention for a sore throat. The incident sparked an investigation with the goal of compiling the evidence necessary to court-martial Lieutenant W.

The investigators found five soldiers who had accepted Lieutenant W's offers and had spent nights with him at the YMCA and two others, including the medical orderly, who testified that he had made sexual advances to them at the depot. Some of the men who were called to answer questions regarding Lieutenant W's behaviour had gone out with him as much as six months earlier. In order to secure the testimony that would convict Lieutenant W, the investigators presumably made deals with the witnesses ensuring that they would not be charged for their part in the affairs. In one case, a soldier had slept with him on at least eight occasions. Nevertheless, he, like the others, testified that he had been an innocent victim, surprised by the lieutenant's sexual overtures. That the police were able to find seven men whose connections to Lieutenant W dated back to September 1943 is testament to the thoroughness of their enquiries among the men in the barracks. It also reveals that many soldiers knew of Lieutenant W's connections with their comrades. The men who were approached by the police did not come forward out of their own volition, and some were reluctant to help the investigation.

The part played by one witness in this case offers insight into the tactics employed by the special investigators and the support they sometimes found within the ranks. The duty clerk was asleep in the room next to that of the medical orderly with whom Lieutenant W was sleeping on the night in question, and he was awakened by the disturbance caused when the third man, a corporal, arrived for medical attention at four o'clock in the morning. Fifty-seven years later, he says that he clearly remembers the night because it was one of his two wartime encounters with homosexuality, to which he remains resolutely antipathetic: "I only know I'm so dead against it, when I'm approached I'll never forget it." He also clearly remembers being approached by the special investigators whose reputation had preceded them: "As soon as you mentioned [the special investigation section] when you were in the army, you knew what it was." He recalls his interview with the investigators as being quite casual. The evidence he supplied them with was enormously helpful in painting Lieutenant W as a pervert. In the transcriptions of both his statement and his testimony in court, the duty clerk testified that after the corporal had left with the sick soldier, Lieutenant W had come into his room and molested him: "I went to bed at Lights-Out, which would be at approximately 2215 hours, the 15th of January 1944. During the night I was suddenly awakened by someone who had ahold of my testicles. The person who had ahold of my testicles was [Lieut. W], the accused here present. I shoved Lieut. W's hand away from my testicles and asked him what time it was. As I recall it, the accused said it was some hour after four o'clock. I then rolled over in the bed but did not get up. The accused stayed in my room for about half a minute and then left the room." If this account were true, it would clash with Lieutenant W's behaviour in the six other charges that he faced. In all other cases, he had socially courted the men with whom he had sexual relations. Even on the night in question, he was undressed and in bed with the medical orderly in the adjacent room when they were disturbed. In the case of the duty clerk alone, Lieutenant W was accused of a wanton act of lechery.[23]

Today, fifty-seven years after the night in question, the duty clerk is quite certain that Lieutenant W never interfered with him at all. He remembers the night and the disturbance in the adjacent room; he recalls being awoken, not by the pressure of someone's hand on his testicles, but by the nearby commotion. He also remembers being interviewed by the police and testifying at the summary of evidence and the court, but is surprised to discover that the verbatim transcriptions of these events record him making the claim that he had been molested. He does concede that the idea of homosexuality, then as now, "absolutely infuriates me, so I'm biased on that." He recalls that it was well known at the Exhibition Barracks that Lieutenant W courted soldiers, although before the investigation it was discussed only in whispers.

Why the disparity? The duty clerk's wartime account of Lieutenant W's actions on the night in question coincided with his own acknowledged disgust with homosexuality. Both the police and the duty clerk might have agreed that it was against such debauchery that society needed protection. At that early stage in the investigation, the police would have needed some corroboration that the lieutenant was a threat to the young men in the district. The duty clerk conveniently offered them exactly the evidence they required, including the exact time. (In fact, the proposition that he asked Lieutenant W for the time at the moment that he was being sexually molested would seem to diminish the story's credibility.) However, it does not follow that this frame-up of Lieutenant W was an explicit conspiracy between the investigators and the duty clerk; rather, it was more likely the result of men who shared a certain morality pushing their 'truth' to a more convenient location. In fact, the defence had no rebuttal to the clerk's fabrication, and Lieutenant W was found guilty of the charge as framed by the duty clerk.[24]

Special investigators in the RCAF were equally ruthless. In one case, for instance, following up on information uncovered through censorship, in which love but not sex had been communicated, the police wanted to secure the confessions that homosexual acts had been performed. Consequently, they presented themselves as civilian gay men to the airman under suspicion in England. The levels of camouflage and subterfuge in the underworld of homosexuality were staggering: while the police were impersonating homosexuals and civilians, their target in this case was a female impersonator in an entertainment unit who pretended to be a straight man in real life. By gaining his confidence and eliciting a confession, they were able to gather enough evidence to charge him and his lover, a pilot, with "disgraceful conduct of an indecent kind."[25]

In the same way that damning evidence could come to light through censorship practices, it was not unusual for special investigators to stumble across homosexual affairs while investigating other crimes. For instance, while looking into a case of stolen property among the Royal 22e Régiment in England, the special investigators found that the kit bag of a soldier whose nickname in the unit was "Anna" contained large quantities of cosmetics and Vaseline. Lance Corporal Carriere of Number 1 Provost Company reported: "I asked him what he was doing with the powder and vaseline that I had found. He replied that he was using them in his business [tap dancing] and that he used the powder on his face. When I observed that it was a great quantity of cosmetics for a soldier to use, he became angry and replied: 'If you want to know, I use the powder for my arse.'" The soldier's homosexual affairs were well known among his comrades within the Royal 22ᵉ Régiment. However, in the absence of any sustained association with him, the military police viewed him as a pervert rather than a comrade. Private Anna seems to have resented their unsympathetic intrusion into his private life. The police continued their investigation until they were able to intimidate one of Anna's lovers in the regiment into confessing their sexual activities. Thus, a homosexual relationship that had been accepted within the family of the Royal 22ᵉ Régiment was outed by the unwelcome intervention of the investigators. In this way, the military continually worked against itself: an equilibrium that had been established within the regiment was disrupted by police charged with applying a code of morality to which many people and units, in the actual practice of their lives, did not adhere. In fact, investigative police were not welcomed by units, which had more than homosexual secrets to keep. While all men knew how they were supposed to feel about homosexuality, many were more merciful in the privacy of their minds and in practice. Men judged each other on a wide range of issues. Only in the abstract were men reducible to a homosexual disposition. Actual men, for the most part, were judged on the basis of their whole character.[26]

A large portion of the special investigators' work involved probing the activities of the many Canadian soldiers who had absented themselves without leave from their units in England. Since these soldiers had thereby cut themselves off from their army pay, they were known to be without means of support. All authorities took an interest in how such men survived, since it was against the law, both in Canada and England, to employ or knowingly assist a deserter. Once a deserter was apprehended, the investigators interrogated him to determine his survival strategies. Quite frequently they found that soldiers (of various sexual orientations) had lived with homosexual British men. In fact, the police discovered that the homosexual underground was the first stop for many soldiers absent from the army. Prosperous homosexual civilians helped the deserters find employment and offered them shelter and comfort in exchange for sexual favours. Similarly, many absent soldiers relied on women, both married and single, for such assistance. The military police worked closely with civilian police in infiltrating these networks and, in the process, exposed many British men as queer. The civilian forces were especially thankful for the help in their war against vice. In one operation that exposed a queer subculture from Manchester to London and its intimate connection with Canadian soldiers, Scotland Yard compiled detailed files on the homosexual civilians involved, remarking, "The movements of [three gay civilians] will be closely watched in future, as it is quite obvious that they are a moral menace to society."[27]

The commitment of the police and the military's laws and regulations dovetailed with common-sense notions of the period. The laws and policing around 'vice' were not imposed on society, but in step with it. At the same time, they gave support to anti-homosexual attitudes and practices, reading them as patriotic, ethical, and manly. Queer men were sometimes entrapped by phobic comrades, lured to the point of committing themselves to a homosexual act and then exposed as perverts. Soldiers who betrayed their homosexual comrades to the authorities were not always appreciated by the other men. The attempt to augment one's own position by destroying a man's reputation and career could itself be seen as unmanly. Nevertheless, at the height of the manpower crisis, while the almost fatally divisive conscription debate was raging in Canada, well-trained and highly praised infantrymen were being taken out of the front lines in Italy and court-martialled for having sexual relations with their comrades. The temporary loss of infantry power (for they were always sent back to the line after serving their sentences of detention) and the energy needed to hold the courts would seem counterproductive to the war effort. Most of these cases, however, were initiated not by special investigators, but by non-commissioned officers (NCOs) and junior officers outraged over the sexual goings-on in their units. Certain commanding officers apparently saw such courts as a way of maintaining discipline and not as a waste of personnel and energy. That judgment was itself grounded in the assumption, constantly articulated publicly, that homosexuality among men was destructive.[28]

Soldiers were sometimes more conveniently placed than provost police or security officers to carry out investigative work. By observing the behaviour and habits of their comrades, soldiers might come to witness or suspect homosexual relations. In August 1942, in England, Lance Sergeant Kopanski became suspicious when Sergeant Major John O of the Hastings and Prince Edward Regiment "was very familiar with" Private Mike A, a sixteen-year-old runner with the Edmonton Regiment: "[O]n one occasion he shared cookies with him in the runner's room ... and on numerous occasions, I saw him standing on the hallway leading to the R.S.M.'s office talking to

Pte. [Mike]." Feeling that a sergeant major "should not be familiar with a pte. who was a runner," he reported his suspicions to the company security officer. At Sergeant Major John's eventual court martial for "disgraceful conduct of an indecent kind," Lance Sergeant Kopanski stated: "The Security Officer at that time, Major MacArthur, instructed me to be very careful and keep my eye on the accused as regards any repetition of an incident such as I have described." Several nights later, Lance Sergeant Kopanski secured the help of two NCOs and followed the two suspects as they left the Sally Ann canteen and turned off the road into the forest. They quietly pursued them through a convoluted pathway, listening for evidence of indecency. One of the observers testified: "Together we went back along the path into the bush to a point where we could hear voices. We listened for a few minutes and I heard a couple of slight screams muffled; I took the flashlight and rushed into the bushes where I found the accused and Private [Mike] in a state of undress. Pte. [Mike's] trousers were below his hips, his shirt undone and his tunic off. I could not see the front of the dress of the accused's clothing as he had his back to me when I came upon them." The sergeant major was found guilty of "disgraceful conduct," reduced to the ranks, and given ninety days detention. However, the president of the court, Lieutenant Colonel Redman of the Calgary Highlanders, questioned Kopanski repeatedly regarding his authority to investigate his comrades: "When were you first told to investigate this matter concerning the accused?", "Who gave you the authority to do this or was it just a command from the officer?", "What definite instructions did you have?" While the court punished Sergeant Major O for his sexual crime, it appears to have been equally suspicious of a sergeant who concerned himself too much with the vices of his comrades.[29]

It is difficult to know what soldiers or officers actually felt about homosexuality. Military regulations and concern for one's reputation encouraged most servicemen to distance themselves from any queer, or queer-friendly, public image. When an unlucky soldier was found out, his fate depended on the sympathy, camaraderie, or intolerance of others. During the occupation of Germany, craftsmen Bill M and Dietrich of the 9 Canadian Infantry Brigade Workshop had been sharing a tent for approximately a month in Oldenburg. Craftsman Dietrich described to the adjutant of their unit an event that had taken place a week earlier:

At about 2230 hours 31st of August 1945 I left the tent to get some water. I went to get the Guard's Jeep to get the water then I thought that it would be better if I took a thermos bottle to get some tea at the same time. I had to return to the tent to obtain the thermos bottle. When I opened the flap of the tent I found Cfn [Bill] sitting on his bed with a man who appeared to me to be a Jugoslavian soldier inasmuch as he had on a Jugoslavian uniform and was wearing a Jugoslavian hat badge. One Jugoslavian was sitting on the bed and the other was standing in front of [Cfn Bill] and in the best way that I know how to put it [Cfn Bill] was 'sucking him off.' I went out of the tent, there was nobody around at the time. I went back into the tent again and the two Jugoslavians were running out. I hit one on the side of the jaw, I grabbed an empty beer bottle and threw it after the other one. They ran out along the road and that is the last that I have seen of them. I reported the matter the following morning to S/Sgt Gabel, and the Corporal of the Recovery section of this workshop.

At the subsequent court martial, Craftsman Dietrich said that he had been on "friendly terms" with Craftsman Bill. Dietrich testified: "I have asked him to go out with girls but he didn't bother with them." Craftsman Bill testified that he and Dietrich had spoken about the girls who had been in the camp that evening and then began "to drink the Schnapps seriously and that is the last that I remember until I woke up the next morning." Bill claimed that the first he knew of the incident was the following morning when Dietrich told him, "You turned fruit on me last night," and refused to ride with him in the truck. Bill claimed that "there is nothing in my past history to indicate any abnormality. I think Dietrich made up his story to get rid of me because I am cold one minute and hot the next." Craftsman Bill denied evidence that he had been overheard telling another soldier that he loved him and assured the court that he "had intercourse quite often with girls."30

The court found Bill not guilty of gross indecency. Since deliberations were always held in camera, it is seldom possible to know how officers on court martial boards arrived at their verdict. In this case, they could have spared Bill because they felt that homosexuality was too onerous a burden to saddle him with or because they thought the incident trivial. Bill's defending officer had cautioned the court: "I feel that [the prosecution] has not made a case that warrants disgracing this man for the rest of his life." Whatever men felt about queer behaviour, they were aware that labelling a man homosexual could indeed have serious consequences. The incident defines the limits of the military's regulations. The case came to trial because Bill was unfortunate in sharing a tent with an unforgiving soldier whose righteousness may have forced the commanding officer to instigate court-martial proceedings. However, Bill was fortunate in that the major and captains who sat in judgment were merciful. While the great majority of men denounced homosexuality in public pronouncements, few were willing to destroy men's lives because of their sexual difference. At the same time, even though he was acquitted, Bill had been forced to undergo an unpleasant ordeal that could have profound consequences. The military supported servicemen and women of any rank who chose to prosecute their queer comrades. On occasion, it also came to the aid of those accused by clearing their reputations.

The pervasive and often subtle anti-homosexual propaganda to which most Canadians had been exposed from birth affected the self-images of many homosexual men. This was evident in the self-policing that can only be explained by the guilt that could accompany homosexual desire. For example, late one night in 1944 in the hills of Italy, far from any critical gaze, a soldier stopped a jeep at the request of the officer he had been assigned to chauffeur. The officer felt the soldier's crotch, as he had on various occasions earlier in the evening, pulled him from behind the wheel, and gave him a blow-job. The driver enjoyed the pleasure, laying his hand on the back of the officer's head, following the rhythm of the movements. After he had ejaculated, he drove the officer back to camp and they bid each other good night. The incident played on his conscience for three days before he confessed the 'crime' to his corporal. Until then, no one could ever have found out about the episode; no one need ever have been court-martialled for his secret pleasures. Although no one's life would have been altered dramatically by the incident, the soldier felt the need to confess his crime to his superior to relieve himself of his guilt. Such incidents reveal the reach of society into the consciences of citizens.[31]

THE RCAF SEARCH FOR A POLICY

Evidence compiled through investigations was the basis of courts martial whereby the final disposition of the accused was left to the discretion of the court. Military law inherently accepted the possibility that men might behave indecently, but operated on the assumption that they could be dissuaded from such activity by making the repercussions unpleasant. However, military officers could not reconcile that perspective with the expanding category of the homosexual. Deterrence would have a limited effect on the constitution of a person whose desires were fixed and directed towards the same sex. Therefore, as the number of homosexual courts martial rose in late 1943, the RCAF looked for a more efficient way to handle the problem. A brief look at the debates of 1944 sheds light on the effect of the concept of the homosexual on military policy.

It was presumed by the policy-makers that homosexuality was contempt-
ible and that homosexuals were unworthy, degenerate, and a threat to the
forces. That formula underwrote all public discussion regarding the issue in
the military. Nevertheless, there were differences regarding how to identify
a homosexual. Since homosexuals were bad men, good men were reluc-
tantly and infrequently marked as queer and same-sex sexual behaviour
was not interpreted as indicative of a homosexual character. The courts
were often willing to overlook considerable evidence that someone was homosexual, and psychiatrists were reluctant to diagnose servicemen as homosexual on the basis of queer behaviour. Meanwhile, the police, working
independently of the courts and psychiatrists, often had difficulty gathering
sufficient evidence to prove that suspects had engaged in homosexual acts.
Therefore, even those men who did face courts martial for homosexual offences could escape conviction or serve terms of detention or imprisonment
and then rejoin the air force family. In April 1944 the chief of air staff (CAS)
asserted in a memorandum that it had become clear that prison terms
would not "produce any reformation in character" or "deter other personnel with similar tendencies." The concept of a homosexual orientation, as
opposed to a man who succumbed to immoral temptation, underlay the
search for a new policy.[32]

As a result, throughout 1944 the RCAF tried to arrive at a policy that
would assure the discharge from the service of men known to be homosexual. Within the context of the RCAF's evolving personnel management
strategies, the search for a homosexual 'type' was congruent with attempts
to detect servicemen predisposed to cowardice through a "lack of moral fibre" (discussed by historian Allan English). After several months of deliberations, the first directive was issued on 5 April 1944, advising that men
suspected of being homosexual should be discharged, citing merely that
their "services [were] no longer required," and that officers were to be retired. Men were no longer to be court-martialled for homosexual offences.
In cases where civilians were involved, prosecution was to be left to the discretion of the civil courts and discharge to the RCAF. (RCAF personnel were
already being prosecuted by the civil courts in cases involving civilian sexual partners.) Special investigators were to continue their work, bringing to
light hidden queer networks. This administrative policy was arrived at
without any consultation with Medical Services. The fact that a policy
could be debated at the highest echelons of the RCAF for four months without any referral to Medical Services alerts us to the place of medicine in the
mindsets of the administrative officers. They saw homosexuality primarily
as a legal and personnel issue. While the medical model of the homosexual

as a type of person may have contributed to the historic shift in understanding human sexuality that underlay their deliberations, administrative
and legal officers were unaware of Medical Services' earlier categorization
of homosexuals as "psychopathic personalities with abnormal sexual behaviour."[33]

Medical Services took exception to the new policy, arguing that only psychiatrists could determine whether someone was a true homosexual. Men
against whom evidence had been compiled were guilty of sexual misconduct, but 'true' homosexuality was a medical condition. Some suspects
could be medically diagnosed as homosexual but never engage in homosexual acts, whereas most of those who were homosexually active were determined to be sexually normal. The doctors initially argued that most
homosexual men desired to be cured and that medicine could accommodate them. (Personnel psychiatric files do not support those assertions.)
However, they agreed that any long-term cure was difficult and that such
men should not, meanwhile, remain in the service. This criticism gave rise
to the reinstitution of court-martial proceedings in August 1944 and the re-
sumption of deliberations for an acceptable policy. By 23 December 1944,
the RCAF finally issued a replacement directive, allowing the police and the
courts to continue investigating and prosecuting men against whom evidence had been compiled. Meanwhile, both those men and others who
were merely suspected of being homosexual were to be referred to psychiatrists for their opinion as to whether "homosexuality is present." Administrative discharges for homosexuality thus became the privilege of Medical
Services. However, discharges that were part of a court's sentence were out
of their hands.

The RCAF doctors did not try to replace the courts, but merely asserted
themselves as the authorities that determinded which queers were to be
marked homosexual and which were not. Air force psychiatrists argued
that homosexual men who were content with their sexual perversions justly
deserved to be punished. They agreed that the courts were correct in claiming jurisdiction when evidence of sexual misconduct had been collected. By
the terms of the final directive of December 1944, psychiatrists were to be
notified of all impending court proceedings so that they could advise the
defending officers and gain information about the cases. Psychiatrists were
happy to use the services of the police and courts to learn about homosexual behaviour, but they wanted all functions to defer to their medical expertise in the final labelling of suspects. Thus, psychiatry was not, and did not
seek to be, a replacement for law; instead, it was another level of control in
the campaign against homosexuality.[34]

PUNISHING IMMORALITY AND CONTROLLING VICE

The Medical Services' position on homosexuality in the military was grounded in the understanding that while homosexuality was a sickness, individuals were nevertheless responsible for their behaviour. There was no contradiction in claiming homosexuals as the natural subjects of medicine and also seeing them as accountable to the legal system for their actions. Medicine and law used similar methods to achieve their common goal of the elimination of homosexuality from the body and the body politic. The suspect first entered into a discourse that was intended to overwhelm him with guilt and shame. He was isolated and humiliated because of his apparent moral and developmental inadequacies. On top of this psychic torture, his body was subjected to a regimen aimed at the reformation of its sexual responses. In the case of psychiatry, this physical intrusion could target more directly the source of the problem through aversion therapies, designed to punish the body for homosexual responses and praise it for heterosexual. Meanwhile, law punished the entire body through confinement, the elimination of pleasures, and the imposition of hard labour. If either law or medicine was able to claim any success, it was through browbeating their subjects into denying their unwelcome sexual responses.[35]

One irony of the criminal system was that in punishing men for homosexual behaviour, it confined them in all-male environments in which homosexuality could flourish. Men who may not have had homosexual experiences beforehand had the opportunity in prison. Thus, against its own rhetoric, the military became a recruitment centre for homosexuality. Men whom military psychiatrists had confirmed to be homosexuals were deemed unfit for service in any capacity, and yet detention and imprisonment were forms of military service. This administrative incongruity was glossed over by the doctors themselves, who argued that "the lowering of the Pulhems profile to S5 [signifying a homosexual disposition and necessitating discharge] does not automatically prevent a man from undergoing detention." Nevertheless, military authorities were concerned about the prevalence of homosexuality in military prisons. As the war raged on in Europe, the Canadian Army was increasingly challenged to find space to accommodate the many soldiers under sentence (SUS). The British juggled their own prisons to allow the Canadians more space. However, the continuous crisis of the lack of accommodation was exacerbated by the fear of homosexuality among SUS. The deputy provost marshal, for instance, described to his superior at Canadian Military Headquarters in London how the attempt to keep men sexually pure trumped the problem of the lack of

Canadian Detention Barracks, Winnipeg. Soldiers under sentence go through drills on the exercise compound. After the war, some soldiers complained bitterly about mistreatment while in detention, including homosexual abuse by guards. Courtesy of the Directorate of History and Heritage.

Canadian Detention Barracks, Winnipeg. This is the corridor of a cellblock where soldiers served their sentences. The sentences of those convicted of homosexual offences varied from thirty days to years. Courtesy of the Directorate of History and Heritage.

space: "As at 29 Jan 45, there were 591 SUS in the [Canadian detention barracks], with reservations for 30 more to be admitted on 31 Jan. The Commandant had arranged to put 2 men in each cell in A Compound but I explained to him that for moral reasons this procedure would not be approved. Unfortunately the cells have not got sufficient cubic space to allow for three men in a cell." Homosexuality was imagined to be a secret held between two men; introducing a third man into a cell meant that each would patrol the other two. In this way, the military could save on the number of guards required.[36]

The prisoners, however, were not the only source of homosexuality in military detention barracks and prisons. Guards also could strike up sexual relationships with soldiers under sentence. In fact, it was not uncommon for guards to take advantage of their position of power over the soldiers to gratify themselves sexually. During the war and after, soldiers complained about the inhumane treatment they received at the hands of Canadian guards. One staff sergeant, who had been wrongfully convicted and was later declared not guilty of the offence for which he served time at the Canadian detention barracks in England, was among many soldiers who complained of intimidation, beatings, and mistreatment. He related the warning given to the soldiers under sentence by a guard who had just come on duty: "This is my first night with some of you, and I want you to know I am a hard son of a bitch; I'm also a prick and I'm sure that at one time or another you have jerked yourselves off; that is done by rubbing it. Well rubbing me will make me go off, and when I do, I'll splash all over you. It will be your own God-damned fault if I do." The poetic image of the guard as a penis waiting to ejaculate on the soldiers was not entirely metaphorical. Both the army and air force were forced to court-martial guards for having consensual or forced sex with various soldiers. Initially, the size and strength of some homosexual men and their prewar experience in penal institutions had recommended them for work as guards. Moreover, the willingness of experienced and qualified men to enter the service as guards, an otherwise unglamorous position, was welcomed by the personnel officers.[37]

Soldiers under sentence sometimes appeared before the medical officer with a venereal infection that appeared while they were in detention. Since the incubation period for gonorrhoea was not greater than ten days, its sudden appearance required an explanation. On the rare occasions when the medical records do acknowledge that a man probably contracted gonorrhoea homosexually, they tend to leave the obvious unstated. For instance, in one such case at 62 Military Detention Barracks in Canada, the medical officer simply recorded: "He was in prison past the incubation pe-

riod for VDG [gonorrhoea]." In other cases, no mention is made at all of venereal disease. One queer soldier imprisoned at 66 Military Detention
Barracks in Valcartier claimed to have had gonorrhoea nine times, but there
is no mention in his file of venereal disease. The most common theory to
account for sexually transmitted diseases among men who were not in contact with women was that the patient had infected himself. One doctor
treated a patient for gonorrhoea who had been in detention for the previous month. Where the soldier's case sheet required the identity of the sexual
contact, the medical officer noted, "(in detention)(self-infection?)." The rationale behind the theory of self-infection was that soldiers in detention
would infect themselves with gonorrhoea in order to be transferred to a
hospital from which they could more easily escape. While such a strategy
was possible, it was not the simplest explanation for gonorrhoea contracted
in prison.[38]

MEDICAL SERVICES

Controlling venereal disease occupied much of the attention of Medical Services in both Canada and Europe. Doctors, in their temporary roles as medical officers, assumed the front-line positions in a long-standing battle
against sexually transmitted diseases.[39] The powers of control assumed by
the military over the bodies of one million Canadians provided the conditions for a major assault on venereal disease. By means of short-arm inspections, doctors examined soldiers' genitals regularly. ('Short arms inspections'
were surprise examinations in which soldiers were paraded naked so that
the medical officer could survey their genitals for signs of venereal disease.)
They were also advised to inspect "mucosa, anus, and genitalia ... as often
as circumstances permit during treatment and at each probationary inspection." The genitals of officers were spared such intrusions, and these men
frequently sought medical attention outside the military for embarrassing in-
fections. Other ranks, however, were constrained by orders and regulations
to take all available precautionary measures and to report any infection to
medical officers. Since the military could account for the venereal health of
its mostly male personnel, it felt justified in targeting civilian women as the
cause of the continued high infection rate. Overseas, British medical authorities blamed the Canadian troops for the increase in venereal infection
among English women, arguing that Canada had not been as vigilant
against the diseases as England.[40]

The military went to great lengths to stem the loss of manpower due to
sexually transmitted diseases. Venereal disease control units followed the

First Canadian Army across Northwest Europe, providing forward treatment for infantrymen. Approximately one thousand cases were cured each month at the front by one such unit. In Canada, England, and Newfoundland, the military promoted extensive educational campaigns aimed at giving clear and explicit information regarding the avoidance, identification, and treatment of the venereal diseases. While men were urged to abstain from sex altogether, it was recognized that a more practical strategy to lessen the likelihood of infection was to make sex safer by making soldiers smarter. Medical Services worked diligently to dispel misconceptions about venereal diseases. Doctors were constantly urged by their superior officers to eradicate the widespread ignorance regarding sexual hygiene: "*emphatic assurance* must be given that gonorrhea cannot be contracted by the casual contacts of army life and that segregation of infected persons and provision of separate facilities is inefficient and unscientific. Toilets, ablution rooms, food handling, dishes, etc., *do not* play a role in the spread of gonorrhea … The medical officer must not permit popularly held fallacies to jeopardize the scientific, efficient management of gonorrhea in his unit." Scientific objectivity nevertheless came up against the reality of social biases in attempts to communicate the possible sources of infection. Both in lectures to soldiers and educational pamphlets, venereal disease was said to be "contracted *in one way only* – by having sexual intercourse with an infected woman."[41]

Medical Services faced the problem of having to communicate to homosexually active soldiers that assuming the receptive role in the act of anal intercourse was an especially risky behaviour. However, the public discourse overseeing sexuality precluded presenting homosexuality as a fact of military life. The efforts of the medical authorities to reach homosexual men and still obscure the meaning of their communications from others required much deliberation and creativity. For instance, in a widely distributed pamphlet that initially identifies infected women as the sole source of gonorrhoea, the back cover listed ten guidelines:

Remember: –

1. Venereal Disease is 100% avoidable.
2. Venereal Disease is only caught from an infected woman! Other men undergoing treatment are no danger to you!
3. Sexual intercourse is not necessary to maintain Health and Strength.
4. "Wet Dreams" are not harmful but are a sign of well-being.
5. You cannot tell by a woman's looks if she is safe.

6. Prostitutes with medical Certificates or in Brothels are a menace.
7. If you get "Browned Off" – look out! Look out – that's when you are an easy victim.
8. Alcohol makes wise men fools. Look out! Look after your pal if he is drunk!
9. If you DO run foolish risks, take preventive measures.
10. If you get Venereal Disease you can be cured, but only if you take the full treatment.

Buried in seventh position is the warning of the danger in being "browned off." In its most common usage, to be browned off meant to be irked, frustrated, and angry, and it was popularly used by soldiers to refer to their common response to the enforcement of petty military regulations. The expression, however, derived from the experience of being actually buggered and was often used in that sense by homosexually active men. On the one hand, then, those reading the pamphlet at a glance could have interpreted number seven as a reference to the value of not losing your temper – probably good advice, although largely irrelevant in relation to sexual diseases. On the other hand, those who did engage in anal intercourse might have understood that there was a high risk of infection associated with it. The inclusion of the warning to homosexual men is a sign that medical officers were aware of the frequency of homosexual exposure to venereal disease and felt it significant enough to devise ways to overcome proscriptions against the public mention of homosexuality. It is ironic that the authorities chose to deliver their message through double entendre, a practice that gay men had elevated to an art form.[42]

Whether men had contracted venereal disease from other men or from women, they were reticent about cooperating with the authorities. Doctors were the first step in a network of policing organized to identify, locate, segregate, and cure the civilian women identified as the source of infection. At the outset of each case, medical officers were required to extract from the soldier the name of the woman who had infected him. They were trained in interrogation techniques designed to convince the patient to cooperate. For those who did reveal the identity of their sexual partners, the venereal disease control officers often succeeded in forcing the women into treatment centres. Most men, however, were vague about the identity of their sexual partners. Knowing that the information would be used to harass and humiliate their lovers, they instead commonly reported that they did not know her name or place of residence. They may well have told their sexual partners themselves that they were infected, allowing them to find treatment discreetly from their own doctors. Queer men faced the additional problem that the truth would expose both them and their lovers to criminal charges. Consequently, although they sometimes remembered the places and times of encounters, they never admitted the name or sex of their partners. This deceit on the part of both queer and straight men, motivated by a desire to protect their lovers, misled the authorities into believing that venereal disease was overwhelmingly concentrated in the category of "loose women," variously known as "pick-ups," and "amateurs." Whether their sexual partners were well known to them or not, soldiers resisted identifying them. Ruth Roach Pierson asserts that misogyny and gynaephobia informed the construction of the loose woman as a menace to male soldiers. That judgment overlooks the evidence that led medical officers to conclude, naively, that pick-ups were the primary source of infection for soldiers.[43]

While the military administration, including Medical Services, argued for a scientific, value-neutral approach to sexuality, its distaste for sexual diversity was deeply entrenched. Men undergoing treatment for venereal disease were meant to feel like criminals. One private wrote to the prime minister from the military hospital in Saskatoon:

I am a patient in the venereal disease ward and there are over 30 other boys with me. We're not permitted to have anyone but male visitors and we're confined to the grounds only behind the hospital. They wouldn't even let one fellow see his wife when she came all the way from Regina. Now my wife is coming from Montreal shortly and if I'm not allowed to see her there's something wrong. Is there any harm in seeing her half an hour each day in the visiting room? After all gonnorhea [sic] is not contagious *unless* there is intercourse. Also this place isn't even fit for a V.D. ward. It's in the basement of a school and half the time it looks like a pig sty. It's damp and the ventilation is very poor.

The district medical officer dismissed the complaints, saying that he was "not disposed to unduly consider the comfort of venereal patients who are in double deck beds, who have radios, magazines and cards." Far from sympathizing with the soldier's situation, he was "surprised to find that even male visitors are allowed in the wards. Certainly, it is not, in my opinion, reasonable to permit wives or other female visitors to visit venereal disease wards." Venereal disease patients, therefore, as sexual outlaws, were temporarily cast in the role of social pariah. For many, the stigma attached to sexually transmitted diseases caused intense psychological conflict.[44]

Venereal disease, like homosexuality, was something men were expected to have some control over. Moralists believed that those who could not remain either chaste or faithful to their betrothed or wife had failed to fulfil their social responsibility as men. While a great many men and women were sexually promiscuous, they were easily villainized because of the political strength of the moralists. Only the rare man with venereal disease took a public stand in defence of his rights, and the results were unfavourable, since he was already stigmatized. Similarly, while homosexual men occasionally defended their rights to their own sexual desires, defying established authority, they had no popular footing to stand upon. The certainty that homosexuality was immoral and the fact that it was criminal meant that, once marked, men were at the mercy of the established authorities.

MILITARY ADMINISTRATION

Being marked as homosexual within the military could have long-term financial and social consequences. Those convicted by court martial of a homosexual offence were often sentenced to be "discharged with ignomiy," "dismissed," or "cashiered." The administration could also discharge problem soldiers for "misconduct." Under military regulations, a serviceman discharged under such terms forfeited his war service gratuity (WSG), medals, awards, and honours. Soldiers and officers could also be hounded later in life in certain circumstances. Employers sometimes asked to see the discharge certificate, for example, and veterans discharged with ignominy were excluded from employment by the Crown in any capacity. In 1944 the discharge review board (properly titled the War Service Gratuity Board of Review) was established to decide which dishonourable discharges could be remitted, thus allowing men to claim their gratuities.

The WSG was a bonus paid to servicepeople calculated as a percentage of the number of days of qualifying service during the war. As one element in the extensive legislation passed under the umbrella of the Veterans Charter, it was intended to help men make the transition to civilian life, recognizing that a small amount of capital could assist in starting a new business or a family. The veterans' re-establishment and rehabilitation benefits were based on a recognition of war service and intended as compensation for the time spent fighting for the country. In contrast, the 1943 family allowance legislation was informed by the principle of universal entitlement and marked the beginning of the Canadian welfare state. Veterans' benefits were disbursed according to a strict accounting of the "length of service, injury or non-injury, and service overseas or in Canada."[45]

Servicemen were obliged to apply for their gratuities, and the applications of those with unfavourable discharges were forwarded to the review board. The board, comprised of representatives from the three services and the Department of Veterans' Affairs, would review the circumstances of the discharge and decide whether the applicant could be judged worthy of his gratuity. The board's deliberations regarding the claims of homosexual servicemen offer some insight into the way that bureaucrats could turn state privileges against those judged antithetical to the state's interests. Its rationale for denying gratuities to soldiers who had been convicted of homosexual crimes, or who were known to be queer, helps us to understand the expansion of state surveillance techniques. For instance, by September 1946, the board was regularly reversing the discharges of soldiers dishonourably discharged for repeated misconduct and periods of desertion, but consistently rejected the requests of those whose discharge resulted from homosexuality. In denying the claim of an RCAF corporal who had been discharged by court martial for having consensual sex with another airman, the board argued, "The Board considers that acts of sexual perversion should be categorized in such a manner that they can be kept track of in civilian life and therefore a change in his discharge category is not warranted." The board overstepped its mandate by trying to preserve a database for the extension of military surveillance of homosexuals into postwar civilian life. There is no evidence that the state did finally make use of its knowledge of homosexual offenders.[46]

The members' comments on individual cases often reveal the personal disgust for homosexuality that underlay their attempt to write postwar policy from their position on the review board. Highlighting the peculiar problem that homosexuality posed, the RCAF administration forwarded to the review board even those cases where men who had been honourably discharged were suspected of being homosexual. One airman had been convicted of homosexuality by court martial but had been honourably discharged. Therefore, his gratuities should have been uncontested. Nevertheless, the RCAF was "in doubt respecting this application and has been unable to arrive at a decision." After deliberation, the board approved the grant but articulated its reservations:

These cases involving sex abnormality are most perplexing. On the one hand there is usually medical opinion to the effect that the condition is beyond the control of the individual and on the other the fact that offences of this nature are not only repugnant to conventional standards of conduct but are criminal acts under the law of the land. In this particular instance no gross act of indecency was proven, service is reported to have been good and there are no other offences. Sentence of the Court Martial was comparatively light and the discharge certificate states "honourably released."[47]

The board's considerations underline the uncomfortable fit between the medical model of homosexuality and received attitudes toward it. First, although men were expected to control their behaviour, the officers on the board had been introduced to the notion that homosexual behaviour might have been beyond the individual's control and therefore more to be pitied than censured. Nevertheless, the fact that homosexuality was considered both "repugnant" and "criminal" would seem, in their minds, to outweigh any appeal to nature. It was only because there was no hard evidence that they decided to recommend that the airman receive his gratuities. As with all public pronouncements on homosexuality of the time, the condition seems to have been far removed from the experiences of the officers charged with its administration: they comfortably placed themselves as 'normal' men pronouncing their verdict upon an unfortunate (immoral, dangerous, or pathetic) queer. Homosexuality was consolidated as a significant factor in the cataloguing process carried out by the men charged with administering the regulations. 'Straight' men actively placed themselves in a position of power over 'homosexuals' each time they pronounced a verdict, whether merciful or harsh, upon them.

In 1947 the review board was asked to relax its guidelines, as it was felt that it "would be inconsistent with the true spirit and intent of the WSG Act of 1944 as amended to deprive the member of the benefits." Many men discharged for homosexual activity reapplied, sometimes for the third time, and were granted their gratuities in 1947. Several, however, continued to be denied after 1948 on the basis of their having had consensual homosexual relations. The board customarily reviewed the court-martial proceedings on which the sentence had been based. If it found mitigating circumstances, it sometimes changed "discharged with ignominy" to "services terminated in the interests of the Army." There were times, however, when the board rejected requests that the sentence of dishonourable discharge be remitted. Officers, for instance, were never pardoned; the dishonourable discharge was the sole punishment for officers, since they were never sentenced to terms of imprisonment. They may also have prompted a particular sense of indignation among the fellow officers on the board. One ex-captain wrote to all levels of the state over a period of three decades asking for amnesty for his court martial for homosexuality. From his member of Parliament to Prime Minister Pierre Elliott Trudeau, all refused to interfere with the judgment of the court. The military also remained steadfast regarding other privileges. Homosexual servicemen who asked for their war medals and awards were typically advised, "We regret that we can only inform you the Board has decided that any application you may make is to be denied."[48]

THE MILITARY'S QUEER PUBLIC FACE

The National Film Board's (NFB's) 1944 documentary *Future for Fighters* describes the opportunities available to returning servicemen through government loans and grants. It is surprising, given the attitude of the military in general and the Board of Review in particular, to see its apparent approval of same-sex partners. It features two couples appearing before a veterans' land settlement committee comprised of three elderly men. The first couple, a young soldier and his wife, intend to raise a family with a grant that would allow them to establish a farm. After they are successful, the audience is introduced to two returning soldiers, Ed Ryan and Stan Lipchuk, who are applying for a loan "to set up a partnership." They are informed by the Committee that, together, they are eligible for loans of $2,400. The audience sees the men working together on their boat, one a solid-looking middle-aged man, the other young, blond, and handsome. The narrator then tells the audience that the two men are also getting assistance to buy a small farm close to the fishing grounds so that they can set up a domestic, as well as professional, life together. In fact, the two returning soldiers find that they are eligible for twice as much capital to establish a life together as one man was allowed for the purpose of raising a family. While there is no overt suggestion that they are a homosexual couple, they can easily be read as partners in life. Thus, while the state was steadfastly protecting Canadian society against the 'perverts' it had discovered in the military, it could be interpreted as promoting same-sex unions in this NFB film.

The NFB, which had been founded just several months before Hitler invaded Poland, was brought to life in support of the war effort. By 1945, hundreds of films were being shown in theatres across the country each year explaining the progress of the war and Canada's role in it. The military used the infrastructure established by the NFB to promote recruitment and depict life in the forces both at home and overseas. In promoting themselves to the Canadian public, the services sometimes played with suggestions of homosexuality and gender inversion. For instance, *Soldiers All* showed Canadian audiences what life was like for the Canadians garrisoning in the south of Britain in 1941. After presenting scenes of Canadian soldiers helping British women with their domestic chores – washing dishes, putting children to bed, baking – the narrator says that "in return for the hospitality, the [Canadian soldiers presented] 'Sultan Saturday Night,' a dire drama of the Middle East." The film shows soldiers and townspeople (women, men, and children) in a local theatre watching the Canadian soldiers perform a plotless scene set in a sultan's harem. A smooth-skinned,

Mock Wedding. Two male soldiers of the Veterans Guard of
Canada get 'married' in a POW camp on the Canadian prairies.
Sixty years later, as gay men and lesbians secure the right to
marry, the playfulness behind mock weddings like this is no
longer possible. Courtesy of the Glenbow Museum NA-1234-5.

lithely muscular young soldier, scantily clad in fabric draped around his
midsection, performs a seductive dance to the obvious delight of another
soldier dressed as a sultan. The camera pans across the audience to show
the British townspeople and Canadian soldiers responding to the performance with appreciation, the men laughing noticeably louder than the
women.[49]

Hiding Homosexuality. Allusions to homosexuality were often hidden in gendered drag within cultural drag. The Arab world provided a common cultural camouflage for presentations of Canadian soldiers lusting after one another. Courtesy of the City of Toronto Archives, Fonds 1266, File 84539.

If an actual woman had been engaged to play the seductress in "Sultan Saturday Night," it is hard to imagine that the scene would have been a success. In fact, as explicitly sexual, it would have been deemed in bad taste to present it to an audience that included women and children. However, situated within the tradition of cross-dressing in British farce, the sexual element was clearly acceptable and entertaining. One soldier lusting after another on stage inspires laughter in the audience, which is well aware that the object of the soldier's desire is actually a man. Some of the Canadian soldiers in the audience, however, betray a nervous response to the scene.

Jack Clarke Bewigged. L.A.C. Jack Clarke of the RCAF competing for the title of Miss Toronto, 1941. He was encouraged to enter by his squadron mates, who helped to transform him into a viable competitor. Courtesy of the City of Toronto Archives, Fonds 1266, File 75046.

One tweaks the nose of his friend sitting next to him as the camera passes by them. The humour is grounded in the sublimated reality that men could, and often did, attract each other. The men in the audience are protected from any suspicion that they are queerly excited by the performance not only by the gendered disguise of the drag (which, incidentally, reveals the soldier's body), but by the cultural camouflage – after all, if homosexuality is involved, it is Arabic, not Canadian or British.[50]

Treating homosexuality as a joke was a common way to make it palatable for public audiences in Canada. Jack Clarke of Woodstock, Ontario, a leading aircraftman with the Number 2 Flight Exhibition Squadron of the RCAF, had a slight build and a handsome, delicate face. He was entered into the 1941 Miss Toronto Contest by his friends in the squadron, who used makeup supplied by the Women's Auxiliary Force to transform him into a woman. After the judges had eliminated forty-two of the sixty-one contes-

Jack Clarke Dewigged. The master-of-ceremonies exposed contes-
tant number 70 as a man, and an airman, to the delight of the crowd
at Exhibition Stadium in Toronto and the surprise of at least one of
the judges, after Jack had survived several elimination rounds. Courtesy of the City of Toronto Archives, Fonds 1266, File 75047.

tants, Jack was still in the running. The joke was then exposed for the large
audience at the Canadian National Exhibition grounds in Toronto. The *Toronto Telegram* reported: "The crowd, and at least one judge, had no
knowledge that there was a 'ringer' in the line-up until the master-of-ceremonies yanked the wig from the head of the young airman." The *Globe and
Mail* reported: "The two women judges reversed a time-honored procedure
and asked: 'What are you doing tonight?' Without hesitation, and in a shrill
falsetto, A.C.2 Clark quipped: 'I've got a date with my sergeant-major.'"
Clarke's joke was based on the absurdity of an airman having a date with his
superior officer. It is likely that "the record crowd" at the stadium laughed
at the quip. However, as the records that are related in this book demonstrate, men did indeed have dates with each other at all levels of command in
all of the services. Nevertheless, that reality was not incorporated into the
imaginary world. Both inside the services and in the civilian world, people

agreed to laugh at the suggestion that men could date each other. When the truth of that reality did surface from time to time, laughter commonly gave way to more severe responses – anxiety, anger, indignation.[51]

In *Letter from Camp Borden*, a 1941 NFB production that depicts various aspects of basic training from the point of view of a new recruit in Ontario, a key scene presents a talent show featuring Lieutenant Ross Hamilton. Hamilton was a renowned female impersonator from Pugwash, Nova Scotia, who had been a member of the famous Dumbells troop in the First World War and had been re-engaged by the Canadian Army to help organize entertainment units in the Second. His Marjorie character was a classic impersonation of an opera diva, his remarkable soprano voice helping him pass unquestionably as a woman. The soldiers at Camp Borden are shown cheering his performance enthusiastically. The film was shown in theatres across Canada and was one of the most popular wartime documentaries produced by the NFB in collaboration with the army.[52]

Such films, featuring (literally) veiled homosexuality and gender inversion, reveal the place of sexual difference in Canadian society during the war years. All men and women were presumed heterosexual until proven 'guilty.' 'Queer' was a serious charge, not levelled lightly in polite society. Paradoxically, the fact that most people thought that homosexuality was remote and rare allowed it to surface much more casually. Audiences could conceive of soldiers in drag and men seducing men in farcical terms. Both the military and society in general found a measure of control over homosexuality in laughing at it. Such drag scenes seemed to be saying, "Imagine how ridiculous it would be were there actually such men among us." Meanwhile, in the privacy of their minds, many people derived illicit pleasure from such representations.

During the war years, the military was less self-conscious of representations of homosexuality in its ranks than it is today. However, the reality of queer love was far more troublesome. Lieutenant Ross Hamilton, while delighting soldiers with his talented portrayal of an opera star on the stage at Camp Borden, became a disturbing presence for the administration as a result of the more private sexual pleasures he was sharing with recruits in the showers. As was commonly the case in the early years of the war, he was discharged quietly by a medical board in August 1941, "for reasons other than medical." His discharge certificate reads, "having been permitted to retire." Nothing in Lieutenant Hamilton's file suggests that homosexuality was behind his 'decision' to retire from the army. Thus, the very public image of gender inversion and allusions to homosexuality lay side by side with the less visible reality of sex between men.[53]

Ross Hamilton as "Marjorie." Ross Hamilton began
his successful career as a female impersonator during
the First World War with the popular Canadian
Army entertainment unit known as "The Dumbells."
Twenty-five years and fifty pounds later, his rather
delicate alter ego had matured into a more ample, but
always elegant, opera diva. The new generation of
troops appreciated his female impersonations, as had
their fathers, until the army discharged him because
of his homosexual behaviour. From *Canadian Music
Trades Journal* 23, no. 1 (June 1922): 65. Reproduced from the National Library of Canada's website, nlc-4418, www.nlc-bnc.ca.

Lieutenant Ross Hamilton, Second World War. From
National Library of Canada/Music Collection. Reproduced from the National Library of Canada's website,
nlc-4429, www.nlc-bnc.ca.

At first glance, it might seem that the official repugnance towards homosexuality, with its consequent policing and punishments, would be incompatible with public depictions of female impersonators suggesting
homosexuality and promotions of same-sex domestic arrangements. However, in the pre-Kinsey environment of the war years, it was generally assumed that homosexuality was a rare condition. Laws and social pressures
were arranged to give Canadian society the appearance of being homoge-

neously heterosexual. And, in fact, queer people were successful in concealing homosexuality from view in everyday life. As one gay veteran of the
war remarked, "Two men could go and rent an apartment together and nobody was going to jump to the conclusion that they were a couple." Presenting images that could be interpreted as queer was really a sign of the
power of heterocentrism: it was only because the audience for the films (in
fact, all of Canada) was presumed to be universally heterosexual that the
military authorities did not fear homosexual readings of the scenes.[54]

THE WARTIME NEEDS OF THE MILITARY

The military's regulation of sexuality must be understood in the context of
its need for young men to fulfil the nation's martial obligations. Prime Minister Mackenzie King had initially intended that Canada's contribution to
the European war would be limited to supplying materiel and training air
force personnel. However, as the conflict progressed, Canada's need for
manpower increased and, ultimately, more than one million men, one-fifth
of Canada's entire male population, served in uniform. As the ground war
intensified during the final months of the war, still more were required. The
various tactics that the state and society had employed to force all available
men into general service were no longer effective, and so the final reinforcements were conscripted. If the military had been successful in its campaign
against homosexually active men, it would have been disastrous for the
country's war effort. Alfred Kinsey's survey of male sexual behaviour
among the race-cultural group he identified as "American and Canadian
whites" was published in 1948 and relied on interviews conducted predom-
inantly during the war years. He calculated that "*30 per cent* of all males
have at least incidental homosexual experience or reactions ... over at least
a three-year period between the ages of 16 and 55." He also found that "*13
per cent* of the males (approximately) *react erotically* to other males *without having overt* homosexual contacts after the onset of adolescence" (em-
phases in original). The first group would have been liable to court-martial
proceedings if their homosexual experiences had been coincident with their
war service. The second group could have been subject to administrative
discharges as a result of their homosexual dispositions. If Kinsey's results
were accurate, or even approximate, hundreds of thousands of Canadian
soldiers would have been subject to either judicial or administrative proceedings. The loss of manpower and the staff required to administer that
process would have taken Canada out of the war. In other words, the military could not have afforded to be successful in its campaign to purge itself

of its homosexual elements. Still, various military functions, with the support of the upper echelons of the organization, worked towards that end.[55]

That the policies surveyed in this chapter were unevenly applied is consistent with other forms of military discipline. Regulations against driving while intoxicated were enforced only when such behaviour led to traffic accidents and damage to government property. Few men who were guilty of neglect in the prevention and treatment of venereal disease were finally disciplined according to the military's threats. As one officer defending a soldier for neglect in the performance of his duty remarked at a court martial, "The interpretation of the word negligence in this case is very broad, and I am afraid that practically everyone in the Army, regardless of Rank, is guilty of such a thing several times a day. The only difference between [the accused] and 'the everyman' is that [he] was unfortunate enough to get caught." It was easiest to overlook illicit behaviour that did not interfere with the goals at hand. Good officers recognized the diversity among their men and did not interfere needlessly in a well-functioning unit. At the same time, the military's official commitment to eradicating homosexuality meant that some unfortunate men would be caught up in the policing networks. To the policy-makers, thinking in the abstract, homosexuals were not reclaimable as soldiers or as men. However, the actual homosexual men brought before the authorities for that reason were typically effective soldiers. Nevertheless, they would pay severely for pleasures that others enjoyed without repercussions.[56]

The Department of National Defence during the Second World War should not be conceived as one coherent institution, but rather as a loosely unified system of departments often with opposing interests and frequently in competition with each other. The following chapters will show that censors or security officers could uncover and document evidence of homosexual love affairs whose existence commanding officers had wished to keep within the regimental family. Enthusiastic military investigative officers could go to great lengths to build a case against a man whose services were too valuable to be lost. Psychiatrists could be asked to diagnose a man as homosexual and therefore pathological when they actually saw him as fundamentally healthy and well adjusted. The judge-advocate general (JAG) and administrative officers could try to make an example of a homosexual 'pervert' by means of a court martial only to find that their intended target was one of the most popular men in the company. And, on the front lines in Italy, some fighting units disturbed the social equilibrium when morally indignant NCOs brought their best infantrymen to trial at precisely the moment when they were most needed.

THE QUEER POLICY

What was the military's policy towards homosexuality during the war? The issue was addressed explicitly twice, by Medical Services in 1942 and by the RCAF in 1944. However, the medical model of the homosexual as a military misfit to be discharged had a minimal impact on manpower operations; it was applied infrequently even in cases where patients had been convicted of homosexual behaviour through courts martial. The RCAF arrived at its policy only after debates that lasted a full year and concluded several months before the end of the war. However, all of the services dealt with homosexual servicemen, from mobilization until V-J Day, using the resources available to them under the conditions of war. The practices that developed over those years represent the military's de facto policy. This chapter has reviewed those practices, and now the challenge is to articulate them in a more coherent way. If the military had written a policy based on its actual practices, what would it have been? Among the *King's Regulations and Orders*, the following entry would have governed the handling of queer servicemen:

Routine Order * * *

The following procedures will be followed in cases of homosexual servicemen:

1 During recruitment examinations, doctors will quickly gauge the stability of all recruits. Since homosexuals are unstable, all well-adapted men are presumed heterosexual, regardless of their stated sexual behaviour and desires. Military psychiatrists will otherwise play a minimal role in the management of homosexuals, diagnosing only those men who are deemed misfits for other causes.

2 When officers become aware of homosexuals under their command, they are to ignore the situation as long as it does not interfere with the smooth functioning of the unit. However, if the officer or his men cannot reconcile themselves to the presence of a homosexual soldier, said soldier is to be transferred to a more adaptable unit.

3 Men having sexual relations with each other should take reasonable precautions to ensure that they are in a private location. Popular soldiers, who are well established in their units, will be allowed much latitude in romantic attachments with their comrades. However, sensitive soldiers, unsure of themselves and embarrassed by their homosexual desires, should be harassed and intimidated.

4 Soldiers will be court-martialled for homosexual relations in the following cases:

  a) Whenever their sexual behaviour disgusts their NCOs or comrades;

  b) When military police, censors, or other administrative personnel uncover proof of such intimacy and choose to pursue the matter; and

  c) When such activity becomes too overt and threatens to embarrass a unit publicly.

5 The sentences of those found guilty of such indecent conduct should vary according to military necessity. Men in combat units should be sentenced to terms of detention and returned to the line. Efficient soldiers who are, nevertheless, not deemed critical to the war effort should be imprisoned at hard labour and discharged. All officers will be dismissed or cashiered from the service upon a guilty verdict. Hence, when judging important officers, court-martial boards should seriously consider not-guilty verdicts, regardless of the evidence.

Chapter Two

MILITARY LAW AND QUEER
SERVICEMEN

To date, neither military nor social historians have offered a sustained analysis of court-martial records. This is regrettable, for the court martial, as the most severe weapon in the military's disciplinary arsenal, had a profound effect on the servicemen forced to appear before it, perhaps particularly on men charged with homosexual offences. This chapter will outline the place of homosexual offences within the framework of military law, describe the operation of the courts, and discuss the problems that the administration confronted in its attempt to control homosexuality through the application of military law.[1]

In attempting to deter homosexual behaviour by publicly shaming selected servicemen, the courts concentrated the military's anti-homosexual barrage on individual men. These men took the fall for the military's embarrassment and suffered the consequences, often in silence and shame, for decades after the war. I contacted one airman who had been convicted of "disgraceful conduct of an indecent kind," having had consensual sexual relations with another serviceman in 1943. Fifty-seven years later, he was unable to discuss the experience of the investigation and court martial, except to say that "it was a nightmare." So deeply was he affected that he requested that no reference to his case that might be unearthed in the course of archival research be included in this study, regardless of how well his identity was protected. Like many veterans, his war wounds had never healed; rather, he had repressed them in order to carry on in civil life. But unlike most veterans his pain was inflicted, not by the Germans, but by the state he had sworn to protect.

The military, of course, fully intended that such men be disgraced and humiliated, and medical officers were aware that a public recognition of their homosexuality could have severe consequences for many men. Doctors warned that guards should be posted in detention cells to prevent probable suicide attempts of men convicted of homosexual offences. Major Carscallen, a medical officer, discussing a homosexual soldier under sentence in 1944, suggested that the "possibility of suicide is always present. Would strongly suggest that he be watched closely while in detention." In reference to a career soldier who slit his wrists after being convicted of disgraceful conduct, the medical officer made it clear that the effects of the court were entirely foreseeable: "His depression appeared to centre about his present difficulties and did not seem much greater in extent than was warranted by the severity of the stress." The fear of being marked as queer was widespread, and the anguish suffered by men so identified was seen as wholly natural. Many soldiers could steal illicit homosexual pleasures, and when these transgressions were secrets guarded by the soldier and his partner, by his unit, or even by his regiment, they could be sustained. However, to be officially and publicly marked as queer was to be left vulnerable to ostracism at administrative and social levels, which could result in severe psychological stress. It was that fear that the military exploited in its campaign against homosexuality.[2]

CANADIAN MILITARY LAW IN THE SECOND WORLD WAR

The military's battle against homosexuality did not begin during the Second World War. Canada entered the war with the legal machinery in place to combat sex between men. Throughout the war, military law remained the central disciplinary tool to battle a range of unwanted behaviour, including homosexual acts. Military law was a specialized code intended to enable the forces to maintain discipline in their ranks. Many organizations have regulations beyond the concerns of civil and criminal legal codes that help them to function efficiently; for example, employers impose various requirements on employees and members of social and athletic clubs adhere to specific rules. Similarly, when Canadians enlisted during the Second World War, they became subject to the provisions of either the Army Act, the Air Force Act or the Naval Discipline Act. These acts referred to other state legal codes, civil and criminal, generically as civil law.

The Naval Discipline Act, first passed in Britain in 1866, was adopted by the Royal Canadian Navy and served as Canadian naval law until 1944. It specified offences that were not mentioned in civil law, such as "misconduct in action," "corresponding with the enemy," and "mutiny." Otherwise, only five civil law offences were named along with their punishments.

Section 45 decreed, with respaect to every person subject to the act: "If he shall be guilty of Sodomy with Man or Beast he shall suffer penal Servitude" and "If he shall be guilty of indecent Assault he shall suffer Penal Servitude or such other Punishment as is herein-after mentioned." Since a sentence of penal servitude was second in severity only to death, in most cases charges of indecent assault were preferred and punishments of varying degrees of imprisonment, along with dismissal from Her Majesty's Service, were awarded.[3]

The Army Act was initially created and enacted by the British Parliament in 1881, and thereafter it was brought into force annually. By the Second World War, having undergone minor amendments, it was designated the Army and Air Force Act and governed both the army and the RCAF by a like enactment in the House of Commons of Canada. Depending on its application, it was commonly designated simply the Army Act or the Air Force Act. It listed all offences punishable by court martial and specified the admissible punishment for each. Tables 1 and 2 (see Appendix 2) analyse the various sections of the Army Act and list the frequency of charges laid. The great majority of offences dealt with breaches of military discipline that would have directly compromised the ability of the army to prosecute the war, such as desertion or losing equipment. A few other miscellaneous offences can be understood as putting army personnel at risk, thereby constituting an attack on military property. For instance, duelling and attempting to commit suicide were outlawed. Soldiers who failed to take care of themselves, neglecting to follow medical treatments or wilfully or negligently harming themselves and thereby rendering their bodies unfit for service, were sometimes harshly punished. Officers were forbidden from striking or otherwise ill-treating soldiers. The body of a Canadian who was subject to military law was not his or her own property, but was at the disposal of the state for use in its interests.[4]

Two offences were unrelated to all others and were classified under the heading "Scandalous Conduct." Table 3 shows the frequency of charges laid under sections 16 and 18, which punished conduct perceived as shaming the Canadian forces.

Section 16 provided that every officer who "behaves in a scandalous manner, unbecoming the character of an officer and a gentleman, shall, upon conviction by court-martial, be cashiered." To be cashiered was to be discharged in disgrace from the forces, and it was a punishment that could be imposed only on officers. Once cashiered, an ex-officer lost various rights of citizenship for life, including the eligibility to work in any capacity for the Crown. Scandalous behaviour could be of a military or social character, although the act stipulated that this charge should be applied only in the case of social behaviour so grave as to "bring scandal on the service." Although nothing in the section specified homosexuality, in practice, half of the charges laid under section 16 referred to homosexual behaviour. The other charges were for illicit financial dealings or drunken and obscene public behaviour. The limits of scandalous behaviour were debated in a case in which a Canadian Army captain had been charged in England with resisting arrest by two British constables and referring to his commanding officer as "a fucking shit." His defending officer argued that he should not have been charged under section 16, since scandalous behaviour "must be an act which would lead him to be ostracised from the fellowship of his brother officers or decent self-respecting people." While perhaps not proper, berating the superior officer was considered "nothing for which to hold him in abhorrence as a result." In fact, it may have bound him more closely to some of his colleagues. However, defending officers never challenged the propriety of classifying homosexual acts under section 16.[5]

While only officers could be charged with scandalous behaviour, all ranks were subject to section 18, subsection 5, which specified "any other offence of a fraudulent nature not before in this Act particularly specified, or of any other disgraceful conduct of a cruel, indecent or unnatural kind." Thus, this subsection was applied to fraudulent financial transactions as well as to an array of disgraceful conduct – mistreating animals, bestiality, and a variety of other sexual offences. Once again, homosexuality was not specified in the wording of the offence, although the explanatory notes in the *Manual of Military Law* made it clear that the legislation was intended to prosecute this offence. Normally, subsections were much more specific. The other four subsections of section 18, for example, specified malingering, wilfully injuring oneself, disobeying medical orders in order to prolong an infirmity, and stealing property belonging to another soldier. That subsection 5 included, not only fraud, but any behaviour of a "cruel, indecent or unnatural kind" meant that the nature of the offence could not be inferred from a guilty verdict. In practice, 40 per cent of the charges laid under section 18(5) referred to fraud, 2 per cent to cruelty, 1 per cent to heterosexual indecent assault, and 55 per cent to homosexual acts. Seventy-nine per cent of the homosexual charges were described as indecent, and 11 per cent as unnatural, although the difference is not apparent. Soldiers found guilty under section 18 forfeited all good-conduct badges.[6]

Written under the assumption that only male persons would be subject to military law, the Army Act had not foreseen that heterosexual indecency might also obtain among military personnel. In fact, only one instance has been uncovered to date of a charge preferred under section 18(5) that named heterosexual indecency between servicepeople. While travelling by train in Canada, a male RCAF officer assaulted a female airwoman. The servicewoman testified at the officer's court martial: "I woke up ... and this time I saw the accused half way up the bunk. I told him to get off and leave the bed and before I had any time to say more he was right on my bed. He did not have anything on ... I tried pushing him away from me and I told him to leave. The bedclothes were over me; he took these off me. I struggled with him for a couple of minutes and then I couldn't do anything. He just took advantage of me." Having been found guilty, the accused was cashiered from the RCAF, a severe punishment for officers. However, this was a uniquely military punishment; it expelled him from the military ranks in shame and with restrictions on his future dealings with the Crown, but left him materially intact. A guilty verdict in the criminal courts would probably have led to a prison term. Outside of this instance, the military courts ignored indecent assault between male and female servicepeople. It was a charge that was overwhelmingly applied to male homosexual behaviour, almost always consensual, and those convicted were liable to suffer imprisonment with hard labour or a lesser punishment.[7]

Not only was there a curious absence of heterosexual charges, but the legal system did not map itself evenly onto the queer realities of service life. Women were never charged with homosexual offences in any branch of the forces. Commanding officers were aware that women engaged in homosexual relationships, and those troubled by such relations felt that the problem could be solved by assigning the women involved to different units. This response effectively thwarted the maturing of sexual relations between women, but whether it had any effect on the ultimate incidence of homosexuality is doubtful, for it left two women without partners in different units. To employ a common contemporary metaphor, this practice spread the infection throughout the service. Although transferring the culprits offered an alternative to legal proceedings, the absolute absence of charges against women for homosexual activity suggests that other factors were at play. The separation alternative was often favoured in dealing with queer servicemen, but it was never meant to replace the iron fist of the courts. The military's embarrassment in prosecuting male homosexuals was always weighed against the deterrent value of reminding its flock through legal proceedings of the harsh consequences of sexual misconduct.[8]

The absence of both heterosexual and homosexual courts martial involving servicewomen suggests a common cause. The women's services were already fighting a serious public relations battle against rumours that they catered to sexually active women. Families were reluctant to entrust their daughters and sisters to an institution that was open to 'bad' girls. The campaign to assure the public that potential recruits were entering a protected environment would have been seriously undermined if courts revealed that women in the forces were being sexually 'assaulted' by other servicewomen. Whether recruitment would have decreased or increased is a matter for speculation; however, the military brass may have hidden the reality of lesbianism from the public in order to protect the good name of the women's services. Prosecution would have implied that women were controlling their own sexuality rather than submitting to the protection of the institution. The rare court martial for heterosexual indecent assault was certainly not helpful publicity, but it did position the military in the chivalrous and comfortable role of the protector of women's virtue.[9]

Moreover, while the military establishment attempted to mould male sexual behaviour through occasional offensives with the weapons of imprisonment, discharge, and shame, the men who authorized courts martial could see no connection between male and female homosexuality. When the debate was raging over whether servicemen suspected of having homosexual "tendencies" should be discharged or court-martialled, the possibility that such a directive would also apply to servicewomen was used by medical authorities to demonstrate its absurdity: "Homosexual 'tendencies' exist amongst W.D. [women's division] personnel. Treatment of this medical problem under the terms of the directive would, it is considered, be most improper and ill advised." Labelling some men queer was a way of defining the limits of manliness. After queers were rejected from the club, those who remained – unmarked – qualified as candidates for the category of real men. Fags were not-men; women were already not-men. Naming women fags would have had no meaning. Discussions among high-ranking male officers regarding homosexuality in the forces not only discounted the danger of queer women, but saw no need to explain why. While the civil offences of sodomy and indecent assault were defined as male crimes, the military charges preferred against servicemen were delimited in terms of their effect on military order and discipline. When women were admitted into the ranks of all services during the Second World War, an order was passed stating that, for administrative purposes, all references using masculine pronouns in laws, orders, and regulations were to be read as including women. Thus, if there had been any will to do so, the way was clear to apply sections 16 and 18(5) to homosexual women as well as men. However, male officers, who used the accusation of homosexuality to define proper manhood, had no reason to bring lesbianism into focus. Consequently, queer servicewomen were not court-martialled and military records are almost entirely silent regarding female homosexuality.[10]

Section 41 of the Army and Air Force Act was a porthole through which civil laws could be introduced and prosecuted by court martial. Thus, treason, murder, manslaughter, rape, or any other offence under the Criminal Code of Canada, when committed by a person subject to military law on active service and more than one hundred miles from a city or town containing a "competent civil court," could be tried under section 41. Likewise, the *Manual of Military Law* stipulated that "offences of an indecent kind against children and young persons of the female sex" should be charged under section 41 and not under section 18(5). Therefore, in Canada and Great Britain, instances of rape and indecent assault against civilian women and girls were handled by the criminal courts. Homosexual offences involving soldiers and civilian men and boys were also tried most frequently by civil courts in those jurisdictions. However, in continental Europe and Africa, sexual offences involving civilians were prosecuted by court martial. A survey of approximately half of the courts martial held during the Second World War has uncovered thirty-six charges of rape laid against Canadian soldiers under section 41 and two cases of indecent assault on females under section 18(5) in continental Europe. When the army was forced to try such cases by court martial, the punishment stipulated by Canadian criminal law applied.[11]

Under section 40, an officer "guilty of any act, conduct, disorder, or neglect to the prejudice of good order and military discipline" was liable to be cashiered in the most extreme cases. Soldiers or airmen judged guilty could be imprisoned with hard labour. In the case of homosexual offences, it was most commonly used as an alternative to either section 16 or 18(5). A charge under military law consisted of the offence, which needed to be cited in the words of the Army Act, supported by particulars. If the facts as noted in the particulars of a charge were not proved by the evidence, the court would have to return a finding of not guilty. Likewise, if the facts were proved but the court judged that they did not constitute the offence charged, the accused was acquitted. In order to allow courts more latitude in such cases, alternative charges were often laid, either specifying different particulars or offering another offence. For instance, Private C was charged under section 18(5) with an alternative charge under section 40. The charges specified his service number, rank, unit, and then the offence and particulars:

FIRST CHARGE   DISGRACEFUL CONDUCT OF AN

SEC. 18(5)   INDECENT KIND

Army Act

in that he

at Listowel, Ontario, at about 0100 hrs., 22 April 1943, was in bed in a partly
naked condition with another soldier, ... Pte [M], in a naked condition, who had
his both arms around the body of the said Pte [C], and had the lower front part
of his body and his private parts in close proximity to the buttocks of the said Pte
[C] and was moving his hips and body back and forward.

SECOND CHARGE   CONDUCT TO THE PREJUDICE

(Alternative)   OF GOOD ORDER AND

Sec. 40   MILITARY DISCIPLINE

Army Act.

in that he

at Listowel, Ontario at about 0100 hrs., 22 April, 1943, was in bed in a partly
naked condition with another soldier ... Pte [M], in a naked condition, who had
his both arms around the body of the said Pte [C].

A court was not able to convict on both charges but could find the accused guilty in the alternative if the evidence did not support the original
offence. In this case, the court chose to convict under the alternative charge.
Since deliberations were held in closed court and not recorded, there is no
way to know whether the members of the court judged that the particulars
of the original charge were not proved or that the acts specified were not
"disgraceful conduct of an indecent kind" but "conduct to the prejudice of
good order and military discipline."[12]
    Section 40 was vague and could be used by commanding officers to con-
trol a wide range of behaviour, allowing them to define what was and was
not acceptable comportment for a military man. It could be applied, for example, when the conduct was offensive precisely because it suggested homosexuality. In North Africa, a captain was charged under section 40 as a
result of his behaviour when drinking. His commanding officer told the
court that on one occasion "he was a little outrageously fay [sic], on which
occasion I warned him of the danger of drinking anything to excess in this
climate." Acting "outrageously fey" could be considered conduct to the
prejudice of good order.[13]
    Homosexual behaviour was not actually mentioned in any of the three
charges available under the Army and Air Force Act. In each case, the court
was the judge of what behaviour should be considered scandalous and

indecent. However, in describing the civil offences of sodomy and gross indecency, the *Manual of Military Law* stipulated that "most of the charges of indecency which are brought before courts-martial will be laid under" section 18(5). Thus, the intended use of that section was clear, even though civil law was itself vague concerning what constituted a "grossly indecent act." The members of courts were therefore charged with determining what behaviour between men should be censured. They were consistently advised that the words forming the charges "have no special or technical meaning. They mean just what they would mean to a reasonable man." They were told to look to their own military experience to determine what behaviour was scandalous, disgraceful, indecent, unbecoming the character of an officer and gentleman, or prejudicial to good order and military discipline. These concepts were thus constantly being defined by the courts that were asked to consider them. Who were the men whose own experience and moral principles were being called upon to determine military standards?[14]

OFFICERS AND RANKS

Most homosexual offences were tried by general courts martial, which had greater powers of punishment than district courts. Only general courts could try officers. They consisted of at least five officers, each of whom had held a commission for a minimum of three years. The president of a general court martial was a general or colonel, while at least four members needed to be of ranks not below that of captain. When officers were on trial, no member of a court could be junior to the accused if others of equal or senior rank were available. Thus, those charged with homosexual offences appeared before officers who had established military careers. Military justice did not include the notion of trial by a jury of one's peers. It was an authoritarian system intended to protect the institution through the judgment and will of those most committed to it. A selection process had already established, in a very general and imperfect manner, who within the system would be available to judge.[15]

The attitude towards homosexuality expected of an officer is suggested by Commander Little, the director of naval intelligence during the war, who, fifty years later, recalled that "there was an iron door and the door simply closed [against 'queers'] ... You had nothing to do with people like that. I guess there were plenty of occasions when you didn't know whether a guy was or wasn't, but if you had any thought that he might be, close the door, we don't want anything to do with that guy. And that was the general view as far as I was concerned, although I certainly didn't waste any time on it." Commander Little had come from a strong Anglican background in small-town Ontario and had attended Upper Canada College in Toronto. His candid account of his peers' negative disposition towards homosexuality is thoroughly supported by the records. But it also suggests the complexities that governed social relations. Typical of the official attitude was the combination of a strong antipathy towards homosexuality and the assurance that little thought was devoted to the issue. Since notions of individual honour and a respect for privacy were fundamental to officers, the iron door was left ajar for those who had mastered the double life. In fact, the interview from which this quote is taken had been arranged by another retired, but younger, officer who had been his close associate and protegé in the navy. Until the issue of this research was raised, Commander Little had been unaware that this long-time, respected colleague was himself gay. The champions of the officer class imagined themselves as belonging to a superior caste of men who set the standards for performance and morality within the organization. Entrance to the officer class and expulsion from it were governed by military policies and regulations ever vigilant against queers. But homosexual officers who had mastered the double life easily slipped past investigative techniques.[16]

In Canada, entrance to the officer class was partly protected by vetting procedures designed to judge an applicant's suitability in various respects. The personnel files of officers frequently record the reports of credit bureaus that had been engaged to investigate the financial dealings and social status of those being considered for a commission. Detectives sometimes interviewed business associates, personal friends, and neighbours, who would be asked about the "character" of candidates. The entries in subsequent reports suggest the intrusiveness of their enquiries: "clean young folk of temperate habits," "social life seems limited to entertaining in his own home," "informants state he lives well, entertains in a nice manner." The assessments reflect the middle-class standards of those interviewed. Detectives relied upon evidence from "clean young folk" to ensure that only "clean young folk" be granted admission to the officer fold. Of course, what the informants did behind closed doors would have required still another level of investigation. In any case, the respect for privacy that existed on a personal level among officers was violated at an institutional level. That the administration had assumed the task of enquiring into private lives meant that individual officers would already have been sanctioned by the military. Thus, a standard of behaviour was expected and individual privacy respected. One belonged to the officer class by virtue of being there.[17]

In the field, boards of officers interviewed and judged those being considered for commissions. In the United Kingdom, the Officers Candidate
Training Unit (OCTU) at Hove put prospective officers through physical
and psychological tests to determine their cracking points. Bert Sutcliffe
was sent to the OCTU from the Dutch front after Christmas of 1944. He remembers controlling his anger when asked by the board "if I would like to
have sex with my sister." To resist such baiting was to demonstrate a cool-
ness under pressure considered valuable in an officer. Bert had been nurturing parallel social and military careers since his arrival in Britain in 1941.
While rising steadily through the ranks in the Intelligence Corps through
diligence and good work, he came out in the unique and extensive homosexual underworld of wartime Britain. A more effective training ground for
deception and self-preservation could not have been found. Bert passed the
course. On the other hand, another prospective officer, Ralph Wormleighton, appeared before a similar board of officers in Italy. Although highly intelligent and called back for a follow-up interview, he was finally rejected as
officer material. He says, "Looking back, I can see the reason. I was still
immature and obviously so." He ascribes that immaturity to his inability at
the time to come to terms with his homosexuality. He feels that the total repression of his sexuality had retarded him socially. Clearly, a homosexual
orientation was a complex social and personal challenge. While everyone
needed to hide the queer truth from the military's gaze, individuals could
choose for themselves whether or not to remain privately ignorant. Bert
saw his active homosexual life as part of his personal growth, which in turn
made him a more valuable asset to the military.[18]

The officer class and other ranks mapped themselves, albeit imperfectly,
onto Canadian social-class divisions. Nevertheless, other ranks could be educated, articulate, and cultured men, while officers could come from working-class backgrounds. The most important distinction between officers
and ranks was that the former had the power and responsibility to enforce
discipline on the latter. Men were expected to demonstrate solidarity with
their peers, regardless of which side of the rank divide they found themselves. Soldiers' memoirs commonly describe their commitment to their
comrades. However, they identify a sharp divide between officers and ranks
in Canadian military society. Gwilym Jones, an American who joined the
Canadian Grenadier Guards, chose to decline a commission rather than betray his loyalty to the ranks. He observed: "My feelings about the army
caste system probably stemmed from my being raised in the States but was
exacerbated by various traditions or customs adhered to by the Guards regiment. Personnel of different ranks were not allowed to walk out with each

other (even if the other person was your brother); officers could not associate with other ranks. Even the Sergeant's mess was hallowed ground. I was reminded of that salutation that describes the system so aptly: Officers and their ladies, Sergeants and their wives, and men and their women."

While soldiers nurtured solidarity within their ranks, the military expected officers to abstain from any familiarity with the men. The following charge against a lieutenant with the Royal Regiment of Canada for "conduct to the prejudice of good order and military discipline" eloquently expresses the army's attitude towards the role of the officer: "At Guildford Surrey, at about 2250 hours on the 23rd day of January, 1943, did adopt towards subordinates methods of command and treatment such as to cause disrespect for authority and loss of those feelings of self respect and personal honour essential to military efficiency, in attempting to lay hands on ... Cpl. Page, R. and referring to other ranks Canadian personnel as 'French Canadian Bastards.'" The twin concepts of respect for authority and "personal honour" were protected by the system of military law. Homosexual officers forfeited their honour, upon which rested their claim to authority.[19]

The administration was able to use the system of military law to ensure that the officer class remained nominally heterosexual. Soldiers, sailors, and airmen convicted of homosexual crimes received a wide variety of sentences, from imprisonment with hard labour and ignominious discharges to short periods of detention. By contrast, officers found guilty were universally dismissed from the military. In this way, the justice system selected for the military those officers and gentlemen who remained unmarked by homosexual scandal and who could therefore command the repect of their men. However, military law supported officers who were shown disrespect for other reasons. Some soldiers resented taking orders from certain superiors of particular racial or ethnic backgrounds. For instance, Trooper Marshall told his superior officer, "You are nothing but a Frenchman and a Frog, and I would sooner take orders from a German than from you." Private Hughes declared, "No God Dam Jew is going to give me any orders." Signalman Jacobi told Lance Corporal Quon, "I don't like you because you are a damn Chink. You shouldn't have a hook [chevron] because you are lower than a white man." These three soldiers were all court-martialled and disciplined for their defiance of constituted authority. However, by dismissing officers whose homosexuality was proven, the military was never forced to support them against similar insubordination.[20]

Most officers would serve on court-martial boards from time to time. Those of superior rank would sit as court members, while lieutenants and captains would be appointed defending or prosecuting officers. Moreover, the judge-advocate general often used courts martial for homosexual offences as training grounds for "officers under instruction." Here they learned more than military legal procedures. All involved in the courts were apprised of the great shame that accompanied a homosexual charge. The unique mood of courts that dealt with these crimes was reflected in the language employed. Typical is the following excerpt from a closing address by the defence: "I need not stress to you of course the serious nature of these charges or the painful duty that was yours in listening to the evidence in this case. It is shown by your painstaking attention how you appreciate your heavy responsibilities for you are acting as judge and jury in this case affecting a man, the most serious charges and the most serious consequences that can affect any officer in His Majesty's Service." The pain, shame, and gravity of the charge are framed as a burden on the court rather than on the accused. Many courts responded with anxiety to such proof that homosexuality was already concealed within the officer class. All were meant to feel the ignominy of being condemned by one's peers. The iron fist closing the iron door against homosexuality could be a cautionary experience for those present. But not all responded with trepidation. Occasionally, court members revealed a lack of concern over the presence of homosexuality in the forces.[21]

Although court members were employed in the service of the Naval Discipline, Army and Air Force Acts whose caps were set against queers, their personal sympathies could remain judiciously covert. Bob Grimson was an RCAF officer from Toronto who served in Canada, the United States, Britain, North Africa, Malta, Italy, and Greece. He was actively, enthusiastically, and discreetly queer throughout his wartime career. In Algiers, while seconded to the RAF, he was appointed to sit on several courts in judgment of RAF airmen accused of buggery. Along with the other court members, he felt compelled to find the airmen guilty: "The evidence was that [they] had buggered someone … I would have preferred to say 'bugger off' to the court." Homosexual officers appointed to courts could not practically argue that they considered queer behaviour acceptable and not "disgraceful conduct." To have voted in favour of the accused could have turned suspicious eyes towards Bob himself. Shortly thereafter, while stationed in Malta, Bob was detailed to guard another officer awaiting trial for having sexual relations with a sailor. For three weeks, Bob commiserated with the officer over his bad fortune and his impending dismissal from the service. None of these incidents dissuaded Bob from pursuing his own romantic and sexual desires, and he felt that his masculine demeanour saved him from suspicion. Moreover, Bob had already weathered discrimination back in Toronto and survived. After being fired in 1936 from his first job in an accountancy firm because he was Jewish, he found employment in a Jewish firm. When he was discovered to be homosexual, however, he was no longer welcome there. Gentiles had seen him as Jewish, Jews as homosexual. The RCAF was his third stop.[22]

Besides the court members who heard the case, the defending officer, prosecuting officer, and judge-advocate were key courtroom players. The accused could request the services of a particular officer, or retain civilian counsel. He had the right to challenge any appointment. Lists of those qualified to serve these functions were prepared by commands, and the adjutant appointed all court officers. Legal officers attached to military districts often prosecuted cases or acted as judge-advocates. By long-standing tradition, they were not available to act as defending officers. Many defending and prosecuting officers had had some legal training before enlistment; others learned on the job. Military historian Lieutenant Colonel MacDonald recalled that the Second World War saw the office of the judge-advocate general explode "from a cozy shop for legal advice to a major legal firm with offices around the world." The main function of the JAG branch was to give legal advice. In Canada, assistant judge-advocates were appointed at district headquarters and deputy judge-advocates were assigned to corps and headquarters reinforcement units overseas. Because of the great number of courts and the scarcity of judge-advocates, very few courts had the benefit of their advice during the war. Normally, the president of the court resolved legal questions. However, the *Manual of Military Law* required that "a judge-advocate should be appointed in all [offences of an indecent kind], whether at home or abroad, in order that the court may have the benefit of his advice, particularly with regard to the danger of accepting the uncorroborated evidence of witnesses who are known to be accomplices." Except in isolated cases in continental Europe, judge-advocates did attend courts dealing with homosexual crimes. In cases involving both officers and soldiers, they gave consistent advice regarding legal process and requirements.[23]

Officers were particularly reluctant to find fellow officers guilty of homosexuality. Of seventy-six courts martial from the three branches, fifty-nine tried soldiers, sailors, or airmen and seventeen prosecuted officers. In most courts, the accused faced multiple charges relating to separate homosexual acts; however, a conviction on one charge resulted in a sentence comparable to multiple guilty findings. In 42 per cent of the cases, courts found their fellow officers not guilty of all charges. However, when the accused were from the ranks, the courts cleared only 7 per cent of those charged. In part, this may have been a result of the officers' ability to mount a more effective defence. Fellow officers worked diligently to defend a peer, and on occasion, court-martialled officers employed civilian barristers to argue their cases, something soldiers never did. On the other hand, military police and prosecuting officers prepared much more rigorous cases against officers than against the ranks. In fact, cases in which an officer was charged with a homosexual offence were consistently the most time-consuming, detailed, and contested of all courts.[24]

There were noticeable differences in the sentences imposed on officers and soldiers. While fewer officers were found guilty, they were nevertheless more severely punished. In all three services, without exception, officers found guilty of homosexual offences were discharged dishonourably from the service. Sixty per cent of the army officers were "cashiered" and the others were "discharged with ignominy," the lighter sentence. RCAF officers were ignominiously discharged, and all of the convicted naval officers were "dismissed from His Majesty's service." However, it was common for soldiers, sailors, and airmen to serve sentences of detention or imprisonment and rejoin the ranks. Eighty-five per cent of the soldiers (army) found guilty of homosexual offences were sentenced solely to periods of detention; 15 per cent were discharged with ignominy. Twenty-nine per cent of the naval ratings and 24 per cent of RCAF airmen served time and then resumed their work. In all of the forces, men who were marked by the courts as queer but were not discharged were able to complete their service and secure honourable discharges, thus qualifying them for government assistance after demobilization. Clearly, the three services, and notably the army, did not let homosexuality interfere with the need for trained and efficient soldiers. The purpose of the courts was to punish unwanted behaviour and deter others from acting on their homosexual desires. Practically, it could not afford to lose queer soldiers. Detention was assessed as an aspect of active service, part of the soldier's continuing training. Queer soldiers in detention were not lost to the forces, but were undergoing discipline in the military's effort to correct their behaviour.

ARGUING QUEER CASES

A number of courts relied on the confessions of the sexual partners of the accused, usually obtained through military police investigations. Under the law, any person voluntarily involved in a homosexual act was guilty. When there were no other witnesses, the prosecution's case rested on the evidence of the partner, an accomplice to the crime. In respect to sexual crimes, an accomplice was defined in law as "a person who consents to the commission of an unnatural offence with him or her." The main function of the judge-advocate in cases of "disgraceful conduct" was to warn the court of the dangers of convicting an accused on the basis of the uncorroborated evidence of an accomplice. As the deputy judge-advocate for the First Canadian Corps advised one court in Italy, it "would be so easy for one man to frame another in cases like this." While courts were asked to look for some material evidence that corroborated the particulars of the charge, it was within their discretion to convict upon the uncorroborated evidence of an accomplice and they sometimes did. When a respected officer stood to be convicted on such evidence, the courts often chose not to accept the evidence of witnesses who were willing accomplices. If their testimony was true, then they had themselves engaged in criminal activity and were untrustworthy. It was often easier for courts to ignore the offence altogether. Since witnesses could not be compelled to incriminate themselves, the fact that accomplices testified to criminal acts suggests that they had incentives to do so. Considering that they were never charged, it follows that they were coerced to testify by the military police. In most cases, witnesses testified that they had been drunk, asleep, or unwilling during the sexual activity. Courts consistently accepted these attestations, no matter how unlikely. One defending officer argued (unsuccessfully) that, even if such witnesses had been unwilling participants, they became accomplices by not reporting the sexual offence committed upon them until questioned by the military police.[25]

The accused themselves did not fare as well when using drunkenness or sleep as a defence, and judge-advocates were often called upon to clarify the law. With respect to the state of sobriety of an accused, the *Manual of Military Law* asserted that an accused could be acquitted if he had been so intoxicated as to be unable to form the intent to commit the crime. This defence was never successful, since a man incapable of forming the intent would also not have been cogent enough to perform sexually. Prosecuting officers frequently quoted the *Manual of Military Law*, which also stated that "evidence of drunkenness falling short of a proved incapacity in the accused to form the essential intent, and establishing merely that his mind was affected by drink so that he more readily gave way to some violent passion does not rebut the ordinary presumption that a man intends the natural consequences of his actions." In fact, alcohol was understood to lower one's resistance to homosexual behaviour: the underlying intention was always there, alcohol merely facilitated its expression. Consequently, drunkenness was more successfully submitted in the mitigation of punishment. Underlying this legal principle was the notion that homosexual desires were commonly present but were held in check by moral men.[26]

Judge-advocates also ruled on unforeseen legal matters that sometimes presented themselves in individual courts. When Lieutenant C was charged with scandalous behaviour in that he "indecently did permit another male person ... to place his head near the genital organs of the said [C,] who at that time had the front of his trousers undone," his defence counsel asked that the court be closed, "having regard to the officer's character." The court, which sat in Toronto, granted the request and the four-day trial sat in camera in the spring of 1943. After a finding of guilty on an alternative charge of "conduct to the prejudice," the court proceedings were forwarded to Ottawa for approval. (All guilty findings were reviewed by the JAG office before the sentence was promulgated.) The JAG, with the support of the justice department whose advice he sought, ruled that the court had had no jurisdiction to sit in camera. The rules of procedure specified that military courts, like others, were to be "in open court and in the presence of the accused." They had the "inherent power to sit in camera if necessary for the proper administration of justice." The JAG interpreted this to mean that a court would be justified to sit in camera only "in a case where the witness's testimony if given in open court would convey information useful to the enemy or be prejudicial to the safety of the state." The request in this case had rested solely on the basis of "sparing the accused's feelings and minimising the degree of notoriety and publicity concerning his alleged indecent conduct." The JAG's ruling meant that all courts concerning homosexual behaviour would be open, which was against the wishes of those on both sides of the charge.[27]

COURTS MARTIAL AS DETERRENTS

The courts induced shame in the accused, but the military was also embarrassed when it was forced to air its dirty laundry in public. Orders in 1944 instructed military districts in Canada to transfer civil offences (offences not strictly of a military nature) to the civilian criminal courts for investigation and prosecution. The civil authorities, though, were no more willing to prosecute homosexual offences than the military was willing to relinquish control over them. The Quebec government decided not to prosecute "any officer or other rank notwithstanding that there is evidence available to make a prima facie case." In the case of Lieutenant C, the Toronto police undertook the investigation but did not want to prosecute. The military was content to maintain control, since "there would be adverse publicity if he were to be tried by civil court." The administration also feared that if he were "tried by the civilian courts, a very strong plea for leniency might succeed and the court might be swayed by his age, his position in the Army, and the heavy consequences of conviction" - that is, civilian courts might be unwilling to interfere with military personnel during a time of war. In the end, although the military was unable to close the courts, it retained significant control over the publicity that might accompany them. In Lieutenant C's case, the JAG argued that because the evidence adduced at his trial "was for want of a better expression, unsavoury in character, as might be expected," "the court would have been justified in requesting women and young persons to leave." The principle otherwise espoused was that there was no legal basis to close courts martial in order to spare individual sensibilities. Nevertheless, this opinion was "shared by all of those legal officers of [the JAG] staff with whom the matter has been discussed." This act of chivalry had the effect of removing from the courtroom an audience whose esteem the manly institution of the military coveted. While justifying the policy in terms of protecting these groups, the military was, in fact, protecting its own self-image as a masculine, morally upright organization. The issue of access to courts martial for homosexual offences was an instance of the paradox that faced the military generally: how could it ensure that personnel were aware of the interdiction against homosexuality without suggesting that it was widespread in the organization?[28]

In the interest of deterrence, the army and air force publicized the details of certain courts martial. Particularly undesirable offences were clearly described at the beginning of each edition of the *Routine Orders*, published weekly. For instance, as part of the RCAF's campaign to coerce its men into showing respect towards female personnel recently introduced into their ranks, Charles S was charged under section 40 in that he, "in a letter written by him did make improper statements concerning personnel in the RCAF (WD) [Women's Division]." While his offence was minor, the administration was using the medium of the *Routine Orders* to influence a widespread sexism and chauvinism that was hurting the recruitment of women and undermining their position in the RCAF. Similarly, to curb the problem of theft of air force property, one routine order reported that an airman had been convicted of "being in improper possession of nine sheets, eight pillow slips and seven shirts, the property of the public." It was necessary to describe the offence in such detail in order that the publication of these crimes should have its intended salutary effect.[29]

Homosexual convictions were frequently cited in the *Routine Orders*. Table 4 (see Appendix 2) lists the total number of district and general courts martial published by the RCAF throughout the war. Homosexual offences, tried by general courts martial, were listed with the more serious charges. Only 14 per cent of the total courts published were general courts martial, and 13 per cent of those citations related to homosexual offences. However, never were the particulars of homosexual offences mentioned. For homosexual charges alone, the citation consistently stated that the accused had been "found guilty on a charge under section 18(5) of the air force act." So, while the sole intention of the publication was to mould behaviour by naming the offence, the administration was unwilling to specify the behaviour to which it referred. And since section 18(5) could designate fraud as well as "disgraceful behaviour of an indecent kind" (itself imprecise), the reader was left uncertain of the actual crime. While queer acts and individuals could be favoured topics for discussion among the ranks, the administration could never bring itself to mention, in print, the thing that it wanted to proscribe. This silence reflected the discomfort of the officer class and shrouded homosexuality in a haze of shame. Such obscure references to ignominy could instil a sense of anxiety among young servicemen and women who were coming to recognize their emerging sexual desires.[30]

The deterrent value of publishing the results of homosexual courts martial, which, paradoxically, neglected to mention homosexuality, must have been limited. The RCAF was itself deterred by the ignominy of exposing in print the queerness in its ranks. However, within its family, the RCAF found other tactics to control queer behaviour. Al Hawkshaw joined the RCAF in 1941, was seconded to RAF squadrons, and fought in North Africa, the Middle and Far East, and Europe. Throughout his wartime career, he tried to hide his homosexual desires and behaviour from public view. Even so, he had sexual and romantic affairs with other RCAF and RAF servicemen. He returned to Canada in April of 1945 and was stationed in Dartmouth, Nova Scotia. While there, he witnessed a ritual that had precisely the intended effect upon him: "One day we were called out on parade. Standing in lines the C/O called one guy to the front. He was a Flying Officer. I don't recall the words but it was because he was a homosexual. They tore off his wings, his medals, the F/O ribbon on his jacket and he was kicked out of the RCAF. I was terrified. All the other guys were mad that they had to do that. Why not just let him go?" Such degradations could follow guilty verdicts by court martial. The terror Al felt should alert us to the material effectiveness of some forms of social control. Throughout his career, he remembers hearing no official reference to homosexuality otherwise, and so the significance of this cautionary event loomed large in his experience. According to his account, the men at the Dartmouth station saw themselves as a community that included the flying officer marked as homosexual. At the end of the war, men who had suffered and triumphed together had come to appreciate one another. They valued their comrades according to their reliability and did not denigrate them according to their failings. Comradely support for servicemen who had passed the tests of combat was common. In this instance, as was frequently the case in its regulation of homosexuality, the military administration, with heavy-handed self-righteousness, pitted itself against the ranks of its men.[31]

SEX TALK IN COURT

One of the few official forums in which homosexuality was accorded a public hearing was the courtroom, despite the initial attempts to close those courts dealing with the issue. Owing to the nature of the legal process, this otherwise nebulous or vitriolic discussion often became biologically precise. For instance, in St. John's, Newfoundland, in October 1943, the prosecuting officer questioned his witnesses along these lines:

Q96: Now, whose cock was in whose mouth?
A96: Pte [A]'s cock was in Pte [V]'s mouth.

In Italy in September 1944, a lance corporal of the regimental police of the Carleton and York Regiment was pressed to provide the following details: "They were covered with a blanket and I took it off. I noticed the [accused] had no pants on and his underwear was down to his knees. His rectum was covered with slime. Pte [M] had no pants on, his shorts were down and his penis was covered with slime." Courts dealing with homosexual crimes required such graphic testimony in order that the facts as stated in the charge be proved. While broadcasting such details may have been humiliating for the accused, it had the effect of making sexual relations between men sound commonplace. The passion that may have accompanied the original crime was stripped in the retelling, but details of sexual techniques and individual preferences were discussed with scientific disinterest. Men who previously may not have considered the possibility of homosexual relations learned how others cruised, courted, and copulated. They were asked to put themselves in the position of the accused to judge him. In one case, they took that task literally. Two officers of the court went to the Robert Simpson Company in downtown Toronto to see if it could have been possible for two servicemen to have oral sex in a cubicle in the fifth-floor washroom. Back in the courtroom, they demonstrated the positions attempted and gave their opinion as to the accused's chance of success in that location. Thus, the actual court proceedings had the potential to undermine the rhetorical insistence that homosexual activity was beyond the pale.[32]

The military further lost control of the courtroom discourse relating to homosexuality when the accused, rather than the administration, raised the issue. In 1944 Private Anderson was being tried for desertion in Vancouver when his defending officer asked him to comment on his physical "make-up." He replied, "Upon reaching the age of about 15½ I discovered I would rather be with boys than with girls ... [S]ince here at Little Mountain I have acted like a soldier, but the fact remains that if you have the desire you are going to slip and I would just as soon let that be known. I am not ashamed of it and I don't try to hide the fact." He saw this assertion as clearing the air. He was eager to complete his training and be sent overseas, but wanted to continue on his terms, unashamed. He was aware that to "act like a soldier" was to behave heterosexually. In mitigation of punishment, his defending officer argued that "there is no reason in the world why a young man of his education, strength and appearance should not prove as efficient [a] soldier as we of the Canadian Army would like to have." A light sentence would allow Anderson "to prove that he is capable of becoming a first-class Canadian soldier." In fact, the court did heed that advice, found him guilty of AWOL (absent without leave) rather than desertion and sentenced him to a minimum period of detention. At the same time, the defending officer suggested that the "difficulties" in Anderson's "nature ... need proper treatment of a psychiatrist or medical officer."[33]

Thus, when homosexuality was not on trial, its introduction into court proceedings tended to shift its significance. In England in January 1944, Private Smith of the Westminster Regiment was charged with AWOL, a common offence among impatient young soldiers waiting for the Canadian Army to be sent into action. His homosexuality was used by his defending officer to gain the sympathy of the court. The officer asked "the court to use their imaginations with regards to a boy growing into manhood, knowing that he had an overpowering obsession which led him to do acts that he knew full well were shunned by society." He told them that when Smith's woman friend in Canada had become pregnant by another man, Smith married her in March 1940 "through an unselfish urge to protect her reputation." But while Smith was serving in England, she took up residence with another man back in Canada. Smith resented that his assigned pay was now going to support another man's family, and when he was unsuccessful in having it discontinued, he went AWOL in order to stop her payments along with his pay. His homosexual orientation and activities were highlighted in an attempt to secure a minimum sentence: "I would respectfully suggest that this boy, through his abnormalities has never had a chance in his life. Medical opinion is that this sexual state cannot be cured and I forsee [*sic*] a life of unhappiness and shame ahead of him, even though he be normal in every other way. I respectfully suggest that where medicine and science has failed prison walls are not likely to succeed. I put it to you Gentlemen that this boy is more to be pitied than censored [*sic*] and I respectfully place him on the mercy of the Court." While Smith was being tried on a charge of AWOL, his defending officer made his sexuality the central issue. A light sentence was urged because a long one would not cure his homosexuality. Ironically, if Smith had been tried for homosexuality, the court might well have used this admission as cause to impose a more severe sentence. In the case of AWOL, the subject was mobilized to inspire pity. The tactic was unsuccessful, and Smith was sentenced to nine months detention. He was released in August 1944 to accompany his unit to France.[34]

BEING MARKED QUEER

Private Smith acknowledged leading a homosexual life while stationed in England, and his defending officer offered the court the names of his various lovers in case they doubted him. Nevertheless, he was never charged with any homosexual offence, and there is no record that the army considered discharging him. Neither does it appear that Smith himself ever asked to be released from the army. The same was true for countless others whose homosexuality was known to various military authorities. Medical officers, psychiatrists, commanding officers, personnel selection officers, military police, courts martial, and courts of enquiry documented the homosexual lives of servicepeople without prompting court-martial proceedings or discharges from the services. Within units, queers could be accepted quite openly. So why were some charged and dealt with so severely? What was the purpose of courts martial within the wider system of regulating homosexuality?[35]

To understand how some people came to appear before a court charged with a homosexual offence, we must consider the three arms of the military independently. Different factors determined the protocols for dealing with homosexuality within the army, the air force, and the navy. First, the nature of each service affected the possibilities for queer sex and romance. Being

with an army unit, in a bomber squadron, or on board a corvette determined one's sexual options to some extent. Moreover, within each service
there were a variety of postings that could either facilitate or inhibit homosexual relations. Second, more important than the frequency or visibility of
queer activity in any particular environment was its perceived threat to the
service in question. The court martial was one element along a spectrum of
possible responses to homosexual behaviour. Its primary value was as a coercive tool to mould behaviour through deterrence. If any service wanted to
rid itself of homosexual activity, it could have saved time and resources by
simply discharging any personnel suspected of being queer. Medical discharges for homosexuality were employed for exactly that purpose. However, their use depended primarily on manpower needs. When men were at
a premium, it was necessary to shape their behaviour through fear of punishment and shame. In other words, the greater the need for men, the
greater the number of courts martial. Of course, the court-martial option
was sometimes motivated by moral, as well as personnel, imperatives. The
actual recourse to any regulation depended on the attitudes of the individual commanding officers and military police in the position to initiate
charges. The third factor determining protocols around homosexuality had
to do with the ability of military police and officials to uncover homosexual
relations.[36]

The Canadian Army appears to have had the lowest incidence of courts
martial for homosexual offences of the three services. Why were there any?
Why weren't there more? Sexual intimacies between two men could become the subject of a court martial in various ways. Military police were
trained to investigate homosexual offences. Sometimes they responded to
investigations carried out by civilian security services, hotel detectives, or
civil police whose reports could form the basis of charges. Complaints
could be made by soldiers or officers threatened by queer behaviour in their
environment. In all cases, upon hearing the accusation, the officer commanding the accused was responsible for either dismissing the charge or in-
stituting an investigation. Investigations took place in the morning,
according to military custom, and witnesses were questioned in the presence of the accused. The commanding officer then heard the evidence for
and against the accused. At that time, he could cause a summary of evidence to be taken, whereby, in his presence, the deposition of each witness
would be transcribed along with any cross-examination by the accused.
The commanding officer would then send the application for a court martial along with the summary of evidence to his superior officer whose rank
permitted him to convene a trial. In the case of homosexual offences, copies

were also submitted to the JAG before a trial could be ordered. The convening officer then ordered either a district or general court martial. The *Manual of Military Law* cautioned that no offence against any section of the Army Act was to be sent to trial unless there was a "reasonable probability" that the accused would be convicted. Exceptions were cases involving disgraceful charges where a court martial afforded "the only means to the accused of clearing his character."[37]

These tasks were administratively independent. The military, like other large institutions, was a complex organization comprising various elements that often worked against each other's interests. The majority of cases that came to trial in the army were not initiated by commanding officers. Usually, commanding officers had little to gain by advertising that there were queers in their units. Moreover, they had more practical options if they chose to rid themselves of homosexual subordinates, such as transferring the suspect to a queer-friendly unit. Rather, commanding officers were commonly forced to apply for courts martial when their men were indiscreet and discovered 'with their pants down' by a third party. Once a report was brought to his attention, a commanding officer may have felt compelled to defend the honour of his unit by demonstrating an intolerance towards immorality. He may have had little choice if the event was well known. On the other hand, some commanding officers were disturbed by the presence of homosexual relations in their units and initiated proceedings themselves. But the views of officers convening courts could be quite different from those sitting as members.

In the case of Lieutenant C, the district officer commanding and the assistant judge-advocate for Military District 2 (Toronto) read the summary of evidence and decided that court-martial proceedings were warranted. The director of administration wrote that the accused would "have great difficulty escaping conviction" as a result of the police reports. All of these parties reported to the adjutant-general, in charge of all administrative and legal issues in the army. His office predicted "that any officer who is sitting on such a court would feel that an officer convicted of such an offence should not be retained in the service, and consequently would award either cashiering or dismissal." The trial was expected to demonstrate "that such behaviour as alleged is not tolerated by military authorities, particularly in an officer." However, appearing as a witness, the commanding officer of the accused commended him highly as an officer and a gentleman. He had been forced to proceed with a summary of evidence when the homosexual incident became known outside of the unit. His testimony supports the proposition that commanding officers tended not to interfere with units

that had found their own equilibrium, especially with court-martial proceedings. It is essential to separate the rhetoric that guided discussions of
homosexuality at an official level from the application of the resultant policies. Moreover, there was much confusion and little consensus among policy-makers over the effectiveness and value of military law in regulating
homosexuality.[38]

The highest echelons of the RCAF struggled throughout 1944 to establish
policies governing the use of courts martial in prosecuting homosexuals. In
December 1943 the director of provost and security services (DPSS) reported to the supervisory board that "certain cases have arisen of a homosexual nature, and this condition of affairs is under close investigation, as
there appear to be nine other personnel implicated." Consequently, the air
member for personnel (AMP), the DPSS, the director of personnel (DP), and
AMS(Air) met to discuss the handling of such cases. On 5 April 1944 the
chief of air staff issued instructions to all commands in Canada concerning
"personnel suspected of homosexual tendencies." While assuring the commands that "such cases are rare," he "considered that a uniform policy
should be adopted in dealing with them." The new policy challenged the effectiveness of military law in achieving its goals of reform and deterrence:
"Having regard to the characteristics of such persons, it is considered
doubtful whether disciplinary action will produce any reformation in character or will deter other personnel with similar tendencies." Punishment
was thus of little value. However, the idea of retaining homosexual servicemen was unthinkable, since they would "come into contact with other service personnel." He further argued that "in the majority of cases coming to
the attention of this headquarters difficulty has been experienced in procuring sufficient evidence to warrant prosecution." Instead of initiating disciplinary action, therefore, commanding officers were directed to
immediately discharge such personnel from the service. The chief of air
staff's argument hinged on two distinct considerations – the ineffectiveness
of the courts in altering behaviour and the expertise of homosexuals in
evading surveillance – but he contended that many would not elude suspicion and the RCAF would free itself of the burdens of proof required by the
Air Force Act.[39]

While the April policy highlighted the weaknesses in the legal system in
dealing with homosexuality, the director of medical services (DMS[Air])
took "strong exception" to the directive's assumption that homosexuals
could not be treated by medical science and that lay military men had the
expertise to identify a true homosexual. But if not all queer men were homosexual, then it followed that the military had had it right all along. Pun-

ishing men for their criminal and immoral activity was reinstituted by August of 1944. Psychiatry laid claim to the mind but left the body and its nefarious behaviour to the courts. By December 1944 a new directive was finally forged to reconcile the medical and legal claims to queers. It cited as justification "the number of recent cases wherein servicemen have been proven to be homosexualists or homosexual tendencies have been suspected." The senior medical officer (SMO) of the unit was to be notified immediately in all cases. Disciplinary action was to be taken whenever possible. If convictions did not result, then the accused was to be interviewed by a psychiatrist who would determine whether "homosexuality is present." If the patient was found to harbour homosexuality, then he was to be discharged. The SMO was to be notified of the date and place of the trial so that he could advise the defence if "there exist medical facts relevant to the case" and also to gain "a first hand knowledge of the facts." Thereafter, doctors and disciplinarians formed an uneasy union in their different interpretations of what it meant to control homosexuality.[40]

The search for a policy drew attention to the question of just what it was the courts were discovering. In principle, the courts were concerned with crime, psychiatry with desire, and administration with military effectiveness and appearance. The purpose of the court-martial system was to modify behaviour. Whether its victims were true homosexuals or not was irrelevant to that end. It was enough that the knowledge circulate that homosexual behaviour exacted a heavy penalty. But as the war progressed, the army, like the RCAF, came to distinguish the types of men who were being caught in the campaign against homosexuality. For instance, in 1944 Lieutenant Colonel MacDonald, assistant adjutant general (AAG) at Canadian Military Headquarters in London, commented to Medical Services: "I suppose there are various degrees of this physical (?) defect – ranging from the true homosexual to the man who ... uses the practice as an 'outlet.' From our point of view the legal guilt of the man varies accordingly but inversely to the degree of his true homosexual constitution." Evidently, some within the army administration intended to render unto medicine that which was medicine's, and unto law that which was law's. However, separating the homosexual chaff from the queer straw was no simple matter for the martial courts or the administration. Moreover, such opinions as Lieutenant Colonel Mac-Donald's had little influence on the real administration of courts martial. In fact, his assumptions about whom the courts were targeting for the most severe punishment is mistaken. Policing functions, commanding officers, and individual courts tended to target true homosexuals – those whose desire and behaviour coincided. In this, they were less informed by a respect for

the medical model of the true homosexual than by a moral, gendered distaste for perversity. Sometimes men were charged for no more than fondling
each other. Since they lived in close proximity and touched each other frequently, by the very nature of military life and camaraderie, the intention of
the accused became the measure of whether he was guilty of indecency or
not. In other words, the offences as named were so vague that the differences between horseplay, acceptable physical intimacy, and perversion were
determined only by the intent of the accused. Courts, like psychiatrists,
probed the desires of men. Whether they found homosexuals was a matter
of judgment.[41]

A brief survey of several charges that proceeded to trial reveals how military justice looked beyond behaviour in prosecuting homosexuality. In fact,
the evidence shows that the military preferred to prosecute homosexuals
rather than homosexuality. Captain K was charged when he "*did attempt*
[i.e., did not actually] to handle the private parts" of a soldier, and Corporal G was charged when he put his hand on the penis of another soldier
"*with intent* to commit an act of sexual perversion." In both of these cases,
the courts were concerned not only with the actions of the accused but also
with the motivations behind them. In other contexts and performed by
other personnel, the same gestures could have been innocuous. Flying Officer Harold S was charged with being "in bed naked with Leading Aircraftman [W], also naked, performing unnatural movements." Aircraftman
W, on the other hand, was not charged, since he "had a clean record in that
respect and had not been the subject of any suspicion in the past" and "it
was believed he was a passive agent." Thus, accused were not brought to
trial simply on the basis of having been discovered engaging in sexual relations, but after a determination of their basic sexual orientation and the
threat they posed to the service. True homosexuals were dangerous. In fact,
commanding officers were not always able to articulate, as with Flying Officer Harold S and Aircraftman W, how the actions under charge were specifically sexual. Private A was charged with being in bed with another
soldier under a blanket and "permitting a sucking sound to issue from under such blanket." The navy also allowed itself considerable discretion in
characterizing homosexual acts. For instance, one seaman was charged
with an "act to the prejudice, etc. in being with another in a state of undress in a cabin in HMCS *Longueil* with the lights out and the door closed."
Nothing in the charge is specifically sexual; rather it reflects the will of the
superior officer to charge homosexuals even without homosexuality. The
nature of the offences allowed all of the services to fashion a charge to fit
the circumstance.[42]

Some trials make no explicit reference to homosexuality but nevertheless suggest how soldiers might find acceptable cover to satisfy desires for physical contact with each other. Aggression, for example, was accepted as a part of barrack-room life. In the course of one trial, Private Hunter describes the events in his barracks that led to an accident: "I saw Private McIndoo and Private Sheppard wrestling around the bed, which I took as fun, just wrestling in fun. In the meantime they were rolling around the bed and then they came into a clinch, the two of them, and they rolled down on the floor and Private Sheppard's head struck the floor and drew blood." The corporal in charge of the hut testified that friendly wrestling matches were "an ordinary procedure around the hut." That soldiers might have been satisfying homosexual desires through aggression rather than through lovemaking was never raised by the courts.[43]

It is often assumed that medicine differed from law in that it looked beyond the evidence of homosexual acts to the psychosexual makeup of individuals. Medicine thus had a primary influence in creating a new social entity, turning 'homosexual' from an adjective into a noun. The social category thereby created ultimately positioned itself in opposition to those authorities who named it. The argument asserts that the law, on the other hand, had not stipulated the sexual orientation of the men that it prosecuted; under the law, homosexuality was a crime to which any weak man could succumb, and did not describe a type of being. Likewise, religion viewed homosexual vice as a sin shunned by moral men. The notion of the homosexual as a member of a cultural minority, either tolerated or outlawed, is indeed unique to modern Western societies. Still, the power of psychiatry in creating the identity at the basis of that movement must not be overstated. The military courts concerned themselves with the type of men that they were prosecuting. Men who were already suspected of being homosexual were more likely to be targeted by those in a position to lay charges. The homosexual, as a social role, had its genesis as a reaction to legal injustices. Psychiatry and law were involved in a similar project of naming and defining the species 'homosexual.' During the war, psychiatrists, as experts in abnormal psychology, were sometimes called by defending officers to attest to the sexual nature of the accused. However, with or without scientific expertise, the courts addressed the question of men's sexuality.

The term homosexual did double duty, designating both behaviour and desire. Consequently, many observers were confused over whom it was meant to describe. Two scales, one each for desire and behaviour, would have charted responses to the psychosexual and social pressures facing individuals during wartime (and modern-day) Canada. References to the true homosexual in the military courts tended to point to the intensity of homosexual desire. It was the man whom they judged to be psychosexually queer that the courts tended to punish most severely. As the war progressed, policing functions had matured in their ability to target men who loved each other. The extensive use of censorship, for example, aided the administration and police in their search for true homosexuals. Sometimes, even when men were physically chaste, they were nevertheless charged solely on the basis of their desires. In early 1945 in England, two leading aircraftmen were charged with "conduct to the prejudice of good order and Air Force discipline" on the basis of personal letters in which, the attendant psychiatrist wrote, "intimacies were exchanged and words used suggesting a 'love affair' although no actual mention was present of homosexual activity."[44]

The courts thus gradually moved towards an assault on homosexual desire. But this assault was never complete and, to a large degree, was out of the hands of the administration. Charges laid at the unit level depended not primarily on maturing policing functions, but on someone's misfortune in being caught by the wrong person in an act of homosexuality. Soldiers already suspected of being predisposed to such behaviour might be watched more closely. Two Canadian corporals in a British pub/hotel, for example, grew suspicious of the growing intimacy they observed between a sergeant and private and conspired to catch them in the act by barging into their room. On the other hand, men who did not consider themselves queer could be more indiscreet than those whose deeper, true homosexual dispositions had brought them to a clearer understanding of the social consequences of being uncovered. For instance, in Italy in July 1944, when Privates M and A were discovered having "unnatural intercourse" under a blanket on the ground, they simply dismissed two curious comrades who came upon them and continued to pursue their sexual interests. More sophisticated transgressors would have been less likely to be still *in flagrante delicto* when the regimental police came to investigate twenty minutes later. Of course, it is equally possible that the two men were beyond caring about the consequences at that moment, both having experienced heavy fighting and gunshot wounds at Ortona and the Hitler Line.[45]

Within individual courts, members often addressed the issue of the true sexual nature of the accused. In support of Lieutenant Colonel MacDonald's claim that the legal guilt of an offender was inversely proportional to the queerness of his nature, the homosexual disposition of an accused could be introduced by his defending officer as a plea for mercy. The defending officer's decision on whether to present the accused as normal or as constitutionally deviant could depend on the strength of the evidence against him. Private A's defending officer argued that his "fixed" homosexuality demonstrated that "the human being at best is a very frail mechanism and can easily be unbalanced by alcoholic stimulants." The prosecutor replied that "the law does not make any stipulation as to whether or not the accused is or is not of a sexual nature." Although one might argue that this is evidence of the law's indifference to the homosexual as a type, it is equally clear that the prosecuting officer had been drawn into a discussion of the accused's sexual orientation. The possibility that the accused was homosexual put the prosecution on the defensive: "[I]t has not been proven that he was [homosexual] and if it was proven that he was, it would not make any difference to the charges as laid." It was upon the testimony of a psychiatrist that the defending officer rested his appeal for mercy. In that way, psychiatry entered the courts as the conscience of law. Faced with the medical insight that homosexuals were suffering from a disease beyond their control, the courts sometimes lost confidence in their moral rectitude. However, it was more common for defending officers to champion the sexual normalcy of the accused. Private C's defending officer brought out in evidence that on the night of his homosexual encounter he had also allegedly had sex with a woman: "I suggest to the court this is an indication of a normal sexual attitude on the part of the accused. This evidence is supported by the statement of L/Cpl Kimmel, who, having lived in close proximity of the accused, over a period of sometime [sic], is of the opinion that he is a clean chap, and in his opinion had given no evidence of immorality, as far as he could see." The defence routinely asserted that the accused had normal sexual interests, and the prosecution would frequently respond by trying to prove that he had a reputation as a queer within his unit. In response to a defence of frivolity (that an action had been meant as a joke) or the claim that the act in question was not sexual in intent, the prosecuting officer was allowed to call witnesses to testify that the accused had also propositioned them, which implied a queer disposition.[46]

The number of prosecutions was never a measure of the incidence of queer activity. Rather, courts provide a glimpse into the determination of the military to seek out homosexuals, the wiles of queers in evading detection, and the power of the personnel and medical authorities to have cases referred to them for treatment or medical discharges. The RCAF articulated these issues in its search for a policy, but the same dynamics existed in the other services. In all cases, one crucial variable never entered the debate: the will of individual units to protect their queers from law, the administration, and psychiatry. Policy-makers based their positions on the proposition that all decent men would abhor homosexual activity in their midst. This reflects the limits of the official, public discourses on homosexuality. Actual officers and men were far more pragmatic, forgiving, and complex. Certainly, not all were purely heterosexual or heterosexually pure.

The absence of courts martial is as intriguing as their actual incidence. Section 40, "Conduct to the prejudice of good order and military discipline," was a conveniently unspecified offence that gave military authorities a free hand to punish unwelcome behaviour mentioned nowhere else in the Army and Air Force Act. Significantly, this section was never used to dissuade Canadian servicepeople from attacking their queer comrades because of their sexual orientation or effeminacy, although such attacks occurred. Occasionally, soldiers defended themselves against charges of "striking a superior officer" with the assertion that the victim was apparently queer. It is quite possible that such officers were queer and had made sexual overtures to their attackers. It is equally possible that the soldiers were fabricating the accusation of sexual impropriety. It would have been an inspired defence tactic, slandering the officer and the institution as corrupt at the same time that they positioned themselves as morally upright. However, the forces did not allow officers to be slandered as homosexual. Precisely for that reason, officers marked as homosexual could not be retained in the service.[47]

The Canadian Army, interestingly, used section 40 liberally to punish German prisoners of war (POWs) detained in Canada who beat their own homosexual German comrades. The army oversaw approximately forty thousand prisoners of war during the Second World War. By the terms of the Geneva Convention, POWs were subject to the laws, orders, and regulations of the Canadian Army in the same manner as Canadian servicepeople. Held primarily in POW and lumber camps across the country for as long as six years, some prisoners objected to the prevalence of homosexual affairs within the POW community. Rather than ask the Canadian authorities for help in combating this immoral and illegal activity (under both Canadian and German military and civil law), the prisoners held unofficial courts martial. Prisoners found guilty of homosexual immorality were punished in various ways, including savage beatings and murders. The Canadian Army, responsible for good order and military discipline among prisoners of war, determined that anti-homosexual activities were far more damaging to military interests than homosexual relations, at least among Germans. Consequently, the army court-martialled German prisoners who assaulted their homosexual comrades. Throughout the life of internment operations, Canadian military intelligence and the RCMP observed the process by which homosexual German soldiers were intimidated and, finally, terrorized into asking the Canadian authorities for protection from their comrades. Ironically, while the Canadian military prosecuted its own homosexual servicemen, it was forced to come to the rescue of queer German soldiers in the interests of good order and military discipline. Prosecutions against German anti-homosexual attackers were in part motivated by a desire to stem the increasingly heavy expenses carried by the army's Medical Services for treating seriously beaten prisoners. The belief that homosexuality was socially ruinous was deeply entrenched at all official levels of Canadian discourse, but German homosexuals were not seen as a threat to Canadian society.[48]

CONCLUSION

Did the military courts intend to prosecute homosexual desire or behaviour? In fact, they prosecuted both. While there were varying opinions as to whether true homosexuals were more guilty, more pitiful, or more disgraceful than those whose heart was not in their perversity, the justice system accepted whomever the police, commanders, or busybodies threw its way. The value in courts martial lay in their coercive potential; from the point of view of the upper echelons, it was less important who was actually being prosecuted than the fact that someone was. Taking good men out of the front lines, out of squadrons, and off ships and subjecting them to court proceedings, which required a further drain on resources, would appear to have been a waste of scarce personnel. However, courts were meant not only to punish but also to deter other servicemen from behaving in a similar manner. When men could not be spared, and given that the authorities wanted them to appear straight, it was most practical to use the stick of military law to banish homosexuality. The upper echelons might have had some intuition of the disaster that would have befallen the forces should the justice system be successful in prosecuting all instances of homosexuality. The harsh system of military justice was intended to ensure that there never would be an open and honest correlation between desire and behaviour. To that end, it was largely successful. However, while it could thwart openness and honesty, military law could not quash love and passion. Before exploring the resourcefulness of queer servicemen, 'true' and not so true, in evading military discipline, the relationship between Medical Services and homosexual servicemen must be addressed.

Chapter Three

MILITARY PSYCHIATRY

In reviewing applications for courts martial, the JAG office sometimes changed the wording of the charges submitted by commanding officers from "disgraceful conduct of an unnatural kind" to "disgraceful conduct of an indecent kind." The Army Act would have allowed either formulation, and the military legal authorities offered no justification for their preferring to describe homosexual actions as indecent rather than unnatural. The two words suggest different ways of thinking about sexual deviance. Was homosexuality a mistake of nature or a failure of the individual to live according to the standards of Western society? To describe it as an offence against decency was consistent with nineteenth-century legal discourse. Homosexuality was one of various male vices, especially conspicuous in the course of industrialization and urbanization, that needed to be controlled by legislation and a variety of other techniques. The appeal to nature was more problematic in the twentieth century than it had been in its religious incarnation, as the sin *contra natura*, in earlier days. Science had challenged religious discourse since the Enlightenment and, by the war years, positioned itself in many circles as the authority on the natural world. As a middleman between science and society, medicine had developed theories that placed the "unnatural" vice of sodomy in the natural world, as either an inborn predisposition or a developmental anomaly. Thus, the debates that have since been framed within nature/nurture or essentialist/social constructionist binaries were all part of a scientific explanation for the phenomenon. The opposing viewpoint, upheld by religious and judicial interests, continued to see homosexuality as a moral transgression.[1]

This chapter will explore the place of medicine in the overall regulation of homosexuality in the three branches of the military. The first part locates psychiatrists within the military hierarchy and homosexuality within the medical profession. The second part studies the relationships between medical officers and their patients in the three branches. In framing the discussion in terms of the actual influence that psychiatrists and servicemen had on each other, this study follows one recent historiographical trend. Much of the early literature took as given the historical significance of psychiatry. Michel Foucault read the work of nineteenth-century sexologists as instrumental in creating the modern category of the homosexual. In their enthusiasm for classification, they came to define men and women according to a variety of sexual desires and behaviours, including homosexuality. Medicolegal structures applied this new category, and queer men came to define themselves within its parameters. Working within that framework, Jeffrey Weeks and others focused on the actual pronouncements of the sexologists and psychiatrists whose individual works represented more or less coherent systems of thought and were readily available for historical analysis. Thus, most research into the medical construction of homosexuality has emphasized the constructs of experts. However, recent research has looked more closely at the relationship between scientists and homosexuals. Henry Oosterhuis, for example, has demonstrated that Richard von Krafft-Ebing's work relied on the input of hundreds of homosexual men. Many homosexual men saw Krafft-Ebing as an ally in that he pushed their interests as far as was politically possible in the context of nineteenth-century Austria. Thus, in that country, homosexuals were in fact present at their own 'creation.' Likewise, as shown by historian Jennifer Terry, gay men and lesbians of New York in the 1930s resolutely and effectively resisted the attempts of medical authorities to explain their lives and behaviours pathologically.[2]

This chapter will show that doctors had a wide range of theoretical constructs available to them in their treatment of homosexual servicemen and that they drew upon all of them. But it would be a mistake to believe that the influence of doctors was limited to their diagnostic and prognostic capacities. Although the scientific position they represented cast sexual deviance as either a developmental or biological problem, many continued to see it primarily as a moral failing. Meanwhile, others were sympathetic to homosexual servicemen. Many had encountered homosexual patients in their prewar practice, and those who were open-minded had come to appreciate the variability of human sexuality. High-ranking medical officers, able to influence policy, tended to echo conservative, anti-homosexual biases. Military records favour such unsympathetic accounts; a public defence of homosexuality as morally neutral and harmless to military interests would have been radical and politically foolhardy. However, as their confidence increased, some medical men did try to influence the military to replace its moral position with the scientific (itself not always sympathetic to sexual difference). They had limited success.

More important, however, were the effects that medical officers had in their actual daily interactions with officers and soldiers. The medical records of homosexual servicemen suggest that those relationships were as varied as the men themselves. Most doctors were unwilling to apply the military's psychopathological categories to their homosexually active patients, and so the majority of these men were left in the military stream. Many case histories suggest that doctors comforted servicemen who found themselves in dishonourable and dire straits. For some, the reason was personal. Allin Hawkshaw, a homosexual RCAF airman, had already fought throughout the European and Asian theatres when he was stationed back at Goose Bay, Labrador, during the war. Officers at Goose Bay, an isolated base, had become familiar with the homosexual culture that flourished there. The consulting psychiatrist diagnosed only two of five airmen who had been court-martialled as true homosexuals, although all were discharged from the RCAF. Meanwhile, Allin's experience with the station medical authorities was more congenial:

[W]hen off work about midnight I dropped into the hospital for a coffee from an orderly there. One eve we wound up on the operating table having a "go." He was always the only one on duty. But that night in came a nurse. She told the Station Commander. I got called in and asked how many times [I had been] there … "No more, I'll send you to see the Doctor.["] He was kind [and] after a couple of questions [he] said I should see the other [doctor]. Turned out he was gay. Had some sex [with him] but very very careful. I was sure lucky with that Stn Commander.

Such evidence helps immeasurably in understanding the medical files. While Medical Services categorized homosexuality as a pathology requiring immediate discharge, the actual doctors were much more lax. Not only did Allin have a sexual affair with the doctor assigned to diagnose his pathology, but the other medical officer happily acted as the go-between. At least for Allin, the medical department at Goose Bay acted more as a dating service than as a treatment centre for homosexuals.[3]

Allin's story alerts us to another important role for Medical Services during the war. Few commanding officers were willing to lose good, effective homosexual men to an ideology that defined them as unmasculine, immoral, and unwanted. As usual, it was only when a report was tabled, this time by a nurse, that a commanding officer was forced to react. By sending Allin to Medical Services, he absolved himself of the problem. It is unlikely, however, that the commanding officer would have allowed the doctors to discharge Allin without his approval. In this instance, everyone got what they wanted. This particular case reminds us of the practical, institutional factors that underlay the very different worlds of policies and practices. The medical officers who labelled homosexuality pathological and inimical to military life were playing to an audience that would not have accepted a more sympathetic account. On the other hand the commanding officers would not have allowed that category to be wielded to the detriment of their units. These contradictory paths were both determined by military necessity. The following pages will explore doctors, patients, and homosexuality within the context of military life.

PSYCHOPATHIC PERSONALITY WITH ABNORMAL SEXUAL BEHAVIOUR

In November of 1942, a committee within Medical Services produced a system of classification of mental disorders that would be adopted by the three services. The committee, known as the committee on nomenclature, was chaired by Lieutenant Colonel Richardson, in charge of the Canadian Neurological Hospital in Basingstoke, with members Major Moll, a neuropsychiatrist attached to the personnel selection section at the time, Major C. Gundy, a regional neuropsychiatrist, and Colonel Van Nostrand, consulting neuropsychiatrist at Canadian Military Headquarters. The category of 'psychopathic personality' would come to be the diagnosis most frequently applied to psychiatric patients on both sides of the Atlantic. Psychopathic personality was a clinical label with a contentious, changing history within the psychiatric profession. By the war years, it was in common usage in Europe and North America. In the Canadian military, it described a person whose reaction patterns were constant over a long period of his life and therefore predictable. He was characterized by "faulty adjustment socially, failure to profit by experience or punishment, usually egocentricity, lack of concern for the feelings of others, emotional instability, and impulsiveness." The committee members intended to employ the term in a manner "suitable for army purposes" to define a "group of social misfits who are not mentally defective, psychotic, or neurotic." They argued that the "Army does not tolerate as wide a variety of individual behaviour as a civil community; the Army confronts men who are at best 'wobbly' with frustrations and deprivations and takes away the props that have supported their weak egos." For this reason, they stipulated that many men falling into this category could more properly be called "military misfits."[4]

The category psychopathic personality was subdivided into three groups: "inadequate," "anti-social," and "with sexual abnormality." Both the inadequates and anti-socials were characterized by "defective social adjustment and emotional abnormalities." The inadequate type expressed these failings by withdrawal and evasion, whereas the anti-social type was rebelliously aggressive. In both instances, it was the behaviour of the individual that revealed the mental disorder: "Many inadequate psychopaths come to light because of frequent, usually petty, infringements of regulations and breaking of laws." Anti-social psychopathy could be revealed through "inconsiderate, malicious, or sadistic behaviour, or it may be the cause of accidents which expose other people to danger, or it may appear as agitation, stirring up dissatisfaction to authority. It may, on the other hand, show itself as crude, cold and egotistical behaviour." The inadequates and the anti-socials were both distinguished by the inability to change; they were locked within destructive patterns of behaviour and were incapable of learning from experience.

The committee had much less to say about the third psychopathic personality, homosexuality (abnormal sexuality): "Psychopathic Personality with Abnormal Sexuality is the diagnosis used when abnormal sexual behaviour is the basic feature of the case, and is not apparently based on mental deficiency, psychosis or psychoneurosis." Whereas each case of inadequate and anti-social psychopathy was to be dealt with on its own merits, with the proviso that "very few of either group are suitable for full combat duties," the committee claimed that sexual psychopaths exerted "a very bad influence on their fellow soldiers and are, therefore, unwanted in any unit." Once a diagnosis of psychopathic personality with abnormal sexuality (in general practice, a synonym for homosexual) was made, the psychiatrists were required to grade the individual so that he would be automatically discharged from the service. Under the PULHEMS system of personnel classification, the final category measured the soldier's stability, S, on a 5-point scale. Under a grading of 5, the individual was deemed unfit for any military service. Homosexuals were to be graded S5 and discharged as a matter of course.

In their discussion of the differences among the three types of psychopathic personalities, the committee did not apply the same nuanced understanding of the range of human behaviour to homosexuality as it did to the other manifestations of psychopathy. They inferred that the diagnosis of homosexual would be unproblematic. However, the inclusion of homosexuals within the category of psychopathic personality would be especially problematic for subsequent diagnostic evaluations. Psychopaths, as a genus, were marked by an inability to adapt to new situations, a characteristic that manifested itself in abnormal, inappropriate, and destructive behaviour. According to the heterosexist standards used by the committee, homosexuality was abnormal, inappropriate, and destructive, and so active homosexuals were psychopaths. When homosexuals were effective and adaptable soldiers who habitually showed intelligence and insight, it was difficult to support the argument that they were psychopaths. In fact, they were psychopaths in their sexuality only. Psychiatrists argued that, by not behaving heterosexually, homosexuals had not adapted to society. The ironic truth, however, was that homosexuals were constantly adapting to society – especially to a military society – that was set against them.

The qualification that the category of psychopathic personality with abnormal sexuality should not be used when the homosexuality was "apparently" based on mental deficiency, psychosis, or psychoneurosis effectively meant that few men would be diagnosed as homosexual. The only servicemen who were referred to medical officers were those who had difficulty adapting to military service, and as would be expected, many of these men demonstrated some form of psychiatric disability. If they happened to be homosexual as well, the committee advised that they be classified within the larger psychiatric category to which they belonged. Within this framework, homosexual behaviour was seen as a symptom of a more general degeneration.

Mentally deficient soldiers were those who had demonstrated a "defective learning ability." Following this criterion, psychiatrists sometimes attributed homosexual behaviour in soldiers with a low "mental ability" rating (M on the PULHEMS scale) to their "suggestibility." The inference was that they lacked the intelligence to overcome homosexual desires. Psychoneurosis described various symptoms, mental or somatic, that appeared when the soldier was under stress. Such a patient differed from psychopathic personalities in that his behavioural patterns, either constitutional or originating in his childhood, were a reaction to specific stressful situations. A psychotic patient differed from a psychoneurotic in the intensity of his symptoms, his lack of insight, and often the presence of delusions and hallucinations. Some psychiatric authorities classified homosexuality as a psychoneurosis during this period. By excluding all of these types from the category of psychopathic personality with abnormal sexual behaviour, the committee offered doctors a great deal of flexibility in their diagnoses of homosexually active men.

In summary, homosexuality could be a symptom of a neurosis or the basis of a psychopathy. It could only be diagnosed as homosexuality in the latter instance, in which case the serviceman was otherwise healthy and productive. Therefore, the only time it could be applied was in reference to men the military did not wish to lose. Those men were seldom referred to psychiatrists and, if they were, did not often discuss their homosexuality.[5]

WHO OWNS HOMOSEXUALITY?

Over the course of the war, science became increasingly forceful in its claim to expertise in the categorization and control of personnel. In the RCAF, psychologists devised methods to test the physiological capabilities of potential pilots, thereby maximizing personnel efficiency. By treating men suffering from 'battle exhaustion' in the army and 'lack of moral fibre' in the RCAF, psychiatrists performed a critical function in recuperating many trained personnel for continued service. At the same time, psychiatric claims to special insight into human behaviour did not go unchallenged by commanding officers, who saw themselves as experts in managing and motivating men. Psychiatrists did not have access to all personnel, but treated only those problem cases referred to them. Still, in that capacity, they had considerable authority to determine the future, within the military or outside of it, of those patients they diagnosed. Civilian psychiatrists were commissioned and medical officers were trained in psychiatry, primarily in order to diagnose anxiety states among combat servicemen. By 1944, they had established themselves as crucial to effective personnel management. During this same period, homosexual servicemen were being increasingly referred to individual medical officers for disposal and psychiatrists sat on medical boards charged with deciding the future of men diagnosed as homosexual. Thus, at the same time that their star was rising within the military, psychiatrists were gaining insights into the effects of the administration's procedures regarding known homosexuals.[6]

The chief of air staff (CAS) of the RCAF circulated the directive for the handling of "personnel suspected of homosexual tendencies" in April 1944 without having sought the advice of Air Commodore Tice, the director of medical services (DMS) (Air). Tice was advised, along with other relevant directorates, that files relating to personnel discharged as suspected homosexuals would be forwarded to him for his information. The directive itself claimed insight into the nature of homosexuality: "Having regard to the characteristics of such persons, it is considered doubtful whether disciplinary action will produce any reformation in character or will deter other personnel with similar tendencies." The highest military echelons understood the "treatment" of homosexuals to fall within the policing, legal, and administrative functions. This, in fact, was an accurate reflection of the state of affairs within all three services; psychiatrists were an afterthought. The issue for the military administration was whether it was possible to alter immoral sexual behaviour through punishment. Subjecting men to courts martial and subsequent detention was the judicial equivalent of medicine's aversion therapy. Deserters, thieves, and disobedient soldiers were similarly punished in order to dissuade them from acting in ways antithetical to the military's interests. Incorrigibles were discharged for misconduct. However, no competant soldier was discharged because it was suspected he *might* desert, steal, or disobey. By 1944, the CAS identified homosexuals as a unique category within the military family, one whose criminal behaviour was deeply ingrained.[7]

Air Commodore Tice was disturbed that such a directive should be circulated without the prior consultation of the DMS(Air). He asserted the expertise of psychiatry regarding the "problem" and challenged the CAS for primacy in the field of human behaviour: "Sexual irregularities are primarily medical problems. Those who are the subjects of such irregularities are by no means always criminals. Neither are they always beyond help. Many can be treated and relieved of their abnormal sexual propensities. This directorate would feel derelict in its duty were it to ignore the necessity of medically investigating each such case with a view to restitution." In protesting that homosexuals were not "always" criminals, Tice helps us to understand the received, common-sense notions of his era. The underlying tone of frustration in the arguments of medical officers advocating a scientific approach to homosexuality suggests that their opponents' view – that it was a moral failing – was deeply embedded in the culture. Meanwhile, Tice's argument was designed to appeal to an institution with a manpower shortage. His claim that homosexuals could be cured would have been difficult to defend against informed medical experts. Nevertheless, just as psychiatry was recovering for the services a percentage of men who had broken down in battle, it now promised that it could return sexual deviates to heterosexual normalcy. Speaking on behalf of the patients whom he seemed to be defending, Tice asserted that only "the most chronic and advanced cases associated with gross psychological abnormality do not wish whatever help can be given them." This choice of rhetoric kept medicine from being construed as soft on vice; employing medical terminology, it named "chronic" homosexuality as corrupt. Tice based his scientific position in the moral: good men try to undo nature's mistake. At the same time, he deconstructed the directive itself to demonstrate that only medical experts, as scientists, had the objectivity to deal with homosexuality. An example of the "emotional" response common to the lay mind could be found in the wording of the directive itself, "which implies that 'tendencies' are in themselves reprehensible and justify discharge from the service forthwith." Thus, doctors would be able to protect (for the service) those who had the decency and strength to fight their homosexual constitution. Tice's argument kept Medical Services from appearing amoral and unmasculine.[8]

Tice also signalled the opposition of the medical profession in principle to the policing of homosexuality. He claimed that some soldiers "who are sexually maladjusted seek medical advice because of their own desire to obtain help." The privileged knowledge that doctors obtained about their patients' sexual proclivities would not be betrayed in the course of police investigations: "No reputable physician will so far forego his professional privilege as to consider himself obliged to inform the C.O. or any other authority of what has come to his knowledge through the confidence of his patient." Tice argued that those merely "suspected of homosexual tendencies" were the natural subjects of the medical profession. His distinction between innocent and irredeemable homosexuals was framed primarily in terms of the age and experience of the suspect:

By no means all such suspects are actually abnormal sexually. Many are immature individuals just emerging from adolescence who, having discovered no heterosexual outlet, nor having learned any compensation for strong sexual urges, are easily led into irregular practices by confirmed perverts. These youngsters are entitled to medical aid. They must be differentiated from the pervert who is a constitutionally psychopathic individual. The latter should be discharged from the service as soon as identified, as has been the custom in the past.

There were bad homosexuals and good homosexuals. Bad queers accepted their homosexuality, good ones deferred to medical expertise. Tice implied that Medical Services had more experience than other military departments with the issue of homosexuality. The CAS was impressed by the arguments of the RCAF's highest-ranking doctor, and the next directive provided that in cases where no disciplinary action was taken, the senior medical officer was to be responsible for taking "proper medical action."[9]

Tice portrayed the medical profession as enlightened and disinterested, in contrast to the lay military departments, which tended to react "emotionally." His approach was based on a commitment to healing, rather than punishing, homosexuals. That such a course was in the best interest of homosexual men is highly contestable. Those who fell into the 'enlightened' arms of the medical 'experts' could suffer from their beneficent contempt. And yet, even though Medical Services classified homosexuality as a sickness, many doctors did not accept the possibility or value of changing homosexuals into heterosexuals. However, it would have been difficult to argue at mid-century that homosexuality was a natural, morally neutral, inconsequential occurrence. Air Commodore Tice may have been trying to balance his own viewpoint on homosexuality against an appreciation for which arguments would be creditable and would enhance, rather than diminish, the authority of Medical Services. Meanwhile, in the privacy of their practices, doctors frequently found themselves defending queer servicemen in the face of devious police tactics and severe prison sentences.[10]

In the spring of 1945, an airman who had been convicted in England of indecent conduct with another airman and sentenced to ninety days detention was referred to Squadron Leader Kershman, a consultant neuropsychiatrist stationed in Canada. Although the sentence did not include dismissal from the service, such a course was recommended by the air officer commanding, RCAF overseas, notwithstanding the prevailing policy to refer homosexual cases to Medical Services for disposal. The service police had entrapped the airman by befriending him while in civilian clothes, not identifying themselves as police, and eliciting a "confession." Squadron Leader Kershman, recording his opinion on the patient's case file, fumed, "I can see no just cause for the procedure followed in this case. It is medically absolutely wrong to turn this man into a criminal with a discharge for service misconduct. He is a medical problem and should be so treated. There seems to be a strongly sadistic feature in the way these cases have been handled by the police and administrative departments overseas. The methods used are tricky and mischievous, with no regard for the consequences or enlightened understanding of the problems involved." He commiserated with the airman, who said that the police treated homosexuals like "lepers and criminals." However, in Dr Kershman's view, the airman was "a good case for endocriminological treatment and possible psychotherapy." His record of the interview indicates that the airman was cooperative, supplying the psychiatrist with considerable information about his family, work, and sexual history. After having suffered the court martial, the period of detention, and the threat imminent discharge, it is not surprising that he may have responded positively to someone who seemed sympathetic. However, the doctor's recommendation had the potential to cause more long-term stress and harm than that imposed by the legal apparatus. In this case, as in others, it was only because "it is not practical to carry out [the treatment program] in the service" that the airman was finally discharged. Nothing in the record of the interview suggests that the airman was interested in converting to heterosexuality. Indeed, he reported that he had tried to have sex with one woman in England. The doctor recorded ambiguously: "This was not successful. He felt no emotion and was very disappointed." The psychiatrist, who saw homosexuality as a sickness, seems to have interpreted the airman's experience with heterosexuality as a temporary failure, but since the airman subsequently pursued a satisfying relationship with another serviceman, his heterosexual experiment could more positively have been seen as a moment in his sexual self-discovery. Dr Kershman was bound by his anti-homosexual, albeit 'enlightened,' position to view the airman's acceptance of his homosexuality as a failure.[11]

In the RCAF policy debates in 1944, the administration made no reference to Medical Services' established procedures regarding the treatment of homosexual servicemen. In 1942, it had been decided that air force doctors should use the morbidity codes outlined by the army's medical officers, which designated homosexuality a psychopathic condition. The RCAF, however, continued to see the issue as criminal. In aggressively challenging the administration for medical control of the homosexual problem in 1944, Air Commodore Tice was operating from a stronger position than his colleagues had held two years earlier as a result of the increased influence of psychiatry within Medical Services. Moreover, those two years had provided medical officers with much insight into the detrimental effects of military law and policing on competent, queer servicemen. The choice made in 1942, which determined the official medical position throughout the war, reflected little insight into the diversity among homosexually active men. In addition, it clearly positioned homosexuality as deviant and universally inimical to military interests. In doing so, the policy was acceptable to administrative authorities but provided medical officers with an ambiguous diagnosis, difficult to apply.

MEDICAL MODELS

Doctors brought their own academic and personal histories to bear in their interviews with queer servicemen. Medical officers would have been briefly exposed to various theories concerning the aetiology and treatment of homosexuality in the final years of their training. Throughout the two decades prior to and including the war, the Faculty of Medicine at Queen's University required that students pass two courses in psychiatry in the fifth and sixth years of the program. The eight texts assigned for the courses offered remarkably scant, and contradictory, information on homosexuality. Those who specialized in psychiatry would have been more conversant with the various theoretical models current in the first half of the century.

Their sympathy for a particular approach is sometimes apparent in their reports, although there is little evidence of a coherent understanding of homosexuality among psychiatrists generally or individually. While they commonly (at least in their official declarations) classified homosexuality as pathological, a few doctors drew upon alternative theoretical models more sympathetic to a diversity of human sexual behaviour.[12]

Wartime psychiatrists had access to equally valid theoretical models that could lead them to conclude that homosexuality was innate or acquired or both, related to gender inversion or separate from it, restricted to certain individuals or a potential in all men, a serious threat to civilization or the basis of high culture, a disease that must be cured or an innocuous variation of human behaviour. The committee on nomenclature's judgment that it was a dangerous pathological condition (the scientific equivalent of an unpardonable sin) represented one choice among many possibilities, albeit the one least likely to upset the upper echelons of the military and most consistent with prevailing attitudes.

Medical writings on homosexuality at the time drew upon the research and interpretation of a range of thinkers. The idea that homosexuals constituted a third sex was introduced into nineteenth-century medical thought by Karl Heinrich Ulrichs, who imagined the sex drive to be distinct from the anatomical sex of individuals. Since attraction to men was assumed to be a feminine drive, male homosexuals were male bodies with female psyches. Ulrichs, a homosexual, sought to position homosexuality – or sexual inversion – within the natural world, thus making its persecution unreasonable. In the twentieth century, this approach was pursued by Magnus Hirschfeld, who argued that homosexuality was a natural and integral part of a individual's personality and that to attempt to change or punish it was to do violence to the person.[13]

Krafft-Ebing accepted Ulrichs's claim that homosexuality was innate, but argued that it was a sign of the degeneration of the species. The strains of modern life had affected the nervous systems of weaker specimens, who then passed down their afflictions to their offspring. Homosexuality was symptomatic of an inferior, and degenerate, line of evolution. His distinction between "sickly perversion" and "moral perversity" echoed throughout the diagnoses of military psychiatrists: sickly perversion was a constitutional, uncontrollable condition (Medical Services' psychopathic personality with abnormal sexuality), whereas moral perversity was the result of a temporary weakness of will. Havelock Ellis shared with Krafft-Ebing a view that homosexuality was inborn, although for Ellis, it was in the early stages of embryonic development that the homosexual was created. Certain people were thus considered to have been congenitally predisposed to homosexuality. In contrast to Krafft-Ebing, Ellis also argued that homosexuality, at least in the upper classes that he studied, was a harmless and sometimes valuable trait, although he noted that it could be acquired as a result of a bad environment. This allowed him to distinguish lower-class homosexuals as a different, more dangerous threat to society. Many medical officers would also draw distinctions between homosexual men of their own station in life and those of the lower classes. They may have derived their ideas from Ellis or arrived at them from a similar class perspective.[14]

Finally, Sigmund Freud's psychogenic theories can be found throughout the case files of the military psychiatrists. He, like Ellis, arrived at his theories after observing the middle and upper classes of European society. For Freud, all people were born with an undifferentiated libido and passed through developmental stages on their way to a mature heterosexuality. Homosexuality was a phase through which all sexually mature people passed and at which homosexuals had stopped. Although he criticized the view that homosexuals were a threat to society, his theories provided many psychiatrists with ready-made tools for pathologizing and persecuting gay men. Two Freudian concepts were frequently applied in psychiatric assessments. Medical officers often identified "latent homosexuality" in patients who were referred for a variety of causes, including homosexual infractions. Within Freudian theory, latent homosexuality – the result of unresolved conflict in the process of sexual and social maturation – was the cause of many neurotic traits in overtly heterosexual individuals. Alcohol could trigger an overt homosexual act in an otherwise 'normal' man. Freud also distinguished between sexual aim and sexual object: the aim of one's sexual desire shaped the manner in which one sought sexual satisfaction (active or passive, tender or violent) and was distinct from the gender of the sexual object. Freud felt that the sexual aim, rather than the object (male or female), was the more important determinant of the health of a sexual encounter. This distinction allowed doctors to discuss the homosexuality of masculine soldiers, whereas the concept of inversion – which viewed homosexuals as identifying with the opposite sex – could not account for the great diversity in sexual and gendered behaviour.[15]

It is impossible to reconcile the military category for homosexuality – psychopathic personality with abnormal sexual behaviour – with all of the competing scientific theories regarding the genesis of homosexuality. The military category recalled Krafft-Ebing's sickly perversion formulation, but the forces' concern with the effect that homosexuality would have on military life also related to Krafft-Ebing's "moral perversity" concept and

Freud's "latent homosexualism." Medical officers tended to see sexual perversion through their class biases, as did Havelock Ellis and Sigmund Freud. They identified more easily with upper-class homosexuals and tended to see lower-class 'perverts' as socially dangerous. Whether rooted in a biological degeneration of the race or in adverse environmental conditions, homosexuality in the lower class represented a more serious threat to the civilized world. A moral revulsion towards sexual deviance, which scientific training had not always extinguished, was common among military psychiatrists, although compassion and respect were sometimes evident as well. However, it is important to remember that the doctors who showed the greatest respect for homosexual servicemen were those who excised references to homosexuality from their patients' files. The medical records tilt towards antipathy.

MEDICAL OFFICERS AND HOMOSEXUAL SERVICEMEN

Psychiatrists' ability to diagnose and discharge homosexuals was severely limited in practice. Men were not referred for a psychiatric examination unless they were a problem in their unit or were court-martialled for homosexual behaviour. In Canada, there was never a psychiatric screening of personnel to vet homosexual servicemen as there was in the American forces during the Second World War. Even after the committee on nomenclature had identified homosexuals as a restricted category in November 1942, Canadian doctors who assigned the stability ranking to recruits did not diagnose homosexuals as such, even when the men freely acknowledged their homosexuality. More significant was the psychiatrists' aversion to apply the category in cases where other military functions had marked men as homosexual.

Out of a sample of fifty-six cases in which men appeared before martial courts for engaging in homosexual relations (six from the navy, seventeen from the RCAF, and thirty-three from the army), only twenty-nine were subsequently interviewed by a psychiatrist. Of the men not interviewed, most were given minor sentences of detention and returned to their duties, frequently combat; several others, though willing accomplices to homosexual relations, were never charged. Of the twenty-nine interviewed, the psychiatrists diagnosed four as homosexual and one as latent feminism, a term used to describe a submissive personality. The psychiatrists offered no diagnosis in three cases, found the evidence in three others to be inconclusive as to whether the patient was homosexual, judged another three men to be normal, and determined three to be mentally deficient and four to be psychopathic personalities (anti-social type). The balance of the diagnoses identified the effect of the court martial or the stress of combat on the men: anxiety state, hypertension, post-traumatic neurosis, and hysteria. Thus, in only 14 per cent of those cases in which servicemen were known to have had sex with each other did psychiatrists diagnose them as homosexual.[16]

Predictably, diagnoses of homosexuality were even more rare in cases of troublesome servicemen who had not been marked by the police or courts as queer. References to psychiatric reports from Europe consistently show insignificant numbers of patients diagnosed as homosexual. A report by Major Kirkpatrick compiled in January 1944 names one diagnosis of psychopathic personality with abnormal sexuality out of 728 cases. Similarly, over the period from 15 January 1944 to 16 May 1944, the Canadian neuropsychiatric base, attached to 14 Canadian General Hospital, admitted only two homosexuals out of 1,027 cases. Table 5 (see Appendix 2) shows the distribution of psychiatric casualties in the First Canadian Corps during a four-month period of the Italian campaign. Only one case, or 0.1 per cent of the total, was diagnosed as (latent) homosexual. Overwhelmingly, the most common diagnosis was psychopathic personality, inadequate type. No one was diagnosed with psychopathic personality with abnormal sexuality. Doctors may have avoided using that category for a variety of reasons, not least of which was the unwillingness to lose even inefficient men because of their homosexual behaviour. For instance, in examining a twenty-six-year-old gunner in December 1943, Major Burch, a medical officer, identified the problem as "Instability. Problem of sexuality reported, not admitted. Long crime sheet. Volatile." Apparently, the soldier's homosexual activities had been reported by a third party, probably his superior officer. Major Burch diagnosed him as psychopathic personality, inadequate type and recommended reallocation to a pioneer unit. Only men who had thus established themselves as 'military misfits' were referred for psychiatric consultation in the absence of a court martial. And only when soldiers discussed their homosexuality with the examining doctors could homosexuality possibly be identified as the main feature of the case. There was little will or need to refer to the medical authorities queer soldiers who were doing their jobs effectively.[17]

Lieutenant Colonel Richardson, the neuropsychiatric specialist at the DMS branch at Canadian Military Headquarters in London, surveyed the total number of medical boards that had downgraded soldiers for neuropsychiatric disabilities in Europe during the first six months of 1944. The Canadian Army Overseas (CAO) was at that time implementing the PULHEMS profile system and so reclassified 23,373 soldiers. Thirty per cent

(5,349) of these boards resulted in the lowering of the M (mental ability) or S (stability – psychiatric) categories. Gradings of 5 (on the scale of 1 to 5) resulted in repatriation to Canada and military discharge. Tables 6 and 7 analyse the 2,430 soldiers who were diagnosed as psychopathic personalities. Only 0.7 percent (seventeen cases) of psychopathic personalities were classified "with abnormal sexuality." However, as can be seen from Table 7, 82 per cent of those cases were also classified M1, the highest level of mental ability. The figures suggest that targeting men exclusively because of their sexuality was self-defeating. Those men who either could not, or would not, hide their homosexuality during this reclassification did not lack the intellectual ability required to soldier effectively. However, that classification entailed their disharge from the service.

The Royal Canadian Navy established a psychiatric service at the Royal Canadian Naval Hospital at Halifax in June 1941 that saw approximately nine hundred patients within its first eighteen months. Surgeon Commander Marvin Wellman studied a hundred consecutive cases in 1942 in order to determine the effect of sea service on mental health. The results are displayed in Table 8. Wellman excluded neurological and disciplinary cases from the study so that only the more severe psychiatric problems would be analysed. That exclusion probably explains the relative absence of psychopathic personalities in the sample. However, it is notable that of the hundred cases, only one was labelled homosexual. In his discussion of the findings, Surgeon Commander Wellman identified the sailor as having registered "anxiety over unethical behaviour." In common with the psychiatrists from the other services, he avoided any detailed discussion of homosexuality in the navy. Nevertheless, his passing comment sheds light on the general attitude towards homosexuality among the naval medical officers: only those servicemen who had a problem with the problem needed attention. While doctors diagnosed those men forwarded to them after courts martial for homosexual offences, they had no interest in increasing their already heavy workload by treating well-adjusted queer sailors. Surgeon Commander Wellman found that naval life, including the long periods of service at sea under difficult conditions, could precipitate a high number of psychiatric casualties. The Royal Canadian Naval Hospital, inundated with such patients, seems to have left the courts to deal with homosexuality.[18]

The army's committee on nomenclature had advised that homosexuals were to be diagnosed on the basis of abnormal sexual *behaviour*. The statistics presented suggest that medical officers did not follow that counsel, for in only 14 per cent of the cases in which men had demonstrably engaged in homosexual behaviour (and then been interviewed by a doctor) were the psychiatrists willing to label them homosexual. If men were not caught by the authorities having sex with each other, there was very little likelihood that their homosexual behaviour would become a military problem. However, using behaviour as an indicator of a homosexual disposition was consistent with the committee's advice on how to identify other psychopathic personalities; a person's conduct was the outward thing that revealed his inner conscious processes. The same problem that had confronted the military's legal experts dogged the psychiatrists: when was homosexual behaviour indicative of a homosexual disposition? The military was not so concerned with whether men were psychically queer or normal, just as long as they renounced homosexuality. Psychiatry, however, concerned itself with the workings of the mind and, therefore, probed more deeply into both expressed and repressed sexual desires. What did they find? What were they looking for?

THE MEDICAL OFFICER AND PATIENT ENCOUNTER

It is not possible to identify a psychiatrist's theoretical allegiance on the basis of case histories. Doctors probably drew on various models in diagnosing different individuals. The same doctor may have used Ulrichs's notion of sexual inversion to classify an effeminate soldier who liked to take the passive role in anal intercourse and Freud's to account for a masculine soldier who regularly penetrated his comrades. A masculine infantryman who found pleasure in submission could be an instance of individual or racial degeneracy. More likely, his transgression would be overlooked as anomalous and not indicative of any sexual disorder. Although some patients were seen over an extended period, doctors usually made their diagnoses on the basis of relatively brief meetings with patients. Those who were sent to psychiatrists as a result of court-martial proceedings were usually examined once. The psychiatrist made a determination of the accused's orientation on the basis of that meeting. Men (queer and straight) who were committed as psychiatric patients for reasons other than their sexual orientation could receive much more dedicated attention over a period of days or weeks.

Psychiatric examinations followed a set pattern. The patient's complaint, or the reason for his referral to the psychiatrist, was recorded first. He was then questioned on his family history; unstable personality traits in his parents and siblings and the nature of family relationships were noted. Then the patient's personal history was covered, including his memories of early childhood and school, his work history, recreational interests (most commonly sports and hobbies), sexual habits, domestic life, and military career to date. The psychiatrist then recorded his impression of the patient's personality as revealed through his answers to questions "as to mood swings, reactions to danger, attitude to physical health, obsessional traits, aggressiveness or recessiveness, military morale," and any other issues deemed appropriate. The present condition of the patient was then transcribed along with any physical problems. Finally, the psychiatrist arrived at a diagnosis and recommendation for the patient's disposal – either back to his unit, a transfer within the force, return to Canada if overseas, or discharge.[19]

The reason for the patient's referral to the psychiatrist likely had some impact on the nature of the encounter. Air Commodore Tice asserted that some servicemen visited psychiatrists voluntarily with a view to finding help 'recovering' from their homosexuality. If such cases did exist, they seem not to have been committed to paper. Psychiatrists, in such circumstances, may have followed the precedence of their spiritual forebears – religious confessors – in respecting the privacy of their patients. Records that do exist in the personnel files of servicemen indicate that the usual reason men were referred to psychiatrists was, not homosexuality, but because they were a problem for a commanding officer. The officer would send the soldier to the army examiner responsible for allocating manpower efficiently, who may have recommended a psychiatric evaluation. Medical officers, who had minimal training in psychiatry, also treated queer men who were having trouble in their units. Gunner Burwell Snyder saw his medical officer four times during the first week of May 1944 in Terrace, British Columbia. He asked the doctor for help with his anxiety over being harassed by the other recruits because he was queer. While he asked the doctor to help him secure a transfer to another unit, the medical officer merely prescribed phenobarbitol to calm his nerves.

Sometimes men appeared before medical boards that were responsible for allocating problem cases. The consultant psychiatrists' reports on those soldiers contained detailed statements on their sex lives, such as their habits of masturbation in adolescence and their frequency of sexual intercourse. Ranking medical officers felt that such disclosure in a document that was "not strictly confidential may possibly be prejudicial to the man's best interests." As a result, psychiatrists were advised in September 1943 that "intimate details of sex relationship will be omitted from the documents except ... cases in which sexual abnormality is the cause of the patient's maladjustment in the army: e.g. psychopathic personality with homosexuality ... or sex abnormalities are the basic cause of the patient's psychiatric disability." The effect of this directive was to position the 'normal' sex life outside of psychiatric scrutiny. While the sex habits of queers could be dissected in detail, the sexual behaviours of those unmarked by their orientation were given a pass.[20]

The interview was recorded by the psychiatrist during the course of the meeting, although his impressions, diagnosis, and recommendation were added later. A careful analysis of the record offers insight into the interview itself. A paucity of notes does not necessarily mean that the interview was unsuccessful, for the psychiatrist may have been directing his attention to the patient rather than recording the proceedings. A great deal of detail, however, does tell us that the patient was forthcoming in his answers. By contrast, when the psychiatrist recorded a succession of negative responses, such as "normal childhood, average school record, no problems," it is probable that the soldier was less than interested in sharing his past with the doctor. The doctor's impressions reveal something of his own tastes in men and show that the encounters were subject to the dynamics that order all relationships: "a very pleasant man," "a vigorous straight-forward, rather irresponsible man of good morale," "throughout interview he was pleasant, freely accessible." When the psychiatrist jotted down that the patient denied a particular proposition, it is likely (although not certain) that it was put to him by the doctor. For instance, the comments "He denies anal intercourse" and "always lacking in aggression" describe issues that the psychiatrists thought were significant in determining a homosexual disposition. Similarly, comments on military processes and defences of homosexuality can be assumed to have originated, probably unsolicited, from the soldier: "[O]n no occasion were his activities public or a source of social scandal. His defending lawyer took very little interest in his case – did not take it seriously enough." Psychiatrists often revealed their own biases and class positions by the way they recorded simple facts: "He states without any emotion whatever that his mother is a prostitute." When the words are in quotation marks, or are inconsistent with the rest of the transcription, it is probable that they were spoken by the soldier. Thus, in a multitude of ways, the soldier's own words can come through the record written by the doctor and we can learn something of both parties.[21]

In most cases, psychiatrists determined a man's sexual orientation on the basis of a relatively brief encounter. What evidence allowed them to make this judgment? The diagnosis drew its authority from the psychiatrists' claim to privileged knowledge of the workings of human consciousness. The following case illustrates this point. Captain Egan was called to the stand at Private A's trial for disgraceful conduct in having sexual relations with another private while stationed in St John's, Newfoundland. Egan testified: "I have studied psychiatry and have had previous experience in this sort of thing on medical boards." He said that Private A's "mental examination, as one completed on Saturday, showed two particular peculiarities that were at all noticeable." Egan was making it clear that his subsequent remarks would be based on the observations he had made in the course of a proper medical examination in his official capacity as doctor. However, Private A had worked with Captain Egan as an orderly since the doctor's arrival in Newfoundland. As the trial progressed, Egan's testimony slid between knowledge that he had acquired of Private A in the course of working with him and knowledge acquired through the official mental examination.

In support of his argument that Private A was probably homosexual, he presented the following "clinical" evidence: "One, chronic alcoholism which was sufficiently controlled that it did not interfere with military duties, and second is, a noticeable absence in the amount of female companionship that he experienced in proportion to the average soldier, especially in this area." Both of these claims could have been the result of his casual observations of Private A over the period of their association in the medical ward. His expert testimony that Private A was probably a case of "fixed or developmental" homosexuality rested on three facts: "(1) new sex habits are seldom acquired in the latter stages of life and (2) through various conversations with the accused while on duty he has stated his service in the army to be of long duration marked by lack of female association and (3) he has a definite inclination to associate with much younger men." It was clear that the doctor required no psychiatric examination to arrive at the facts upon which he based his diagnosis. Asked if, from his observation, he had formed a "definite medical opinion that [Private A] is perverted," the doctor replied, "I do not think that this would ever manifest itself so strongly to a casual observer." Thus, he seemed to be privileging the facts derived from the mental examination. It is conceivable that he was simply uncomfortable calling a close associate a pervert in open court. Were it not for his complex psychoanalytic interpretation of the facts, Captain Egan would have had nothing more to offer than another witness, Private Reed, who testified that the other soldiers "talked amongst ourselves about it [Private A's homosexual affair with another soldier] at times. Everybody was talking about it."

Captain Egan told the court that there were acquired and developmental types of homosexual. His model echoed Ellis's and Freud's theories that homosexuals could be created by environmental conditions or in the embryo. The defending officer had wanted to know if "a man can be born with inherent perversions and how his battle in life to beat it down can be affected and also what effect age might have on his perversion?" There is a sense of certainty based on extensive learning in Captain Egan's testimony:

If the acquired type continues on the perversions for a number of years the oral reflexes of sexual satisfaction become more or less permanently established and, therefore, it is to be considered in the same light as a developmental case. In such cases, the individual is extremely vulnerable in that cure, as far as is known, cannot be obtained with the institution of punishment. Early acquired types, however, are quickly broken of the habit by the removal of the causital individuals from their presence because at that stage of events, the genital stage is relatively strong and can come forward to dominate.

Such public pronouncements on the aetiology and prognosis of homosexuality were rare and must be treated with caution. Theoretical models espoused by individual doctors were not necessarily accepted by others. Captain Egan's testimony regarding the futility of punishment in cases of fixed perversion, such as Private A's, might have been designed to push the court to an acquittal or light sentence. However, in this instance, the doctor's opinion had little impact and Private A was sentenced to six months imprisonment at hard labour and discharge with ignominy.[22]

ACCEPTING HOMOSEXUALITY
WITHOUT HOMOSEXUALS

Given the ambiguity of the category of psychopathic personality with abnormal sexuality and the competing theoretical models, what did psychiatrists actually look for in identifying homosexuals? The most common indicator of homosexuality was the assertion (sometimes insistence) of the soldier himself that he was queer. Most men, of course, had learned to renounce their homosexual impulses in all but sympathetic social situations. There were few occasions in polite society where a man could expect to be questioned about his sexuality; psychiatrists, however, were required to probe into the sexual histories of their patients in the course of their interviews. Men who responded honestly to the psychiatrists' requests could come to regret their candour. If the doctor was particularly hostile to homosexuality, the soldier could find himself on a ship back to Canada. For instance, one private was referred to a medical officer at Basingstoke, the Canadian Army's psychiatric hospital in England, because of a speech impediment that rendered him unable to talk to officers. Captain Fraser managed to complete the interview by narcoanalysis (while the soldier was in a sleeplike state induced by barbiturates). The soldier told Captain Fraser that he liked training and soldiering but was afraid to go into combat. The doctor found no physical impediments to his continued service, describing him as "well-developed and well-nourished." Regarding the private's sexual history, the doctor recorded:

About the age of 14 began masturbating. Says he was taught by another lad his same age. Later they practised fellatio & coitus and with the pt usually in the active roll [sic]. This affair continued until pt came o/s [overseas]. States he has ... felt sexually attracted by other men in the army but has never had relations with other men. In addition he masturbated fairly frequently at times every night. Age 17 he had a book which stated that this would lead to brain damage & he would lose his voice. From that time forward he has had trouble speaking to strangers.

Captain Fraser diagnosed the soldier as psychopathic personality with abnormal sexuality, a category that entailed his return to Canada and discharge from the army. Whether Captain Fraser would have forgiven the soldier's homosexual past had he not been suffering from the speech disorder (diagnosed "hysteria," meaning there was no somatic basis to the condition) is impossible to know. But were he not referred because of his speech impediment, his homosexuality would not have led to his disharge.[23]

When psychiatrists found some homosexual experiences in a soldier's sexual history, they commonly assumed that these experiences were symptomatic of a wider pathology. However, since they did not see men who were not "military misfits," they had no access to a control group to test homosexuality as a factor in adaptability. A form used by psychiatrists at Basingstoke to assess each patient's personality listed categories such as "endowment factors, developmental factors, functional capacity, physical, psychological, social," and provided two columns, one for the psychiatrist to list the man's "assets" and the other his "liabilities," both to be determined after a lengthy interview. Captain Armstrong, a medical officer, interviewed an army private in January 1944 who was referred because of "behavioural difficulties." He filled three pages of notes, which suggests that the patient had been very talkative. In recounting his colourful past as a fastidious hobo during the Depression, the private told the doctor that he "intermittently as circumstances dictated would indulge in homosexual relationships or masturbation." This was offered in the context of an otherwise heterosexual life; in fact, part of his current trouble had been a string of AWOL offences committed so that he could visit his English girlfriend. On the personality assessment form, Captain Armstrong left the assets column blank but thoroughly filled the liabilities side, noting "intermittent homosexual" among the soldier's other "shortcomings." Finally, however, he tentatively diagnosed him as psychopathic personality with abnormal sexuality. An inclination to indulge in homosexual relations proved what the doctor had already determined on the basis of other evidence – that the patient was unstable. Such a diagnosis discounted the psychoanalytic notion of homosexuality as a universal phase of sexual development preceding the mature genital stage characteristic, as Freud argued, of heterosexual relations.[24]

Like Captain Armstrong, many doctors left traces in their records of their feelings towards their patients' homosexual experiences. A class bias often underlay such sentiments. When one soldier openly discussed his homosexual disposition at his court martial for AWOL, the chief medical officer of Pacific Command referred him for a psychiatric examination. Comparing the impressions of the personnel officer with those of the psychiatrist illustrates how military officials applied their own preferences in their dealings with their subjects. In July 1944 the personnel officer had written: "[The recruit] is a tall, well-built soldier with an engaging air and a good background of training in the US Army Air Corps. He led a rather roaming and unsettled life prior to joining the Army in Jun 41. He drifted from one job to another in both Canada and the US for a number of years and the basic reason for this was probably his broken home life ... [H]is adjustment will probably be normal since he claims he likes Army life." If the recruit did mention his homosexuality, it was not written down. While the personnel officer noticed the "instability" in the recruit's work history, it is clear nevertheless that he was favourably impressed by his manner. The soldier described the same unsettled family conditions and work history to Major Armitage, the psychiatrist at Military District 11 reception centre (Vancouver) six months later, after his court martial for AWOL. The doctor could barely contain his personal dislike for the man: "This man is a very glib talker and is aggressive and assertive and opinionated, and feels rather offended by his treatment. He is completely lacking in any sense of responsibility and most unreliable and is, I believe, a pathological liar. He has an extremely bad family and personal background and I am half inclined to believe that his homosexual tendencies are authentic." The "engaging air" that had charmed the personnel officer impressed the psychiatrist as "glib" and "opinionated." Of course, it is possible that the recruit had behaved in a charming manner to the personnel officer and aggressively towards the psychiatrist, for any number of reasons. It is curious that the doctor was only "half inclined" to believe the soldier's own account of his homosexuality. He had made it clear that he wanted to remain in the army and so would have had no motivation to lie about his sexual orientation. The major's choice of words more probably signals his own surprise to encounter a man so incautious in his self-representation.

Major Armitage carefully recorded a history of the soldier's love life: "He says he lived with his father for 6 months [at 16 years of age] until he had a fight with him when his father found out about his homosexual activities. He returned to Vancouver, B.C. and lived with a man there for 5 months, then went to Seattle, where he lived with another man for 6 months, and has lived with other men off and on for short periods of time … He was in jail many times, he says, for homosexual activities and for drunkenness." This disinterested, scientific account of the soldier's sexual and romantic history sits uncomfortably with Major Armitage's notes regarding his patient's attitude: "[H]e rather defiantly says that he has had these [homosexual] tendencies for many years and that he is quite satisfied with the results." The defiance that the doctor records may well have been a response to his own disapproval of the soldier's sexual life. The doctor's frustration at having his authority undermined by a patient, a non-expert who claimed his own knowledge of homosexuality, comes through the one-sided record. Major Armitage labelled him a psychopathic personality with abnormal sexuality, thereby forcing his discharge from the service. He believed that it was "most unlikely that any psychological treatment would ever be of any value" and that "it is unfortunate that there is no medical legal machinery in Canada to deal with this type of person." The soldier's defiant defence of his homosexual life led Major Armitage to despair of the power of psychiatry to heal him: "I believe it is absolutely hopeless to try to recommend any type of employment for this man in civil life and that rehabilitation would be useless and that he will do whatever he wishes to do after he is discharged."[25]

Psychiatrists could respond differently to homosexual men with whom they felt an affinity and who acknowledged their position as experts in matters of human behaviour. Even doctors who had insight into the nature of these relationships could profit from their patients' deference. When Colonel Hyland initially began treating Captain K at Basingstoke in England in January 1942, he was unaware of the ordeal that had preceded the captain's sudden physical ailments. Two days earlier, Captain K's superior officer had shown him the result of an investigation; these were communications from several soldiers describing Captain K's homosexual advances towards them. Captain K fell ill and was hospitalized. The doctors at 14 Canadian General Hospital judged his symptoms to be hysterical and transferred him to Basingstoke, where Dr Hyland began treating him.

Captain K described the prejudice that his family had experienced in small-town Ontario during the previous war because of their German ancestry. He also discussed his university education and his devotion to his widowed mother. Since 1930, he had worked as a trader at an investment firm. The doctor recorded that, in the army, he drank moderately and was "one of the most popular officers in his mess." The two men seemed to share a sense of class roots and traditional values. There is a scientific distancing evident in Dr Hyland's record of their developing relationship during the ten days the captain spent at Basingstoke. Before the doctor became aware of the homosexual scandal looming over Captain K, he observed:

Pt [patient] is an introspective unstable individual who complains constantly of a great variety of symptoms all of which are described as "terrible" or "awful." He talks freely & on different interviews appears with a number of his symptoms or emotional reactions written down so he won't forget to tell me about them ... He is very conscious of the examiner's opinion of him & quite evidently anxious to create a good impression ... He is very suggestible during examination & shows a childish reliance on the examiner. He asks questions sometimes such as "Do I have to eat lunch?" When told he must do so he obediently goes.

The doctor seemed concerned that Captain K's deference to medical authority was too easily obtained. Nevertheless, it facilitated treatment. The doctor learned through another officer in the ward of the impending court martial and questioned Captain K about it. In his notes, Dr Hyland recorded that "he did not mention this to me previously because it had not been worrying him ... & denies being upset because he states there is absolutely no truth in it." (More likely, he wanted to retain the doctor's respect.) Hyland, however, deduced that the captain's medical complaints were a reaction to the accusation and that a normal response would have been much more vigorous: "It is noteworthy that in conversation pt shows no normal indignation. It was pointed out to him the hysterical nature of his symptoms & their motive. He finally accepted the explanation but even then showed no proper reaction to the situation." For the remainder of Captain K's stay at Basingstoke, the imminent scandal seems to have dominated their conversation.

Distinctly different from the dynamics that animated relations between psychiatrists and working-class homosexuals, the common social ground shared by doctors and officers tended to work in favour of the patient. Captain K came to share with Hyland his thoughts regarding a defence to the charges: "Pt feels that there are 2 factors in the case. 1. He is being framed. 2. He was incorrectly identified. If it [is] 1. he does not wish to take any action in the matter. If it is 2 he wishes to clear his name but has no idea how to do it. Pt discusses the matter with little show of enthusiasm. He now admits that he has been under great strain in his unit ever since coming overseas owing to a knowledge that he was not wanted by the major." There are hints in the records that Hyland suspected the truth of the accusations. His entry that "Pt attributes his failure to personally interview his accusers or to ascertain exact details to lack of time" suggests that the doctor had asked questions based on the assumption that an innocent man would have responded differently to the crisis. Nevertheless, the final records reveal that Hyland had become complicit in Captain K's attempt to prevail over the accusations: "Pt to be discharged to the Holding Unit & he is being advised to take no action about the charges if he hears no more about them. It would seem best that he make a fresh start & not return to his former unit. Final diagnosis: hysteria."[26]

Middle-class queer men could sometimes reject medicine's claim to expertise in the field of human behaviour, especially when it stripped them of the power to define themselves. Lieutenant DiPierro was twenty-five years old when he returned from Europe, where he had acknowledged and acted upon his queer desires for the first time. At the end of the war, he was spotted by the military police at the Mount Royal Hotel in Montreal, an establishment frequented by homosexuals at the time. He was briefly interviewed by an army psychiatrist before being discharged, "on medical grounds," for being homosexual. He immediately returned to civil life as a professor of architecture at McGill University. However, the experience had been disturbing. Fifty-six years later, he commented, "I was obviously a great nuisance because I was very depressed all the time and they [McGill] sent me to a private psychiatrist up in Victoria Hospital up on the mountain ... and he wanted to cure me, to stop me being gay and all this stuff and it didn't work." After the humiliation of his discharge, the further degradation of having his desires and emotions debased compounded his depression. In the end, he could no longer bear remaining in the country that he felt had betrayed him after he had given it five years of war service: "So depressed that I just had to finally get a ticket on a freighter – a freight boat from Halifax – no, Montreal – to Liverpool ... And I left the country never to go back. It was a traumatic experience and I'd no one to talk to in those days." The experience left him with little respect for the men who he felt had disrespected him: "I find it very silly. I don't like psychiatrists, I think they're crazy. I don't like them because they think up excuses for anything you've got. They blame it on your parents or something. But they were no help at all. I think I was just unwilling to cooperate." Nevertheless, in his state of depression, he did initially accept the proposition put forward by various authorities, including psychiatry, that the road to health entailed changing his sexual orientation. Psychiatrists were able to 'help' such men only when their competence was endorsed, and they were more likely to convince men of their own class to accede to their authority.[27]

While Lieutenant DiPierro was sent to the psychiatrist already marked as queer, Captain K's homosexuality had not yet been named publicly. Captain K also differed in being closer to his doctor's age and station in life and in denying his homosexuality. Possibly, he was perceived as a lesser social threat. Aside from those differences, both of these doctor/patient relationships were generally cooperative, unlike those that tended to exist between psychiatrists and patients from the lower classes. Some psychiatrists looked for the traits in homosexuals that made them identifiable and, most importantly, different from themselves and their colleagues. If homosexuality was pathological, then it should appear to be so. A homosexual who was otherwise identifiable with a doctor and who boasted accomplishments was not in the same category as one whose life was demonstrably different.

While psychiatrists may have been morally repulsed by the idea of homosexuality or trained to see it as a sign of pathology, the actual men who sometimes confronted them could seem in every other way just like home, as in the following case. Dr Musgrove was required to judge whether a private convicted of homosexual behaviour by a court martial was in fact homosexual. The soldier had been described by the personnel officer as "pleasant, agreeable, mature, ambitious and extremely conscientious ... [a] realistic and alert thinker possessing interests covering many fields." He had been a champion chess player, was artistic, had a love of music and a very high score on the military's intelligence test, was an amateur boxer, and had competed on the army team in the Ontario Hockey League from 1931 to 1939. Despite the fact that he behaved homosexually, Musgrove formed this opinion: "I am, however, convinced that this man is not a frank homosexual and that he does not exhibit any gross evidence of psychiatric pathology." If this soldier was not homosexual, then who was? What markers did psychiatrists use to confirm a man's homosexuality?[28]

Even patients who declared their homosexuality were not necessarily taken at their word. Dr Warren was unwilling to confirm a soldier's sexual orientation on the basis of his affirmation that he was homosexual:

This man complains that he went absent without leave from Fort Lewis because the other soldiers there all knew of his homosexuality. He points to the ring on his fourth finger indicating a homosexual relationship, his nail varnish and his dyed hair. He also mentions with considerable emphasis homosexual behaviour which he claims he has indulged in, drawing to my attention pointedly the disturbing element he presents in the Army ... The account that this man gives of his life and of his sexual inclination needs confirmation before it is accepted at its face value ... I cannot say at present whether his sexual orientation is of much importance in itself but I feel sure that the crux of the problem he presents arises from a psychopathic personality.

For Dr Warren, it was not the patient's homosexuality that indicated psychopathy. In keeping with a trend of psychiatric analysis, he suggests that the patient's homosexuality may have been one symptom of a larger pathology. It is curious that Dr Warren thinks that an independent confirmation of his sexual orientation would be necessary. Who would undertake that investigation? Medical services asserted that it alone had the keys to unlock the secrets guarded in people's psyches. In fact, anyone who wanted to be discharged from the army could declare that he was homosexual, as long as he followed up his declaration with queer activity. It is indicative of the depth of anti-homosexual sentiments and the fear of being seen as queer that there seem to be no such cases in the files. In fact, there were easier ways to be discharged than to destroy one's reputation and future in the process. For example, one could disobey orders repeatedly, claim conscientious objector status, or simply desert.[29]

The feminine markers that the soldier had adopted did not persuade Dr Warren that he was homosexual. There was no consistent correlation between a man's gendered behaviour and a diagnosis of homosexuality. 'Secondary sex characteristics' was a common label for an individual's mix of masculine and feminine traits. But what constituted effeminacy in men at that time, and its psychiatric significance, is difficult to determine. An RCAF fighter pilot seconded to the RAF was transferred to Basingstoke Neurological Hospital in November 1943 from a British military hospital where he was being treated for an ulcer. His transfer to Basingstoke suggests that he might have been considered a psychiatric case. In his personal history (written by all psychiatric patients at Basingstoke), he wrote that he was "very satisfied with his branch of the service" but was concerned about his stomach – "a pilot without a good stomach going into battle is like an infantry man without his rifle." After several days, Captain Walters diagnosed him as having "no major psychological problem" and a "normal personality." However, under the liabilities column he wrote that the pilot was an "effeminate type – flighty." This did not lead to an enquiry into his sexual orientation. "Flighty" must have described the pilot's demeanour; since he had had the fortitude to complete his training and assume duties as a fighter pilot in England, it would not likely have identified an inability to concentrate. The doctor, however, saw a frivolous, perhaps whimsical, nature as a "liability" for a man, antithetical to manhood. Further, it was seen as a typically feminine trait. Presumably, the difference in acceptable behaviour for men and women derived from the fact that men were considered responsible for important and dangerous matters, especially during the war, and a masculine personality should reflect that gravity. Ironically, the pilot in question was performing his duties well, notwithstanding his effeminate nature.[30]

While some psychiatrists saw effeminacy as suggestive, if not indicative, of homosexuality, others saw traditional feminine characteristics, like submissiveness, as evidence that a man was not homosexual. By this logic, homosexuality was a vice that required an aggressive, thereby, masculine personality. Lieutenant Church reported on a navy sub-lieutenant who had been convicted of "an act of gross indecency with a rating" : "[I]t appears to me after personality analysis that he would be unlikely to be the aggressor as his personality trends are nearly all on the submissive side as opposed to aggression as usually shown in the male. This suggests latent feminism despite his apparently normal sex history." This, along with the sub-lieutenant's own assurance that he had "achieved heterosexual maturity," convinced the doctor that his "sex development is not abnormal." Homosexuality, for Church, was not connected to gender inversion, but rather to hypermasculinity; in fact, sex was defined by the act of penetration, which was inherently aggressive. (Church was echoing the traditional Christian view of sodomy.) On the other hand, in January 1944 a psychiatrist judged that there was "insufficient evidence" to consider a man convicted by court martial in England of homosexuality to be a sexual psychopath. He described the soldier as a "vigorous straight-forward, rather irresponsible man of good morale" who "likes the army and wants to carry on," and diagnosed him as having a mild form of psychopathic personality, "aggressive type." Homosexuality could sometimes be seen to result from too much testosterone, sometimes from too little.[31]

Most psychiatrists saw factors other than effeminacy as more indicative of a homosexual orientation. Squadron Leader Moorehouse, a psychiatric consultant based in Canada, interviewed five different men who had been found guilty of homosexuality by court martial, and concluded that two of them were "bona fide" homosexuals. One man who he confirmed "may be regarded as a true sexual pervert (homosexual)" was found to be physically normal "except that the patient is immature, secondary sex characteristics poorly developed and has an effeminate habitus and manner." However, his decision was ultimately based on other observations: "The significant factors are that this is a French Canadian airman who voluntarily enlisted in the Service, had no objections to posting to an isolated station, freely admitted a background of homosexual endeavours and experiences, uses words and phrases common to the vocabulary of a homosexual, and finally was found in such practices." In a similar case, Moorehouse again recorded the willingness of a French Canadian to enlist and be posted to a station without access to women as a possible sign of his homosexuality. However, a similar willingness was not a factor in his consideration of English Canadians. It is possible that he assumed that French Canadians would not be motivated by patriotism, and hence found their reason for willingly accepting a posting that restricted them to male company more suspect. Thus, effeminacy in men was, for Moorehouse, one factor in a larger symptomology. He judged one English Canadian airman to be masculine but suspect nevertheless: "He is not effeminate. I am, however, not inclined to accept his statements fully. His manner is not frank and open and he is obviously not telling the whole truth. However, as there is so little evidence to prove inclination to perverted behaviour, and because of serving on an isolated station, it is not possible to state definitely that he is a bona fide homosexual." Serving in an isolated station meant that the patient was removed from women and thus more likely to temporarily engage in homosexual behaviour. Ironically, the same factor – serving in an isolated location – was, for the English Canadian, a sign that his homosexual activity was not symptomatic of a homosexual character; for the French Canadian, it was a sign that it was. The English Canadian was presumed to be there by necessity, the French Canadian by choice.[32]

Psychiatrists considered the circumstances of each case in coming to their judgment about a patient's sexual orientation. Isolation from female company was often seen as a mitigating factor in having "indulged" (a common term in the files) in homosexual behaviour. But only a small percentage of military service was performed in isolated, all-male environments. (Naval service commonly required long periods without female company.) Psychiatrists asked men about their heterosexual experiences and were remarkably trusting of their patients' declarations that they were sexually normal. Middle-aged single men, having been convicted of homosexuality, typically asserted that they preferred heterosexual relations. The overwhelming tendency of doctors to accept these histories suggests that they were either insensitive to the pressures that would motivate men to lie about their transgressive desires or sympathetic in that they did not want to label their patients homosexual. In fact, openly discussing one's heterosexuality could be interpreted by some doctors as evidence of candour, as in the case of a forty-two-year-old single airman convicted of homosexuality who, the doctor stated, "freely admitted" to "normal sexual relations."[33]

As an example of the uncritical acceptance of the testimony of their patients, it is instructive to consider the report tabled by Major Whikower and Captain Cowan in January 1945 entitled "Some Psychological Aspects of Sexual Promiscuity: Summary of an Investigation." Out of their survey of 200 venereal disease patients, only two were reported to have contracted a disease through homosexual contact. The doctors' suspicions about the truth of their subjects' responses should have been aroused by the results of their other enquiries. Of the 105 married men who had contracted a disease, more than half said that they had become infected the first time they had been sexually unfaithful to their wives. In the control group of 40 married men, only one admitted to ever having been unfaithful to his wife, and he only once. While the doctors presented these data as factual evidence of sexual behaviour, it would have been reasonable for them to have considered what factors may have motivated men to misrepresent the reality of their sex lives to the authorities. Doctors, apparently, could labour under the same ingenuousness in dealing with heterosexual soldiers as they did with homosexual soldiers.[34]

The records suggest that doctors readily accepted the more aggressive protestations of normalcy. A thirty-four-year-old soldier who had been "shot up badly at Carpaquet where the unit lost twelve tanks during an attack on the town" and who continued to serve throughout the Normandy campaign was subsequently convicted of homosexuality. After interviewing him, Dr Alcorn noted: "Sexual History – Normal. VDG [gonorrhoea] 1938. Has had plenty of intersexual contacts. Denies homosexual ones and denies absolutely the charges mentioned above. He is easily depressed." In the course of a lengthy interview with a thirty-eight-year-old, single soldier who had been convicted three times of homosexual offences, Dr Sweet recorded: "He denies any masturbation in adult life. He denies stoutly any sexual contact with men except in several instances mutual masturbation. He denies ever having anything to do with homosexuals. Few sexual dreams and the few he has had centre about women not men." The psychiatrist accepted the soldier's resolute denial that the homosexual behaviour to which he was willing to admit was at all indicative of his desires: "In my opinion he is not in the accepted meaning of either a pervert sexually or a homosexual. Alcohol appears to put him on a juvenile level of emotion, judgement and conduct." Similarly, Flight Lieutenant (Doctor) Graham found "no evidence of psycho-

sis or mental illness other than of fellatio" in a forty-two-year-old single airman who claimed a normal sex life: "After some hesitancy he admitted to
fellatio, stating first that they had a 'pretty good summary of evidence' ...
They were both 'pretty drunk.' He states he does these acts only when he
gets drunk and has tried to refrain." Finally, Dr Musgrove found a thirty-
eight-year-old single private with a "pleasant, freely-accessible" manner to
be convincing: "[The] facts ... seem to be truthfully told but, of course, I
have no way of confirming this since I have not seen the actual draft of evidence and have only his side of the story. I am, however, convinced that this
man is not a frank homosexual and that he does not exhibit any gross evidence of psychiatric pathology." Again, the private had argued that the sexual encounter for which he was convicted "occurred while both of them
were intoxicated" and was not reflective of his sexual nature. Psychiatrists
almost universally accepted these denials of sexual abnormality. In doing so,
they neglected Medical Services' own directions to make homosexual behaviour the deciding factor in determining homosexual orientation.[35]

Doctors were invariably more forgiving than courts when it came to the
mitigating effect of alcohol on sexual behaviour. In all three cases cited
above, psychiatrists accepted that alcohol had altered the men's normal
patterns. Dr Sweet's conclusion that alcohol had the effect of making men
regress to a juvenile level of behaviour was consistent with a Freudian interpretation of homosexuality. For the many psychiatrists who diagnosed such
men as normal, homosexuality was a universal possibility held in check by
mature adults. Under the law, however, alcohol could not change a man's
motivation: a drunk man who engaged in homosexual relations was seen to
have been acting according to his desire. Defending officers were unsuccessful in arguing that men were not responsible for their actions because of
drunkenness. Freudian psychiatry, too, saw the behaviours liberated by alcohol as consistent with inner wants, but theorized that all men had passed
through such phases and could therefore regress by a weakening of the will.
But whether or not they were working within a Freudian framework, many
psychiatrists were naive about men's fear of their own homosexual desires.
Flight Lieutenant (Doctor) Bochner recorded an RCAF officer's explanation
of the events leading to his homosexual crime in the following terms:

[H]e states that he drank one or two beers by himself at 2130 hours then met some
friends (male and female) with whom he visited and talked for a while. In the course
of latter there was consumed more beer and also some gin, some rum and some
whiskey. Ultimately he felt a peculiar toxic stage of inebriation in which he realizes
some extremely strange personality changes appeared. He states that the latter

distortion of personality ended quite abruptly and left him grossly shocked over the whole episode. In the history elicited there is no evidence of any earlier questionable behaviour.

The doctor concluded that the officer was not homosexual and that the queer encounter was an "irresponsible reaction" to the alcohol. The doctor found the man's response to his homosexual encounter – "grossly shocked" – as normal. But, if all men had homosexual desires that they held in abeyance, why should they have been so surprised and disturbed by them? Why did doctors find such phobic responses reasonable? In fact, it is indicative of the depth and pervasiveness of the fear of homosexuality that so many different people, including doctors, were willing to sanction and normalise disgust.[36]

Drunkenness was thus accepted by some psychiatrists as having the power to affect basic personality patterns, temporarily turning heterosexual men into homosexuals. But war itself was understood to have a powerful impact on men's personalities. Since the First World War, students of human behaviour had applied their attention to the question of who broke down under stressful combat situations, why war had the power to impair soldiers psychologically, and how it might be possible to prevent or minimize the loss of personnel to battle exhaustion (shell shock). The debate was framed between, on the one hand, a vision of men as rational beings who were individually responsible for controlling their fears by a manly exercise of willpower and, on the other hand, the view that soldiers were subject to subconscious reactions to inhumane situations and hence were not necessarily responsible for their own inability to transcend the horrors of war. Reasonable proponents of either position understood that strict adherence to theory was of limited value in dealing with the reality of men facing combat. Even Lord Moran, in his classic study, *The Anatomy of Courage* (which argues that all men are responsible for fulfilling their duty), acknowledges that, ultimately, each man has a breaking point in war. The military accepted that reality and, in the Italian campaign, for the first time in Canadian military history, sent psychiatrists in support of the troops. For the rest of the war, many psychiatrists tried to separate men who could continue in battle (after treatment or rest) from those who had reached the limit of their capabilities.

Good psychiatrists and effective commanding officers prided themselves on knowing when men had pushed themselves to the limit. Lieutenant Colonel Andrew of the Perth Regiment testified in Italy concerning Captain H's character at his court martial for homosexuality:

He went into action with his platoon on the 17th of January 44 north of Ortona. I saw him several days later after the action and found he was suffering from nerves. It wasn't fear of self as far as I could see and understand from him on questioning him, it was the sight of that which took place around him. He did not want to leave the battle and was not in fear of injury to himself. About the end of Feb 44 I was in command of the Perth R on the Orsogna front and we had been subjected to a great deal of mortaring and shelling. One evening after we had suffered a great number of casualties [H] came down to my Tac HQ and was in a very nervous and exhausted condition. I talked to him and got from him the fact that it was not fear of himself but the conditions of the circumstances surrounding which played on his mind. He went back to platoon. He did not come back to go out of the battle. A short time later he came out of the line and it was then that I noticed that [H] had changed. He was not the person he had been before in that he was nervous, very nervous, and somewhat excitable, but at no time did he say he was in a funk. His temperament just did not allow him to see the sights that other people can face and he was upset. Right up to that time that [H] left the Regiment his conduct, apart from battle, was absolutely that of an officer and a gentleman and if there had been anything happen in the Regiment I would have heard about it.

The lieutenant colonel may have been overstating his knowledge of the men under his command for the benefit of his own reputation as a leader. It is possible that men such as Captain H could have been having homosexual relations under his command without his notice. Meanwhile, his remarks eloquently describe the gauge used to measure men in battle: there was a distinction between those who broke down after having pushed themselves to the limit and those who malingered due to a lack of courage. It was the fact that, having pushed himself to the edge of sanity, he still was unwilling to concede defeat that marked Captain H as a noble exhaustion casualty. Also, the lieutenant colonel implies a certain respect for men repelled by war; to embrace it might have suggested a more troubling example of manhood than to abhor it. Captain H's fear was born not within himself, but from the tragedies surrounding him. Brigadier Lind, commanding the Perth Regiment, echoed the judgment of Lieutenant Colonel Andrew in his assessment of the Captain: "I noticed then that if [H] did not get to the rear he would have a breakdown which would seriously affect his life. He never shirked at a job and as far as I know he had always turned in a first class stellar performance." In fact, men such as H validated their commanding officers' authority by trusting the officers to judge when they should be removed from battle for their own good and that of the army.

While he was out of the line, Captain H asked for a driver to take him to a party at Fifth Canadian Division. Private P was assigned. Once there, Private P waited with the other drivers and batmen while the officers drank in another building. He said that Captain H "came out and brought me a few drinks. He came out with drinks about every half hour. Each time he came out he put his hands down on me and felt my crotch. This happened in the doorway while the other soldiers were inside the room and could not see." Captain H had filled his water bottle with liquor from the party, and on the drive back to their lines later that night, he had Private P stop the car a couple of times to have a drink. Private P said that on the last stop, "I stopped the car and he passed me the bottle. I took a mouthful. While I was drinking he put his arm around me and his hand on my crotch again. He then opened my fly and with his hand played with my penis for a while. I got an erection. He then pulled me over from the wheel, put his head down and sucked me off. I discharged in his mouth and he spit the sperm out." Captain H was found guilty of disgraceful conduct and was dismissed from the Canadian Army.

Two noted psychiatrists, reviewing the case, argued that Captain H should not have been classified as homosexual, since the changes in his personality that had been noted by Brigadier Lind and Lieutenant Colonel Andrew could have affected his sexual behaviour. In principle, of course, the courts were not concerned with his sexual orientation, but with whether he had committed the deed. To that, Captain H had confessed. According to Medical Services' official system of classification, psychiatrists were to use the same criterion. Nevertheless, the doctors argued that it was war itself that had precipitated his flirtation with homosexuality and that the legal proceedings were unjust. Dr William Barraclough, lieutenant colonel in command of 16 Field Ambulance, citing Brigadier Lind's evidence, wrote: "[I]t is my opinion that the offence charged could have been symptomatic of a temporary emotional illness." Dr J.P.S. Cathcart, a noted neuropsychiatrist and the director of the Department of Veterans Affairs, protested the severity of the penalty. After reading the transcript of the trial and meeting with the ex-captain, he addressed the issue of his sexual orientation and how the encounter may have occurred. While acknowledging that "[m]uch of course is expected of an officer and a gentleman," he argued that Captain H had drunk "a little more than his share, with resulted lowering of the bar of conscious resistance to what may have been merely a latent urge." As usual, he lamented the defending officer's lack of expertise regarding homosexuality:

[A]lthough he was pretty meticulous in his inquiries, he might have succeeded better had he received help from a psychiatrist or someone with scientific knowledge of inversion and some of the peculiarities of its habitues ... [I]f [Private P] had been a complete novice at the business of inversion he would have made violent protest regardless of the difference in rank ... It is quite evident to me that [Private P] was a very willing participant and may, if my theory was correct, have been the inticer [*sic*]. On the other hand, the available evidence, including the result of my interview with Capt. [H], seems to indicate pretty definitely that with the latter this was a lone incident.

Whether the war or alcohol was to blame, both psychiatrists argued that the encounter was an aberration for Captain H. Both implied that, with respect to the problem of inversion, the approach of the legal system was crude compared to that of enlightened science. Contrarily, Dr Cathcart argued that a normal man's response to Captain H's alleged proposition should have been violent. Since Private P did not beat up Captain H on being propositioned, it followed for Cathcart that the private himself must have been queer. Thus, the doctor normalized anti-homosexual violence at the same time that he defended a fellow officer against the charge of being queer.[37]

Psychiatrists, like other military authorities, were willing to accept homosexuality without homosexuals. It was the homosexual, whether defiantly proclaiming or tacitly inferring his membership in a subculture, who posed the greatest threat to the established authorities. Psychiatrists like Cathcart viewed men such as Captain H with sympathy. Whether they humbly admitted their transgressions or aggressively denied them, these men posed no serious threat to the heterosexual order.

Men who had clearly given their limit to their combat unit and had not been caught in homosexual relations were spared from invasive questioning on their sexual lives. Major (Doctor) Johnson interviewed Corporal C, who had shot himself in the foot in Holland. Corporal C was described as a timid man who "couldn't stand seeing fights, blood or people injured" in civilian life. The doctor recorded that "he has never shown any interest in the opposite sex and always was lacking in aggression." Although he hated "shooting at the enemy," the corporal continued as a platoon leader with the Argyll and Sutherland Highlanders. Against his own nature, he contributed his utmost. He saw a number of his friends killed and was especially affected when he saw "one good friend [die] before me with a stomach wound." When he became depressed and unable to continue, he shot himself in the foot. Under the circumstances, his lack of interest in the opposite sex was insignificant. Major Johnson wrote, with some admiration: "This man has pushed himself to the limit of his tolerance and only his pride and loyalty to the regiment kept him from breaking down – at the time of his accident he had an acute anxiety state." Thus, psychiatrists, like commanding officers, prized a demonstration of willpower over the trials of life. For many doctors, triumph over one's own perverted nature was equally noble.[38]

CONCLUSION

When doctors criticized the excesses of the policing and legal functions, they did not invoke an appreciation and respect for the diversity of human nature, but claimed dominion over the problem of homosexuality, the right to label homosexuals and cure waverers. Nevertheless, by criticizing the methods and results of the courts, they may have helped to curb some of its excesses. While in the privacy of their offices some psychiatrists (queer or straight) may have helped some homosexual men in a violent, unsympathetic world, their public pronouncements tended to reinforce the sense that homosexuals posed a serious social threat. In fact, the most common response of doctors in dealing with patients suspected of being homosexual was to judge their actions according to what would seem reasonable to the psychiatrists themselves. Thus, Dr Cathcart normalized what he considered acceptable behaviour – beating up a queer man. Most saw actions performed under the influence of alcohol as forgivable and insignificant in the overall assessment of a man's character. Doctors tended to believe agreeable men who protested their normalcy, and they showed a marked disinclination to find men homosexual. Even men who had been so labelled by other military functions were seldom so named by the doctors. It is possible that they were cautious in applying a label that might destroy a man's life. The real source of antagonism for those psychiatrists who wanted control over the problem of homosexuality was the soldier who challenged their claim to expertise. The medical profession (as opposed to individual doctors, who could be queer or straight, sympathetic or antagonistic) could not tolerate homosexual people claiming to know more about what was good for them than the doctors themselves. The queer servicemen's claim to mental health and sexual satisfaction was discounted as a result of the doctors' claim to expertise.

Chapter Four

QUEER SERVICEMEN IN CANADA

In the previous chapters, I have focused on the incursions of military authorities into the queer lives of servicemen. In this one, I turn the spotlight onto the lives of queer officers and ranks in all branches of military service. How does my work differ, then, from the enquiries carried out by military authorities during the war? Like them, I am concerned with understanding homosexuality and homosexuals. Just as the military police interrogated known homosexuals in their search for more suspects, I rely, in part, on the revelations of surviving veterans about their wartime friends and lovers. Wartime police, personnel, and psychiatric reports as well as court-martial proceedings will once again be put to the service of dissecting the sex lives of a harassed minority. Like all judgments, diagnoses, and studies, this one both suffers and benefits from the biases and insights of its creator. In sum, I too offer a particular conception of homosexual life in wartime Canada. But it would be a mistake to conclude that this work is qualitatively the same project as the wartime enquiries upon which it relies. In this instance, the gay men who offered their experiences did so voluntarily, in acts of self-definition and reparation. Likewise, the evidence amassed by wartime policing functions has this time been filtered through a lens sympathetic to homosexuality and removed from the spectre of that world's punishments and rewards.

A number of studies of gay and lesbian life focus on identifiable communities. Unfortunately, there are few published studies of the history of homosexuality in Canada. Recent works have studied the evolution of homosexual minorities in particular cities. Their subjects have self-identified as gay and created communities based on that social difference.[1] This study differs from that literature in that its subjects are tied together by their common association with the Canadian military during the Second World War

and the fact that they derived (or had the potential to derive) sexual pleasure
with members of their own sex. In contrast to urban gay communities, these
men were not fixed geographically, but discovered sexual and romantic opportunities in the camps, bases, and prisons that arose to accommodate
them, in the urban centres through which they passed, in correspondence
with lovers over oceans, and in tents, fields, and bomb-damaged buildings
throughout Britain, Italy, and northwest Europe.

Studies of urban gay and lesbian cultures are often able to presume the
definition of the homosexual. Their subjects had made a prior choice to settle in a community of sexually like-minded people. In that way, they came
to represent the current common-sense notion of gay or lesbian: a person
defined, at least in sexual terms, according to the gender of his or her preferred sexual partner. Moreover, in the modern world, sexuality has become a master category of community formation; people commonly
organize their social lives and living arrangements around their sexual orientation. However, it would be short-sighted to frame a study of homosexuality in Canada's wartime military in such terms. The mobilization for
war brought together an enormous diversity of male recruits: rural and urban, educated and illiterate, effeminate and masculine, married and single,
white and non-white, unemployed and financially independent, French, English, Native, and ethnic. Some entered the forces with an unequivocal appreciation of their homosexual orientation, others had repressed these
unwelcome desires to the point that they were, at the time, unconscious of
them. Some soldiers derived no emotional pleasure from their homosexual
activities, while others created chaste but romantically charged relationships with their comrades. Some gravitated to gay networks within the military, and others lived deliberately on their fringes. In some cases,
homosexual relations were integrated into the life of a unit, but most queer
soldiers looked for sexual pleasure outside its bounds.

How then should a study of male homosexuality proceed? What group
should be separated out of the larger category of "men" for analysis? This
choice will impose a structure on the society under examination. In order
that the significance of same-sex sexuality in Canada's wartime military
culture can be explored as thoroughly as possible, homosexuality is here
defined as the ability to derive sexual pleasure from members of one's own
sex. In this way, the analysis will be able to examine the cultural constraints
on homosexual expression without assuming an emotional commitment
between individuals. Moreover, this definition corresponds to the concept
of queer as understood during the war years. A presentist approach might
confine the analysis to men who were committed to their male sexual part-

ners emotionally, romantically, and physically. Excluded, for instance, would be men who had sex with each other while in detention or on isolated military bases and who had no other apparent desire for homosexual sex. However, for a study to reveal as much as possible about the culture under examination, it should scrutinize the range of meanings assigned to any one act. Individual men interpreted their homosexual behaviour, and that of their comrades, in diverse ways. They also delimited their behaviour and created sexual identities in relation to familial and social constraints and opportunities. As a work of history, this study is particularly respectful of the power of environmental factors in conditioning behaviour. It does not assume that the modern notion of a gay man or lesbian is essentially rooted in nature. Whatever the biological underpinnings of sexuality, a historical document must address the cultural factors that influence behaviour.[2]

What causes men to be homosexual and who cares? As documented in the previous chapter, military doctors, as men of science, represented themselves as experts on the subject. Whether the result of a genetic defect, a hormonal imbalance, race degeneracy, or an unfortunate parental relationship, homosexuality was checked and subdued when its cause could be articulated. Boys and men (and, undoubtedly, girls and women) who confronted homosexual desires in a heterocentric world could also take comfort in the knowledge that there was a reason for their difference. For instance, Don remembers that as a young recruit in the army in 1945, he took comfort in finding the word homosexual in the dictionary. He had heard the term but was not sure of its meaning. He believed that it represented him and felt legitimated, even if marginalized, by the fact that the dictionary acknowledged him as a real being. Knowledge, it is said, dispels fear. However, it is important to note in the case of homosexuality that fear precedes knowledge. While it may be true that people are afraid of things they do not understand, it is equally true that they do not always understand things that frighten them.[3]

A sense of the sexual culture of wartime Canada will emerge out of the evidence presented in this and the following chapters. I will explore the relationship between individual deviants and their larger society, between pairs of illicit lovers, and between whole networks of queer men (and, sometimes, women) and the world within which they operated. In this chapter, I deal with conditions in Canada, in the next, I follow Canadians abroad, and in the subsequent one, I look at the way that queer servicemen fit into their units in all theatres of war. This survey synthesizes a very wide range of experience. Soldiers and officers who appear in these pages came from diverse regions of an enormous country. They brought with them the different attitudes towards sexuality that had been formulated in the decades preceding the war. Nevertheless, I attempt to define the general features of the sexual culture that queer servicepeople created in the military. Self-acceptance, visibility, and social contact were interrelated as queer soldiers developed support systems and self-confidence.[4]

Some broad generalizations can be drawn from my interviews with gay veterans, wartime psychiatric interviews, and military records. While many servicemen entered the war as sexual innocents, heterosexuals did not face the same challenges in sexual self-discovery. As RCAF veteran J. Douglas Harvey writes, "Most of the eighteen- and nineteen-year-old Canadian kids who went to war were incredibly naive by any standard. Not only about the war and the world but about much simpler things. Sex, for instance. It can never be determined how many aircrew died in a virgin state, but it was undoubtedly a very high percentage. The English girls must have thought a flock of eunuchs had landed in their midst. Nevertheless they were delighted to meet us and that was quite evident."[5] In fact, interviews with homosexual men suggest that many recruits may have had more queer than straight sexual experiences. But while many men had enjoyed homosexual relations in their childhood and youths, almost all understood them to be unutterable pleasures. An exception to this nation-wide rule was the case of a prostitute's son from Nanaimo, British Columbia, who was not naive concerning human sexual needs and whose homosexuality was apparently not discouraged by his mother. In other neighbourhoods in cities and towns, boys frequently performed oral sex and masturbated each other. In rural Canada, boys commonly shared beds and sexual pleasures with farmhands, relatives, or friends. Many understood from an early age that these sexual pleasures were to be denied and denounced publicly. Sexual self-discovery was a game of espionage requiring much subterfuge. Typically, players passed through a period of self-deception regarding their sexual needs; others came to accept their deviant desires regardless of the culture's hostility. Many entered military service fully content in the private knowledge of their sexual non-conformity. A number of homosexual charges laid during the war were against officers and ranks from the permanent force. For them, from the point of view of sexual possibilities, the influx of a million men into their ranks was a welcome development.

In public utterances, men who had sexual relations with each other were cast as beyond the limits of decent society. Religious leaders who dared broach the subject spoke of homosexuals in terms of immorality; they were a sign of the degradation of the race as a consequence of any number of social ills. For a great many Canadians, homosexuality, like other sexual transgressions, was primarily understood to be immoral. It was a source of shame and revealed that one had failed the test of manhood. There was no legitimate male role for a homosexual: to be marked as queer meant that one was outside of masculine society. Since gender was fundamental to one's self-image, many men found it impossible to reconcile themselves with their homosexual desires. Others understood that it was society that was naive. However, many came to this realization only after much personal anguish. Some accepted society's edicts, quietly acknowledged their sexual deviance, and lived the prescribed life of married domesticity – normal for all the world to see. Some queer men found fulfilment in the life of husband and father, although their homosexual desires remained hidden from their wives and children.

It is possible to divide the great number of Canadian men who confronted their own queer feelings during the war years into two groups: those who accepted their desires and those who did not. Acceptance required that one first allow the problematic fact of homoerotic desire into one's consciousness. Such an awareness could be purely personal and private. It could be a secret kept by two lovers. It might refer to an individual's relationship with a gay subculture. It could also, for some individuals, be a public stance in the face of authorities. The broader the audience to which one was 'out' as queer, the greater the perceived challenge to the political and social order. Some queer men whose thoughts will be included in the following discussion say that they had so repressed their homoerotic interests during their war service that they were oblivious of them until years later. Consciousness, then, at both the level of the individual and society, the private and the public, is a central theme in what follows. Social mores had a profound psychological impact on the lives of queer men. To keep from thinking the unthinkable about themselves, many did not allow the issue into conscious thought.

Military documentation does not facilitate this enquiry. Since Canadian society was ordered around rewards for appearing heterosexual and punishments for homosexual expression, few were motivated to adopt a public identity as gay. Moreover, when one's private life came under public scrutiny, personal advancement hinged on publicly disavowing one's homosexual desires and actions. Nevertheless, a careful reading of wartime documents reveals that the military was somewhat successful in cracking the borders between private and public and uncovering how people ordered their lives. Interviews with queer veterans have been invaluable in informing the official archival sources.

RECRUITMENT

Individual servicepeople enlisted for a variety of reasons – patriotism, adventure, social pressure, peer pressure, ethical and political convictions, and financial need. Some queer men saw the military as an opportunity to escape communities in which they felt socially constricted. Ralph in Waterloo and Jim in Hamilton were both young men, twenty-one and twenty-five years old respectively, when they enlisted in 1941. Both had repressed their homosexual desires until that time and deferred to heterocentric community standards in imagining and fashioning their social/sexual lives. Ralph remembers those standards in Waterloo, Ontario, as oppressive: "When I was seventeen, I guess, in my last year in high school, it was expected that you would acquire a girlfriend and my former chums were all pairing up, and this girl latched on to me and, for about two years, until I joined the army, I'd see her about once a week; never got past the stage of heavy necking ... it was just a kind of social pressure: you had to do it ... there was no choice in the matter. And it was expected that we would eventually marry and have babies." When she pressed that they marry before he was sent overseas, Ralph protested, " 'No, if I'm not killed, I'll probably be injured or something, you know, it wouldn't be fair.' " In fact, he was relieved to get a letter from her a year later, informing him that she was marrying somebody else. As he came to explore his sexual desires years later, he understood that his early discomfort resulted from his having had no sexual or romantic interest in women.[6]

Jim also felt pressured to marry a neighbourhood girl in Hamilton. Although he had considered her to be a friend, he became uncomfortable when everyone, including the girl, came to assume that they would marry. He, of course, never mentioned his homosexuality, and so "they expected something would happen and I wasn't inclined that way." After enlisting, he was sent to Camp Borden, "which was too far away to be convenient and then suddenly [I] went overseas – that's probably the only thing that saved me [from marriage] ... if I hadn't been in the army and if I had been home all the time and she were home, then it would be put up or shut up, and an awful lot of marriages happened for that very reason." Neither Ralph nor Jim, at that stage in his life, had acknowledged his homosexual desires consciously. Nevertheless, discomfort with the sexual and social roles prescribed for them was at the heart of their decision to enlist. If they were unsure of how to define their sexuality positively, they did know what they were not. Both knew that they were expected to marry even though they did not respond romantically or sexually to women. Many young homosexual men, at the time of their enlistment, had little insight into the significance of their sexual and emotional desires, if they acknowledged them at all. Their communities had offered them no positive help in articulating their needs. Ironically, for many, the war would be a training ground in love.[7]

Until he enlisted in 1940 at the age of twenty-one, Hugh lived in a small village in New Brunswick. There, homosexuality was a matter for action but never for discussion. He estimates that he had had some form of sexual relations with about half of the fifteen to twenty local boys in his generation's "gang" over the course of his teens; they would usually "jerk one another off – something like that. I guess the odd fellow would give you a blow job." He judges that "out of the group there was only one other fellow in the village who was homosexual." Like Ralph and Jim, Hugh assumed that he would marry, but he was more sensitive to his sexual preference for boys: "I went around with girls but I never had the urge, I guess, to cuddle with them as I did with boys." At the outbreak of war, Hugh remembers, "I was going with this friend of mine's sister and I eventually found out that it was him that I was [in love with] ... We'd go to his place and we'd lay on the chesterfield, and his back would be [against me] – listening to the radio, and I'd get this erection." Hugh and his friend "joined up together and figured we were going to go overseas together, but they shipped him out before I went out." Hugh became keenly aware of his passion for his friend in his absence. This self-knowledge, that he could relate sexually and emotionally to men in a way that he couldn't with women, he took with him to Europe several months later.[8]

In a middle-class Toronto neighbourhood, Jim Egan also had been "fooling around with the boys" since the age of thirteen. However, unlike most of his contemporaries, he scoured literature for help in understanding his experiences. Reading Walt Whitman's *Leaves of Grass*, Jim came to the realization that "this is what I am." He found an even clearer self-representation in Oscar Wilde's *The Picture of Dorian Gray*: "And when I read that, I thought, 'Ho, ho! Lord Henry and Dorian are just the same as me.'" But it was the character of Basil Halwood, "madly in love with Dorian," with whom Jim most identified. In his own life, he also "had the hots" for a young man but saw no chance of forming a satisfying relationship: "And one of the reasons that I decided to join the merchant navy was that I wanted to get away from him because I knew perfectly well that he was gay but he himself would never admit it – he'd go to the rack before he'd admit it. But, anyway, when I announced that I was going to join the merchant navy, he announced that he would too, so we ended up on the same ship together." His aggressive pursuit of literature offered Jim positive insights into his sexuality. Queer Canadians who were passive recipients of popular culture were less likely to find sympathetic reflections of themselves. In Jim's life, romance and sexuality were themselves art forms to create and scrutinize. So, by 1943, to satisfy his wanderlust and to escape a hopeless infatuation, Jim joined the merchant navy. He remembers, "So, he came along with me and, eventually – and the funny part of it is, it was not at my instigation because I was very very fond of him and I didn't want to do anything to upset that friendship, but he made the advances and sure, there was some fooling around on board ship and that's as far as it went. Now I could easily have allowed myself to fall in love with him, but I just reasoned it out and I said, 'Don't do it: you're just wasting your time. You're just letting yourself in for a whole bunch of heartbreak.'" By consciously examining his homosexuality, Jim achieved a greater measure of control over his emotional life than those who denied their nature. This control may have protected him from exposure. Those less comfortable with their homosexuality often used alcohol as a tool to release inhibitions and deny responsibility. Ironically, alcohol also impaired their judgment, making them less discreet and more vulnerable to discovery.[9]

Hugh's kind of prewar sexual experiences, in a rural New Brunswick village, resounded throughout rural Canada. In the farming community outside of Warkworth, Ontario, Aubyn also had had sexual encounters in his youth while sharing beds with farmhands during the Depression and, in particular, "with a high school boy that didn't know which way he was. I knew from the time I was three years old that I liked men more than women." His family nurtured his unorthodox gendered identity: "My father was very wise. He was before his time and I liked music. I was quite good at piano and I was having piano lessons and I was reading and I was artistic and the sister below me loved the outdoors and she loved animals. So we more or less changed places. I helped mother in the house. I loved cooking and she loved the outdoors and so we changed places and Dad thought that was perfectly all right." Aubyn describes a role that was socially sanctioned and adopted by many gay men. His "artistic" temperament was seen as justification for assuming a feminine division of labour. A further – unsanctioned and largely personal – slippage allowed him to justify his homosexual desires as part of his uniqueness. The move from art to gender to sexuality allowed many homosexual men to ground their sexual difference in a more optimistic light than the discourses of law, religion, or medicine would allow. The public role of artist translated into the private, and often only vaguely acknowledged, role of homosexual. In prewar

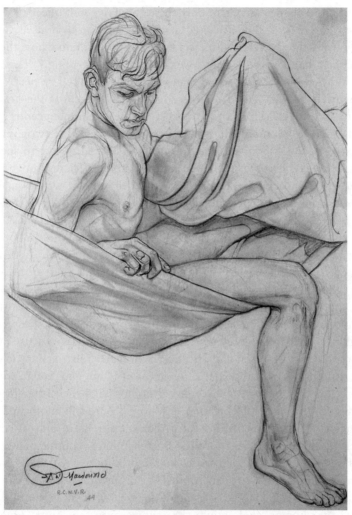

Rise and Shine, 1944. Within the framework of art, men could express their homoerotic interests in a socially acceptable way. In his work, Lieutenant Grant Macdonald explored his relationship with the male bodies that surrounded him in the RCN. His artwork was not only officially acceptable, but at the centre of the RCN's self-representation. There is a voyeuristic element in this study of a young sailor climbing out of his hammock. We enjoy the details of his body – his nipple, even fingernail – in the close quarters of the lower deck. Does he know we (through Macdonald) are studying him in his vulnerable waking state? He is groggy, maybe even a touch grouchy, but does not appear threatened. Courtesy of the Marine Museum of the Great Lakes at Kingston.

Warkworth, Aubyn remembers only the terms fairy and queer to describe homosexual types, and he accepted neither in relation to himself. "I think nobody wanted to be referred to as a fairy ... and you know how they used to flip their hand sort of thing, weak wrist sort of thing." The artistic model allowed him greater social manoeuvrability and self-respect.[10]

Aubyn felt he was suited for the educational branch of the RCAF and drove to Toronto in March 1941 to enlist. At the recruitment centre, he met a handsome Torontonian who was enlisting as aircrew. The two exchanged addresses and corresponded. The Torontonian invited Aubyn to spend the May 24th weekend at his St Clair Avenue apartment. There, Aubyn had his first clearly homosexual encounter: "Well, I thought it was wonderful. I was more relaxed of course and I think he was a little more experienced than I was ... We were quite affectionate with one another. There was no oral sex ... We fondled one another ... it was romantic. And we both came two or three times I think." Thus, Aubyn was recruited into both the air force and a homosexual life at the same time. At that stage in his life, he had insights into his sexual needs but had been emotionally isolated in his rural Ontario community. He saw his recruitment trip to Toronto as the beginning of a new life. The RCAF, despite its repressive policies, represented for Aubyn a place to explore his sexuality. His sexual activities also point to the importance of emotion and affection in his early relationships.[11]

The rural prewar homosexual experiences of Hugh and Aubyn were private but not uncommon; many enlisted homosexual men brought sexual identities forged in the Depression. Economic hardship motivated many working-class Canadian men to enlist. For those most deeply affected by the Depression, the war was not their first encounter with the military. The Department of National Defence (DND) had administered the unemployment relief camps from 1932 to 1936. The nationwide system of camps for unemployed, single men housed as many as 170,000 men. Periodically, men reported that homosexual activity was extensive in the camps. One camp veteran was quoted in the Ottawa daily Le Droit as calling for "a closer inspection over morals, as Petawawa [a military base used as a relief camp] rivals with Sodom." The Montreal daily L'Autorité reported, under a banner headline, "Les horreurs du camp," on "des actes contre nature qui rappellent Sodome." The most visible of the homosexual pairings that arose in the camps was the intergenerational couple, the wolf/punk relationship. The younger partner in such a couple was called a 'bum boy.' In November 1933 the DND held a court of inquiry to address the allegations of immorality in the camps.[12]

While a thorough treatment of the sexual culture of the relief camps is beyond the scope of this chapter, clearly the Second World War was not unique in assembling large numbers of young men and women in same-sex environments. American historians John D'Emilio and Allan Bérubé argue that the Second World War set the stage for the subsequent homophile and gay liberation movements by creating same-sex military communities in which individuals could explore their homosexual desires. While the argument does have merit, it must be accepted cautiously; the First World War and the Depression relief camps in both Canada and the United States resulted in similar social formations with no subsequent emergence of gay-rights politics. In fact, the gendered division of labour under capitalism resulted in the separation of men and women throughout most of the evolution of North American society, although perhaps never to the extent of the Second World War.[13]

TRAINING CAMPS: PRESENTING ARMS AND FALLING IN

Queer men responded differently to war training. One's sexual identity had an impact on the experience of basic and advanced training. The camps brought together a cross-section of Canadian youth. One gay veteran remembers how "all the farm boys and office boys and country boys, factory boys were just herded in" to the Horse Palace at the Canadian Exhibition grounds in Toronto. For most of them, the military was a new world that temporarily would dominate all aspects of their lives – sleeping in barracks of bunk beds with forty other men, showering in groups, shaving whether or not one's body had produced a beard, eating, training, praying, or drinking with people chosen by the institution to be one's comrades. As training progressed, men grouped themselves according to their likes and dislikes. A common sexual identity was one of various factors that might inspire a friendship. But homosexual men were as likely to make their closest and most enduring friendships with their straight comrades. However, there was no escaping the fact that a homosexual orientation made recruits vulnerable at a social and institutional level. Whether one accepted or resisted one's socially transgressive sexual desires at a conscious level, they could still affect one's experience.[14]

For Bert Sutcliffe, who would not come out to himself as homosexual until the following year while stationed in England, training at Camp Borden in Ontario was exciting: "Well I guess by then I was twenty or so but I thought it would be wonderful to drive a tank around Europe and kill Germans." Having been the only male member of his family, he welcomed the fact that "[y]ou were never in anything but male company." From March to November of 1940, he revelled with other young men in the novelty and excitement of war games: "People would come around to me and say, 'Hey, I just fired a flame thrower' or 'We just did a route march of twenty miles' and I never had a chance to discuss anything except with the people who were in my unit." His attention was focused on learning the trade of war, and he cannot recall his erotic potential being aroused. Even the army's attention to his genitals did not encourage him, at that time, to reflect upon his own sexuality: "I was amazed at the things that went on: at six o'clock in the morning the lights would come on and people would come in and tell you to pull your clothes off and get in line for an inspection of your penis and testicles." If other men around him were engaged in sexual liaisons, he did not, or could not, see it.[15]

Aubyn completed his RCAF basic training at Manning Depot on the Exhibition grounds in Toronto. His response to drills, marches, rifle practice, and being surrounded by men was different than Bert's: "I hated it. I liked the showers. There were great showers. Probably there was a hundred showers all in a row and there were all kinds of naked men." He recalls, "I saw one or two men that had erections when they were showering when there were a lot of people around of course and some of the men would say, 'Well look at that goddam fruit' – no, 'fairy.' 'Fruit' was an English term, 'fairy' was a North American term." 'Fairy' referred to a type of homosexual man: one who was not physically imposing or aggressive, an affront to the aggressive masculine standards of basic training. At Camp Ipperwash in Ontario, a recruit marked as a fairy because of his effeminate manner was viciously sodomized by a group of recruits in the showers. He was saved by a homosexual recruit who stumbled across the attack. Not all homosexual men were so tolerant of delicate men. Bud recalled a recruit from St Catharine's during his training with the RCAF: "It just put you right off. I like guys that are men. I hate – what do you call them? ... 'Fairies'! That's it." He remembers the indignation that this fairy aroused in the other men: "One guy said he should have been born a woman – mistaken identity. He [the fairy] was so upset and crying, you know ... I didn't have too much to do with him. He'd be all upset."[16]

The word 'fairy' could refer to a 'sissified' man, as in the case of the RCAF recruit, without any reference to his sexual preference. It could also signify a male homosexual, especially one who was also effeminate, as in the Manning Depot showers. However, in the abstract, any fairy was assumed to be homosexual. For instance, neighbourhood boys who harassed homosexual men in High Park in Toronto during the war years called the

Reveille. Many recruits had to adjust to the lack of privacy in the forces. In *Reveille*, army cartoonist Stewart Cameron playfully imagines a barracks room in which each recruit is self-absorbed. In fact, as training in Canada proceeded, these men came to rely on each other to fulfil a wide range of psychological and physical needs. Some men managed to forge homosexual relations in this context. Cameron shows us a pin-up girl on the table in the foreground. Does he mean to assure us that this all-male, intimate society is heterosexual? Courtesy of the Estate of Stewart Cameron.

activity 'fairy hunting,' without any allusion to the countenance of their victims. This semantic imprecision conflated effeminate men with homosexuals. 'Queer,' on the other hand, was used in the case of homosexual men who presented themselves according to accepted standards of masculinity. Seen from the point of view of gender standards, fairies were more offensive than queers. Although their offence was more against nature than morality, they had equally failed to be proper men. In a world that prized aggression and strength, fairies were often isolated and harassed. For fairies who were unable to project an acceptable masculine bearing, training camp may have recalled the ordeals of their school days. An RCAF officer recalled that one of his earliest childhood lessons in deportment was the example of "Tissie," an extremely effeminate child who was ridiculed and rebuffed by the neighbourhood boys in Toronto to the point of his eventual suicide. He understood Tissie to embody the fears of the other boys (later, men), and he was careful to project a more acceptable masculine image. The Tissies of the world, he thought, represented the homosexual for the general public.[17]

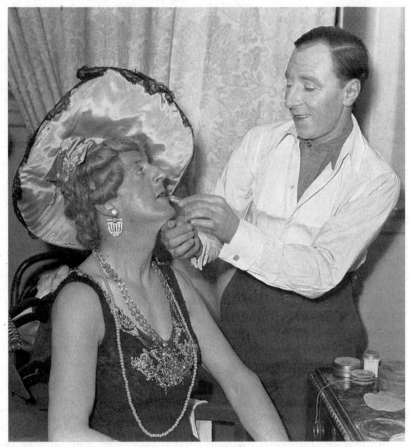

Fairies. Not all men avoided being labelled a fairy. Some male soldiers found pleasure in disturbing the categories of soldier, man, and woman at the same time. The female impersonator from the army's "Kit Bags" concert party, above, sang to soldiers such lyrics as "But on Saturday I'm willing, if you'll only take the shilling, to make a man of any one of you," a popular song from the First World War. Courtesy of the National Archives of Canada/PA151171.

That fairies could be vilified in certain masculine settings does not suggest that all men avoided the label. The sergeant pharmacist in Ralph W's field ambulance unit was "a flaming queen and made no bones about it ... He had the usual limp wrist. He slumped and jiggled. His manner of speaking was a bit flirtatious. That was his ordinary manner of speaking." Notwithstanding his overt femininity, Ralph remembers that "everybody loved Ross." An effeminate nature did not entail a lack of self-assertion. Those who defied the gendered norms unapologetically could gain respect for their inner strength. Nevertheless, they faced challenges that more masculine men did not encounter.[18]

Masculine recruits had to negotiate the showers in their own way. One gay veteran, Edward, an artist, remembers trying not to look at the other boys in the showers at Newmarket. In the early days of training, he felt that most young men were nervous and ill at ease with their bodies, hiding their genitals "because we were all ashamed of it being so little. Now and then we'd see somebody else and just look away because one doesn't do that." While he himself was not ready to express his homosexuality, he was alert to the activity around him: "There was two guys having a shower and I think they were doing something cause as soon as I opened the door they moved apart." At the beginning of the war, he had not yet found the courage to accept his own homosexuality and to act upon it. He recalls an incident in Kingston, Ontario, when another artist had tried to set him up with a queer man: "... and I was taken up to a hotel room and the guy was a stud. He was handed to me ... and I said to the guy, 'Do you want to take off your clothes?' and he did and he was a beautiful thing. And I said, 'Well, you know, you have a nice physique, and I'm a sculptor. You know, that's what I want to be, a sculptor.' And I said, 'I guess you'd better put your clothes back on.' And that's all we did and he was ready to – he thought, 'What am I wasting my time for with this guy?'" Edward was stopped, he thinks, by his inability to see a future in homosexual relations. Of course, the situation he described would have required only his attention at that present moment. But acknowledging his homosexual desires would have meant rewriting his relationship with society. From casual family interactions to public cultural representations, he had been treated as a boy and therefore as a prospective husband and father. Like most of the gay men interviewed, he had passively accepted that he would fulfil those obligations. During the war years, he renegotiated his relationship with society, including his relationships with individual men.[19]

Men who were unconcerned with questions of sexual identity could accept homosexual pleasures less problematically. Now a husband and grandfather, Bud dodges questions of identity but remembers his homosexual encounters in the RCAF: "I was on a train going out west, an older guy – course we had to share two in a bed – and I ... fell asleep and the next thing you know he was poking me ... and he came. But then, in the morning, he didn't say nothing, you know; I guess he was sort of embarrassed. You know, in those days, you would be." For Bud, homosexuality was a recreational activity subject to rules and a part of military life. As long as the bounds that contained it were not crossed, he was not in conflict with society. He took the passive role in his relations with other men. It was not the sexual release from penetration that he sought, but the pleasures of being penetrated. In fact, four of the married men interviewed in the course of this research, as well as many others documented in the military's records, preferred the passive role in anal intercourse. They were not simply looking for a convenient substitute for a woman's vagina, but were finding pleasure in stepping outside of the active male role in intercourse. In fact, the men most likely to practise anal intercourse, as active or passive partners, were those who had had heterosexual experience. Possibly, for them, sexual activity had already defined itself as involving penetration.[20]

The most important rule governing homosexual relations was that one not get caught. Of course, heterosexual intercourse was also performed in private. But for heterosexuals, the maximum price for being discovered in consensual sexual relations was embarrassment, not prison, and the range of sanctioned behaviour was far greater. The barracks in training camps were the antithesis of berths on a train, but after lights out, recruits could improvise privacy. At the RAF radar school in Clinton, Ontario, Bob Grimson befriended a "very handsome-looking" Albertan: "We both slept on lower bunks, he was to my right ... and we used to hold each other's hand [across the aisle]." For them, barrack life inhibited any greater demonstration of their affection. However, they were easily able to arrange a more auspicious setting to further their relationship: "But we went on leave, we went to London, Ontario, and we went to a movie and stayed in a hotel overnight. Made a little love. Became a good friend."[21]

Some pushed the bounds of privacy much further. Twenty-five-year-old Private John L had served in Canada and Newfoundland since the beginning of the war. In May 1944 he was stationed at Camp Borden in Ontario with 11 Canadian Support Troop Training Centre. Just after lights out on 6 May, he was joking with several other soldiers in the washroom that connected the two arms of an H hut. Nineteen-year-old Private Keith S walked by, said, "Hello," and then continued into the barracks and prepared his bed in the dark. The two had known each other by sight several months previously at the Newmarket training camp. John followed and chatted with Keith while he undressed. He then asked if he could climb into his upper bunk with him. The soldier in the adjacent bunk called the attention of the hut corporal to the irregularity. Corporal Hobin struck a match to verify that two bodies were in the bunk and told Keith that his friend would have to leave. Keith replied, "He is just laying in bed with me," and Corporal Hobin returned to his own bed. For the next half hour, the soldier in the neighbouring bed noticed "considerable movement" but heard nothing. Finally, Corporal Hobin turned the barracks' lights on, which caused Private John to jump out of bed and return to his own quarters. Similar incidents suggest that others accepted the risk of sharing a bed in a crowded barracks under the cover of darkness and blankets.[22]

Privates John and Keith were not in the same unit and so had not known each other except by sight. John had spent the night socializing in the Wet Canteen, while Keith had been to the show on base. The ablution room was a very informal meeting ground where potential partners might be casually encountered. Privates Roy C and Charles M at 13 Basic Training Centre in Listowel, Ontario, were luckier in the opportunities that training offered them. Charles was working as a cook and therefore shared sleeping quarters with his corporal in a room attached to the mess, apart from the barracks. When Private Roy was detailed as his assistant, it meant that they would work closely together, separate from the others on base. Both had minimal education, were unskilled workers in civilian life, and were popular with the other recruits. Though underage, Roy was sold a bottle of whiskey by the corporal for use at the weekly dance at the Armories. Charles and Roy went to the dance, a popular social gathering among the recruits and the local girls. Afterwards, Roy decided to spend the night with Charles at the mess rather than return to his barracks. His superiors were accustomed to him sleeping at the mess, since he had to be up early to help prepare breakfast. When the two found that Corporal Foley, Charles's roommate, was not there, they climbed into Charles's upper bunk and made love. Unfortunately, while they were immersed in anal intercourse, Corporal Foley walked in and turned on the overhead light.

Privates Roy and Charles were tempted by the opportunities afforded by their private quarters and naively underestimated the power of moral indignation backed by military discipline. Having been confronted with their lovemaking, Corporal Foley later related to the court, "I know I was pretty mad. I told them they should be ashamed of themselves, and it was disgraceful conduct, and I gave them 10 minutes to get their equipment together, and they were under open arrest, to go to the barracks." Charles retaliated, arguing that "these two hooks carried a lot of weight." Foley acknowledged the truth of that assessment in court: "[I]n fact that is one of the things about it, that they never had to be chased to do anything – they would do their work – you didn't have to tell them to do it, they did it before you told them to." Charles's defiant response suggests that while he was aware of the need for discretion in his lovemaking, he was unprepared for the repercussions. His reaction would have been shared by most of the gay men interviewed who had been unaware that their transgressions had been in violation of military law. In fact, the law was applied so unevenly that it is not surprising that many were seduced into taking inadequate precautions. Some relationships that were clearly romantic but publicly chaste were accepted as a feature of life in basic training.[23]

Jim was aware of his homosexual desires but was unwilling to act upon them or divulge them to others. His memories of basic training at Camp Borden include relationships that were clearly read as homosexual by others and escaped censure. More than fifty years after the event, they are infused with a voyeurism that suggests an uneasily suppressed sexuality:

One of the male nurses was sort of noticeable and he palled around with another boy who was not noticeable, but, nevertheless, I put my heads together [sic] and thought, "Well, there's something going on here," and ... they would go out, if they had a weekend pass, they would probably go to Toronto, they would probably do everything they wanted to do and up at Borden it was not easy in the camp. They might go drinking on a Saturday night ... well, it was in the back of my mind that there was something going on ... well, he was on draft to go to another location ... so, his last night in camp was a thing everybody was sort of celebrating and so on and this boyfriend – the male nurse – was very much in evidence and he had drunk a lot of beer ... so he was sort of overexpressing himself, not seriously, but you could see what he had on his mind ... what he was saying made it clear that he was sort of heartbroken. But to see those two separately, you wouldn't think of them being a pair or that the other one was anything but straight. So those were the uncertainties of war.

How the two men were arranging their love life was a matter of considerable speculation for Jim. Decades after the event, his recollection was still infused with envy for those who were fulfilling their desires while his own sexual needs remained in limbo. The two lovers were showing Jim that it was possible to carve a place of belonging out of Camp Borden society.[24]

George was taught more directly that quite openly homosexual relationships were possible in the RCAF. He enjoyed the technical classes and the camaraderie at the RAF radar school at Clinton, Ontario, and remembers a wide range of men: "The service was a melange of people. They weren't all young, unattached males, by any means. Some of them were four or five years older than I was, and if you're twenty-five, twenty-six – some of them even probably older than that – they were married and had children. When you're in an environment when your colleagues were married people, obviously gay sex wasn't something you would discuss." One of his most en-

Régiment de Maisonneuve. This photo shows a recruitment centre for the Regiment de Maisonneuve in Quebec. Several men overtly register their relationships with their comrades. Notably, in the bottom left-hand corner, two soldiers evince a casual intimacy with each other's bodies. Their physical intimacy, fully exposed among their comrades, reinforces the proposition, supported by both the memories of veterans and the documented evidence, that wartime services accommodated a wide range of relationships to fulfil the needs of a million servicemen. Courtesy of the Montreal *Gazette*.

during, non-sexual friendships from the war was with one such married man. The base was staffed by British officers and included a high percentage of RAF personnel, who offered a very different culture: "One thing we learned at Clinton was the dirtiest songs I've ever heard since ... sung by the RAF personnel in the canteen. Oh, I couldn't believe some of them. They were all sex, sex, sex." In contrast, he found that the "Canadians were essentially uptight at Clinton." Within that conglomeration of men was a Manitoban named Lovell C, about five years older than George, "a very attractive man – good looking and beguiling." Lovell was unlike anyone George had known: "Oh, he was certainly very, very wise to the gay sexual scene and his gay orientation ... he was so damned self-assured and he also knew what he wanted." Nothing had prepared George to be the object of another man's romantic attention: "He obviously found me attractive and he was pursuing me – literally – around the equipment." George cannot remember the reaction of others to the courting, perhaps because of his own bewilderment: "I was too embarrassed to go into it with anybody else." George offers the following reflection on the meaning of that event in his life: "I found Lovell fascinating as a person ... I guess I was easily seduced. I was a kid." Like Jim at Camp Borden, he had not, on his own, been able to visualize an affair with a man. Lovell opened up for him a new understanding of the possibilities of male-male relationships. Thereafter, George nurtured sexual and romantic affairs as well as non-sexual frienships.

At Clinton, George and Lovell found a safe place to consummate their desires: "He was obviously attracted by me and decided to, in effect, seduce me, which he very effectively did ... in one of the woodlots next to the station ... We would go for a walk and end up in the bushes ... You know how nice it is to have your cock sucked? ... That was a strong sexual release." In George's experience of training camps, Clinton was "rather unusual." The next stop in his radar training was Corpus Cristi, Texas, where he found that "certainly in the kind of barracks [there], you couldn't do anything. You have to have a rendezvous somewhere off the base in most instances."[25]

Bob Grimson was sent to Corpus Cristi after his tenure at Clinton and, unlike George, found himself allowed a greater measure of freedom as an officer: "We were assigned to what they called the BOQ – Bachelor Officers' Quarters – and it was tended by black sailors, who were only allowed to do things like making up beds and cleaning floors and changing sheets – doing anything that you would want, you know, to have done, in a servile way. So that was my first experience with discrimination." He was attracted to one of the black sailors, whom he perceived as deferential to whites, a trait that, for Bob, made him "sort of a stereotypical black." Although he had no evidence that the sailor was also interested in him, he remembers that "somehow or other, I signalled him to come into my room, which is a crazy thing to do even in the best of times, you know, even today. Especially with a black one, which would have compounded the felony." Notwithstanding his judgment that the sailor "would have been straight" and an unwilling participant who "was being told what to do," Bob twice used him as a sexual partner: "Anyway, I did him and he was so bloody scared."[26]

Both Bob and the black sailor likely understood the power accorded them by their rank/class and race. In the sailor, Bob identified not just a black man, but a "stereotypical" one – a servant from *Gone with the Wind* or *Showboat*. If the sailor had been white or of a more aggressive demeanour, it is unlikely that Bob would have envisioned the sexual potential. Bob may also have understood that his own whiteness and rank would be interpreted by the sailor as sources of power. His own account of the sailor as "scared" and resigned to the ordeal suggests that the black man understood that he would be unwise to expect the institution to defend his interests. Bob's judgment that "he would have been straight" makes it clear that the event was, in effect, an assault, not a mutually satisfying encounter. Although they had been raised in different countries, separated by thousands of miles, both men seem to have understood each other's rights and constraints in the situation. If Bob had been a black officer (an impossibility, in fact, according to RCAF regulations in 1941, which limited commissions to white Canadians), then the sailor would have been able to register a complaint without fear of insulting white honour.

Although Bob identified this as his first experience with discrimination, the fact that he so quickly exploited the situation to his benefit suggests that the dynamics of racism were not foreign to him at the time. As a Jewish youth growing up on Clinton Street in Toronto, he had experienced the Christie Pitts riot and the ongoing attacks by the "Hitler copycats" who would drive through his neighbourhood "with lead pipes or iron bars and beating up on people. I well remember it." His first "very unromantic" homosexual encounter, as a fourteen-year-old, was with the Chinese man who picked up the family laundry, sometimes asking him, "in pidgin English, 'You hard?' you know, type of thing, and that would lead to a little play." Bob would visit the laundry on Harbord Street on Saturday nights "when [the laundryman's] brothers – whoever they were – were out playing fantan in Chinatown and ... he would lay out the dirty sheets." As to why it ended, Bob suggests, "Maybe I thought I could do better." Perhaps both man and boy were taking advantage of the fact that they were socially protected in their sexual transgression by their differences in age, race, and class. Neither Bob's family nor the laundryman's were likely to cross socially. Quite possibly, the Chinese laundryman was looking to "do better" himself, which could relate to any number of personal or social attributes.[27]

At Corpus Cristi, Bob's sexual encounters with the black sailor ended when Bob began an affair with another officer, the safest homosexual relationship available to members of the forces: "Another time, [I] was going to the cinema at the base. I happened to sit next to a navy lieutenant who started to knee me, you know, and went back to his legitimate [quarters], since we were both officers, and had a do there." Many homosexual romances and sexual encounters began with such a gesture, carefully calculated to gauge the disposition of a comrade. Cinemas, public transit, shared sleeping accommodations all offered the opportunity for an innocent but ambiguous signal. Since officers usually had private quarters, their sexual transgressions could be easily concealed from the public gaze. Moreover, there was nothing suspicious about officers entertaining each other, whereas colleagues often looked askance at those who were too familiar with the other ranks. Moreover, the military police were unable to intimidate officers into testifying against each other, a power they exploited in the case of other ranks who were thought to be partners of officers.[28]

QUEER NETWORKS

Officers in the personnel or training functions came in contact with a great number of men in the course of their work. Queer men passed through their command, and some of the officers were homosexual. Captain Bradley of the Hastings and Prince Edward Regiment actively encouraged a young private, a pianist in civil life, to apply for a transfer to his command. At his trial for absence without leave, Private Archambault said, "I received a letter from this Captain Bradley from Belleville, Ontario, saying that he would be home on the week end [sic] so naturally I know that a Private and a Captain are a different rank but we get along nice and liked music and all that and I thought it was nice of him to send a letter and I asked for a four-day pass and went to Belleville." Since Private Archambault would be discharged from the army in 1943, having been deemed unable to meet military standards, it is curious that the captain had been eager to recruit him into his regiment. That he also invited him to his home suggests that he was personally interested in the youth. For his part, Archambault may have been flattered by the fact that a person in authority was interested in him. If he was aware that Captain Bradley was seducing him, it is unlikely that he would have offered quite so much information to the court. Officers could intrigue other ranks for many reasons, as mentors, role models, or simply engaging personalities.[29]

John had no misconceptions about Major M's interest in him. John was a young personnel officer with Medical Services, responsible for interviewing recruits and grading their mental ability. He had completed university in Vancouver, married, and enlisted in the army all within three weeks. Now stationed in Ottawa, he was one of a group of young married officers who fraternized at National Defence Headquarters (NDHQ). Major M, a district army examiner, had been a respected psychology professor in civilian life.

He often entertained the young officers on his trips to Ottawa. According to John, "They liked him, thought he was an entertaining fellow ... I think they'd all decided that Herman was gay, and that was fine: good company around the mess, great story teller." When the major invited John to spend a weekend in Kingston, his friends became concerned for his welfare: "Anyway I remember these two fellows saying 'Are you going down to Kingston with this fellow?' [I said,] 'Why not. He's invited me down. I've never seen Kingston ...' But obviously they thought, 'Now John, you're young and suggestible.'"

John had an affair with the major, meeting with him both in Kingston and in the major's room at the Lord Elgin Hotel on his visits to Ottawa. For John, who thinks he was naive sexually until then, the affair was "fun" and educational: "Oh I think there was probably kissing. I can't really remember that as much as I can the fucking and sucking." Accepting the passive role in anal intercourse was a delicate question, overlaid with issues of domination and submission: "I very much enjoyed fucking a man, but I – if it was with the right person – it didn't offend me to be fucked. I would take umbrage right off the bat with someone who was making the assumption that I was going to be fucked." Those who equated their acts of penetration as a confirmation of their dominant role in the encounter were also defining their partners as dominated. Some refused the submissive identity associated with being penetrated, while others embraced it. However, the meaning of anal intercourse was predetermined by heterosexual penetration, in which many men defined themselves against, and above, women in terms of their active role. Men like John resisted the notion that penetration should be defined in terms of gendered superiority, and looked for a meaning that allowed them dignity: "I've known a number of friends over the years whose main joy was being fucked ... [M]y longest homosexual [relationship] was just that: we [enjoyed] fucking [each] other." Having experienced the presumption of dominance by other men, bisexuals like John had the opportunity to question the meaning of their own role in heterosexual intercourse.

While John enjoyed his intrigue with Major M, he resisted any further involvement with the gay life: "He would suggest that there were officers [like him]. He also seemed to know other ranks. I chose not to want to be recruited into any subculture ... I didn't want to be the subject of gossip." John had witnessed the limits of acceptance at the University of British Columbia, in which a "very well-known and much respected professor of English" was also known to be homosexual and a centre of the university's queer subculture. John recalled, "I travelled around, most of the time, with

a very heterosexual community who were aware of homosexuals' inclination, and tended to sort of brand anyone who was sort of friendly with Professor Pennyworth as potential recruits. But I can't remember thinking that
it was so awful ... it was just part of the university life that there were these
people around." John had avoided the group, since he "didn't want to be
identified with them ... I was part of a male fraternity and you joked about
things like this." Around his fraternity, queers, freaks, and fairies were the
subject of gossip. To protect his own reputation, he maintained a safe distance and ensured that his public identification was with his fraternity
brothers. In Ottawa he risked his reputation only by his affair with the major. Any further involvement would be difficult to contain, since the homosexual underground was as likely to gossip as his own colleagues were.[30]

Like Major M, other officers in the personnel and training functions
made sexual liaisons among the wide range of men with whom they came
into contact. Thirty-one-year-old Lieutenant W, whom we encountered earlier, was a very efficient administration officer at Number 2 District Depot
in Toronto. From September 1943 to April 1944, he entertained at least six
soldiers at his room at the YMCA on College Street. Usually, Lieutenant W
took the soldier out to dinner, a show, bowling or wrestling matches, and
then back to his room away from the barracks. Most of his partners were
employed at various clerical functions, also at 2 District Depot. He asked
that the soldiers not tell their comrades that they were going out with him,
perhaps in an effort to contain the gossip as much as possible. So, while
Lieutenant W was developing a quite extensive array of sexual partners, he
was not facilitating the formation of a network or subculture.[31]

In August 1940 twenty-two-year-old Bill A left his trade as a grinder of
eyeglass lenses in Toronto and enlisted in the Royal Canadian Navy. Between February and June of 1943, he was detailed for shore patrol work at
HMCS Cornwallis in Digby, Nova Scotia. This gave him some freedom of
movement and the chance to meet servicemen not connected to his unit.
Sapper Doug S of the Canadian Army (Canadian Engineers Reinforcement
Unit) was on leave for two weeks visiting his family in Digby. The two met
and had an affair until Doug was sent overseas. The sexual element of their
relationship took place in Doug's bedroom at his family home, where they
alternated roles in anal intercourse. After Doug arrived in England, they
corresponded with each other. The challenge for gay men and women writing letters was to hide emotional or sexual references from the superior officers and navy censors who surveyed the mail. But Bill's passion and his
playful references to his paramour's penis were too explicit. The letter con-

veyed to the censor a colourful impression of their illicit relationship and references to others whose sexual lives fell under suspicion. It offers much the same information to our historical gaze:

Hello Doug,

Finally received your long awaited letter. To say that I was pleased to hear from you would be putting it very mild. It was a great pleasure.

So very glad to hear that you are very well and enjoying yourself. I'll bet you are getting around England in more ways than one. Okay Bub. By the way how is our "wee" Dougey making out. I only met him twice but it was hardly enough. Get me kid. I only wish that he was here so I could hold him again. I really miss him. He was a lot of fun. How about you, brother? Do you feel the same about yours truly?

Well Doug, I presume that you have noticed my new address. I was drafted out here to the West Coast Dec 20. I finally received my request for "Combined Operations" course. And is it ever tough. I really stuck my neck out this time. But I believe that I will live to see you over there again. As far as I can make out I will be here for about [censored] weeks then back again to the East Coast and overseas. What a happy day that should be.

When I left Digby, all the old gang seemed to be much the same in spirit and health. I ran up to your home a couple of times to get your address. All the family were very well and happy. I did not see Johnnie but hope to receive a short stopover leave on my way back and if so, I intend to go to Digby and Deep Brook for a day or so, and will surely look up our old pals, drunkards and gash.

As for your cigarettes, well Doug, I will get my step-mother to send you some. You understand I am on a small island out here and there is no place close where I can send them to you. So Mrs [–] will do the job for me – okay. I had an aweful [sic] dull time at Christmas but the New Years Holidays were different. Did I ever get stiff in more ways than one. I went to Nanaimo, BC for seven days leave. Hotels, girls, ice and roller skating, movies and dances were the general run of the day. I am with a swell gang out here. They live very fast and loose. We all get on very well together, fun, fun and more fun, with no fights.

Well, Doug, must close for now as I am out of words and deeds. So until the next time, I either hear from you, or see you, I will say so long for now. The very best of luck, kid and look after yourself. Look after my "wee" Dougy for me, until I can stroke him again. Okay brother, bye for now.

Always yours, Bill

p.s. Keep your eyes open for smokes, Doug. It is a pleasure to send them along.[32]

The letter's jocular tone and familiarity belie the fact that they had known each other for only twelve days the previous May. Bill stayed overnight on at least two occasions at Doug's family home. It appears that since that time, in Doug's absence, he was well received by the family.

It is obvious that their relationship was not cloistered. During the time they spent together, they belonged to a group of "pals" given to drinking. After his posting on Vancouver Island, he discovered another "swell gang." As in Digby, they appear to have been heavy drinkers, but their social activities were varied. Bill seems unable to contain something of the group's exuberance and magnanimity. His description of them as devoted to "fun, with no fights" suggests that they eschewed the brawls and disagreements that were common in other military social gatherings. Also, the gang included men and women. The sexual orientation of the other members of the gang is not clear. While three of Bill's four male sexual partners during the war (who were also servicepeople) were married, there is no sense that the group was fundamentally structured around sexual categories.[33]

In his letter, Bill tested Doug's affections, eager to discover if his infatuation was reciprocated. Since Doug had already written to him, his hope was not unfounded. There is even a hint that his request for a transfer to combined operations may have been partly motivated by the desire to be near Doug. He claims ownership of Doug's penis ("my 'wee' Dougy"). However, at the same time, he enquires into Doug's sexual adventures in England and divulges his own in Nanaimo. This willingness to share sexual and romantic partners with others was common. Several gay veterans noted that since one never knew when one would be transferred, romance and sex had to be expedient. So, Bill's optimism that their relationship might have had a future coexisted with an understanding that they were both continuing in the meantime with their independent sexual lives.

Nevertheless, as with many homosexual servicemen, Bill's affairs tended to be distinct and brought to an end by the vagaries of wartime service. During the first two years of his navy service, Bill's only sexual activity was masturbation. Then, in November 1942, he had a sexual relationship with a naval cook in Halifax. They rented a room in the YMCA where they took turns having anal intercourse with each other. Several months later, he and a stoker first class from HMCS Summerside found privacy at the Winchester Hotel in Digby and the Annapolis Hotel in Annapolis, Nova Scotia. Then he had his encounter with Doug. Finally, before he was transferred to British Columbia, he had an ongoing affair with an ordinary seaman aboard ship. In all cases, he and his partners included anal intercourse in their sexual repertoire, alternating active and passive roles.

Why should his sexual relations have had such similar forms? It is possible that the reason Bill chose these lovers in particular is that their sexual interests coincided with his own. That explanation suggests that he had a large pool of potential lovers from which to choose and that there was a discussion of sexual likes and dislikes. Alternatively, the naval police may have limited their investigation (from which this account is drawn) to acts of sodomy, ignoring other practices. However, in other cases, police curiosity was boundless. Most likely, the similarity in their sexual behaviour results from the fact that queer men learned from each other. Interviews and documentary records support the proposition that techniques were passed along.[34]

SEXUAL IDENTITIES AND DENIAL

Bill's letter refers to various new relationships in his life, all of which resulted from the peculiar circumstance of war. His young lover's family in Digby opened their doors to him. Doug's family home was the site of their sexual relationship, and his relatives became part of Bill's social circle once his lover was shipped overseas. In this instance, we can observe a general loosening of the social order that was typical for wartime Nova Scotia. Because of its strategic location, Nova Scotia housed naval, air force, and army bases. The province was totally unprepared to accommodate the influx of servicepeople stationed there. As well, some married servicemen transferred their families from other parts of Canada to be near the base so that they could see them when on leave. As a result, many Nova Scotians opened their homes to servicepeople. Byron was a nineteen-year-old homosexual Haligonian when war broke out, and he remembers the change in his family's response to strangers: "While I came from a family that was very closed and didn't have a lot of social activity itself, mother became very interested in accommodating and being hospitable to the servicemen. Everybody did in a sense. You were hospitable to the servicemen. These were the men that were fighting to keep the world free."

Byron was not accepted in the services owing to a hearing loss and so was employed at the National Selective Service (NSS) office in Halifax. For him, wartime Halifax offered unprecedented social and sexual opportunities. Although from a working-class family, Byron identified with the cultural and social trappings of the elite. He found it easy to meet the cultured and educated officers he admired in the record and book shop on Barrington Street. Many would happily accept his invitation to dinner: "Well, they'd been on the ship for weeks. And confined in quarters ... big big break for them to get away. And I'd say, 'Do you want to stay overnight, you don't have to go back to the ship until tomorrow noon?' 'Oh God, yes!' And it was great and mother didn't mind it. I had my own room and bed and what happened, happened. If it happened. Some of them were not gay really. Were surprised at themselves. But others were only too happy to have the opportunity." For Byron, these men became an important pipeline to the world of New York and London theatre and concerts. His judgment that not all of the men who came to call as soon as their ship docked were "gay" was based on the observation that some "would be so pent up, so randy or sexually repressed after four or five or six weeks at sea that any warm body in a bed was as good as another." Others simply appreciated his family's hospitality. If his analysis is correct, it suggests that sexual behaviour and identities were not constrained by today's insistence on the hetero/homosexual binary. Even bisexuality, which depends on the two poles for its definition, was not how these men defined themselves.

Byron also met many people through his work with NSS. One young RCAF airman from rural Nova Scotia who was training in Halifax would come to visit Byron frequently. Unlike Byron's other contacts, he was "very very shy – very inarticulate ... not a reader and he was not interested in music or anything like that." While on farm leave, he invited Byron to his family home outside Windsor. Byron was given the bedroom of the second son, a serviceman posted abroad. He remembers, "I was in bed about a half an hour and the door opens and he came in in his pyjamas and all the house was quiet and he crawled into bed and we had wild sex which absolutely floored me because I just did not think he was the type at all. It was over and done with and he immediately got up and went upstairs. And I was there for two nights and next night the same thing happened. And that was that. Nothing was ever spoken. Just the act was performed."

Thirty years later, while visiting Toronto, Byron came across the same man, now married and living in Mississauga, Ontario. He seemed eager to reunite, and so the two met at Byron's room at the Royal York Hotel. Byron assumed that it was the memory of their wartime sexual encounters that inspired his old lover to visit, perhaps since that was his own most enduring recollection. However, his sexual overture "shocked the hell" out of his old companion, who then decided to leave. Byron notes, "And I really was shocked and I'm sure he was ten times more shocked. But funny things like that happened which indicated that war – and unnatural conditions – had caused certain things to happen sexually in people's lives that never would have happened probably had it not been for war and had they not been exposed to things outside their milieu ... He would never have met anybody like me on the farm." In fact, it may have been the reverse that was happening: the war may have been offering Byron a glimpse of life in rural Nova Scotia. As was the case with other interviewees from rural Canada, homosexuality was never meant to be acknowledged in the light of day. Nevertheless, it was indeed the war that had brought the two together. It is credible, as Byron suggests, that his wartime lover no longer remembered their sexual liaison decades later. Byron's description of the young man's subsequent behaviour – "it never happened" – may suggest the cognitive process that allowed him to have the experience he wanted without consciously legitimating it.[35]

How did men come to terms with their homosexual desires? If Kinsey's statistics are accurate, or even approximate, a great many men in North American society were faced with the problem of reconciling both their public figure and private self-image with the fact that they harboured severely proscribed criminal, immoral, unmanly desires. While an infantry platoon commander with the North Nova Scotia Highlanders in northwest Europe, Donald Pearce kept a personal diary, against military regulations, on loose pieces of paper. He transcribed keen and subtle observations on human behaviour in war – his own response and that of his men, the enemy, and civilian populations across Europe. In January 1945, in Holland, he ruminated on how people respond to unwelcome and socially proscribed desires. His reflections on free will eloquently address the way many men and women may have dealt with homosexual desire:

We are free to condemn what we desire, but not to determine what we desire, except in the limited sense that gradually we come to develop a feeling, a sort of seventh sense, which tells us what we are going to let ourselves get away with, what it is foolish to present to ourselves, even tentatively, for ratification, at least in its real and unmodified form; and in those cases we either change the appearance of the desire or try to pre-arrange assent by packing the jury – all of which must be done far below the level of consciousness, at a sort of underworld bargain-counter where secret concessions and agreements are made; for we all have foreign correspondents dwelling in the unconscious who are quick to report more than usually suspicious activities, though they, too, have been known to accept bribes. What do we mean by "freedom of will," if we can neither determine our desires nor evade the necessity of limiting their expression?[36]

It is difficult to detail how servicemen reconciled their homosexual desires with their self-image. Lieutenant Pearce's reflections suggest that men and women were continuously challenged to reconcile inner desires and social expectations. In his formulation, alcohol may have been one of many chips in use at the "underworld bargain-counter."

The role of alcohol in the lives of men who attempted to ignore their homosexual desires is demonstrated by the actions of Frederick G, a thirty-six-year-old single airman with the RCAF stationed at Souris, Manitoba, in 1944. He had had at least two previous convictions for homosexual offences. In 1934, while working as a caretaker in a Toronto theatre, he had been arrested by the city police for gross indecency. In 1943, after a year in the RCAF, he had been given a summary punishment of twenty-seven days detention by his superior officer for attempting to commit sodomy with two fellow airmen at the Metropolis Hotel in Victoria, British Columbia. In Souris, Frederick suffered from "boredom and loneliness," which he assuaged in the canteen from opening until closing time, usually drinking between twelve and fourteen pints of beer. He was never belligerent, the alcohol only making him want "to walk about and talk to someone." However, after lights out, he got "in the habit of handling the genitals of sleeping airmen." After several months of this nocturnal nuisance, eight airmen requested to their superior that Frederick be made to leave the barracks, stating that they had each been fondled several times. It is possible that they were sympathetic towards him, for such behaviour might have aroused a more violent response in some units. On the other hand, it is equally possible that Frederick's imposing physique discouraged aggression against him.[37]

While most men who were accused of committing sexual improprieties when drunk denied any recollection of the event, Frederick was rare in admitting freely his unwelcome habit, but he stipulated that he only had the impulse after he had been drinking. He admitted to the doctors that he had engaged in mutual masturbation with men, but "stoutly" denied "having anything to do with homosexuals" and said that his sexual fantasies were heterosexual. It is possible that he was being candid with the doctors, who accepted his self-description. They did not accept him as a medical problem at all, arguing that he was neither a sexual pervert nor a homosexual and that alcohol reduced him to a "juvenile level of emotion, judgment and conduct." This position aligned psychiatry with law, which argued that drunkenness could not alter motivation, only lower the barriers to action. For the psychiatrists, Frederick's recurrent desire to fondle men's genital organs, when intoxicated, indicated a return to adolescence rather than homosexuality. His vigorous protestations at the suggestion that he might be homosexual could indicate that he felt he had to deny what would have been uncomfortable to acknowledge. For Frederick, it was not the actions that he so strenuously denied, but the possibility that they could have been motivated by a sexual attraction to men. Recurrent homosexual fantasies, for a masculine man like Frederick, may well have been constant reminders that he was failing as a man. Decent, healthy men would never have harboured such immoral thoughts.[38]

DEFIANCE

While an intoxicated Frederick pushed his comrades into action against him, other units took advantage of the presence of men who would perform homosexual acts. Sometimes these men were homosexuals and willing participants; in other cases, they were vulnerable to being pressured by their peers to perform sexual services. The RCAF base at Goose Bay, Labrador, was an isolated posting for young Canadian men. The military was particularly concerned with the influence that 'perverts' could have in such settings. In fact, a homosexual culture did evolve under the initiative of a few worldly airmen. Joseph was a seventeen-year-old from Sherbrooke with a baby face that made him appear even younger when he voluntarily enlisted in the RCAF in 1942. He impressed the interviewing and medical officers as intelligent, "[v]ery alert – keen – youthful," and was recommended as "[g]ood aircrew material." In civil life, he had worked as a bellhop in a hotel and on a ship. He did not, of course, tell his interviewers that those jobs had offered him a pool of clients who paid up to ten dollars for his fellatio services. The "good impression" that he made on the personnel officers had been a trick of his earlier trade. They were not at all concerned with his "feminine habitus and manner."[39]

Joseph had no objection to being posted in such an isolated station as Goose Bay. Once there, he soon found sexual partners. Corporal Denis had been a miner in Manitoba before enlisting in the RCAF in 1940. In training in Ontario, he was known to the RCAF authorities as homosexual but had left no "clear cut evidence," and they failed in their attempt, "in those early days of disorganization and expansion ... to have him discharged." He had flown 120 hours before he was grounded for a middle ear condition. He was then sent to Goose Bay in June 1943 to work in the laundry services. He and Joseph became lovers for a period.[40]

Nineteen-year-old John from Ottawa arrived at Goose Bay in early 1944. Like Joseph, he had also worked as a bellhop in civilian life. He impressed the military examiners as "a young man of good build, neat appearance. His mental reactions are rather slow ... [a] quiet, diffident chap who seems lacking in self-confidence." He and Joseph became lovers. As well, over the subsequent months, they worked together offering sexual services to those interested. Joseph solicited clients and John provided the labour, always in the form of fellatio, receiving between one and five dollars for each trick. On 30 June their activities were reported by some airmen and five participants were convicted, sentenced, and discharged.[41]

The events at Goose Bay indicate the influence of individuals' civilian experience on their military careers. Although the development of the relationships that led to the business of sex at Goose Bay is not detailed, the comprehensive psychiatric and personnel reports reveal patterns that obtained in other units. The details of Joseph's prewar prostitution are not known. He claimed that he had performed oral sex himself, but whether he solicited his own clients is not clear. At Goose Bay he may have been assuming a senior role in procuring trade for John, a role for which he had had a model in his own earlier practice. In any case, they were sexual partners in private as well as in the business of sex. Thus, for them, sexuality was a versatile commodity, one that could offer pleasure, perhaps affection, as well as income. It is possible that the psychiatrist was correct in his conclusion that John had been somewhat manipulated into his role as fellator. John complained that, earlier, he had been "picked on and badgered by other airmen all the time, that if there was anything to be done in the barracks, such as making beds, scrub floors, wash windows, he was always picked on to do the job." In similar situations, men who were eager to please could sometimes be manipulated into gratifying the sexual needs of others. In this case, however, there is no evidence that John was acting against his will.[42]

At this remote base in Labrador, Joseph and John's client base was restricted to other airmen and NCOs. However, as their satisfied clientele expanded, they could rely on a predictable supply of repeat customers. Can anything be known about the sexual identities of the men involved? The psychiatrist labelled Joseph as homosexual, since he "freely admitted a background of homosexual endeavours and experiences, uses words and phrases common to the vocabulary of a homosexual, and finally was found in such practices." However, Joseph also said that he enjoyed heterosexual relations. While the psychiatrist categorized all of the participants according to their sexual orientations, Joseph claimed a more practical expertise, asserting, "I can usually spot one every time." Perhaps it was this ability that made him a successful pimp. There is evidence that both John and Denis were involved in other homosexual relations even when posted on bases near urban centres. So, while they were unwilling to avow as much interest, knowledge, or experience as Joseph, it is not improbable that they were homosexual in their private lives.

At least two of Joseph and John's clients denied any interest in homosexual relations and framed their explanations in similar terms. One claimed that "on the night in question he became intoxicated, returned to the barracks to take a shower, found other airmen engaged in fellatio, paid the French Canadian airman to perform the act for him; that he never did it before and has not done it since." Another admitted "having paid another airman to commit fellatio ... says that it happened about 5 months ago and that in a recent similar episode he was drunk at the time, and further, that he and his friends had been discussing sex and he was somewhat stimulated and excited." If their explanations were genuine, and their fantasies were heterosexual while John performed fellatio, then the event was homosexual in a technical sense only. Their sexual satisfaction did not entail an acceptance of homosexual desires. At most, they may have discovered a practical sexual tool. Nevertheless, they paid as severe a price as those who were more psychically attached to same-sex love.[43]

CONCLUSION

In this chapter, I have focused on the challenges and opportunities that queer servicemen faced upon enlistment and during their training and postings in Canada. The evidence has allowed an elementary reconstruction of some of the homosexual practices that evolved in military environments after 1939. Primary attention has been paid to the individual's way of dealing with his homoerotic desires. The main psychic challenge for men with homoerotic desires was acceptance of their existence. Homoerotic desires challenged claims to uprightness and manhood. Most frequently cast (in dismissive or cautionary utterances) as a moral failing, men who harboured homoerotic interests were sometimes tortured by the presence of this original sin. A sexual interest in men could be easily read as feminine. This slippage from sexual to gender inversion was embodied in the role of the fairy. Since gender identity was a fundamental source of private and public dignity, queer men had every reason to resist their deviant sexuality. This represented a widespread problem, since research into sexual orientation has demonstrated that at least a substantial minority of men in North America have experienced homoerotic desires or behaviour.[44]

Many homosexual men, nevertheless, accepted their desires and creatively fashioned self-images that allowed them a sense of dignity. For instance, some saw their sexual difference as a sign of an artistic temperament. Others embraced it as a private, but not unwelcome, resistance to social conformity. Still others accepted it quietly because it afforded them pleasure, whatever the moralists might say. In contrast to today's concept of the exclusively

Intimacies. This wartime photo shows two soldiers in rural
Nova Scotia. The modern-day viewer might be tempted to read
a homosexual relationship into the image. During the war,
most people would have considered that an insidious, slander-
ous assumption. Since many wartime relationships between
servicemen were emotionally and physically intimate, it was
simply necessary to hide the sexual element, usually from people who did not want to see it anyway. Courtesy of Rick Hirtle.

homosexual man, the wartime counterpart was an immoralist who succumbed to temptation. All men needed to control their sexuality, or at least
appear to, in order to maintain their reputations in the mainstream culture;
the potential fallout for queer men was far-reaching. It is therefore not surprising that a great number of queer men chose to eat their cake and have it
too. Denial was not a strategy but a frame of mind that simply refused to allow the unspeakable into consciousness. If homosexuality could not be accommodated into one's self-image, then the mind helped to keep it at bay.
Still, once the truth was acknowledged at some level, denial became a deliberate process of self-deception. Alcohol was commonly used to lower resistance to homoerotic desire and to provide an excuse for uncontrollable, but
indefensible, behaviour.

Of course, homosexual desires and activities, whether hidden or visible, all took place in a public context. In order to better understand both the psychic pressures resulting from homosexual desire and the choices that queer men made, it is necessary to locate these activities within the larger military community. The war setting encouraged intense male bonds, often resulting in friendships that were indistinguishable from romances. Since true homosexuality was commonly assumed to reside in a very small percentage of the population, typified for many by especially flamboyant or flagrant examples of the fairy, most queer men escaped suspicion. Before considering the larger military environment, this study of queer men and their evolution within the forces will cross the ocean with the Canadian forces. The navy, army and air force all came to create new and radically diverse social environments on the North Atlantic, in Britain, and in continental Europe. Queer Canadian servicemen found new opportunities and challenges in these unique settings. Not only did they have an impact on the war, but the war influenced their social and sexual self-discovery.

Chapter Five

QUEER SERVICEMEN OVERSEAS

One week after the event, Private Tom C of the North Nova Scotia High-landers faced a court martial in England, charged with "disgraceful conduct of an unnatural kind, in that he, [i]n the field, at approximately 2325 hours 1 August 44, in Middlesbrough, did commit a homo sexual act with one ... Cpl George C, 86 Station Complement Squadron, U.S.A.A.F."

Eight years earlier, Tom, then sixteen and having difficulty learning, left school after completing grade four. Until war broke out, he delivered orders for his father's small grocery store in Glace Bay, Nova Scotia. His mother had died twelve years earlier in a mental institution, two of his sisters had died of tuberculosis, another was in a sanatorium, and a fourth had been discharged from the canadian Women's Army Corps with tubercular limbs. His only brother had secured a deferment from military service to work in the Cape Breton coal mines. Private Tom enlisted with the Cape Breton Highlanders in 1940 and arrived in England with the Canadian Army in 1941. In Italy he served as a rifleman with the Highlanders but broke down in battle. He was returned to England where he displayed a fear of loud noises. Thereafter, in training, he could not stand guns being fired near him. In May 1944 he was graded mentally handicapped and emotionally unstable, a detriment to his infantry platoon because of his inability to absorb training and his nervous reaction to loud noises. Nevertheless, he volunteered to take part in the Normandy invasion and was sent across the English Channel with the North Nova Scotia Highlanders on D-Day. In battle, he was unable to control his reaction to mortars going off and would unconsciously jump out of his slit trench. Evacuated after one week, he was assessed by the officer commanding 21 Canadian General Hospital as "obviously unfit for combat service." Subsequently, the personnel officer noted that "[i]n action, he becomes a casualty after a few hours and now, he is indifferent and simply does not care although he mentions that he would not like to remain idle."

Now consigned to routine duties in England, he was granted a twenty-four-hour pass two weeks after his release from hospital. He went to Middlesbrough. At five o'clock he reserved a bed for the night at the Toc H Hostel and then went to the pub next door and had a pint of bitters. Tom was attractive and well built. Soon, an American corporal was buying drinks for both of them. They left the pub, went to another, and continued drinking. Later in the evening, they passed one of the many bomb-damaged buildings in Middlesbrough. The doors and windows were bombed out, giving them easy entrance, and they climbed over the rubble on the stairs up to the second floor. The front room of the second floor was completely empty. Although the windows were blown out, they decided that it was secure enough to afford them the privacy they required. The two men undressed, hung their clothes on the back of the door, and then began to have sexual relations. Tom lay down on the floor and the corporal sucked his penis and manoeuvred himself so that his knees straddled Tom's head. In that position, Tom was able to suck the corporal's penis at the same time, sixty-nining. Perhaps it was because they were so absorbed in their mutually satisfying sexual encounter that they did not hear the Middlesbrough police inspector and constable climbing the stairs. Suddenly a flashlight violated the privacy they had gone to such measures to secure and the two military men were aware that they were no longer alone. Police Inspector Walker told them that they had been caught "committing an act of indecency." The American corporal replied, "I cannot deny the charge. I should have known better." Private Tom said, "I do not remember anything." All four continued to police headquarters. The inspector noted that Tom "stated that he had recently come out of hospital, and he seemed to be suffering from nervous strain."[1]

Private Tom's story introduces some of the themes relating to the unique challenges and opportunities encoutered by Canadian officers and ranks in Britain and on the Continent.

First, while the conditions that they faced in war-torn Europe affected their professional, personal, and social development, Canadian soldiers were also influenced by their pasts. Private Tom's retort to the police that he could remember nothing of the event in which he was, in fact, presently occupied may have been an act of self-deception or simply a child-like response to being discovered. Queer Canadian soldiers were not unique in misrepresenting themselves to authorities in Europe. Concealing one's true identity became commonplace in Nazi-dominated Europe: Jews pretended to be Gentile, resistance fighters presented themselves as harmless citizens, Poles said they were German when possible, and after the war, Nazis claimed to have been anti-Nazi.

Second, the conditions such as Tom experienced – the bombed-out building, the American corporal, and the environment that nurtured instant camaraderie between strangers in uniform – were all a direct result of the war. Wartime conditions sometimes facilitated sexual relations, as in this instance, and other times discouraged them. The form of homosexual expression was constrained or facilitated by particular military environments. Although the meeting between Tom and the corporal could have occurred in any pub, London's gay underground had exploded with the continuous flow of Allied servicemen, creating numerous queer bars and public spaces.

Third, the choice of partner was often deliberate and consequential. The corporal and Private Tom might quite consciously have chosen a sexual partner from a service far removed from their own – an American corporal and a Canadian Army rifleman could be assured that their military paths would never cross. For some, this kind of sexual partner could offer a sense of security. However, in many other cases, partners were chosen from among servicepeople's closest associates.

Fourth, the war affected individuals psychologically. It is clear that Tom had been deeply affected by his service in Italy and France. In some cases, such psychological stress may have lowered resistance to socially proscribed desires.[2]

Much of Canada's military history has transpired on and above European soil. No sooner had Britain withdrawn its troops charged with the defence of Canada than it began calling on Canadians to aid in the defence of England. During the Second World War, approximately 494,000 Canadian servicepeople served in Europe. By V-E Day, the army had sent about 370,000 Canadian men to Europe, and the Canadian Women's Army Corps another 1,000. The RCAF had 93,844 men and women serving overseas throughout the war. At the end of the European war, there were 20,354 RCN personnel in Britain, but many others would have been there at different moments during the conflict. A total of 92,757 Canadians served in the Italian theatre from 10 July 1943 to May 1945. From D-Day until the defeat of Germany, tens of thousands of Canadians served in northwest Europe.[3]

Traditionally, Canadian military history has concerned itself with the country's prosecution of wars and the institutional development of the armed forces. Some historians have begun to look more closely at the effects of the world wars on Canadian society. However, military historians have largely neglected social histories of the armed forces in wartime. How did the various men who were brought together during the world wars organize themselves socially? What happened when hundreds of thousands of men from the regions of Canada were arranged into same-sex environments for extended periods of training and service and sent to Europe to fight European wars? Generations of Canadian men have been thus indoctrinated into martial life in their formative years and have either embraced or resisted military ideals. They have judged themselves and each other according to their effectiveness in martial pursuits.

Military records and published memoirs make it clear that Canada's national undertaking was also a personal adventure for individual servicemen and -women sent overseas. During their years in Britain, servicemen established a range of relationships with local women. By the end of 1946, 44,886 Canadian service personnel had married in Great Britain. Those marriages had produced 21,358 children. For many queer servicemen, the transfer overseas represented a break with heterocentric Canadian social structures. In their place, many found new opportunities for sexual self-discovery. However, while external conditions had changed, internal barriers to homosexual expression still needed to be confronted. When the allure of sexual self-fulfilment was stronger than the brakes of conscience, queer men created new social forms within both military and civilian wartime environments in Europe. Many took advantage of the anonymity possible in a foreign country to confront their forbidden homosexual desires. Many homosexual British men welcomed the influx of potential partners from the dominions and encouraged their sexual awakening in a number of ways. The frequent change of personnel within the military also meant that queer men could make passing contacts with soldiers with similar interests. In Italy and northwest Europe, ravaged by war, other unique opportunities arose that often opened the way for sexual discovery.[4]

CONDITIONS IN ENGLAND

For a generation of Canadian men, England represented an adventure, a break from the various social and familial bonds that had channelled and controlled behaviour in Canada. Many men and women had not experienced that world as oppressive or intrusive, but to live healthy lives, homosexual men and women needed to re-evaluate the social strictures that otherwise devalued them. Unfortunately for them, in England, the military placed itself *in loco parentis* for the ranks and assumed responsibility for Canadian medical, spiritual, legal, and cultural conventions. In addition, individual Canadians had brought their moralities with them across the sea. Nevertheless, the unique settings and situations abroad could offer new perspectives.

Many men had their first homosexual experiences during their years in England. Henri, for example, left his highly religious Montreal upbringing to serve with the Royal Canadian Engineers. In England, he confronted the first challenge to what he describes as his sexual innocence:

We were stationed near Aldershot in Farnborough and I used to go to the cinema. You know, nothing else to do in those days. And this army chap next to me started playing with my buttons – we didn't have zips in those days, played with my buttons ... But I remember it vividly because it was my first experience. Young and innocent I was ... We used to go down a passage at the side of the cinema that was private. We were naughty. He sucked me off ... Well, I liked it and always said, "See you next week," but I didn't realize that it was anything except sex. The business of gay emotions and love and things hadn't happened to me yet ... I thought playing with another man's private parts was great fun.

Until one of them was posted away, Henri and the soldier pursued their semi-anonymous relationship each Saturday at the cinema: "And I don't even know his name. Possibly I did. First name. But I can't remember." Canadian city centres also offered cinemas where homosexual men cruised in the darkness, and Henri could possibly have made similar discoveries had he remained in Canada. Nevertheless, the adventure of serving in England coupled with the separation from his home environment seems to have accelerated his sexual education. Henri's contention that his early enjoyment of sexual relations with other men was divorced from romance may have made it possible for him to enjoy sexual pleasures without having to confront the social significance of his behaviour. Historian Jonathan Ned Katz has suggested that the separation of sex and love in male culture in nineteenth-century America meant that men who felt both simultaneously might have experienced confusion. The same dynamic likely influenced men in wartime Canada. In this way, the history of society was replicated in the history of the individual.[5]

Some queer soldiers uncovering their sexuality did so on their own, acting on opportunities as they arose within their military environments. Other novices were fortunate in finding someone who could provide a more formal education. In his autobiography, Bert Sutcliffe writes: "My posting to the allied planning staff in London was crucial to my personal growth, as during the eight months I was with this specialist unit I got to know and love London." Bert has since elaborated on the specifics of his personal development. His first homosexual experience occurred on New Year's Eve, 1941. He and a sergeant, Harry, from his Canadian security section were attending a course at a British Army school. Returning from the New Year's dance, "we went in to have a leak and we both got a hard-on and our hands automatically reached out and I thought, 'Will we fuck?!' So he said, 'Come on, you can sleep with me tonight, cause the British kids are away for the weekend.'" Harry had had experience as a homosexual man in the army: "[H]e had a buddy of his belong to one of the Toronto regiments and he had been a Saturday night soldier before the war and had been into all of this." Harry became Bert's mentor and introduced him to London's gay subculture: "I was absolutely amazed when Harry takes me to all these places and he says, 'That one's gay, that guy's gay, that guy's gay, these two probably are.' And I looked, and as I say, it was like a kid being taken into Laura Secord."[6]

In common with many young homosexual soldiers, Bert was overwhelmed by the sexual possibilities offered in wartime England: "In '42 I was stationed in London for six months and I suddenly found out that Leicester Square, Piccadilly Circus were just hotbeds of gay bars. Just jampacked with them. Of course, I had all kinds of free evenings so I could wander in and out of any of the gay bars in downtown London, which I did ... The Regent Palace Hotel was one bar and also its sister place, the Strand Palace on Strand, was another place." Many other bars in Piccadilly and Leicester Square were exclusively gay and "were just jam-packed with Canadians, Americans, French, Polish, Australians, and Brit soldiers and Brit civilians." Since he had his own room two blocks from Piccadilly Circus, Bert "could take four people back in an evening." The anonymity offered by the large number of available partners and the absence of regulating functions meant that many men could explore their previously repressed desires with impunity. Such sexual freedom was not limited to gay men: "In London you could almost have sex twenty-four hours a day. Almost anywhere. Gay sex. And you could have straight sex too. After all, London was jam-packed with males and females in uniform away from home." Quentin Crisp, one of England's most famous 'queens,' remembers wartime London as "the happy time."[7]

Wartime conditions facilitated illicit sexual encounters all over Britain. Nightly blackouts in all cities and towns meant that privacy was more readily improvised. Even car headlights were outlawed, and people carried pin-hole flashlights. In Piccadilly the pursuit of sexual partners spilled out of the bars: "At the underground station at Piccadilly Circus every night at ten o'clock ... [there were] maybe ten to maybe twenty-five males all gay and all picking up people." Similarly, "most of the urinals in downtown London were places where gays would congregate and all they'd do is stand and look around and someone would catch their eye and they'd go upstairs and talk and off they'd go and it didn't cost a penny." Private Connor described at his court martial the casual process of finding a sexual partner at Aldershot: "I spoke to this soldier in the lavatory, and while we were talking he offered me a cigarette, which I took, and he reached down and felt my person while I was relieving myself, and we walked to the park, and he did the same thing [masturbated me], and I done the same thing." As suggested by Bert, the lavatory was used as a meeting place, and the two soldiers then went to the municipal gardens where they hoped to find a more private, safer location to masturbate each other.[8]

The upper class could be protected from such exposure, having greater access to privacy and being treated more deferentially by subordinates, including police. Bob, a flying officer with the RCAF, remembers when an English officer approached him during a blackout in London and took him back to his rooms at Old Chelsea Barracks. Bob found the ceremony accorded to the officer ironic under the circumstances: "The guard came to present arms, you know, this kind of thing, and here we were to do things [have sex]." The officer had inherited his rooms and, presumably, his commission. Bob remembers "a huge room, and pictures all around of General So-and-So, General This, Lord This, Lord That, and apparently, it went from father to son to son to son, and here was this one, a second lieutenant." The next morning, after they spent the night together, "there was a knock on the door and there was his batman. And the batman looks in, he says, 'Whoops! I guess I need another cup of tea.'" These markings of the British class system were a surprise to Bob, from working-class Toronto: "He had to go to Church Parade. I didn't like the guy at all; he smelled of booze and cigarettes and everything. Besides, in my eyes, he wasn't that good. And anyway, he said, 'Wait for me, I'll come back afterwards.' Then I got dressed and went out. The guards came to attention. It was rather funny, in my eyes anyway." Bert responded in a similar way to aristocratic trappings when he visited the ancestral home in Lincoln of a British officer he had met in Hyde Park – "An impressive and historic moment in the early life of one recently freed from Toronto's Cabbage Town." As had been the case historically, illicit sexuality had the power to bridge the class divide. In Bert's case, the relationship proved to be more meaningful: "For a long time we were lovers. And then when the war ended and I came home, I would have given my right arm to have stayed in London with him, but I couldn't."[9]

During wartime there was a logic to the choice of sexual partners. A concern for one's own standing in the military meant that careful servicemen would choose partners from the ranks of other Allied forces. Bert reasoned,

"I always had a horror of getting involved with another Canadian just in case at a future date, he might be in my unit and I might have to give him orders. And he might turn to me and say, 'You son of a bitch, I'm not going to do what you tell me, I'll tell them what you're doing.'" In this regard, wartime conditions facilitating wise choices for all queer Allied personnel – "In these days, London wore a uniform. Polish-French-Belgian-Norwegian-Australian-New Zealander-Canadian-American ... all ranks and all services, and both sexes." Canadian soldiers often looked for partners outside of their traditional social and military environments. Consequently, homosexual activity tended to bring together members of groups who were otherwise socially or militarily distinct.[10]

The gay world in London was structured according to the demand for particular sexual traits. Bert attributes his success in the bars to his masculine bearing: "I had a very deep voice and I didn't have any gay mannerisms. I wore a uniform and I was a sergeant or a sergeant-major. I looked stern and forbidding and interesting. And so I got picked up by all kinds of people. I'd be taken to other clubs or bars. I'd be taken to their homes. Particularly Brit civilians or American military in London ... I felt all I had to do was just stand in the corner of a bar and drink my beer and not pay any attention to anybody and sooner or later I'd be picked up." Ironically, the demeanour that made him desirable to many queer men was deliberately fashioned to hide his homosexuality within the military: "People sometimes say to me, 'Why do you swear so much?' And really this was something I did to cover over the fact that I was gay. Everytime I turned around I'd say to someone, 'Fuck off you son of a bitch,' and that was considered standard butch and I developed a whole language of offensive words that I felt I had to use to cover up what was inside me."

Other queer soldiers also felt protected within the service as a result of their masculine comportment. But within the homosexual world, a masculine soldier could often assume a passive role in seduction. Bert describes being picked up as a direct result of projecting a manly image. To pursue the masculine was itself interpreted as non-masculine by those who accepted received standards of gendered behaviour. While in the straight world, the man was expected to actively court a woman, in the gay world, it was often the masculine that was pursued.[11]

To admire the masculine from a vantage point outside of the gay world was more problematic. Captain K quite openly mocked the rigid sex-gender system that attributed active, masculine behaviour to men and the feminine, passive role to women. Since it required that sexual roles be defined through supposedly essential gendered differences, that system could not accommodate homosexuality. Captain K developed a camp personality that came to be despised by some of his superior officers. At his court martial, the men he pursued were forced, often against their will, to describe his betrayals of manliness. Corporal Collyer first made Captain K's acquaintance the night he arrived at Tournai Barracks in England. He testified, "I was going out to the sergeant's mess, Capt. [K] said he could show me where it was, he had been here before on the advance, [we] went up together, going up he threw his arm around my should[er] and said, 'My, isn't it dark, I would like to rape you.' I said, 'That will be the day' and walked off." Captain K's pursuit of soldiers within the 1st Armoured Brigade Company had the effect of feminizing them, and it was that process to which the court (and, in a couple of cases, the men) most objected. The corporal's response suggests that he interpreted the captain's flippant overture in terms of the power they retained as men – to be raped was understood to mean submitting to the officer's sexual desire. In the sex-gender hierarchy in which sexual relations were already overlaid with the necessity of male superiority, sex between two men challenged a primal sense of manhood. A soldier acting as the mailman at the base was somewhat hesitant to report to the court the captain's typical greeting to him: "He would say, 'Good morning, soldier,' 'Good morning, dear' or something to that effect." Treating men, in the straight world, as potential sexual partners could threaten their gender identity, for only one in the sexual partnership could retain the privilege of the masculine role.[12]

CANADIAN DESERTERS AND THE GAY UNDERGROUND

Douglas LePan's 1964 novel, *The Deserter*, describes a Canadian soldier's adventures in the squalor of postwar London. Although LePan was himself homosexual, his protagonist is straight. The novel creates a dialectic between anarchy and social order, drawing on the author's wartime experience and observations while posted at Canadian Military Headquarters in London. While arguing that society requires the repression of disfavoured emotions, LePan nevertheless describes with admiration the fearless soldiers of the Footguards who were "not above eking out their pay with some earnings from male prostitution." For LePan, the Footguards symbolized the essence of British manhood, an immense power that was always controlled and in the service of civilization. In contrast to female impersonators and fairies, whose homosexuality was suggested through gender inversion, the Footguards' sexual versatility was grounded in their masculinity. Their willingness to engage in homosexual activity was part of their unwillingness to submit to any social constraint. While fairies could be seen as 'not man enough,' the guards were the epitome of raw masculinity. From LePan's perspective, they were a powerful masculine force, all the more intriguing because of their position at the heart of the empire, charged with the protection of the monarchy: "It was odd to think of all that primitive carnal energy brought together and combed and kennelled, its coat made glossy to serve as an emblem of order, indeed as one of its supporters, as a kind of bear tethered to the court by a golden chain."[13]

While waiting in a public square, LePan's protagonist witnesses a guardsman's solicitation tactics. The guardsman notices a man loitering in the area he patrols, and after determining that he is a potential client, he approaches him cautiously: "A few minutes later a guardsman came up and asked him if he had a light. In reply he struck a match and held it out. In its tiny glow he noticed that the guardsman, as he bent to light his cigarette, was looking up as though debating whether to say anything further. Finally he asked, 'You waiting for someone?' When there was no answer, he added after a moment, 'You been here quite a while.' But when there was still no answer he walked away." The guardsman trades on his image of hypermasculinity. By soliciting another man for illicit sexual relations, he does not feminize himself as fairies do, but suggests that he sees into the secret repressed desires of other men. His caution is required by the possibility that the loitering man may not acknowledge his own homosexual interest, in which case the guardsman would be cast as immoral, rather than unabashed. He is creating a space in which he can be pursued. (Of course, practically, the guardsman could be vulnerable to indecency charges.) Similarly, Canadian deserters developed their own strategies to find homosexual British partners and played on their desirability as soldiers.[14]

Many young Canadian soldiers who absented themselves without leave in Britain during the war used their sexual attractiveness to their advantage. Once AWOL and cut off from their military pay, they had no source of income. Since it was illegal under Britain's (and Canada's) wartime regulations to employ deserters, they were forced into the underground economy. Many homosexual British men took advantage of the wartime demographics to pursue romantic and sexual relations with attractive servicemen. Homosexual British authors describe prewar England as sexually repressive and intolerant. Many travelled abroad in search of homosexual relations, most commonly to Germany prior to the Nazi terror. During the war years, the situation was reversed. Monied British homosexuals could remain at

home and enjoy the influx of sexual partners and an environment conducive to sexual transgression. However, there were risks involved for both
servicemen and their lovers.[15]

For some, the Spartan life of a deserter had precedents in Canada. Since
his enlistment in October 1939, Private Robert B of the Perth Regiment had
spent most of his time in Britain either AWOL or in detention for that offence. He told the personnel officer that he had left school after grade eight
during the Depression. Captain Watson recorded that he had spent his subsequent teen years riding the rods in Canada and the United States, living in
hobo jungles, "begging with occasional odd jobs – preyed upon sex perverts." In the same language, the medical officer wrote: "First started preying on sex perverts in 1937 since then has 'worked' in eastern Canada and
San Francisco and Los Angeles." In this formulation, the adult middle-class
homosexual partners became victims of the worldly underclass youth. In
Britain, in 1944, Robert described his life to the military authorities: "I
worry about no one. I live a life to suit myself. I can keep up to the best of
men, drinking. I do not like the army ... I tried to soldier but no one wants
me so I have given that up. When I am free I make a fair amount of extra
money by homosexual methods." Major-General Montague, the judge-
advocate general at Canadian Military Headquarters, complained that
Robert "indulges in homosexual practices; that he has no sense of moral or
social responsibility ... that he is unreliable, self-centered and has a poor attitude towards authority." The Canadian state, which had turned its back
on the unemployed during the Depression, now demanded Robert's un-
qualified allegiance. He had learned to survive during the harsh conditions
of the Depression and was applying that education while soldiering in England. To the authorities, he represented the danger of a man no longer concerned with social dictates. A fallen man was, in their eyes, a great threat to
the social order. Once marked as homosexual, he personified the desires
that successful men controlled. Men such as Robert were not signifiers of
homosexuality because of their effeminacy; instead, their homosexuality
was part of their anti-social character. Indeed, many prided themselves for
not submitting to social pressures.[16]

Canadian military police investigated cases of AWOL in Britain. The army
was interested in how soldiers survived, cut off from their military income.
Since it was illegal to harbour deserters, both military and civilian police
joined in the pursuit of absent soldiers and their employers. Occasionally,
soldiers revealed that their work as prostitutes was far more lucrative than
soldiering. Under questioning by military authorities, a private with the
Cameron Highlanders of Ottawa seemed to brag of his success: "Some

nights I stayed at the Stratmore Hotel, Richmond. The most of the time I have stayed and slept with 'Queers' that I met in Kingston, Richmond and Hammersmith. These 'Queers' have paid me as much as 4 and 5 pounds a night to sleep with them." For this private, homosexual prostitution was the most profitable of a range of activities, which included "bumming off American officers," gambling, and theft. Other soldiers lived with homosexual British men, financially supported by them. One private with the Seaforth Highlanders of Canada described his sojourn "with a fruit what they call a pansy in London." Some Canadian soldiers lived similarly with British women. In both cases, the romances often appear to have been genuine. Sometimes, however, the soldiers were clearly taking advantage of their sexual and romantic attractiveness. In the words of the military authorities, some were indeed "preying" on their British hosts. These strategies for survival recall the patterns of relationships between working-class youth and wealthier men described by historian Steven Maynard in his survey of criminal prosecutions in urban Ontario in the early twentieth century. It is probable that, in some cases, we are witnessing not only the same forms of social interaction, but the same men.[17]

One particularly detailed account sheds light on the sexual orientations and camaraderie of the deserters involved in Britain's gay underground. Privates Stan S and Bill H went AWOL from the Saskatoon Light Infantry in May 1941 and hiked and hitchhiked from Surrey to Manchester. Having only four pounds between them on their arrival in Manchester, they went to the YMCA, where they met Morris M, a German Jew who was working as the restaurant manager. Private Bill later reported: "This man became friendly with us, particularly with [Stan] and when our cash ran out he made immoral suggestions to [Stan]. He paid for our food and beds and [Stan] told me that [Morris] had tried to play around with him but that he refused to have any part of it." Whether or not Stan had resisted Morris M's advances, Morris remained interested in the two Canadian soldiers and offered to see that Bill was also "fixed up" with Captain C, the manager of an aircraft production plant. Bill remembered that at Captain C's flat, "we all had drinks and the captain made suggestions to me and admitted that he was a 'man-lover' or as we call it, a 'fruit' ... Later we had supper and then [Morris] and [Stan] went out and it was clear to me that the Jew was getting jealous of the Captain who also fancied [Stan]." Bill claimed that when he resisted the captain's advances he "was suspicious of me and asked me if I was a crook. I suppose he thought I might put the 'black' on him because I had found out that he was a 'fruit.' " While he admitted taking only two pounds that night, it is clear that both men recognized the captain's vulnerable position.[18]

The underground deserters' economy relied on monied British homosexuals for stability. Whatever their own sexual orientation, deserters entered into the gay subculture in order to identify potential benefactors and gauge the risks involved. Bill reported: "[A]t the YMCA I met Norman [B], a seaman, aged 22, who was also a 'fruit' ... [Norman] told me that [Morris] was quite well off and only did this voluntary work at the YMCA to get hold of young men and boys for immoral purposes." Morris M was connected to a number of middle-class gay men, each interested in using their financial resources to attract lovers. Gay British men had always been vulnerable to blackmail, but the wartime network of military deserters increased both their sexual opportunities and vulnerability, as shown by Bill's next acquaintance:

A couple of days later I met a young chap who I knew as Max [B]. He was in the uniform of the Royal Canadian Artillery with "Canada" on his shoulders. He told me that he was staying with a 'fruit' named Alfred [S] at Flixton. [Alfred] is manager of a shoe department at Lewis's Store at Manchester and is a friend of [Morris]. I became friendly with [Max] or "Pinky" as I used to call him. He told me that he had stolen 17 pounds from [Alfred] and suggested that as our uniforms were getting dirty we should get some new ones and he said he knew where he could get them. We went to Newcastle-under-Lyne and at a barracks there we traded our uniforms and 2 pounds for 2 new battle-dress with some Cameron Highlanders [a British regiment].

Eventually, Alfred forgave Pinky for stealing the money. Rather than turning himself in to his own unit as a deserter, Pinky used Alfred's identity card to join the Royal Welsh Fusiliers. Bill's earlier "fruit" acquaintance, Norman, helped him get an identity card from a man who "said he got them from a Mortuary Attendant who got them from Air-Raid victims." Norman then helped him get a job as a "chucker out" (bouncer) at the Sportsdrome in Manchester.[19]

While Bill's sexual orientation is not clear, the subculture he had entered was not primarily structured around sexual orientation. For instance, the "fruits" Norman and Pinky entered Bill's narrative as comrades. This culture was based more fundamentally on class lines – those who had resources to offer as against those in need. These two groups were secondarily distinguished by age differences. While the orientation of the soldiers varied, the civilians were always homosexual. One homosexual Canadian soldier who frequented London's gay bars during the war observed, "And you would see the occasional Brit in cities, and usually he was in a restricted job, and he wasn't allowed to join the armed forces. But they'd come into the gay bars in cities and they'd pick anybody up and take them home. The guys they picked up weren't gay, they just wanted sex, on their own terms." Beyond the dangers inherent in associating with deserters, including the potential for theft, blackmail, or violence, harbouring runaway soldiers also could bring homosexual men to the unwanted attention of the police. For instance, a single, thirty-nine-year-old owner of a café invited two soldiers to stay with him. When the police found Canadian Army uniforms in his room, he admitted that the men had stayed there. He was charged with "receiving army uniforms and equipment" and "assisting [the soldier] to conceal himself, knowing him to be a deserter," both offences during wartime. The detective who investigated the case reported that this individual "had never previously come under notice of police and it is clear that he assisted these two men because he was carrying on an immoral association with [the soldier], who is known to be a homo-sexual." The police described the soldier as "very well-built," suggesting that he traded on the desirability of his body.[20]

OFFICERS AND THEIR PRIVATES

Wealthy civilians were not alone in their pursuit of attractive young soldiers. Canadian officers had access to a great number of young men and developed an equally wide range of relationships. Captain K was notorious for his pursuit of handsome soldiers within the armoured companies of the Royal Canadian Army Service Corps. Normally, the shower room of the ranks was off limits to officers, but Driver Hiebert described an encounter with Captain K in Aldershot, England, while he showered and the captain looked on: "First of all he commented on the showers, whether they were satisfactory or not, he was walking up the aisle and he approached me on the subject of buggery, and mentioned stuff like corn-holing, and sucking off, and jerking off, and he asked me if I wouldn't jerk him off, he hadn't had intercourse for so long he was uneasy, and I refused, he then offered me ten shillings if I would accept. He walked up and down the showers there, came back several times and asked me if I wouldn't change my mind. I finished my shower and walked out of there." The Canadian Army was a rigidly hierarchical organisation that relied upon obedience to authority. The officer in this instance used his superior rank and access to the soldier for his personal sexual gain. When that was unsuccessful, he reverted to an offer of money, which would have prostituted the soldier.[21]

Queer soldiers' responses to such tactics were governed by the attitude of their superior officers and their own interests. Henri DiPierro, who was a young lieutenant with the Royal Canadian Engineers in England, remembers a French Canadian colonel "who promised his wife in Canada he wouldn't touch another woman while he was overseas but he said nothing about other men. And he used to try and get me to do things sexually to him all the time. It was a rather funny experience because I was young and innocent anyway ... He would come into my room and invite me into his room and take his tiny penis out and ask me to do things to it. Very explicit!" Lieutenant DiPierro interpreted the colonel's advances as an abuse of his constituted authority. While he was discovering and exploring his homosexuality within consensual relations with other servicemen, he took exception to the colonel's presumption: "I was a lieutenant in those days. He was a colonel. I think he thought he could push me around. I just refused." Meanwhile, Bud, an observer with 6 Bomber Group in Yorkshire, was also happily exploring his homosexuality with other aircrew in the RCAF. Although he chose not to accept the propositions of his commanding officer, neither did he resent them: "Wing Commander ... he got killed. He was a nice guy. He sort of had the hots for me too. Nothing happened ... He kept saying, 'Bud, we must.' Well, you know how you get talking, and he said, 'Well, we'll have to go out together and we'll spend the night together.' You know, 'on a weekend pass' sort of thing." Bud interpreted the suggestions of his wing commander as non-coercive, leaving the power to reject or accept in his hands. For Henri, the colonel intended to retain his superior position in sex as in the military chain of command. Although both Bud and Henri declined, they interpreted the proposals differently.[22]

Even when the soldier was inferior in rank and felt constrained by that relationship, the offer of sex was not always discouraged. Upon taking command of his unit, Major Jean-Phillippe K asked Private André P if he would act as his batman. André served in that capacity until he was posted elsewhere. He described an evening in June 1943 when he had arrived at Major Jean-Phillipe's room to return his laundry and polish his buttons: "Il m'a demandé de m'asseoir sur son lit et de débouttonner [sic] mon pantalon. Il m'a dit qu'il aimait les hommes et m'a demandé de le laisser s'amuser et que ce serait en même temps une jouissance pour moi. J'ai déboutonné mes pantalons et j'ai sorti ma verge, il l'a alors sucée. Je n'ai pas refusé vu qu'il était un major et que je travaillais pour lui. Il ne m'a pas demandé de faire quoique ce soit sur sa personne et je ne lui ai rien fait." It is possible that André felt constrained by the superior rank of the major whether or not the experience was pleasurable. However, the evidence recorded here was obtained in court against Private André's will. Moreover, the event could not have been altogether distasteful for him, since, upon returning to Major Jean-Phillippe's unit from a different posting, he again asked to serve as his batman. The major declined the offer. In their sexual relations (as well as in those between Major Jean-Phillippe and another soldier who gave evidence), the military hierarchy was reversed; the major asked to assume the more submissive role of giving sexual pleasure to his subordinates.[23]

SAFE AND UNSAFE SPACE IN ENGLAND

Relationships between older homosexual civilians and young queer servicemen were not necessarily sexual or exploitative. Older men could act as mentors, providing a safe environment to pursue relationships. For instance, when Aubyn was posted in Cambridge with the RCAF, he wrote to a local piano teacher recommended by the university. The professor "wrote right back and he said, 'Oh I'm so delighted to help someone who's Canadian.' ... [H]e said, 'You must come and have lessons with me ... My charge is one packet of cigarettes and that's it.'" Professor Timberlake had transformed his large Cambridge home into a cultural drop-in centre for queer and queer-friendly servicemen: "Well, he had quite a few servicemen that came in for music lessons and there were quite a few of them that knew the score. They were ... mainly American and I was the only Canadian and there were some Britishmen ... He was gay too, of course." On the weekends, the teacher would hold piano recitals "and we'd come in and we'd stay all night." While Professor Timberlake "never made any passes or anything like that" at his guests, he was delighted if romances should grow among them: "And my best friend Harry – Oh, he was nice and we got to know one another and we had a few [sexual] experiences there. Harry and I slept upstairs and Professor Timberlake slept downstairs and we'd stay over the weekend if we had a pass ... He was in the American airforce and ... he was a great guy, very gentle and very sincere." Their relationship was strong enough that they planned to renew it after the war. Unfortunately, Harry "was just home and was demobbed in Chicago less than a month when he was killed in a motor accident. He'd gone through all the war and flown I don't know how many missions."[24]

British homes had been most generous in opening their doors to Allied soldiers; homosexual Britons such as Professor Timberlake could be equally considerate of the special needs of their 'family.' Protected by the professor's status, his private home, and their common interest in music, young

queer servicemen were free to socialize together and perhaps form relationships. Sometimes the music was secondary to the environment. The professor was fond of Aubyn's American lover, for example, and "he composed a
simple piece that Harry could play. Harry was a rank beginner on the piano." In the absence of such a safe meeting place, queer servicemen were
always under the potentially antagonistic gaze of fellow servicemen and
police.

Private Nazaire H also used his talent as a pianist as a way of meeting
other servicemen. His experiences at a pub nearby the First Canadian Division headquarters at Old Heathfield in England demonstrate the dangers
that could accompany even discreet homosexual flirtations in an unpro-
tected environment. During January of 1943, Private Nazaire frequently
played the piano at the Half Moon Hotel in the evenings, accepting requests and drinks from the other Canadian servicemen who gathered there.
On 2 February, Sergeant Gordon C, who was billeted at the hotel, bought
him a drink, a customary sign of appreciation for a pianist, and they began
to get acquainted. While they became increasingly occupied with each
other, two NCOs in the pub dedicated themselves to following the progress
of Nazaire and Gordon's involvement. Already suspicious of Nazaire as a
result of his demeanour and gregariousness, they arranged with the land-
lady to listen at the door of Sergeant Gordon's room later that night for
signs of homosexual impropriety. Bursting into the room, they caught the
servicemen in an act of fellatio. While the majority of the hotel's clientele
may have been unconcerned with the sexual lives of Sergeant Gordon and
Private Nazaire, it required only two corporals to take offence to jeopardize the careers and lives of the two men.[25]

Hiding one's homosexual desires from all but like-minded servicemen
was a common strategy for queer soldiers. While it was not uncommon for
military units to accommodate themselves to the presence of homosexual
comrades, to gain a reputation as queer could be dangerous. Although he
was highly regarded as a soldier in the West Nova Scotia Regiment, Sergeant James's reputation as a "pervert" dogged his career. Twice convicted
by courts martial for indecent conduct, he served detention terms in both
England and North Africa. One July night in 1940 at Cove in England, he
met three soldiers from his regiment on a country road leading to their barracks. As in other similar incidents, he was intoxicated when he asked Private Skanes if he would spend the night with him. Private Skanes asked his
two comrades to come along to James's room. There, according to one of
the soldiers, the sergeant locked the door and said,

"I'll blow all of you if you don't blow on me." Pte. Skanes was sitting on the table and Sgt. [James] was sitting on the bed. Sgt. [James] unbuttoned Pte. Skanes' fly and took his penis out. He gave it a couple of shakes and Pte. Skanes said he guessed it was no use as he had had a couple of drinks of beer to-night. Sgt. [James] got down with his head between Skanes' legs and took it in his mouth. Skanes pushed him back and said "There, that is all I want to know of you, I'll report you in the morning." Sgt. [James] offered us ten shillings that night and ten shillings in the morning not to report him but we wouldn't take it.

At the summary of evidence, Sergeant James asked Skanes, "If you did not want to do this why did you come to my room?" Skanes replied, "To find out the truth about the thing. I had heard rumors of it before … [I]t is pretty hard to keep your ears closed to the public. I have heard it in pubs, inside billets and outside." James had served in France during the First World War and for several years in the permanent force during the interwar period. Although he was clearly known within the regiment as queer, he vehemently denied to all military authorities ever having engaged in any homosexual activity, and perhaps he used alcohol as a tool to distance himself from his own problematic sexuality. His immediate offer of a bribe as soon as he understood that he had been entrapped suggests that he was familiar with the 'rules of engagement.' It is also probable that although he was twice prosecuted for such offences, his offers were normally tolerated or accepted.[26]

Sergeant James may have been looking for more than simply sexual relief. Private Skanes reported that on the road to the barracks, "[h]e asked me to go to his billets and sleep with him for the night." It would appear that Sergeant James's primary need was for affection and, perhaps, emotional support. As it turned out, he found hostility and betrayal. Others were similarly exposed when looking for love within their own unit. Lance Corporal Jeffrey R of the Queen's Own Cameron Highlanders of Canada described the actions that led to his court martial in the spring of 1943 in England:

I was alone in the stores, writing a letter home. Pte. Smith, who was Company runner, on this date, was sitting in the Orderly Room reading a book. Due to the fact that I wished company, and as I had a fire on in my stores, I invited Pte. Smith in. He lay down on my bed and was listening to the radio while I finished writing my letter. After I had finished my letter, I sat on the side of the bed and listened to the radio also. I made advances towards Pte. Smith, and he didn't say anything; he didn't say to stop or go on. I asked him if he wished to stay in the stores all night and he said he would ... I realized at the time that I was doing the wrong thing, but seemed to lose all self-control and will power.

After Private Smith related the event to "one or two of the boys," it reached the ears of the company sergeant major, who ordered an investigation. While Lance Corporal Jeffrey voiced clearer insight into his sexual/emotional needs than had Sergeant James, his choice to fulfil them within his own unit was unfortunate. The power of the social proscription against homosexuality on the individual echoes in Jeffrey's statement that he was most repentant of succumbing to the desire that he conceded to be immoral.[27]

Different levels of discretion could be required by homosexual lovers, depending on the social boundaries that individual regiments or units established. A regiment could be a relatively safe space to pursue a relationship, but homosexual comrades were always vulnerable to enquiries of those outside of the secret. In the course of investigating a case of theft, military police found that Private Jean-Paul D of the Royal 22e Regiment (Vandoos) had purchased a pair of stolen boots from the thief for Private Paul H, also of the Vandoos. They asked why one soldier should buy an expensive present for another. Perhaps their relationship came under increased scrutiny because Private Paul was known in the regiment as "Anna." Private Jean-Paul acknowledged the nature of their relationship under interrogation: "J'ai connu le soldat [Paul] il y a environ un an, au mois d'octobre, a East Preston j'ai commencé a sortir avec le soldat [Paul]. Un soir de paye nous avons été au 'Three Crowns' et on s'est soules. Sur le chemin en revenant, j'ai dit a [Paul]:– 'Susses-tu, oui ou non?' Il m'a repondu 'Oui.' Et nous sommes allés sur le gazon et il m'a sus et je lui ai remis son change [*sic* all]." The framing of Jean-Paul's question to Paul, "Do you suck, yes or no?", suggests that it was not an uncommon request. Jean-Paul said that their intimate relationship had continued for several months. Like Lance Corporal Jeffrey R in the English-speaking unit, he registered a sense of shame over the affair: "Depuis le premier de janvier, je n'ai pas eu de relations intimes avec lui, et j'ai rarement sorti avec lui, parce que je voulais finir cette intimité." While such an expression of remorse would have been to Private Jean-Paul's advantage in the circumstance of his interrogation, it is possible that he saw resistance to his desire for his comrade Paul as a moral obligation. For his part, Private Paul referred to Jean-Paul as "mon meilleur ami" and "mon Chum."[28]

Before the interference of the military police, queer soldiers appear to have been accepted as part of the culture of the Vandoos. When asked by the police about a ring in his possession, Private Paul told the police:

Il y a environs 9 ou 10 mois, j'étais a Londres en passe de 7 jours avec les soldats Belanger G. et Leo Beaudoin. J'ai rencontré un civilien qui m'a dit que son nom était Bob, nous étions dans un "Pub" dans la rue Dean. Nous avons bu pour quelques temps et je l'ai accompagne à sa chambre. J'étais sous l'influence de la boisson. J'ai passé la nui là, et le lendemain matin, on s'est rendu à un restaurant Grecque, là on rencontré Bélanger et Beaudoin. Bob le civilien portait une bague de fiancailles à son doigt, et je lui ai demandé si il voulait me la prêter. Il me l'a prêtée [sic all].

Paul's account makes it clear that Privates Beaudoin and Belanger, whatever their sexual orientations, were privy to his queer romantic activities in London. He told the police that he had continued to see Bob over the subsequent months and that Bob had travelled to Caterham, where Paul was stationed, to visit him. Finally, Bob gave him the engagement ring. When asked by Private Dufour of the regiment where he had obtained it, Paul replied "que c'etait [sic] une bague qui m'avait été donnée par une de mes 'trousse' [sic] à Londres." This casual reference to his "tricks" in London suggests that his homosexuality was part of the regimental culture. Private Paul's queer romantic adventures, inside and outside of the Vandoos, were apparently widely known and accepted within the regiment. Nevertheless, as a result of the military police involvement, he was sentenced to detention for two years for his sexual activities with Private Jean-Paul.[29]

SOLDIERS AND LOCAL BOYS IN EUROPE

Nowhere is the 'truth' of the historical record more passionately debated than in accounts of sexual relations between adults and children. Those who appeal to the courts in later life regarding sexual abuse suffered in childhood are challenged to prove that their memories are accurate. It is often impossible to obtain corroborating evidence. Moreover, accounts of sexual relations between adults and children that appear in the historical judicial record can be especially difficult to interpret. Individuals who appear before courts frame their evidence in ways designed to serve their interests. Those accused of participating in homosexual relations typically claimed to be drunk, asleep, or the victim of assault. The narratives people use to represent their experience reflect cultural assumptions about acceptable and unacceptable behaviour in any historical period. Some historians conclude that the documented record, therefore, reveals nothing beyond the text itself. For them, the study of history becomes a study of the way experience has been framed, rather than a study of actual events. My own reading of textual (and oral) evidence assumes an inherent connection between experience and its representation, notwithstanding the fact that historical actors are often motivated to colour the record in their favour. Courts martial involving soldiers and children contain qualitatively different evidence than those concerned with adult sexual relations. Perhaps because the evidence of children is usually mediated through police officers and court officials, there is often a sense that they do not entirely understand the narratives being employed to frame their experience.

In his study of sexual relations between boys and men in early twentieth-century Ontario, historian Steven Maynard discovered "narrative fragments of both coercion and consent" often residing together in individual court files. As a result, his analysis avoids a facile interpretation of complex relationships between boys and men. Like him, I find that such relations as they appear in court-martial records, personal interviews, and published memoirs resist facile categorization as either totally coercive or consensual. Consent does not always apply here, not only because the sexual relations were partly coercive, but because young children are not capable of consenting, their deference to adult authority making them vulnerable to being manipulated into providing sexual services. The soldiers in these cases were seen to have betrayed the trust that society had bestowed on them as adults, but they were not all treated in the same way. Soldiers were punished according to the nature of the sexual acts performed, whether they had been with a boy or a girl and whether they were tried by civil or martial court. Meanwhile, homosexual veterans often remembered themselves as having been active agents in their childhood sexual experiences, frequently being frightened and excited at the same time.[30]

Several men remembered being the initiators in their earliest sexual experiences with men. Allan remembers that, as a boy in Alberta, "I had an uncle who was staying with us and we were sleeping three to a bed and he used to dream at night and maul me and call me Rosy, which was the name of the girl upstairs. I knew it wasn't a homosexual thing with him and I didn't even know the word, but I was very turned on … I liked feeling his erection and stuff – would play with it until he woke up and realized what was going on and would turn over." Similarly, Peter, who would become a padre in the postwar Canadian Army, fondly recalls his first sexual experience during the Depression in rural Saskatchewan:

I was seven or eight years old and I had nothing to do. Anyway, there was a farmer down the road who was a great friend of my uncle's; his name was Bill too. And so, one Sunday afternoon, I said to my grandmother, "I think I'll walk down to Bill's." "Okay, fine." He was only a mile down the road. And that started a relationship I had with him. And we went to bed together every Sunday afternoon in the summertime ... I loved to go to bed with him. He never touched me; all he wanted to do was cuddle me and let me touch his genitals, which I loved. I thought I'd died and gone to heaven. It was a wonderful time with him ... And he said, "Don't tell anyone about this." ... I wasn't going to tell them anyway.

Recalling such experiences in their adult lives, the men interviewed remembered satisfying their sexual curiosity in relationships with adults. Not all sexual experiences in the home were pleasant, however. One gay veteran remembered being abused by a much older brother until he appealed to their father to rearrange the sleeping assignments.

The sexual possibilities that boys found outside of the home could include an element of danger. Allan remembers that when he was thirteen and living in Calgary, "a cousin of one of the boys was down there [St George's Island] and he told us there was a soldier down there and he was giving candy to kids if they would play with his dick." Allan recalls being "curious":

So, anyway, I went back down to the island by myself one day and went for a swim in the river and wanted to go for a walk on one of the little islands. I was curious, so I went. He sucked me off and then he wanted to fuck me. And I tried and it hurt, so I backed off, but he'd given me a whole dime to meet him the next day. A dime was a fair amount of money, you could go to a movie for that. He told me to meet him in the washroom, the men's washroom. So, I did that. We repeated the same thing but I didn't let him try to fuck me this time ...
Q: Was he attractive to you?
A: Well, I think I was more curious ... I was terrified to tell you the truth.

The memories of these sexual experiences contain elements of pleasure, fear, fondness, and disgust. The same range of responses is suggested in the wartime military files documenting sex between men and children. However, while the military documents only hint at the active role that children might play in such circumstances, the memories offered by some men interviewed tend to focus on their agency.[31]

Various sexual acts were interpreted and punished differently. Allan successfully resisted the soldier's attempt to penetrate him anally. The act of sodomy with a boy as the receptive partner was the most harshly punished of all sex-related crimes during the war, including rape. For instance, a Canadian soldier who was convicted by court martial for forcing an eight-year-old English girl to perform oral sex on him was sentenced to eighteen months detention, whereas another who sodomized an eleven-year-old boy was sentenced by the British courts to seven years at hard labour. It is difficult to unravel the factors that may have contributed to such a disparity in sentences. Perhaps the British court was intent on controlling Canadian soldiers who were misbehaving in England. However, that sentence was the harshest imposed on a Canadian soldier for sexual misconduct by any British court.[32]

It is not clear why the Canadian military chose to prosecute cases involving local children. According to military regulations, these could have been handed over to the civilian criminal courts. It appears that when the crimes were discovered by military personnel, the military chose to keep them out of the British courts and press. When such crimes were discovered by civilian police forces, the British exercised their right to prosecute. Private M was court-martialled for "disgraceful conduct of an indecent kind." The eight-year-old girl he was accused of assaulting testified against him. While she may have been coached by the prosecuting officer, there remains an innocence in her words that suggests sexual inexperience:

A: He took me into a great big bunch of tall grass and then he undone his trousers and pulled out that big long thing. He told me to suck it.
Q: What else did he do?
A: He sucked my little thing.
Q: Was there anything else?
A: No.
Q: Did any other soldier come along at that time?
A: Yes. He asked him to let me go.

It is difficult to believe that, in using these words, she is framing her story in a narrative form calculated to be effective with the court. At the same time, her words reflect her sexual education in British society. While she surely knew the names of other body parts, genitals were identified simply as "things." Since the court members found Private M guilty and sentenced him to eighteen months detention, it is probable that they accepted the girl's story that she had performed oral sex on the soldier. However, if the sentences were indicative of the seriousness of the crime, that action was deemed considerably less depraved than Private Arthur's abuse of an eleven-year-old boy.[33]

Private Arthur saw battle in Sicily, Italy, and France and was returned to England for hospitalization in May 1945. He had been raised by a highly respected family in western Canada. His father was the town mayor, and his two brothers were distinguishing themselves in the RCAF. Wondering how such an exemplary youth could be accused of sodomizing an eleven-year-old boy, military authorities from all three services suggested that "perhaps [he had] learned this abominable practice in his many strange environments." It was too late to claim that he had been unfit for combat and unacceptable to imagine that a fine Canadian soldier could behave so repulsively. It was most consoling to imagine that this foreign vice had infected the soldier on foreign soil. While it is entirely possible that Private Arthur's experiences on the Continent had influenced his sexual behaviour, his case fits into a range of homosexual relationships that were part of Canadian and British culture.[34]

Private Arthur had been billeted at the home of Mr and Mrs M in 1940. The assistant JAG personally investigated the case after Private Arthur's conviction and reported that the couple had taken "a great fancy to him and he has made their place his second home ever since, having spent several leaves there." In June 1943 Arthur had accompanied the Canadian troops to Sicily. He had fought in the front lines until captured in France. On 11 May 1945, he was returned to England. He soon renewed his relationship with his adopted family, visiting them on leave and introducing them to his friends. In early August, however, Mrs M received letters from Private Arthur from an English prison, in which he wrote: "I am not going to tell you why I am in here or how long I will be here, that is, not just yet anyway." Her emotional support was deeply valued: "Thanks a million for the letter that I received last night, I was never so glad to receive a letter in all my life. Thank God I have a friend." Although he was not ready to divulge his crime, he described how he was trying to position it for her, and perhaps, for himself: "What I did Edna wasn't anything crooked. I didn't steal anything or attempt to harm anyone. What I did was just a foolish prank while under the influence of liquor." While he was able to describe his crime in such innocuous terms, his letters also betray his comprehension of its gravity. He swore that he could never return to Canada because of his shame and he hoped to settle in Italy upon his release from prison. A "foolish prank," once discovered, had been transformed into an abominable crime. Private Arthur's rationalization of his molestation of an eleven-year-old was much like that of men who buried the shame of consensual homosexual relations with their peers with alcohol and self-denial.[35]

On four occasions, he had met the boy at a public lavatory next to a pub. Mediated through the police investigator is the account of the boy, describing their first meeting:

About six weeks ago I was looking through the window of the dance hall at the Wheatsheaf at the people dancing. I was standing near the open window by the gents lavatory, I think it was a Saturday evening. After a short while I went into the lavatory and while I was in there a Canadian soldier came in. He said to me, "Hullo" and I said "Have you any gum chum?" He said, "no gum chum." He then said, "Do you want some easy money?" and I said, "What is it[?]" and he said "Come in here" and took me into the lavatory and locked the door behind me saying "Don't you shout." He then undid my belt and took down my trousers and began shaking my dicky for a few minutes. He then undid his fly buttons and took out his and sat on the seat and pulled me on top of him and put his in between my legs and worked it up and down and I felt something wet on my legs. He told me to get off and he put his dicky away and rubbed the wet off between my legs with his handkerchief, and told me to pull my trousers up, gave me two shillings and said, "Don't say nothing about it" and walked out.

This account is substantially the same as that given by Private Arthur, both before the trial and afterwards from his prison cell, with the exception of his admonition to the boy to not shout. The police transcribed the details of the three other encounters from both sources. From the boy's perspective, the police wrote that Private Arthur forced him in each instance to cooperate, that he "caught hold of me by my belt and pulled me into the lavatory" and covered his mouth to muffle the boy's calls. Private Arthur, while in accord with all of the material evidence, claimed that the boy had agreed to meet him on each occasion in return for chewing gum and money. It seems less likely that the boy would have been repeatedly overpowered in the same public place than that he simply returned to collect the money and gum. In fact, the military's judge-advocate, who witnessed the proceedings and reported to Canadian Military Headquarters, considered it a fact in evidence that at least two of the meetings had been "by arrangements."[36]

It is impossible to know, at this distance, how the boy understood these encounters at the time and their ultimate effect on him. If the police manipulated the evidence so as to suggest the soldier's physical coercion, it would make that question all the more difficult to answer. At their third meeting, the soldier attempted to penetrate the boy, causing him pain. Private Arthur maintained that the boy returned of his own free will the fourth time and asked that they do it the original way, since penetration was painful. The police, however, positioned the boy absolutely as a victim. To some extent, they may have been driven to do this by legal considerations. Men could not be charged with having sexual relations with a minor (a child under sixteen) if the minor was a boy. Since all homosexual relations were criminal, the law did not stipulate an age of majority for male-male sex. The boy was either a victim or a criminal (juvenile delinquent) guilty of sexual immorality. His statements, although perhaps coloured by the interests of the police, suggest that the episodes had financial as well as sexual import for him.[37]

During the same period, Private C was working as a movie projectionist for the Canadian Army in England, and he would welcome local boys to join him in the projection room. On 1 February 1945, four boys went up to watch the evening's movie with him. As the movie ran, he fondled the penises of the boys. Their testimony at his court martial suggests that his behaviour was not entirely unwelcome. Thirteen-year-old Jack sat on Private's lap for the entire show. He was questioned about this experience:

Witness: ... I sat on the arm of the chair. He said if I sat on his lap I could see better and so I sat on his lap and he started to play with my penus [sic]. I didn't say anything to him. He asked me if I had any sisters and I told him I had two one 7 and the other 10 years old. He asked me where my father was and I said he was in Chesire.
Q. Did you ask him to stop playing with your penus [sic]?
A. I told him to shut up.

As he relates the experience, Jack seems to have been more concerned with the movie dialogue than with the sexual groping. To that end, he was apparently not so intimidated by Private C that he could not make his wants known. While Private C did "shut up" for the rest of the first reel, he also continued to play with Jack's penis. The boys who did not welcome the activity held their coke bottles in their crotch, successfully impeding his access. According to their testimony, they discussed the soldier's behaviour among themselves and felt, as a group, in control of the situation.[38]

While there was a clear tendency among some military officials to equate homosexuality with paedophilia, there is little evidence to support the claim. Wartime military psychiatrists and administrators who assumed a connection saw both as signs of degeneracy. Most of the sexual crimes against minors committed by Canadian soldiers that were uncovered by the police were directed against girls, but it was not always clear whether the soldiers were attracted to the gender or the youth, or both, of the children. For instance, in December 1948 Donald Staley was executed in Lethbridge, Alberta, for the murder of a six-year-old boy, but when he was a soldier with the Canadian Army stationed in England in 1945, he was imprisoned for eighteen months for sexually assaulting a five-year-old girl.[39]

The most detailed account of a wartime relationship between a Canadian serviceman and a boy is the basis of a novel by Rudi Van Dantzig, *For a Lost Soldier*. Van Dantzig confirms that the novel "is a true story, told more or less the way it developed and felt – for me anyway." In 1944 Jeroen is sent from Amsterdam, where food is in short supply, to rural Friesen in the north of Holland to live with a fishing family for the duration of the war. There, he passes through puberty and suddenly becomes aware of his body's desire for the sight, smell, and touch of his neighbourhood friend, who has been sent to a nearby farm. Dantzig eloquently describes Jeroen's confusion at this unexpected and inexplicable response to his friend's body. On several occasions, while alone with his friend, he panics in the face of this inchoate sensual desire. When he has a wet dream one night, he begins vaguely to comprehend his friend's earlier allusions to the pleasures offered by the body's genitals. His sexual pleasure is accompanied by an equal measure of shame. While he struggles to find words to describe his passionate need to be near his friend, there is no one with whom he can discuss his longing.[40]

When Friesen is liberated from the Germans, the Dutch hold celebrations in honour of their freedom and the Canadian soldiers. The local people look upon their liberators with gratitude, curiosity, and a measure of awe. One soldier, Walt, offers Jeroen chewing gum and favours him above the other boys by lifting him first into an armoured car. Jeroen is frightened of the foreign, adult soldiers and runs away. However, on the way home, he begins to see his ordeal as a "glorious adventure" : "I forget how passive and terrified I had been, how, paralysed with fear, I had just allowed it all to happen, and how I had run away as fast as possible." Already, before Walt makes sexual advances towards him, Jeroen is both captivated and frightened by the soldiers. Also, Van Dantzig makes it clear that Jeroen's fascination and dread of his own homosexual passions preceded Walt's arrival. Although related by Jeroen (remembered in adulthood, of course), their sexual affair can be considered from both his and Walt's viewpoints.[41]

Behind a secluded and unfamiliar barn, Walt first pulls Jeroen towards him and kisses him passionately: "Then I am aware of real fear, a panic that pierces straight through me: I should never have gone with him." Walt's actions articulate the desire that Jeroen had not yet brought into focus: "Unspoken and formless, it had been present from the very start, it had been lying in wait all along and now it had pounced." The physical intimacy of lovemaking repulses Jeroen: "The grating surface of his jaw rasps across my skin, crushing my eyes and tearing my mouth"; "He is licking the inside of my ears, I think, and they're filthy, when did I last wash them? I am filled with shame, not because of the tongue licking my ear, but because of the yellow that sometimes comes out of my ear." However, it is the psychological intimacy that most distresses him: "We melt and fuse together, he turns liquid and streams into me. I look into strange, wild eyes right up close to my own, searching me. I am being turned inside out, shaken empty." Jeroen is left alone in his discovery of the emotional and physical power of sex, for he and the soldier speak no common language.[42]

Although Jeroen is frightened of the unknown physical rituals that accompany love, he nevertheless seeks his company and eventually falls in love with him. Finding Walt sunbathing on a dyke, he sits next to him and is embarrassed when Walt catches him admiring his body. When Walt takes Jeroen's hand and guides it over his body, including his growing erection, the boy resists, wanting to escape. However, when Walt's comrades join them at the dyke and Jeroen later sees, from a distance, one of them performing fellatio on Walt, he becomes jealous: "The soldier is pummelling Walt's stomach with quick short thrusts, grimly and silently at work as if giving him artificial respiration. I know exactly what is happening, I know from my suspicions and vague fantasies. And yet these baffling and ominous goings-on make me ill at ease; why does Walt let him do it, has he forgotten that I am here?" Ultimately, Jeroen wants to be liberated from his life by Walt. He fantasizes that Walt will take him away from school, his families (adopted and natural), and Holland and become his protector and lover. When the Canadians leave Friesen, he is devastated to find that Walt has abandoned him.[43]

Through Jeroen's eyes, we see a small group of carefree, playful Canadian soldiers at ease with each other in their homosexuality. He watches from the "safe distance" of the dyke as Walt and two other soldiers romp below: "Walt comes running back out of breath and both of them fall into the grass, fighting and kicking like schoolboys. Then both the soldiers grab Walt's arms and pull the wet shirt off him. Walt struggles to break free and kicks out with his legs. Yet he is laughing." He continues to watch as their boisterous play becomes sexual. In that historical moment in Europe when the daily routines of life were suspended, both liberators and liberated took liberties that had been proscribed in their earlier lives. For Jeroen, it meant a unique coming-out experience that, for all its tensions, he cherished once it had ended. For Walt and his comrades, the stresses of combat and the euphoria of success in northwest Europe may have combined to lift their self-imposed restraints at the same moment that opportunities for various intimate relationships were presented.[44]

A young soldier with the Royal Canadian Corps of Signals, also in Holland during the liberation, relates his own affair with a local boy: "In Holland, I had a boy. And ... we had lots of good times. We had sex together. We played ... And one time I was walking with him and the other kids starting hollering at him and then I never saw him again. They were accusing him of having an affair ... They made fun of him: 'Sucking off the soldiers again, eh?' It was all – there was nothing vicious about it. And I had very nice Dutch friends." Since their affair had ended as a result of the chiding of his mates, their relationship was likely socially problematic for the soldier's young lover. Nevertheless, it is notable that, like Jeroen, he seems to have been an active agent in his relationships with the liberating soldiers. Unlike Jeroen's, his interest in a soldier did not go unnoticed within his Dutch community. The negative attention his affair aroused was possibly less welcome than the anxiety felt by Jeroen in his isolation.[45]

Battle conditions in much of the European campaign facilitated anonymous sexual relations. Both soldiers and local inhabitants could avoid severe social and legal repercussions by engaging in sexually transgressive acts with one another rather than within their own group. The threat of exposure was reduced when sexual partners belonged to exclusive social communities such as army units and remote villages. The danger was further reduced by the knowledge that the soldiers' presence was temporary. Such was the situation for the following soldier passing through Ravenna in northern Italy: "I remember once up there I went to a stone factory, a stone quarry, still operating, doing the civilian thing, making stones. And a couple of old guys and a young kid, sixteen or fifteen or something, he was there. And I huddled him into the back room and let him have his way with me ... And I went on my way and never came back." The soldier's account makes it clear that the young Italian was a willing participant. While younger, he assumed the active sexual role, considered dominant. Similarly, back in England, the innocence of adolescence was sometimes called into question. In reviewing one case of a Canadian soldier charged with indecent assault against a sixteen-year-old English boy, Major-General Montague, JAG, argued that "it is difficult to regard the boy ... as anything other than a definite accomplice." However, Captain Ruddy, also of Canadian Military Headquarters' JAG office, thought that the boy's obvious mental limitations should be taken into account by the court. He suggested that "his mental capacity might bring him to consent to some degree." In other words, age was used as a marker of worldliness, intelligence, power, and, therefore, responsibility. Such a view was challenged by the existence of simple-minded men and worldly boys.[46]

THE CONTINENT AND WAR

The army's first Canadian concert party unit, known popularly as "The Tin Hats" consisted of two female impersonators, Trixie (Bill Dunstan) and Trilby (Johnny Haewood), and an eight-piece band. From the beginning of 1942 until the end of the war, they played to formations from all services in England, Italy, and northwest Europe under very demanding conditions – blackouts and air raids in England and hastily constructed tents and amphitheatres on the Continent. In the first eleven months of their career, they performed two hundred shows before a total of 87,030 military personnel. As the war progressed and they were sent to entertain troops in action, their schedule increased to two shows daily. Both impersonators were thin and graceful and presented themselves as glamour girls. Their performance material makes it clear that they exploited the romantic potential of that role. One program lists Trilby performing "Ma, He's Making Eyes at Me" and Trixie singing "Apple Blossom Time" and "Yum Yum." Audiences responded enthusiastically. The war diary for the unit reported that in April 1942 seventy gunners from the 1st Heavy Anti-aircraft Battery "would not stop their applause in order that the concert could be completed." At Aldershot, "the person announcing the show told the audience that there were female impersonators on the bill. This did not add to the easy running of the show." By disrupting the 'natural' alignment of sex and gender roles, female impersonators aroused passions in their audiences that could be hard to contain.[47]

Johnny Haewood (Trilby) used his work as a female impersonator to launch a successful theatrical career after the war. His colleague remembers, "He was primarily a dancer and gay. He sang with us as well. He did a song and dance but as a female. Later on, after the war, he stayed in England and joined with a troop of girl dancers ... He went to New York for some time. He did the choreography for *The Boyfriend* which was quite a successful show, and *Irma la Douce*." While Johnny was actively homosexual during his service with the Tin Hats, the troop's other impersonator was straight. However, Bill Dunstan's stage persona, Trixie, convinced some soldiers that he was sexually available. Recalling a party hosted by the Loyal Edmonton Regiment, he says, "I remember an occasion in Italy where a very big fellow spoke rather affectionately to me and he wanted to know what I did for entertainment and I said, 'Well, I screwed,' and he said he was going to do that to me and I said, 'Like hell you are,' and he offered to punch me in the nose if I wouldn't ... he wanted me to go out with him in a jeep and pick up a few Germans. And I'm sure he wasn't too intent on that, but I said no."

Bill was insulted by the infantryman's presumption. He felt that he had been threatened with rape and resented the attack on his dignity: "This pugnacious type – I went to see him the next day and told him that wasn't my style and I resented it. So he said he didn't remember a thing about it, he was drunk." To have been exposed as queer by a man in a dress may have been too great a challenge to face sober. Meanwhile, Bill was not insulted by other, more gentlemanly overtures from soldiers. But clearly, some wrongly assumed that a man who could so effectively invert his gender could also invert his sexuality. Whether they interpreted their sexual overtures as homosexual depends on whether they were responding to Bill as a man or a woman. For those unwilling to acknowledge their socially repulsive desire, a female impersonator allowed them to have sex with a man but to maintain that they had been attracted by his feminine traits.[48]

The closer one moved to the centre of the masculinist world, the more difficult it became to express homosexual desire. An infantryman was a man and, therefore, not homosexual. 'Homosexual' was not a subset of the category man; rather it was that which real men defined themselves against. In the military, infantry units were the nucleus of masculinity. While the Canadian military opened many positions to women for the first time during the Second World War, it emphatically excluded them from the job of killing the enemy. This remained the burden and privilege of men. Of course, queer men served in infantry units as they existed everywhere else, and they counted themselves among the 'men' of their regiments. But society resisted any acknowledgment of that presence. Records reveal that some actively homosexual infantrymen forged roles for themselves in their units only by a common agreement that their transgressions would be overlooked. For the most part, they merged into the 'men' of their units, a category already, and inflexibly, defined as heterosexual.

From 1943 until 1945, Hugh fought with the Seaforth Highlanders of Canada in Italy, serving at the core of an intensely arduous campaign. In fact, Hugh participated in arguably the most severe conditions of the war, fighting alongside Smokie Smith on the Savio River on the night he won the Victoria Cross. Hugh remembers with ambivalence his military experiences as a homosexual man: "It was a rough life all the way through, to tell you the truth. But I did love the army." Typical of homosexual men, he saw its appeal as "the comradeship that you had in the army – not necessarily on a sexual basis." A sexual connection to other men could not be reconciled within the brotherhood of comrades: "As far as the army days, it's a matter of going out drinking and not going back to camp or staying at a hotel because you're drunk ... And even then, you know, if something did take

Bill Dunstan as Bill Dunstan. Private Bill Dunstan could arouse passions in soldiers as both a man ...

... and a woman. Bill Dunstan as "Trixie." Both photographs courtesy of Bill Dunstan.

place, the next morning, neither one would speak about it. It was something that didn't happen. It was a crazy situation." When he had "a chance to stay out overnight," Hugh remembers sleeping with a "young Italian boy." Parsing his sex life from his world of comradeship and fighting was, for Hugh, the most viable option. Others took greater chances, and military records reveal the dangers involved. Captain Eby of the 48th Highlanders of Canada testified at the court martial of Private M: "I have known Pte [M] since 28 Nov 43. He came to my platoon at that time. He has been a very willing and hard working soldier. He was through the heavy fighting crossing the Moro River and afterwards, and as long as I was with him, he did his work extremely well without any urging." The night of 21 February 1944, Private M and the rest of his platoon were billeted in a house in a rest area, played cards and sang around a fire. Late in the evening, Private M fell asleep and Private H took him to bed. With the rest of the house asleep, the two shared the same bed and made love. Their groans were heard by the company's new officer, Lieutenant Cox, who laid charges. If men did not voluntarily repress their homosexual desires, some military authorities could be quick to force compliance.[49]

Men who chose to combine sexual and affectional needs within an infantry unit came up against strong resistance from those who would not sanction the possibility of such a connection. Nevertheless, military records leave a trail of the successes of some soldiers on the front lines in achieving sexual relationships with their comrades, to the discomfort of some others. These relationships could be carried out during periods of very stressful combat conditions. The relation between that environment and homosexual activity is difficult to gauge. For Hugh, who came to see himself as exclusively gay, the relative lack of homosexual activity during his army career and the fact that his few sexual encounters were thoroughly unromantic were results of the constraint of serving in a masculinist, anti-homosexual environment. He effectively controlled his homosexual desires throughout the brutal Italian campaign. It is possible, however, that soldiers who were more emotionally affected by the war – those who experienced battle exhaustion – found that their resistance to loving other men had been lowered.

Private Joseph landed in Sicily with the Carleton and York Regiment and was wounded soon after. He related his battle history at his court martial: "After hospital I rejoined the unit in November and saw action at Ortona, the Dundee Cross Roads ... During the Hitler Line battle I was sent to the M.O. because of nerves from shell shock and he sent me to 14 [Canadian] Gen[eral] Hospital." Joseph was assigned to a special employment company upon release. On the night of 22 July 1944, he visited his friend Private Romeo at his former unit with a large bottle of cognac. The two had fought together on the line throughout the previous winter. That night, under a blanket along the Unit Lines, they had prolonged sexual relations with each other. With almost no attempt to conceal themselves, they continued their lovemaking despite the fact that two different soldiers interrupted them, lighting matches to be sure that they were indeed two men, and not a woman and a soldier. In fact, Joseph and Romeo resented the intrusions, telling the meddlers to "put the light out" and leave them alone. Their apparent disregard for convention may have been a consequence of the fact that society's rules had already been disordered by their combat experiences. Barriers to acts otherwise proscribed by society – such as killing – had been challenged and broken, often at the cost of much mental anguish. Many soldiers who had previously been indoctrinated to see homosexuality as another vice became less accepting of society's valuations of right and wrong.[50]

Italy also challenged the men of the Cape Breton Highlanders with severe hardship. The courts martial that resulted from the charges preferred by one outraged NCO reveal that a number of front-line soldiers consistently engaged in homosexual relations. Lovers shared each other's pup tents at night and organized their sleeping arrangements in order to be with their preferred comrade. The evidence from the trials also offers insights into the needs that their sexual play was addressing. Most sexual encounters were prolonged affairs and involved a variety of activities; the men were clearly making love as opposed to simply relieving sexual tensions. At their trials, the accused offered no defence other than character witnesses. Their officers praised them as soldiers – "one of the best in my section," "did duty cheerfully," "dependable and willing worker," "always smartly turned out" – and as men – "seemed to have many friends in pl[atoon] – noticed him laughing and joking with men," "good living soldier," "have been buddies for long while." The silence of the accused in the face of the charges is symptomatic of an inability to accommodate the reality of homosexual desires and relations to the requirements of masculine environments. That there was no sanctioned social role for them, however, does not mean that these men were unable to satisfy their needs. Under the trauma of front-line combat, soldiers sought and received physical comfort from each other, notwithstanding the psychological, social, and legal barriers.[51]

Some homosexual soldiers fighting in Europe eschewed any thought of love or romance because of the dangers of exposure. Bert Sutcliffe, who had recently come out to himself in the exciting atmosphere of London, chose to bury his desires throughout the Normandy campaign. Others looked outside their unit. A signalman's memory of one incident helps us to understand the fleeting, impromptu connections that could be made in each new location throughout the two years of the slow-moving Italian campaign: "In a village in Italy, I went downtown one night because we were billeted nearby and I saw a soldier standing at the corner. He propositioned me and I returned. He sucked me off and I thought it was great. I hadn't had my cock sucked for some time ... And of all things, I went downtown the next night and there he was again. He just, 'Oh, you again' – standing in the same corner." It is evident that the soldier was using a corner in the village to cruise for homosexual contacts, and it is probable that the men in his unit were aware of his activities. In the context of the Italian campaign, in which the army often exercised little control over its soldiers, his queer behaviour might have been less remarkable than it would have been back in Canada. Bob, an RCAF flying officer seconded to the RAF, remembers that "in Casanza, a wonderful little town, the town square, [it was] surprising how many people you would see who you knew who would be cruising around the square ... at night." In such environments, queer servicemen formed a community based on desire.[52]

After Italy's surrender to the Allies, Italian civilians looked for business opportunities that might bring in Allied currency. Bob remembers a variety of enterprises serving the homosexual military market. Attendants who collected money at public toilets could easily be bribed to stand watch while two men used one *gabinetto*. Near Garibaldi Square in Naples, an Italian woman rented a bedroom by the half hour to servicemen and their male lovers, either locals or other servicemen: "And not only that but for an extra couple of hundred lyra she had a peephole where you could see what was happening in the bedroom that she was renting to others like you. And I visited there about three or four times and after awhile you don't care who's looking at you if you don't see them." A nearby bar "was wild: soldiers pretending they were in drag and all this type of thing." Bob remembers that bar as being very similar to 'Momma's' in the Galleria Umberto in Naples, described by John Horn Burns in his wartime portraits of Italy. Burns's fictionalized account of a real establishment and the characters that congregated there offers insights into the gay culture created by Allied servicemen in wartime Italy. In 1944, despite being harassed by military police because of her gay clientele, Momma's was allowed to open, as were other bars, from 4: 30 to 7: 30 daily. Burns felt that "[h]er crowd had something that other groups hadn't. Momma's boys had an awareness of having been born alone and sequestered by some deep difference from other men. For this she loved them. And Momma knew something of those four freedoms the Allies were forever preaching. She believed that a minority should be left alone."[53]

Burns obviously had an intimate knowledge of the bar and was a keen observer of the types of men who frequented it. In eloquent detail, he describes, from Momma's point of view, the clientele and the dynamics that governed their behaviour. Detailed accounts of the Allied homosexual culture are rare, but Burns's work is an excellent source of insights into queer types, psyches, and social relations, one that has been enthusiastically endorsed by an RCAF officer who was himself intimate with Naples in 1944. The men who assembled at Momma's in the evenings to drink, cruise, and perform for each other were as much influenced by the hierarchies of rank and gender as were the militaries and societies that deprecated them. However, since love, sexuality, and gender performance were all concentrated in one sex, new roles emerged particular to the homosexual military world.

Momma's was ordered around a relationship between the masculine and feminine. At one pole were those most unashamedly in search of 'real men.' The most aggressive in their quest were conspicuous by their adoption of feminine markers of dress and speech – the queens or Nellies. There were many expressions of camp, but Burns describes two ageing British sergeants, Esther and Magda, as the most notable. They are as despised as they are despising: "Their conversation was a series of laments and groans and criticisms of everyone else present. They called this dishing the joint. They were disdainful and envious and balefully curious all at the same time." Their willingness to acknowledge their dependence on real men for love and support marks them as feminine. The tragedy of their lives lies in the paradox that when they succeed in seducing a real man, they demonstrate that he was a counterfeit, for a real man would never sleep with other men. Momma identifies "a lost air about them that made her prefer not to look at them, as though the devil had put her a riddle admitting of no solution, and a forfeit any way she answered it."

The queens see themselves in competition for men with the local equivalent of their British type: "An Italian contingent always came to Momma's on schedule. They entered with the furtive gaiety of those who know they aren't wanted, but have set their hearts on coming anyhow. They wore shorts and sandals and whimsical little coats which they carried like wraps around their shoulders, neglecting to put their arms into the sleeves. Momma knew that her Allied clientele didn't care for them ... They just sat around and mimicked one another and sniggered and looked hard at the Allied soldiery." They include former military men and *carabiniere* whose

muscles are overlaid with "scented silk or pongee." The British sergeants
compete with them for supremacy in camp style: " 'Why the nerve of you
Wop queens! Glamor!? Why you've got as much allure as Gracie Fields in
drag.' " The author, who generally sympathizes with the Italians in the face
of Allied arrogance, has them simply laugh in response: "This laughter
hadn't a hollow ring. It was based on the assumption that anything in life
can be laughed out of existence." In fact, the psychological well-being of
queer Canadian soldiers often rested on that basic human capacity.

The opposite pole of the British and Italian queens enters the bar in the
persons of parachutists and sailors, and immediately Momma is frightened
that there will be trouble: "From the way they shot around their half-closed
eyes she knew that this wasn't the place for them. They had an easiness and
a superiority about them as though they were looking for trouble with infi-
nite condescension." Their sense of masculine entitlement is conveyed by
the observation that they were "taking up more cubic space than they
should have." The camp element in the bar welcomes the tension. A flamboyant black American, a second lieutenant, exclaims, " 'Gracious …
men!' " Magda, the British sergeant, pines, " 'Look Esther … look at the essence of our sorrow … What we seek and can never have' … And each side
hates the other. The twain never meet except in case of necessity. And they
part with tension on both sides." When one of the 'men' – a parachutist –
understands that they are surrounded by queens, he "flipped a wrist, and
bawled: 'Oh saaaay, Nellie!' " Soon the Italians are upon them, lighting
their cigarettes, "a swirling ballet of hands and light and rippled voices."
Heterosexual norms are again reversed in that it is the queens who actively
pursue the men and perform such courtship rituals as lighting their cigarettes. This twist allows the men to retain the disinterested posture that
keeps them from being marked as homosexual.

In between these masculine/feminine poles is an assortment of queer men
who define themselves less rigidly on gender lines. One blond English youth
broods at the bar, sipping wine, "the handsomest and silentest boy
Momma'd ever seen … Momma wondered if at Tobruk or El Alamein
someone in the desert night had cut his soul to pieces. He'd loved once –
perfectly – someone, somewhere. Momma would cheerfully have slain
whoever had hurt him so." He arouses an Italian count pining for his lost
Axis love: " 'You look so much like the German officer. I was happy with
him. He said he was happy with me … Would you like sometimes to come
to my house in the Vomero, sir?' " A South African lance corporal an-
nounces his marriage to the Grenadier Guardsman who saved his life in Tu-
nisia. A British marine, a boxer, "observed everyone with a cool devotion"

and is "on the most basic and genial terms with himself and the world." In this community of men are those who define themselves, in varying degrees, according to whom they love, how they see themselves, and how they want others to see them. With all of the evidence before her, the "masculine and the feminine weren't nicely divided in Momma's mind as they are to a biologist. They overlapped and blurred in life. This trait was what kept life and Momma's bar from being black and white."

The patrons define themselves as men, but through their class. In the military, rank is largely coincident with social class. Only men from the most active and hazardous formations – in this case, parachutists and sailors – can fulfil the desire of the queens for a real man. Real men are necessarily of working-class origin. They embody manliness: it is their courage, daring, and physical strength upon which the nation ultimately depends for protection. The essence of femininity for the queens is a need to be protected in a dangerous world. Paradoxically, they turn for protection to the very element in society that most immediately threatens their security – the real men who protect their ranks against the taint of homosexuality. Their entry into the bar is filled with the tension that derives from uncertainty as to whether they will attack the patrons or rescue them. To the British sergeant, they are "the basis of life and love and cruelty and death."

Officers also make their presence felt at Momma's, projecting images of manliness in keeping with the functions associated with their rank: command and administration. There are two sophisticated French lieutenants with their sailors in tow. A "distinguished" major from the medical corps and a second lieutenant who was commissioned for valour in combat at Monte Cassino wear wedding bands but prefer not to speak about their wives in America. The "climax of every evening" is the entrance of Captain Joe, who "stalked cool and sombre in his tank boots, a green bandana tucked round his neck in the negligence of magnificence," and his devoted lover, a young Florentine, whose "faces complemented one another as a spoon shapes what it holds." Their devotion and ease with each other gives "out a peace, a wild tranquillity." The captain describes their success in life as a function of self-acceptance. Happiness, he tells Momma, "is a compromise, signora, between being what you are and not hurting others ... Genius knows its own weaknesses and hammers them into jewels."

Burns observed a diversity of men who had cultivated unique relationships with their homosexuality, the objects of their love, and the world at large. The types of men and homosexual relationships he describes are also found in the military records and in interviews with queer veterans. While some relationships were ideally structured upon a marriage of masculine

and feminine, most did not assign fixed gender roles to either partner. The
fact that biological males sought each other for sexual pleasure and emotional fulfilment qualifies the relationships as homosexual. But masculine
and feminine traits were not simply defined, so that it does not follow that
male homosexuality also entailed a desire for the masculine. Most markers
of gender were superficial, expressed through dress, gestures, and speech.
Gender assignment was most clearly a function of self-image and presentation: a queen was willing to see himself/herself, and be seen, as feminine,
while a real man identified inflexibly as male. When a real man toyed with
feminine gestures, it only highlighted his masculinity, much as blackface ac-
cents the whiteness of a performer. Attributes that stand outside of gender
(although expressed through gendered individuals), such as compassion,
patience, and humour, could be more alluring than the more commonly
recognized masculine qualities of strength and aggression. Men were attracted to a range of physical and behavioural characteristics in others:
older were attracted to younger, younger to older, and like to like; some felt
comfortable when they outranked their lovers, others looked to superior
officers for love, most loved within their peers; some veterans remembered
the personality of a wartime lover, others his appearance, others the sexual
play. Most significant is the great diversity in desires and behaviours.

CONCLUSION

The most obvious and vocal displays of homosexuality became the stereo-
type and stood for the totality of homosexual experience in the popular
consciousness. In Canada, fairies and queens have largely occupied that
space throughout the twentieth century. However, homosexuality prevailed
throughout the Canadian military, in all types of formations and among all
types of men. The fact that gender was so closely allied to sexuality meant
that homosexuality was most visible in those who adopted outwardly feminine characteristics. But this survey of Canadians in Europe makes it clear
that homosexually active men are not easily classified. It also reveals that
they were largely successful in creating satisfying sexual and affectional
lives within an unsympathetic environment. This discussion also suggests
that sexual relations, in the homosexual world as in the heterosexual, were
ordered by differences in claims to power and legitimacy. Age, rank/class,
appearance, gender, race, ethnicity, and intellectual ability informed individual relationships in complex and sometimes unpredictable ways.

Chapter Six

ESPRIT DE CORPS, COHESION, AND MORALE

Since the Second World War, a substantial literature has addressed the question of what motivates men to fight in war. The tone was set in the postwar era by a number of officers and psychologists who commented on the behaviour of soldiers on both sides of the conflict. They argued that men were primarily sustained in battle by the knowledge that they were supported by their comrades – men fight for each other. This observation may have been a corrective to the wartime emphasis on ideology, since, during the war, national propagandas had emphasized the need to defend one's country and way of life. Subsequently, scholars have given varying weight to the different forces that influence human behaviour in war. Sociologist Frederick Manning identified three distinct factors that affect combat motivation: esprit de corps, cohesion, and morale. Esprit de corps is the phenomenon that binds people together in the absence of personal contact. It operates at the level of an army or regiment and creates, in Benedict Anderson's terms, an effective "imagined community." Any group of people ideologically and emotionally committed to an organization, cause, or nation has a measure of esprit de corps. Cohesion is the result of the bonds that hold a particular group together. Morale measures the level of commitment of an individual soldier to his or her unit. The three concepts are related but not dependent on each other in any predictable way.[1]

The issue of unit cohesion has become central to the debate over the effect of homosexuals on armed forces. Militaries have resisted the trend in all Western societies towards the extension of basic human rights to lesbians and gay men. Their central argument has been that the presence of openly homosexual soldiers would disrupt unit cohesion. Queer soldiers would be a disturbing influence, weakening the bonds that hold a group together and making it less effective. An army that accepted homosexuals would have less prestige and, therefore, a lower esprit de corps. Who would want to belong to an organization that accepted social misfits? Morale would also suffer for the individuals forced to work side by side with 'perverts.' Esprit de corps, cohesion, and morale are thus tied together by concepts of self-respect, honour, and dignity, which many military authorities continue to see as incompatible with homosexuality. As psychologist Theodore Sarbin has noted, politicians and military officials in the United States continue to base their defence of exclusionary policies on the construction of homosexuality as sin.[2]

The opponents of the military's ban on homosexuals use the wider literature on cohesion in primary groups to bolster their arguments. They attack the twin pillars of the military's position: that homosexuals disrupt cohesion and that cohesive groups are more effective. Various studies have demonstrated that gay servicepeople have served with distinction and have been accepted by their comrades. Meanwhile, scholars have distinguished between social and task cohesion. Social cohesion is the force that binds people who are attracted to each other; a group is socially cohesive to the extent that its members enjoy spending time together. Task cohesion, on the other hand, measures the efficiency with which members of a group perform their duties. The people we like to be with are not necessarily the ones with whom we work effectively. Studies in sports, labour, and military environments have discovered that a high level of social cohesion can diminish productivity. Similarly, unit cohesion has been shown to work against the interests of military objectives under certain conditions. Fraggings, mutinies, and acts of disobedience can all have their basis in closely knit units that define themselves against their superior officers and the institution.[3]

In this chapter, I will consider the effect of homosexuality on esprit de corps, unit cohesion, and morale in the Canadian military during the war. As a document in social history, it avoids the parameters established by the current political debate over the right of gays to serve in the military – proponents of both positions may find evidence to support their agendas. It is important to approach this discussion with a clear understanding that there could be no debate at mid-century over the right of gays to serve in the military. While some bold men did take a public stand in defence of their sexual difference, they were lone voices who defended themselves as individuals, not as members of a minority. Most queer men played the game according to the unofficial regulations and were careful not to let their sexual deviance show in situations where it could become an issue. But that changed from unit to unit, over time and as a result of military circumstances. As a rule, homosexuality was a greater concern in units that were in the process of formation. As men jockeyed for position, they used whatever attributes were available to them to gain status. Race, ethnicity, physical prowess, aggression, and intelligence could all be mobilized in support of one's own standing in a group. It is wise to remember, though, that most men entered basic training intimidated by the prospect of fighting overseas and facing death. Survival could be a more immediate concern than status. Thus, this chapter will study how units in very different wartime settings dealt with the issue of homosexuality.

MASCULINITY, HOMOSEXUALITY, AND THE MARTIAL SPIRIT

The discussion that follows is successful to the degree that it is sensitive to the attitudes towards sex and sexual deviance that held sway during wartime Canada. Masculine status was, in part, a function of a man's sexual behaviour and his ability to soldier. Thus, the relationship between masculinity, homosexuality, and martial capabilities needs to be explored. Other societies have seen male homosexuality in fundamentally different terms in relation to warfare and masculinity. The literature on cohesion, dominated by military, sociology, and psychology scholars, generally accepts the terms set by contemporary Western cultures: that homosexuality is either inimical to or, at best, neutral regarding military pursuits and masculinity. Before studying cohesion in Canadian wartime units, we will look at the relationship between warfare, masculinity, and homosexuality in three very different societies. We will consider esprit de corps, cohesion, morale, and homosexuality in the Sambian culture of Melanesia, the armies of classical Sparta, and the Airborne Regiment of late twentieth-century Canada.

The Sambian culture of the Eastern Highlands of Papua New Guinea has been extensively studied by twentieth-century anthropologists. In common with Western societies, Sambians are concerned with the uses of semen. However, their social relations are structured around the assumption that semen is a finite commodity and the source of strength and manhood. The transmission of semen from youths and adult men to women and boys defines those relationships. Sexual relations, understood in terms of either pleasure or work (procreation), are highly regulated in the interest of conserving semen and expending it responsibly. Of interest to the focus of this chapter is the ritualized passage into manhood mandatory for all Sambian boys. Males approaching puberty are taken from their mothers, with whom they have had very close relations, and introduced to the separate culture of men. Their passage to manhood entails their complete separation from

Sambian women for a period of years. Their bodies can mature in strength and manliness only by ingesting the semen, through fellatio, of those already initiated into the world of men. Strict rules govern the choice of fellateds and fellators, those related maternally being restricted from one another. The source of semen is most commonly the older youths, already initiated, from neighbouring hamlets. These same youths can become enemy warriors in subsequent years. The bonds that develop between the fellateds and fellators are not simply functional, but homoerotic. Attractive boys are often preferred by the fellateds, and the boys choose youths who appeal to them.[4]

In the Sambian culture, homosexual relations are central to the concept of masculinity. When transmitted homosexually, semen has a spiritual power that it otherwise lacks. Boys pass into manhood and become warriors only through sexual relations with those who have already attained that status. However, while sexual relations between male Sambians separated by age is obligatory, other forms of homosexual intercourse are strictly forbidden. Similarly, heterosexual relations (limited to oral or genital sex) are permitted only between a husband and wife. Sambian women are kept ignorant of the male initiation cult; boys are forbidden, upon pain of death, from divulging the secret of their passage to manhood. Thus, the men are tied together by the common secret that the semen they share unites them in martial prowess. While their methods of attaining masculine status are antithetical to Canadian standards, the concept of uniting warriors is not. Sharing semen is, for the Sambians, similar to sharing regimental traditions of bravery and heroism for Canadian servicemen. The semen that the Sambians share is the source of all strength and courage; Canadian soldiers are united to their brave ancestors through membership in a regiment. In both Canada and Sambia, esprit de corps is maintained by membership in an elite group. However, in the former case, homosexuality is seen as a source of weakness, in the latter, a source of strength.[5]

Sparta was the greatest military power of the Greek world in the fifth century, BC. Spartan society was organized around its army, which was built upon deeply cohesive small units of soldiers. The highest caste in Spartan society was the "Similar," a male member of the warrior elite. Sons of Similars who were judged inferior at birth were left to die of exposure; the fit began military training at seven years of age. Like the Sambians, they spent years isolated from the rest of Spartan society, undergoing a rigorous process of masculinization. New recruits were divided into "herds," in which they were harshly trained by older boys. They fought, drilled, and suffered deprivations together throughout their youth in order to attain a standard of toughness and devotion to their comrades. Historian Josiah Ober describes the place of homosexuality, masculinity, and martial spirit among the Similar caste: "[H]omosexual relations between boys and young men were regarded as standard. Indeed it was a mark of shame for a boy not to be courted by an older youth. The Spartans believed that homosexual relations between young men encouraged unit solidarity and battlefield valor, reasoning that a lover would surely not shame himself before his beloved by flinching back from the line." The Spartan army was organized around the mess unit of fifteen men who lived and fought together. Those who could not meet the demanding standards of fidelity, bravery, and ability were expelled from the Similar caste and became "Inferiors" or "Tremblers." Similars enjoyed privileges of citizenship denied other castes in Spartan society. Unit cohesion was thus the basis of the Spartan military. Spartan society supported this arrangement by extending the highest prestige to its Similars, an honour that, in turn, nurtured their morale. Homosexual relations helped to define successful warriors, who represented the highest ideal of Spartan masculinity.[6]

In the 1990s, Canadian society was disturbed to learn about the cultural practices of the Airborne Regiment, its elite, all-male fighting force. Following an investigation into the murder of a Somali youth by members of the Airborne deployed in Somalia in 1993, the regiment's initiation rites came under limited scrutiny in the course of two subsequent enquiries. It was discovered that recruits were welcomed into each of the three commando units by an initiation ceremony lasting several days. Entry to the group required initiates to perform the most degrading actions that their prospective comrades could imagine. While almost insensibly intoxicated, they ate bread saturated with their comrades' urine and vomit and performed push-ups into human faeces. A black initiate, with "I Love KKK" written in large letters on his back, was leashed and required to walk on all fours. Such rites were designed to test the limits of loyalty of the initiates; those who allowed themselves to be humiliated, who sacrificed their individuality in deference to the group, became part of the Airborne family. Initiates were required to dance erotically with each other, dress in drag, and go through the motions of performing sodomy. Thus, homosexuality and cross-dressing were introduced into the initiation rites as the antithesis of masculinity; a soldier willing to degrade himself to the point of appearing to be gay was demonstrating his ultimate commitment to the group. In this formulation, masculinity and male heterosexuality were inseparable, defined through each other. To be a member of Canada's elite combat unit required a commitment to each, and therefore both. In the Canadian model, heterosexuality was defined as not homosexual. In contrast, the Sambian and Spartan warrior cultures did not see hetero- and homosexual behaviour as mutually exclusive.[7]

Once accepted into the unit, soldiers had to be careful to disavow any hint of homosexual desire. They accomplished that by mocking it. In a series of interviews, sociologist Donna Winslow uncovered the Airborne's attitude towards gay comrades. One soldier related that "[w]hen you're working two or three or even six months with guys and you don't see any women, well sure you get some different behavior, jokes and stuff." The different behaviour – homosexuality – was admitted into the group in the form of jokes. When the chance arose, it became imperative for the "borderline" soldiers to prove their heterosexuality: "[W]e're so homophobic that when we get free time, we go out and get ourselves a woman, just to prove that we're not homosexual. When we go out, the woman becomes a machine, an object that we'd use as much as possible, and talk about as much as possible." If soldiers were borderline but did not prove their heterosexuality, "someone will start a rumour. If they start a rumour, you find yourself with broken legs. Really physically broken." Another soldier put the issue simply: "We can't accept homosexuality because it represents weakness."

The three different societies alert us to the fact that there are no inherent, essential relationships between homosexuality, masculinity, and the martial spirit. The significance of any sexual behaviour depends upon its historical context. In the case of the Canadian Airborne Regiment, there was an insistence on the heterosexuality and maleness of the members of the group. In the wake of largely successful feminist and gay liberation movements in the late twentieth century, the soldiers sought to identify themselves with their concept of Canada's more glorious past. According to one Airborne soldier, "We've still got the old 1950s values, when it [homosexuality] wasn't acceptable." He saw the military standards of masculinity in the 1980s and 1990s as more pure than the nation's: "[I]f a homosexual keeps it to himself, it's his own business ... It's like that in the civilian world, but in the army if you have any particular behavior, you'll get harassed ... One guy got his leg broken, boot-kicked, just so he would leave." In fact, the assumption within the Airborne that they were remaining true to a tradition of anti-homosexuality among comrades was inaccurate. The Second World War signified for them the glory days of the Canadian military – an unambiguously just war fought by brave and manly men. Yet the relationship in mid-century between homosexuality, masculinity, and martial spirit was much more complex than subsequent generations of soldiers have assumed. While the Airborne in the 1990s defied the government by aggressively excluding homosexuals, wartime units often protected their queer soldiers from the intolerant state. They also protected such men from the label that could destroy their lives. Lieutenant C's ordeal addresses the nature of cohesion and assumptions about masculinity and homosexuality in wartime.[8]

ONE OF THE BOYS

At ten o'clock on the morning of 3 June 1943, Lieutenant Ernest C was brought before a general court of seven officers at the Fort York armouries in Toronto. He listened as the charges against him were read in open court:

The accused, Lieutenant (Quartermaster) Ernest Albert [C], No. 2 Engineer Service and Works [ESW] Company, Royal Canadian Engineers, an Officer of the Canadian Army placed on Active Service is charged with disgraceful conduct of an indecent kind in that he in a public toilet in the Robert Simpson Company, Limited, Store at the City of Toronto, Ontario, on Tuesday, 20th April, 1943, at about 1400 hours indecently did permit another male person, to wit, ... Leading Aircraftman Richard [S], an airman of the Royal Canadian Air Force, Special Reserve, to place his head near the genital organs of the said [Lieutenant C] who at that time had the front of his trousers undone.

An alternative charge using the identical wording was laid as an offence under "scandalous behaviour unbecoming the character of an officer." A third alternative charge under "conduct to the prejudice of good order and military discipline" referred simply to his being in the toilet compartment with the airman. He pleaded not guilty to all charges.

During the first two days of the trial, the prosecuting officer presented seven witnesses to prove the particulars stated in the charge. A draughtsman from Lieutenant C's own unit had been commissioned by the prosecution to prepare a detailed plan of Simpson's fifth-floor washroom. He had visited the crime site along with a captain from the Engineers and had taken precise measurements of the size of the room, the height of the urinals, mirrors, basins, air dryers, the shape of the cubicles, and the position and diameter of the flushing ball. Three employees from Simpson's furniture department related how they had become suspicious of a Chinese RCAF airman who had been seen cruising the washroom weeks earlier. When he reappeared on the day in question, they called the store detectives. Together with the city police, they conspired to observe the "Chinaman" and Lieutenant C engage in sexual relations in a toilet compartment. A detective sergeant with Toronto city police quietly entered the adjacent stall and peeked over the partition to observe the act described in the charge. Both accused were taken across the street to Toronto City Hall and questioned by city detectives and a sergeant from the RCAF Service Police. The prosecution's case appeared to be irrefutable.

Over the subsequent two days, the defending officer, Major Bristol, presented sixteen character witnesses to testify on behalf of Lieutenant C. By the rules of evidence, they were allowed to testify to his reputation for good character generally or in special respects. Witnesses could discuss his reputation for honesty or morality but were not permitted to relate specific instances of these attributes. Major Bristol's strategy soon became evident. To lay the foundation for their judgments regarding his reputation, witnesses were questioned at length regarding their personal relations with Lieutenant C over twenty-seven years in the army. He had been a member of the permanent force since the First World War as a soldier, an NCO, and, now, an officer. In those twenty-seven years of service, there had not been a single entry on his conduct sheet. The testimonials from his comrades came to outweigh the seemingly conclusive evidence against him. The court was faced with measuring the observations of trained detectives and store security officers against the assurances of a seemingly endless line of respected military men who insisted that Lieutenant C was the quintessential army man.[9]

Most of the character witnesses were other members of the permanent force whose careers had dovetailed with Lieutenant C's. Without exception, all praised his soldierly bearing and his work with the Engineers. Colonel Milligan, who had recommended him for his commission, supported him unequivocally, stating that "his conduct was exemplary" and that he "carried out his work faithfully." As to his character, Colonel Milligan said that "there was nothing, never anything occurred of any suspicious nature that would make me think he was other than a very upright man." Major Young, who had worked with Lieutenant C for twenty years, claimed that "he was one of the finest N.C.O.s and Warrant Officers that we have had in M.D.2" The refrain, played repeatedly by the witnesses, was that his reputation for honesty and morality was "above reproach." No one had ever doubted his moral character. The court seemed impressed by the claim of one elderly witness that he would trust his daughter with Lieutenant C. The inference was that homosexuality signalled an immoral man, not a homosexual man. A man who would have sex in a public washroom with another man could not control his sexual desires; therefore, he would be heterosexually untrustworthy as well. Others assured the court that he was so upright that he would not tolerate "smutty" stories. But the most compelling witnesses described Lieutenant C as fitting seamlessly into 2 Detachment, Royal Canadian Engineers. In fact, he was described as having been the centre of the social life of the unit throughout his youth and adulthood.[10]

The court heard that after the First World War, Lieutenant C had lived each summer with two other young veterans on a sixteen-foot sloop, sailing over from Hanlan's Point or Ward's Island each morning for work in Toronto. They swam in the nude in the harbour and at the YMCA and then showered together, quite naturally. A clerk with twenty-five-years experience with the Royal Canadian Engineers recalled that Lieutenant C was always "one of the boys" in the unit: "I have served with him under different circumstances, in camps, barracks, and down at the office, and I could not say one word against him." An avid sportsman, Lieutenant C played handball with several comrades from the Engineers. He played in their softball and bowling leagues and coached the hockey team. He kept a sailboat, and in the summer, his room at the Toronto Islands was a centre of social activity for the detachment. Many men stayed the night with Lieutenant C; none were remotely hesitant to acknowledge sharing his bed. Several witnesses were questioned explicitly about sharing tents and beds with him on numerous occasions throughout their military careers. Never had Lieutenant C given his comrades any cause to believe that there was "anything untoward in his habits." Such testimony made it clear that there was little separation between work and social life in the military. While sports teams and parties helped to bind members of the detachment together socially, the experience of sharing tents and beds at training camps meant that soldiers' personal and private lives were inseparable. Many of those most closely associated with the unit described Lieutenant C as more than one of the boys, but someone who, throughout his career, had championed the value of army life and was loved by all ranks.

Regimental Sergeant Major Douglas related that when he was leaving Ottawa to drive to Toronto to testify, he "got calls from five officers, well-knowing Mr. [C], and they said, 'You are going down,' and they said, 'convey to him our best wishes.' I have never heard no one say a bad word about him." Colonel Milligan had observed that the other ranks who worked under him "liked him. They all knew he worked hard and expected them to work hard, and I never had any occasion to have any complaints as to any ill-treatment of any of the men." Regimental Sergeant Major Bond claimed that "[C] has been responsible for many, probably fifteen or twenty, young men getting a splendid start through the Army in life." One young recruit verified that Lieutenant C "was thought a great deal of by all the staff in our office and I respected him myself very highly. I think just as much of him as I do my own father." Regimental Sergeant Major Studd, asked to comment on Lieutenant C's morals and character, epitomized the long litany of tributes by saying, "Well, I would say they were – would 'perfect' be a good word to use there."

The court found Lieutenant C guilty of the least serious charge, of being in the toilet compartment with the airman, and sentenced him to be severely reprimanded. Although it is impossible to know how they arrived at that finding, it would seem that the character evidence must have undermined the powerful testimony of the police. In fact, the case put the army on trial against itself. While the administration had been certain that the lieutenant would be found guilty and cashiered, his colleagues were just as determined to defend him against the institution that he was known to cherish. Moreover, if Lieutenant C was indeed a sexual pervert, then suspicion could fall upon the many servicemen who fearlessly acknowledged sharing his bed over the years. That he was found not guilty of the homosexual charges against him was not a vindication of his right to belong to the forces as a homosexual man; rather it was a demonstration of the court's unwillingness to overlook the adamant wishes of sixteen officers, NCOs, and soldiers. The court faced a dilemma: one horn was a highly respected career serviceman, the other a homosexual who made sexual contacts in public washrooms. The court went through the middle by finding him guilty of bad judgment in being in the toilet stall with the airman. The question of Lieutenant C's sexuality was judiciously avoided.

Lieutenant C's comrades emphatically asserted that he belonged with 2 ESW Company, and the lieutenant felt himself to be a part of it. These are the two cornerstones of group cohesion. Each individual must feel that he has a right to membership in the group, and the group must accept each member's claim to belonging. These two links are distinct, but related: it is easier to feel welcome where it is the case and easier to welcome someone who feels a natural right to belong. In the case of Lieutenant C, the evidence suggests that the possibility that he was queer was overlooked by the group. That oversight, however, may have been either myopic or calculated. One of his long-term friends argued that "this charge I heard about, if he committed it he must be a Doctor Jekyll as far as I know." On the other hand, the defence was notably silent regarding his relationship with the opposite sex. No effort was made to suggest that he had ever been romantically or sexually involved with women. Only homosocial relationships within the military were paraded before the court. Whether or not any of them included a homosexual element is, from a public gaze, as uncertain now as it was then. What difference would it have made to unit cohesion? The unit wanted Lieutenant C, and although he made no pretensions towards heterosexuality, he had upheld his part of the bargain by being discreetly queer. The verdict suggests that that, finally, was acceptable.[11]

BEING WELCOMED, FITTING IN

Psychologists and military analysts have defined cohesion in different ways. United States Army Colonel William Henderson's definition is the most cited in military literature: "[C]ohesion exists in a unit when the primary day-to-day goals of the individual soldier, of the small group with which he identifies, and of unit leaders are congruent – with each giving his primary loyalty to the group so that it trains and fights as a unit with all members willing to risk death to achieve a common objective." Henderson argues that for a unit to achieve that state, it is imperative that a soldier's primary allegiance be to his group and that "a strong sense of mutual affection [exist] among unit members." Furthermore, army life must be "an all-consuming experience" in which strict codes of behaviour are constantly reinforced. For instance, soldiers should be accompanied by their comrades when on leave to ensure that "unit norms are maintained." Henderson sees conformity as central to effective unit cohesion. Soldiers must "view deviance as a violation of group trust concerning common expectations about individual attitudes and behavior." In the same light, "dissimiliar characteristics within a unit, such as language, religion, race, history, and the values that accompany these characteristics, tend to hinder cohesion." Strongly nationalistic and homogeneous populations, he argues, produce more cohesive armies.[12]

Henderson bases his argument on the presumption that a primary group is held together by the sameness of its individual members, but nothing in his definition of cohesion disqualifies a diversity of individuals tied together by mutual respect. While an imagined sameness may hold nations together, military units are composed of real people whose differences become fully apparent as they interact. In common with most of the military literature on cohesion, Henderson focuses exclusively on combat units. Evidence from the Canadian wartime experience does not support the proposition that diversity disrupted cohesion on the battlefield. However, not only is unit cohesion a difficult commodity to quantify, but its effect on unit performance is ambiguous. Whether cohesion enhances performance or success induces cohesiveness is an open question. Consequently, the discussion that follows will focus on the subjective testimony of combatant and non-combatant personnel gathered from court-martial records, interviews, memoirs, and diverse wartime military documentation. The influence of queer servicemen on unit cohesion and performance will be discussed as one aspect of the complex relationships that developed between homosexual people and their colleagues. As a document in social history concerned with cohesion in combat and non-combat units, this discussion will be guided less by Henderson's definition than by Leon Festinger's classic formulation: "Cohesiveness of a group is here defined as the resultant of all the forces acting on members to remain in the group. These forces may depend on the attractiveness or unattractiveness of either the prestige of the group, members in the group, or the activities in which the group engages." The forces that operated on soldiers to remain with their units or desert them changed over the course of soldiers' careers. Equally, relationships among comrades matured over time and in the light of shared experience. We will now explore that evolution and the place of queer servicemen in groups.[13]

In principle, the military did not welcome homosexual servicepeople. Official medical policy stated that homosexuals exerted "a very bad influence on their fellow soldiers and are, therefore, unwanted in any unit." Military law actively tried to deter men from engaging in homosexual behaviour. Was homosexuality, in fact, an enemy of morale? Could queers belong as queer or only by leading double lives, as appears to have been the case in Lieutenant C's unit? I argue, combining elements of Festinger's and Henderson's definitions, that cohesion depended on an appreciation of the value of the members of the group and their commitment to a common goal. In pursuing that goal, morale was strengthened to the degree that individuals believed they belonged to their unit and that their units valued them.[14]

Morale rests upon both the individual's desire to belong to a group and the group's acceptance of his or her claim to belonging. A group is cohesive to the extent that individuals feel that they are welcome and support one another. For Lieutenant C, a career soldier, the bonds that held him to Number 2 ESW Company had developed over a period of twenty-seven years. Similarly, units that matured on active service, often under the enormous stresses of battle, could forgive a range of anti-social behaviour as long as it did not threaten the group. The homosexuality of some members of a unit, along with many other individual peccadilloes, came to be known. The homosexuality of a cooperative comrade could be insignificant, whereas an unreliable and disagreeable peer, although heterosexual, could harm group morale. Indeed, a thoughtless or careless soldier could, in battle or training, actually cause the death of his comrades. However, one of the most difficult situations for queer soldiers, reliable or not, was training camp, where bonds were not yet formed and recruits, all of whom were unsure of how they would fit in, jockeyed for position in the group. Court-martial proceedings, courts of enquiry, and psychiatric reports are an inventory of social tensions. Class, ethnic, linguistic, gender, and intellectual differences were commonly mobilized to estrange recruits. Some found the inner resources to resist being limited by such intimidation, others did not.

In training camps throughout Canada, language differences often had the power to isolate individuals from the group. When isolation was compounded by deeper ethnic tensions and prejudice, many recruits chose to absent themselves without leave rather than suffer humiliation. Private Dubé, raised on a farm in rural Quebec, enlisted at Number 3 Company, Canadian Army Service Corps Training Centre, where he was surrounded by other French-speaking recruits. When transferred to Number 4 Company, he "found himself without friends and unable to understand his instructors or to be understood by them." When he became "very lonesome" in this anglophone environment, he decided to absent himself without leave. At his court martial, his defending officer noted that these circumstances were "similar to that of a number of other French Canadian lads who have appeared before this Court." In fact, this response was perceived to be so common that English Canadians came to refer to absence without leave as "French leave," adding another log to the fire of French-English tension. Ironically, anglophones used that moniker to refer to their own illegal absences, thereby disowning their transgressions. In some camps, this ethnic antagonism isolated groups rather than individuals. For instance, the English majority at Number 1 Field Training Regiment refused to allow the French minority to speak their own language among themselves. When recruits found themselves harassed and set apart by such tactics, they could not always rely on the intervention of officers, since officers often shared the biases of the men. Thus, Private Ayotte absented himself without leave when his superior officer referred to him as a "dirty Frenchman." Throughout the chain of command, the army missed opportunities to show leadership and thus assuage French-English tensions. In one such example, it called a court of inquiry into the 'problem' of French Canadian nurses "insisting" on speaking French among themselves in Medicine Hat, Alberta, when they understood English.[15]

Men were often harassed because of their racial differences. Some chose to stand their ground. Gunner Izzard was charged with "conduct to the prejudice of good order and military discipline" when he struck Gunner

Smith at A23 Coast and Anti-aircraft Artillery Training Centre. Smith had been trying to incite the other men in his unit to run Izzard, a black man, out of the hut. Private Hendrix, also a black recruit, deserted the Winnipeg Light Infantry after being harassed by his comrades. His defending officer begrudgingly acknowledged that racial prejudice could dishearten a recruit: "While the color line in this country is very lightly drawn, no one can deny that there is not [sic] one and to a sensitive chap, such as Hendrix, obviously is, a little bit goes a long way particularly when he is clad in his country's uniform." Fearing the social effects of alienating men such as Hendrix, he urged the court to impose a light sentence: "A little mercy in this case would certainly help to put one young man back on the road to useful citizenship and help to lift him out of this pit of racial inferiority which he had been forced into by the stupid actions of some criminally stupid whites."[16]

Rifleman Kozak, a Russian, chose to return to the comfort of his home after his poor reception with the Oxford Rifles: "I went AWOL because I was called 'foreigner' and 'immigrant,' as I am not naturalised – treated me pretty rough in my unit, and since I come into the army, so I wanted to get away from my unit, because I wasn't treated right." Members of linguistic, racial, and ethnic minorities who felt overwhelmed by the animosity of their comrades often returned to their home communities, where their differences were the norm. But for many young homosexual people, training camp could be the place where they became aware of their sexual orientation. Such people knew of no community to which they might belong. Under the stressful conditions of basic training, the sense of alienation could be unbearable.[17]

Gunner Burwell Snyder, a single twenty-eight-year-old man from Kitchener, enlisted in the army on 6 July 1942. His personnel selection form describes the impression he made on the army examiner: "Intelligence: High. Appearance: Clean cut, quite well built. Personality: Wholesome. Social attitude: Friendly. Emotional stability: Stable." At that time, the personnel officer wrote: "He is a bright normal young man of quite high intelligence. Should become an N.C.O. with training." However, on 3 May 1944, the army examiner at Terrace, B.C., referred Snyder to the psychiatrist because, as a homosexual man, he was having great difficulty fitting into 48 Light Anti-aircraft Battery of the Royal Canadian Artillery. Two days later, Gunner Snyder found his own way out of his pain by turning his sten gun on himself. The subsequent court of enquiry into the circumstances surrounding his suicide sheds light on the extreme stress experienced in certain environments by some people marked as queer. In his despair at being mocked by his peers, Snyder received support from neither his superiors nor the medical officers.

The doctor who examined his dead body had been too busy to pay serious attention to his live one on sick parade two hours earlier. Instead, he gave him phenobarbitol tablets to calm his nerves. He was well acquainted with Snyder, who had appeared on sick parade four times that week asking to be transferred. Snyder had told the doctor "that he could not stand where he was because the men were calling him names and because he just got out of detention barracks" where "he seemed to think the people ... had persecuted him." He also told him that that experience had "ruined" him: "He was saying he could not go on like that and did not want to stay with that unit because they were talking about him, and the men and his buddies were against him." The court did not ask the other men on Snyder's gun crew to clarify the nature of the persecution he had suffered. Typical is the exchange with Gunner Musty:

[Question 15.] Did he associate around with the boys very much in the unit?
[Answer:] He always was a friendly man before, but the last while I do not know. He was just a little different. I did not talk to him very much.

The distance such responses maintain may help us to understand the isolation Snyder was experiencing. Associating with a man marked as homosexual could bring a soldier under the suspicion of his peers in the competitive environment of training camp.

Snyder had gone to his commanding officer on 3 May "in a very nervous state and said, 'I just can't stand it any longer.'" The officer told the court, "The first time I talked to him he kept stressing the fact he thought everybody was referring to him by terms that indicated homosexuality. I investigated this by reference to several other men and assured myself that there was nothing whatsoever in it." In Canada, terms that indicated homosexuality during the war included queer, cocksucker, and fairy. They were intended, of course, to denigrate the object, just as the terms nigger, kike, and moron assailed people for other differences. Snyder had been aware that the campaign against him was working, and he had asked for help in coping with his ordeal. The army, however, itself as anti-homosexual as the young men at Terrace military camp, could offer no solace. Snyder's request to be transferred to another unit had been denied. His needs were outside of the artillery's capacity for personnel management.

Snyder responded to the attempt to marginalize him by feeling marginal. He was hurt by the fact that, marked as queer, he was refused entry into the group. Tragically, he found himself under a commanding officer who lacked the insight of others who would have transferred him to a more accepting environment. Perhaps Snyder's timing cost him his life, for at that point in the war, artillery officers may have been less willing to part with good men than they had been earlier. But his tragedy tells us how powerful the need to belong can be. In order that a group be cohesive, its members must feel they belong. A campaign had effectively convinced Snyder that he did not. His commanding officers had not responded sympathetically to his predicament. While he had told them exactly what was tormenting him, they refused to support him. At that point, he was isolated from all sources of comfort. Ironically, the local coroner did not call for an inquest, but used the evidence from the military court of inquiry and investigations by the B.C. police to conclude "that a morbid psychosis, due to maladjustment to Army Life was contributory to the action of the Deceased." In fact, wiser military authorities were commonly adjusting to the presence of homosexual servicepeople.[18]

Some causes for rejecting a recruit were unconnected to race, ethnicity, or sexuality, and were rooted instead in anti-social behaviour. Gunner Anthony of 9 Light Anti-aircraft Regiment was thought to be a thief by his fellow soldiers and decided to absent himself rather than face the constant abuse. His defending officer related how "he was being hounded by rumours and by his fellow-soldiers who called him 'thief' every time he appeared."[19]

Men who were an obvious threat to morale were commonly discharged from the military after being diagnosed by psychiatrists as psychopathic personalities (anti-social or inadequate). It was in basic training camps that military authorities and their comrades came to gauge each recruit. Some men were able to fit in with ease, others found the atmosphere challenging or even threatening. Whereas in civilian life men had had a measure of control over the activities they might pursue and the type of man they would become, camps tended to set a more rigid standard of manhood.

Basic training was a physically challenging ordeal, designed to 'make a man' out of a recruit. For those who were not athletic or were poorly coordinated, it could also become a psychological test. It was common for men who fell behind to suffer the ridicule of the more physically capable recruits. Sapper Kerns had been a student of commercial art and music in civilian life before enlisting voluntarily in the army. At 131 Canadian Infantry Basic Training Centre in Calgary, he found that "he was not doing as well as the remainder of the boys in the platoon owing to his physical state. He subsequently became the subject of ridicule among his comrades." Whether his homosexuality contributed to his harassment as well is unclear. The defending officer at his trial for deserting the camp said that the training "tended to break him down rather than build him up so much that he finally had to obtain artificial means to get to sleep." The training camp environment prized physical prowess, and weaker, less-confident men could be singled out for failing the test of manhood. Whether the derision had serious consequences could depend on one's own inner resources and the good fortune to find some measure of support. Many of those who suffered ridicule for their inability did receive support from sympathetic men who themselves had been successful in basic training.[20]

When athletic incompetence was compounded by an effeminate nature, the recruit could face great pressure in the competitive, sometimes juvenile world of training camp. Russ was a young homosexual man who underwent basic training at Camp Ipperwash, Ontario, in 1944. He remembers one very effeminate recruit in his barrack: "You could see he was one of those unfortunate kids that, you know – his voice, I mean I had a high voice, I'm sure, at that age (I probably still do), but it was so obvious, I mean, he stood out like a sore thumb. And, of course, the guys picked on him." Russ remembers that this recruit had to suffer not only verbal intimidation, but physical and sexual assaults as well: "At one time I came back in [the barracks] and I heard this commotion going on in the showers and I went in and, I don't know, there was certainly three or four – maybe five or six – of them and they had him in there and they had him naked and they were doing things to him ... they were fucking him ... they were raping him." Russ's immediate reaction was to protect the man under attack. "I was never big, but I waded in to stop them and pull them out ... in each barracks, there was, sometimes either a sergeant or a corporal, and they had their own little room at the end of the barracks. I went and got the sergeant, and a couple of them were charged."[21]

Such criminal violence was sometimes sanctioned by the NCOs who supervised basic training. The victim of the sexual assault at Camp Ipperwash was fortunate that Russ was present, and Russ was fortunate to have been able to appeal to a receptive sergeant. In other camps, sergeants saw their role as being to create aggressive men not given to displaying compassion as Russ had done. Many recruits abhorred the kind of manly prowess preached by belligerent sergeants. Private Jamieson had been raised in a religious Scots-Irish home where "sex was never mentioned, we were not allowed to play cards, and generally our home life was different from the average Canadian home." He was posted to Currie Barracks for advanced training, where his "instructor, Sergeant Hawkins, continually referred to us as 'girls' and also as being 'green' and 'yellow.'" In his trial for deserting the camp, he described a "lecture" by Sergeant Black, a veteran of the First World War: "Relating his experiences he almost boastfully told [us] that on

taking a town they looked for young girls ten or eleven years of age which
they raped and on finishing stuck a bayonet into them. These he claimed
were the best pieces he ever had. I could not adjust myself to this talk. I had
been raised in a religious home where sex was never mentioned. Life in the
army had at Camrose [basic training] been very pleasant, and at Currie all
my ideals seemed shattered by my instructors." Men such as Jamieson, who
had understood the enemy to be Adolf Hitler and the Nazi terror, were especially repelled by the suggestion that one's manliness could be demonstrated by the conquest of eleven-year-old girls. However, instructors such
as Sergeant Black were positioned to set the tone of infantry training
camps. In response, Private Jamieson chose not to belong to the unit. Thus,
while some men lamented the fact that they were not welcomed (Snyder, for
example), others rejected the group itself. Of course, such rejection was illegal under the Army Act and resulted in lengthy periods of detention.[22]

Sometimes men absented themselves not because they abhorred the crude
conception of masculinity current in their camps, but because they knew
they could not kill. Some of the men forced to serve under the National Resources Mobilization Act (NRMA) could not reconcile themselves to the
very purpose of their training. Trooper Anderson found that "the idea of
killing" was making him sick and giving him nightmares. Private Andre of
the Winnipeg Light Infantry said at his trial for desertion that "from the
start I was forced into the Army. I felt that I would never have the nerves to
fight or kill or be with a combatant unit." Not all of those who rejected the
work of the infantry did so out of an ideological pacifism; some were simply pragmatic. Private Johnson at Number 2 Canadian Infantry Basic
Training Centre was charged with "conduct to the prejudice ..." when he
behaved uncooperatively. He said that he "couldn't kill a fly anyway, so
what's the use of learning drill." But rejecting the fighting units could be
costly. 'Zombies' – those who refused active service abroad – were objects
of scorn and aggression throughout Canada. Authorities in basic training
camps encouraged the harassment of men who would not sign up for active
service. Such aggression was sometimes directed at any soldier not in a
fighting unit. For instance, Corporal Joanis and Private MacRae were harassed and beaten in Toronto by members of an infantry unit because they
belonged to the dental corps.[23]

BONDS BETWEEN AND AMONG SOLDIERS

Much of the literature on cohesion overlooks the bonds that form between
individual men in all-male settings. In some armies, individual relationships
are institutionalized through the buddy system, whereby pairs of soldiers

rely on each other for support in battle and in daily military life. Canada's wartime army was structured on the regimental system, whereby the men who fought together in platoons were drawn from the same geographic region. As the war progressed, reinforcements could originate from other areas. Nevertheless, platoons generally remained units of men who shared personal histories rooted in particular regions. The regimental system encouraged esprit de corps, each regiment promoting its own traditions and glories. Sons would likely belong to the same regiment as their fathers and friends. This regional, historical, and social continuity did not exist for those who enlisted in the navy or air force. However, the emphasis on group cohesion and esprit de corps fostered by the regimental system did not replace the friendships that developed between men. Soldiers formed bonds with individual comrades as well as with their units, both of which must be examined.[24]

Soldiers' memoirs consistently provide evidence of the importance of individual friendships between men in military environments. Whether in Canada or overseas, men relied on each other for emotional and psychological support. Pierre Berton remembers "male marriages" as the predominant social arrangement in his wartime experience at Currie Barracks in Alberta:

Harry and I were inseparable. In fact, because of the static situation, a curious kind of male bonding was taking place among many of the twenty-third class at Currie. At least half our number formed themselves into partnerships that were often as binding as marriages. Some men remained loners without any single close buddy, but the pair bonding dominated. Many of these partnerships continued long after the war. In one case, when a man married, his buddy actually went along on the honeymoon. In another dramatic instance, Tommy Tomkins of the Loyal Edmonton Regiment saved the life of his buddy, Rob Spencer at Arnhem ... I don't think that any of us noticed this phenomenon. Harry and I were similarly bonded, but neither he nor I nor anybody else discussed or even thought of these male marriages. It only occurs to me now as I look back on that period.

Few memoirs are as explicit as Berton's regarding the intimate bonds that connected men during wartime, but most contain evidence in support. Of course, most were written during the Cold War and coloured, no doubt, by its anti-homosexual politics. In his autobiography, Alexander Ross addresses the difference between postwar and wartime sexual cultures. In the same way that military psychiatrists and administrators were unwilling to mark men as homosexual, most people were not trained to 'see' homosexuality. Ross and his army buddy rented a room in Kingston with one bed. He judged that there would have been no cause for speculation on their sexual normalcy at that time: "We defined 'gay' as 'disposed to mirth' or 'showy' and read A.E. Houseman happily free of that poet's homosexual propensities. That Hugh and I shared the same bed witnessed only to our need each night for as much sleep as we could get and invited no scurrilous labelling." That his contemporaries were "happily free" of the knowledge of the extent of homosexuality in their culture suggests that they sanctioned much behaviour that subsequent generations would abjure. At the same time, they feared the label homosexual, which was reserved for a small percentage of particularly serious, or just unlucky, offenders.[25]

In this environment, men accepted a wide range of friendships between comrades. As time passed and bonds intensified, as in Berton's unit, many relationships had the appearance of romance; those that were also sexual needed only to conceal the forbidden deeds to remain above suspicion. Men who did not hide their homosexuality successfully could pay a high price. Desmond Taylor was a twenty-seven-year-old single Torontonian who played lacrosse, hockey, and rugby and was a professional singer. When he enlisted in the RCAF in September 1940, he was described in his interview report as "healthy," "rugged," "clean and smart," "confident," "mature," and "pleasant." His flight officer summarized him as a "[f]ine clean cut type. Above the average in intelligence and deportment. Would recommend as officer material." During his training, he read a book on psychology that suggested committing to paper incidents from his personal life that had become a source of anxiety. He subsequently lost his signed "confessions" that revealed his homosexual past. Soon he was being blackmailed. He deteriorated rapidly, failed two ground subjects, and was discharged from the air force. In early 1942, he enlisted with the Queen's York Rangers and was sent to Camp Borden for training. Over the next few months, he became a problem for his superior officers, who described him as "queer." He revealed his problem to only a few friends and was obviously under stress. His commanding officer told him that "after he joined the army he should forget his personal problems and devote his time and attention to the army." Taylor, however, could not bear the fact that the dreadful secret was literally out of his hands, and alone in the early hours of 28 May 1942, he shot himself on the bayonet course. In giving testimony at the court of inquiry into his suicide, Private Spirnyak prefaced his remarks by claiming that "Private Taylor D. S. has been my best friend since I came to Camp Borden and he considered me his best friend. He was quiet and friendly and like a brother to me." Taylor had discussed his predicament with Spirnyak, asking for advice on how to change his name. He considered moving to Mexico, where he would be safe from his tormentors, but finally chose death. Such evidence allows us to read Berton's description of male bonds at Currie Barracks with caution. It is clear that when evidence that "male marriages" had been consummated came to light, the psychological stress could be intense.[26]

Individual bonds between soldiers formed within larger units of men who usually were drawn from a particular community. When Private Dallaire from Ottawa absented himself without leave from the Perth Regiment while stationed in England, his defending officer attributed his action to the common difficulty of fitting into an established unit: "It is the old story of taking a man from one battalion and putting him in another amongst new men, men from a different part of the country, men with their own habits, men from the same home town who stick together more or less and those from other units find it very difficult to fit themselves into the picture. This is not a solitary case, he was in the Footguards, he went with the Perth Regt." Private Dallaire had been a talented hockey player in Ottawa and was thought to have promise as an infantryman. The same rivalry that fuelled competition between sports teams representing different Canadian towns underlay the rivalry between regiments. Thus, cohesion was strengthened when men saw themselves as part of a regimental team in competition with others. The following testimony of an NCO describing the outbreak of a brawl between two groups of Canadian soldiers on a street in England demonstrates how volatile such loyalty to one's regiment/team could be: "Corporal Brooks and myself and Rifleman Dunand were walking from Fleet, and the accused and two other men passed on the road and one of them said, 'Regina Rifles' and Corporal Brooks repeated 'Royal Winnipeg Rifles No 1 Company' and the accused turned around and grabbed hold of Corporal Brooks and knocked him down, and Corporal Brooks got him around the neck and held him there. Corporal Brooks and I started for the camp and the accused came up behind Corporal Brooks and struck him, then the Provosts came along." Regimental solidarity was rooted in Canadian regionalism. Once in combat, however, the Germans became the common enemy and internal regimental rivalries subsided. As units matured under active service, the bonds became deeper. Different rules for inclusion in the unit also developed.[27]

HAPPY SHIPS

While Canadian Army platoons were encouraged to work and play together in order to strengthen the many bonds that held them together, the crew of a corvette in the North Atlantic had no choice but to share all facets of life. Surgeon Commander Wellman, the Royal Canadian Navy's highest-ranking psychiatrist, studied the effect of naval service life on the mental health of ratings after the first three years of war. He concluded that the primary cause of psychiatric casualties in Canada's small ship navy was an inability of ratings to adapt to the requirements of group life on board ship:

In a fighting force they are moulded into a form of group life. There is almost complete regulation of almost all activities. They train, they play, they eat, they sleep, they even eliminate as a group. This impersonality of environment, with its strict accountability, forces them to become, at least ostensibly, members of a group with all its emotional requirements ... Most men are accepted and accept the group to which they are allotted. Others, however, may be overtly accepted but never feel themselves part of the group. Still others are never accepted and become lonely figures attached to it. From those who fail to be accepted, arise most of our casualties.

The familiarity that existed in all military units was magnified for those who served at sea. Wellman understood that successful inclusion in a group was a two-way street; however, he also put the responsibility for failure on the shoulders of the individual rating. It was the job of the individual to not "fail to be accepted." Evidence suggests that, as a result of the conditions articulated by Wellman, homosexuality was granted an even wider berth than it was in the other services.[28]

In principle, a corvette establishment, at thirty-five men, was similar to an infantry platoon. However, while platoons were usually understrength, corvettes tended to be considerably over, with the result that the already small quarters were severely cramped. Corvettes were themselves transgressive of military masculine ideals. James Lamb, who served with the RCN during the war, describes the effect of naming corvettes after flowers:

Right from the beginning, there was something suspect about corvettes in the eyes of right-thinking professional navy men; what was one to make of a man-of-war that looked like a fish trawler and called itself HMS *Pansy*? For the Admiralty, in a moment of inspiration, had designated the new ships as the Flower class, a tradition in escort vessels begun in the first world war ... There was a *Convolvulus*, a *Saxifrage*, and a *Cowslip*. But even a Board of Admiralty has a heart; eventually, HMS *Pansy* was allowed a change of name by a repentant Ships' Names Committee. She became HMS *Heartsease*.

The corvettes that were built by the Royal Navy and then taken over by the RCN retained their floral designations, but those built by the RCN in Canadian shipyards were named after Canadian towns. These small fighting vessels played a huge part in the Allied victory, protecting convoys in the North Atlantic from German U-boats. Lamb discusses the psychological effect of their nomenclature:

It was widely believed in the wartime Allied navies that the naming of the Flower class was part of a form of psychological warfare practised on the enemy by a vengeful Britain; there must be an added ignominy, it was felt, to being sunk by HMS *Poppy*, as U605 was, or to being outfought and captured by a fierce HMS *Hyacinth*, as was the Italian submarine *Peria*. It was one thing to perish in the Wagnerian splendour hankered after by Hitler, but quite another for the proud Teuton to be vanquished by *Rhododendron*, as U104 was, or sunk by *Periwinkle*, like U147.

Lamb argues that this "faintly comic" element crossed the Atlantic with the corvette and that Canadian crews cherished it as part of their "jealously preserved attitude of enlightened amateurism in a world of professional inanity."[29]

Lamb's appreciation for irony was exhausted when brought face to face with genuine sexual outlaws on board corvettes. He tells us that when he, as captain of a corvette, asked for a watch-keeping officer for the Normandy assault, he was "sent another problem child from barracks; this one proved to be not only incompetent and insubordinate, but a homosexual to boot." Lamb may have been currying favour with his audience by positioning both reader and writer as heterosexual. Also, it is possible that the replacement officer was insubordinate insofar as he was unwilling to conceal his sexual difference. We will go below decks to find out how accommodating the ratings actually were to the homosexuals among them.[30]

The cramped quarters and long periods at sea meant that the crews of corvettes became extremely familiar with one another. Most ratings were young men of eighteen to twenty years old who, distinct from the infantry platoons, hailed from various regions of Canada. Joe remembers the hardships aboard HMCS *Sackville* with great fondness: "The Sackville was a happy ship ... Everybody seemed to be happy. Maybe you had your mess decks and your hammock over the table and you'd be eating and you'd smell someone's feet and sit down to eat and – splash! – your dishes would go down to one end of the table." A "happy ship" was navy slang for a contented, effective crew, the equivalent of a cohesive army unit. On board ship, men who worked together tended to bond most closely together: "... seamen mess together, stokers mess together, signalmen, there might be four signalmen." While Joe was not involved in homosexual relations himself,

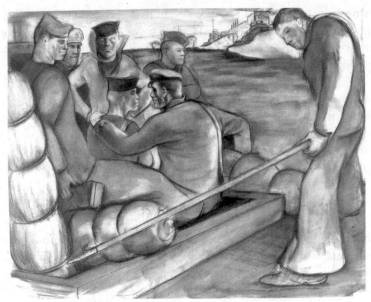

Sailors in Harbour Craft Leaving for Ship, 1944. The RCN's war artist Lieutenant Jack Nichols presents graphically the place of homosexuality in military units during the war. The sailors in the middle of the composition, separated only by years, gaze intimately into each other's eyes. Their mates form a circle around them, protecting their relationship from outside meddlers. The obviously phallic position of the grappling iron held by the sailor on the dock suggests that Lieutenant Nichols intended the viewer to read homosexuality into his composition. Source: AN1971026I-4309, © Canadian War Museum.

he remembers that the sailors who were involved were not shunned by the rest of the crew. He suggests that privacy could be found for romantic trysts only in the crow's nest. Meanwhile, pairs of ratings aboard the *Sackville* "would snuggle up together" in the lockers where hammocks were slung side by side. Joe remembers that it was not unusual to "just look over your hammock and you'd see them" caressing one another. On board the *Sackville*, "everybody knew" that various men were involved in homosexual relations, but Joe thinks that, without privacy, "they never got anywhere ... but, at night, you don't know." Such relations were treated on board as "a joke," and sailors would laugh when they managed to spy their shipmates in a mutual embrace. At the same time, Joe remembers that being marked as queer was not an issue on board a happy ship: "They still do their job and people [are] still friendly with them."[31]

Survivors of HMCS *Athabaskan*. Intimacies such as Pierre Berton and Alexander Ross describe leave their traces in photographic images of the war. These sailors had survived the sinking of the Canadian destroyer *Athabascan* only to be taken prisoner in Germany. The two sailors on the left clearly wanted to document their relationship for the camera, for posterity. These deep emotions may underlie the nostalgia of many veterans' war memories. Courtesy of the National Archives of Canada/ PAI66528.

While ratings were sometimes court-martialled for homosexuality in the RCN, the sexual transgressions that were apparent to the entire crew were part of a wider range of secrets that it was in everyone's interest to protect. The crew of the *Sackville*, like other units in all three services, were bound together through a range of activities. "Lots of guys," according to Joe, were involved in "a little racket on the side. Buy liquor in Newfoundland for say four or five dollars in those days. Stock up on that. Stock up on coke. That's the ratings, nothing to do with the officers. So you get into Ireland ... sold the cigarettes to the taxi drivers. Then the liquor, sold it for 25 dollars to the Americans." One of the key contributors to unit cohesion was the fact that all comrades were involved in hiding such schemes from a range of military authorities. Homosexuality was one of many infractions to be kept from military police and superior officers. This is one of the elements that separated the social organization of training camps from mature units in all services.

Bitterness did result aboard the *Sackville* when homosexuality appeared to violate the separation between the upper and lower decks. The ratings noticed that the lieutenant, who was generally thought to be homosexual, appeared to have "his favourites, they were always together." During a particularly stressful battle with a U-boat, one of the lieutenant's favourites, also known to be homosexual, froze at his action station. While others in the crew yelled at him to fire the Orlicon gun, he was unable to respond. Nevertheless, he was awarded a Mentioned in Dispatches, having been recommended by the lieutenant. While he himself was forgiven for his inability to respond, the affair left a bitter legacy with others aboard who had been more alert on this, and other, occasions.

The relationship between officers and ratings in the RCN was contentious throughout the war. Lamb argues that disciplinary problems were the result of officers trying to be either too familiar with their crews or too officious. While the captain of the *Sackville* had found an effective balance, Joe remembers serving on a frigate that was a much less happy ship because of what the crew interpreted as the petty tyranny of the officers. He remembers serving guard duty in port on one occasion and being confronted for insubordination: "So I saw [the captain] coming down the gangplank, I had the rifle and just turned around the other way and he [says] 'Come here! Don't you know enough to salute an officer?' ... I says 'I did salute ya.' (I didn't at all.) He says 'Go back aboard and get the coxswain to teach you how to salute.' I didn't go back. You get sick of it." On the other hand, officers who were too familiar – sexually or otherwise – with individuals under their command could create an atmosphere of distrust. Lamb remembers being chided early in his career for violating the separation between officers and ratings: "My first corvette captain, suspecting me of 'sucking up' to the signalman on watch, told me bluntly to make up my mind whether I was to berth in the messdeck or in the wardroom, for in this ship I wasn't going to do both" The *Sackville*'s lieutenant, therefore, threatened the cohesiveness of the crew by transgressing, not primarily sexual norms, but the structure of authority. In so doing, he created a situation in which ratings had reason to believe that they were not being treated consistently. The great majority of charges for homosexual activity in the navy were instances of relationships between officers and ratings. Once named as homosexual in a charge, defendants were marked in a manner that would have serious repercussions. Homosexuality became the crime. However, it was not sex, but inappropriate familiarity between classes, that disturbed the balance of navy command.[32]

Whereas homosexual relations between men were either severely punished or, more commonly, ignored, the navy was paternalistic in response to lesbian relations. Margaret was a Wren posted as a censor in Halifax during the war. Not lesbian herself, she nevertheless witnessed the navy's response to various homosexual officers and ratings. A new officer was appointed to her unit in an effort to tighten discipline, "and believe me, she did," recalls Margaret. "But it turned out that she was very gay indeed. She had two other Wren officers part of her little entourage to the point where again it became a terrible scandal and the Navy solved that by moving her to a different position up in Ottawa, sending one of the girls up to Sydney, I think, and the other one out to the west coast. In other words they broke it up and then they brought in a different WRCN officer." By separating the lesbian women, the naval authorities assumed that they were thwarting immoral relations. In fact, they were interfering with the bonds of emotional support that the women had established.

The navy brass assumed that such relationships hindered group cohesion and effectiveness. As Margaret states, "These things were not tolerated if they came to light for morale purposes." But how, in fact, did the officer's staff respond to her departure? Her staff had respected and trusted her, and Margaret insists that it was the navy's persecution of a popular officer that was detrimental to morale: "She was the best officer we ever had. She was very firm, she knew what she was doing, but she was pushed into Outer Mongolia as a result of her personal activities ... I think everybody respected her as an officer. This was an unfortunate loss." By confining her romantic interests to her fellow officers, she did not make the mistake of the homosexual officer aboard the *Sackville*. Of course, it was much easier to find homosexual partners among the officer class on land than in a small ship on the Atlantic.[33]

QUEERS IN COMBAT UNITS

The Cape Breton Highlanders faced the fiercest fighting under some of the worst conditions endured by any regiment of the Canadian Army. After twenty-three months in England, they sailed for Italy on 27 October 1943. Fighting with 11 Canadian Infantry Brigade in the line north of Ortona, they first faced the Germans on 13 January 1944. Two days later, news of their first comrade killed in action "hit each soldier with a shock." After two more days, they had suffered fifty-one casualties. By June of 1944, at a cost of hundreds of casualties, they had mounted patrols and fought battles at Arielli, Orsogna, Monte Cassino, the Hitler Line, and the River Melfa. As the campaign progressed, "battalions were rotated in and out of contact with the enemy frequently in order to relieve the stress of constant engagement." While out of battle, platoons (units of thirty men, although usually well understrength) engaged in training, exercise, and drill. The army emphasized

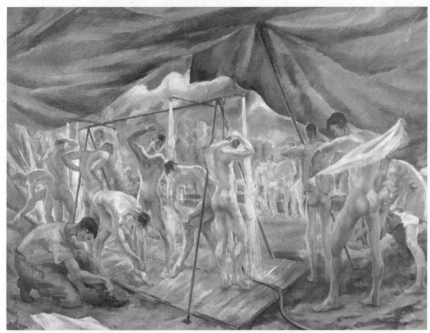

The Mobile Bath (1944) – an Artist's Impression. This painting by official army artist Captain George Douglas Pepper documents a common sight throughout Italy and northwest Europe during the war years – naked Canadian soldiers taking advantage of a mobile bath unit. Pepper's rendering can easily be read as an homage to the beauty of wartime Canada's male youth. In the background, partly hidden behind the shower of water in the centre of the composition, he includes a naked soldier sitting on the grass whose head is being caressed by another standing next to him. As in Lieutenant Nichol's *Sailors in Harbour Craft Leaving for Ship* (page 244), the two men physically in contact are not hiding from their comrades, but are in a casual relationship with three other soldiers, also naked. If this was not a homoerotic fantasy during the war, it will be in the future. Source: AN19710261-5313, © Canadian War Museum.

platoon cohesion because that unit "had to live and fight together and have confidence in one another." In reflecting on the Italian campaign, a veteran of the Highlanders echoed classical military wisdom when he said that soldiers "may have in their minds some idea of national purpose or that they are fighting to preserve democracy, but at The Front during battle, they fight for and with their comrades."[34]

In the case of the Highlanders, the men had grown up in the social and economic conditions of Depression-era Cape Breton. While labour historians have studied working-class social formation, few have tried to incor-

A Mobile Bath – the Reality. Here, some of the members of Canada's first parachute battalion dry themselves off after a bath. Soldiers claimed public space as masculine by performing normally private functions there. It is impossible to imagine that the army would have allowed female soldiers to shower in public. Courtesy of the National Archives of Canada/PA169249.

porate homosexuality into their work. Most historians have presumed working-class culture to have been exclusively heterosexual. However, there is no reason to assume that the bonds that developed among comrades fighting together in the mountains of Italy were unlike those that existed in Cape Breton culture. In fact, the great majority of the ranks who appeared before martial courts for homosexual offences had been part of Canada's working class before the war. Likewise, after the war, the experience of Italy and northwest Europe would be taken back to Cape Breton. Historian Steven Maynard's call to Canadian labour historians to include homosexuality in their analyses of working-class culture has not yet been heeded. Thus, a study of homosexuality within a platoon of the regiment offers insights into the practices of a segment of Canadian working-class society.[35]

During the summer of 1944, the Highlanders were taken out of the line and engaged in training, exercises, drills, rest, and recreation. It was during such rest periods that disciplinary action could be taken to alter unwanted behaviour. In the case of 5 Platoon, two sergeants determined to put an end to the sexual practices that had evolved as the unit had become battle-hardened in the Italian mountains. Pup tents were commonly shared by two men. It was a simple matter for comrades to alter sleeping arrangements so that those who most wanted to sleep together could share a tent. Over the months, patterns became apparent. By mid-August, at least nine homosexual charges were laid in order to put an end to the obvious fact that many men were involved in sexual relations with their comrades.[36]

The trials beg the question of why some men were charged while others who were apparently consenting accomplices were called only as witnesses. The proceedings reveal a willingness on the part of army authorities to avoid transparent implications arising out of the evidence. For instance, while the platoon was still on the line at Capua in May, Private N came to Lance Corporal Adolph's tent one night and asked if he could sleep with him. They spent the night together, and according to Private N's testimony, for three hours he resisted as Lance Corporal Adolph attempted to masturbate him. Adolph was charged with placing his hand on Private N's penis "with intent to commit acts of sexual perversion" and was sentenced to six months detention. Private N was never charged. The court never asked Private N why he had wanted to sleep not only in Adolph's tent, but in his bed. Neither was the court curious as to why Lance Corporal Adolph might be so solicitous of Private N's sexual satisfaction, for, according to the testimony, he concerned himself exclusively with N's orgasm. Private N told the court that various times throughout the night he had "rolled over to avoid 'explosions.'" Lance Corporal Adolph claimed that he and Private N had been "chummy all along."[37]

Lance Corporal Adolph was also charged with two counts of intending "to commit an act of sexual perversion" with Corporal M, a twenty-two-year-old rifleman and anti-tank gunner. Corporal M, like Private N, would not be charged at all. The Highlanders had just come out of the line in early June when Corporal M, who had slept with Adolph previously, asked him if he could share his bed again. He told the court that Lance Corporal Adolph "put his hand on my penis" that night. Nevertheless, he slept with Adolph again the following night. Once again, with both men wearing only their shorts, Adolph "put his hand over on my penis and let it rest there." For the two subsequent nights, Corporal M continued to sleep with Adolph. He told the court that he had lost his blankets at the front and so needed to share Adolph's. Corporal M had been friends with Adolph for a year, and his discomfort at being forced to testify against him was apparent throughout the trial. At the summary of evidence he had admitted that Adolph was "trying to pull me off," while at the trial he claimed that Adolph's hand was merely resting on his penis that happened to be out of his shorts. At trial, he tried to minimize the gesture, claiming that he could not be sure if Adolph was asleep or awake. His choice of words also suggests that he wanted to sway the court to see the actions as insignificant: "that's all that happened."[38]

Similarly, the other trials suggest that charges were being laid selectively and uncomfortable questions were simply avoided. While the platoon was on an anti-tank training course in late June, Corporal B was sharing a pup tent with Private John F. Corporal B described how Private John came into the tent late one night after drinking heavily. Corporal B put him to bed and then went to sleep himself. He claimed: "While sleeping I dreamt I was having sexual intercourse with a woman and I woke up to find that I had had an ejaculation and that Pte. [John], the accused had his hand around my penis working it back and forth." Corporal B testified that they were sleeping in the same bed. While Corporal B was not charged, John would spend a year in detention for "disgraceful conduct of an unnatural kind." Surprisingly, the court never asked Corporal B why it was that if he had been responsible for the sleeping arrangements that night, the two men were in the same bed. Also neglected was the unlikelihood that a "staggering" drunk could so deftly perform such a delicate sexual operation without waking the patient.[39]

Lance Corporal James G faced four charges of disgraceful conduct and was sentenced to six months detention. He was known to be homosexually active before the Highlanders had arrived in Italy. While in England, sexual partners would have been easily available to him from outside the regiment, but in Italy, especially on the line, his options would have been narrower. Private C, echoing Corporal B's disclaimer, testified that he had fallen asleep one night along the side of the road while in the company of Lance Corporal James and another private. He awoke to find that James "was rubbing my testicles and penis ... He then made an effort to get me on top of him but he was unsuccessful." The other private testified that Private C had not fallen asleep. Lance Corporal James faced another charge as a result of being caught one morning in Private R's tent. Private R admitted to Sergeant Slaney "just a few words of what had happened" throughout the previous night. His argument that he had spent the entire night resisting Lance Corporal James's romantic advances was, once again, accepted by the court.[40]

What does the evidence from the summaries of evidence and courts martial tell us about homosexual practices within the platoon? How were partners approached and what needs did sexual relations satisfy? Why were James, John, and Adolph, in particular, sacrificed? What effect did the trials have on platoon cohesion? Finally, why did the Highlanders choose to prosecute and lose the services of three trained infantrymen at the height of Canada's manpower crisis?

All of 5 Platoon involved in the homosexual courts were working men from Cape Breton. They ranged in age from twenty-two to thirty. Before the war, they had learned to shift for themselves in the inshore fishery, in coal mines, and as farmhands in Nova Scotia. A couple of the men did not specify the details of their working lives, listing themselves simply as labourers. One frankly stated to the army examiner that he had never had a "legal job" in his life before the war; another that he had been a bootlegger. Almost all had had varied working experience. One man who served a lengthy period in detention for his homosexual activities appears to have weathered the entire ordeal of war, court martial, and detention in good spirits. The examiner's notes for his final interview before his honourable discharge on demobilization reads: "Was cheerful and pleasant and seemed to have given considerable thought to the rehabilitation legislation as provided ... [Intends] to return to former employment as coal miner in which he was engaged for 13 years. Appears to know all aspects of this work as he freely discussed the different occupations in a mine at great length. His physical condition is good." The homosexual practices as revealed by the courts were possibly rooted in these all-male working environments of Cape Breton.[41]

On board the *Monterey* from England to Italy, the troops were bunked in pairs. They slept side by side, between piping that ran the length of the deck. Protected by the piping on each side, there was nothing between the men. For Corporal James G, sharing such accommodations may have been not unlike conditions for farmhands or lumbermen back home. By casually allowing an arm to come to rest on the body of his bedmate, James could test the receptivity of Corporal W. For two successive nights, Corporal James, although he seemed to be asleep, had fondled Corporal Wile's body. Corporal Wile told Lance Corporal Adolph G of the situation, and Adolph offered to change places with Corporal Wile. He suggested that if James tried the same thing with him, they could then be sure he was a pervert and have him put up on charges. The following morning, Lance Corporal Adolph told Corporal Wile that James had made no overtures and so all was well. However, since, over the subsequent months, Adolph's own homosexuality came to be a part of the platoon's sexual culture, it is quite possible that his motivation in changing sleeping quarters with Corporal Wile was to position himself to be able to proposition James. At that period in the regiment's history, there may not yet have existed a clear homosexual subculture. James and Adolph appear to have been unaware of their common sexual desires, even though they were in the same platoon. The care that needed to be taken to protect their secret is evident in the machinations involved in creating the circumstances in which they could safely make love.[42]

Casual nighttime gestures calculated either to lead to homosexual relations or to be excused as unconscious movements were widespread and effective. Even when the courts tried to prosecute, they found it impossible to attribute intention to such motions. Was the perpetrator awake or asleep? On the other hand, if such gestures were successful, then there was little chance that they would ever need to be explained. As 5 Platoon matured militarily and socially and more comrades came to participate in its homosexual culture, it became more and more difficult to protect the secret. It also became less necessary. By the spring of 1944, soldiers were regularly contriving to spend the nights with chosen comrades. Sometimes the trysts were designed to satisfy the participants' needs on a single night. Other times, as with Lance Corporal Adolph and Corporal M, they could be ongoing arrangements. Sexual activity was also no longer confined to the protective covering of pup tents and nighttime. Lance Corporal James and Private C, for example, made out at the side of a road on the way back from the local village in the presence of another soldier. Why did homosexuality come to play such an integral part in the lives of these front-line soldiers? Why did it take the form that it did?

Equally valid, although it would have been less obvious to mid-twentieth-century Canadian observers, is the complementary question: why was homosexuality seemingly so absent from Canadian society in general and military units in particular? The Spartan and Sambian cultures show us that homo- and heterosexual acts could be viewed as equally normal, although each kind was meaningful within particular social contexts. By contrast, Canadian society did not sanction any form of homosexual activity and insisted that this taboo stand even when it removed its citizens from all other social supports and then subjected them to extraordinary pressures. The men of the Cape Breton Highlanders responded by taking care of their own emotional needs. In order to understand how homosexual behavior served them, it is necessary to have as clear a sense as the evidence will allow of the actual sexual practices that prevailed. This cannot be a straightforward matter of consulting unproblematic sources. Men had every reason to lie, to withhold the truths of their sexual desires and behaviours. Not only did they face prison terms, but they risked expulsion from the group to which they had come to belong. Nevertheless, the records for 5 Platoon are extensive and patterns of behaviour are apparent. It is evident that the men were commonly involved in mutual lovemaking. The behaviours described in the courts suggest that these relations were more than simple attempts to relieve individual sexual tensions; rather they were, above all, passionate affairs committed to giving as well as receiving pleasure. In each case, men were charged with concerning themselves with the orgasms of other men, not their own. Even through the falsehoods encouraged by the court settings, the encounters appear to have been mutually satisfying. For instance, Private N's admission that he had been close to "exploding" several times over the course of the night he had spent with Lance Corporal Adolph is typical. The other witnesses likewise describe events that took place over a period of hours. Most of the evidence refers to fondling and mutual masturbation, although there is some suggestion that at least one of the men enjoyed anal intercourse.

What difference did physical and gender 'types' play in the sexual culture? The personnel files of the men involved in the court cases each contain various entries by personnel officers, army examiners, psychiatrists, and Department of Veterans Affairs officers. These documents usually contain the impression that the subject made on the interviewer and are consistent for individual men. The following are descriptions of the men charged: "a huge, strongly built man, appears shy, but is pleasant and has a definite rural background," "a tall, well-built man who appears to be a strong worker," "a quiet mannered, well built, rugged looking single man." The men involved in the sexual relations who were never charged were generally described in less masculine terms: "a happy, healthy looking soldier with no disability," "tall, with slim physique." However, there is little correlation between sexual practice and masculine characteristics. Sometimes a younger, less virile soldier approached a more typically masculine type. Other times the pursuer was of a more brawny demeanour. And there were times when both lovers were typically masculine in description. Those labelled as virile were equally affectionate and considerate of their partner's sexual satisfaction.[43]

The sexual practices, therefore, did not attempt to reproduce the ideological standard of a sexually active, masculine subject and a passive, feminine object. Neither was the sexual culture that evolved a substitute for heterosexuality. Most of the charges were laid for homosexual offences that took place while the platoon was within walking distance of a village that offered a heterosexual brothel. Moreover, the Highlanders continued to pursue their heterosexual desires throughout the campaign. It remains a fact that, even without societal sanctions, homosexuality was integrated into the Highlanders' culture. It should be easy to imagine how men who were risking their lives, forgoing all domestic comforts, and living under considerable stress should also feel entitled to find emotional support and physical pleasure where they themselves chose to look for it. Most social niceties had been left behind in Canada and England, and soldiers may have responded to war's unique circumstances by freeing themselves from social restraints as well. This was clearly evident in the way that some soldiers aggressively sought to satisfy heterosexual desires in Italy. The many cases of rape prosecuted by Canadian martial courts in Italy and northwest Europe suggest that many soldiers adopted anti-social behaviour in the circumstance of war.

The homosexual culture, insofar as it is reflected in the courts, was free of the violence that came to accompany many soldiers' heterosexual pursuits in Italy. Since the homosexual relations took place within a different context, it is not surprising that they also assumed a different form. The men who became involved with each other sexually were also comrades who had come to depend upon each other in myriad ways. The army's emphasis on platoon cohesion meant that they trained, exercised, worked, ate, and slept together. They knew that they depended on each other for their lives. Under those circumstances, it is not surprising that their sexual relations might be based on mutual respect. It is also clear that men who sought homosexual relationships were being served psychologically by them.[44]

Nevertheless, at least two sergeants in the platoon were disturbed by the growing homosexual culture and resolved to put an end to it. By late spring 1944, various men in 5 Platoon were openly discussing their sexual relations with their comrades. In light of the practice of lovers sharing tents and beds, it is unlikely that such a tight-knit group could remain ignorant for long. Eventually, there would have been little benefit in hiding what everyone already knew. The character evidence offered by the comrades of the accused makes it clear that the men most bold in their homosexual affairs were not marginalized in any way in the platoon. Neither were they merely tolerated – they were appreciated. Sergeant Samson, however, targeted the younger, less-imposing men in order to intimidate them into admitting what transpired in the pup tents at night. Since none of the men who told their story to Sergeant Samson were charged, it seems likely that he used the threat of prosecution to extract confessions. Sergeant Slaney assisted Samson in gathering evidence. When he burst into Private R's tent one morning to find Lance Corporal James putting on his shoes, he demanded that Private R tell him if he had "got fucked" the previous night. Under such pressure, Private R made a partial admission.[45]

What effect did the trials have on unit cohesion? Clearly, Sergeants Samson and Slaney must have felt more comfortable in a platoon in which homosexuality was no longer apparent. For the others in the platoon, it was not homosexuality that had threatened cohesion, but the trials to eradicate it. Lance Corporal James, for instance, was praised by the officer commanding the platoon at Orsogna as "one of the best" soldiers in the section. Lieutenant Nelson, who had been James's commander for a year, said that he "seemed to have many friends" in the platoon and that he often noticed him "laughing & joking" with his comrades. Likewise, he characterized Lance Corporal Adolph as a "smart, first class man." Corporal Wile claimed that Adolph, like James, "was popular" in the platoon. Other soldiers testified that they had slept with them in trenches and barracks without incident. The soldiers who were forced to testify against them were obviously reluctant. It is hard to imagine an environment more detrimental to unit cohesion than the court martial for homosexual offences. Soldiers were given the choice of betraying their comrades or facing charges themselves. Others watched the friends that they had depended on during six months of a gruelling campaign be sentenced to long terms of detention at a time when the platoon was well understrength. It would seem that the commanding officers determined that the unit was best served by prosecuting popular, effective queer comrades.[46]

Sergeant Slaney, now an honorary colonel with the Cape Breton Highlanders, authored its regimental history, *The Breed of Manly Men*. Slaney makes no reference to the trials of August 1944 or to the manner by which the manliest of men satisfied their sexual and physical needs and desires. Nevertheless, he himself was involved in bringing a select few of the offenders to trial. Regimental histories are seldom probing documents and are intended instead to present the institution in a light that flatters its favoured features and hides its warts. The authors of immigration, ethnic, and working-class histories also avoid homosexuality for fear of discrediting their subjects and offending their readership. *The Breed of Manly Men*, however, does pay tribute to a couple of soldiers who, while they did not face courts martial for homosexual offences, were as much involved as those who were charged. Perhaps the decision of whom to charge and whom to protect was influenced by personal likes and antipathies. Throughout the entire military, soldiers were sensitive to the politics of favouritism. Homosexual men and women did not always suffer from such dynamics, but only they could be prosecuted because of their desires.

OVERSEAS SUPPORT UNITS

There were various military environments in which homosexuals were protected by their superiors and where a homosexual identity could be expressed quite openly. Ralph Wormleighton's 24 Field Ambulance Company followed the front lines throughout the Italian campaign and then into Holland, where it remained until war's end, establishing a main dressing station and an advanced dressing station. Its ambulances would bring wounded soldiers back to the advanced dressing station, where they would be examined by a medical officer. Those with head wounds were diverted to an advanced surgical unit, and others would be sent back to the main dressing station.

Just as Margaret's superior officer was transferred out of her censorship unit because she was a known lesbian, Ralph remembers men entering his ambulance company for the same reason. One soldier was transferred to his unit because "he'd been caught sucking somebody's cock" in his infantry unit. Ralph remembers "six or seven people that I'm quite sure were gay that were in the outfit." He feels that his unit's "exceptionally tolerant" attitude towards its queer members can be attributed to the fact that the officers were all medical doctors. A sense of the unit's approach to sexual and gender non-conformity is conveyed in Ralph's account of Ross, the company's sergeant pharmacist: "One [homosexual] was our sergeant pharmacist who was a flaming queen and made no bones about it ... When he arrived to join the unit he was interviewed by the colonel who was, of course, a doctor. At that time he had added all sorts of fancy things to his uniform and, as I said, he was a flaming queen. The doctor took one look at him and he says, 'I don't care what you do on leave, but you take all those decorations off your uniform around here.'"

The most significant difference between 24 Field Ambulance Company and the Cape Breton Highlanders, whose steps the company followed across Italy, is that the queer members of the former were supported by their officers. Ross, like the less fortunate Highlanders who found themselves serving lengthy detention sentences, was popular in the unit. Ralph remembers him with fondness: "The thing about it was that he was completely accepted in the unit. Everybody loved Ross."

Perhaps in deference to the colonel's request, it was on leave that Ralph suspects most of the sexual activity took place among members of the company. At the time, his own homosexuality was repressed, but in looking back at his wartime service, he realizes that "there were two or three persons made passes at me. Even within the unit. I remember an invitation to go on leave with them." As for Ross, Ralph recalls, "I did run into him after the war and I was asking him how he made out, and he says, 'In the unit, hardly at all.' At one point in a rest area in Italy, there was one of the French Canadian drivers got hard up and used to drop into his tent and screw him occasionally, but that was about it." However sexually active the queer element of the unit was, it is clear that their presence had no detrimental effect on morale. In fact, a flamboyant queen like Ross may well have been popular because of his success at self-expression in an authoritative institution.[47]

Ralph's portrait of his field ambulance unit tells us that the sergeant pharmacist had adopted the tactic of presenting himself in an outrageous manner, adopting feminine markers to signal his sexual difference. Gender inversion – itself legal, if risky – was thus employed as a code for homosexuality. It was, nevertheless, one step removed from an open expression of homosexuality, and Ralph's account shows that the actual crime was not visible in the unit. Such flamboyance, in fact, was the legitimate business of certain military units. Each of the three services had entertainment units that toured Canada and the theatres of war to perform for the troops. The Tin Hats was an entertainment unit of fifteen men that included actively straight, gay, and bisexual men. Bill Dunstan, one one of the two female impersonators in the unit, remembers that the other one was "obviously effeminate" as well as openly homosexual: "I don't suppose he used to boast at the top of his voice [about his sexual interests]. No, there was not much doubt about his being effeminate and he didn't make any bones about it."

Regarding the diversity of sexual interests, Bill concludes that the Tin Hats was "probably considerably more tolerant than other units ... That's the way it was and we went along with it. Some of us were gay and some were not." Whereas in other units comrades conspired to keep the group's sexual secrets from the view of outsiders (and insiders who may have posed a threat), members of the Tin Hats were cavalier in their pursuits: "I don't think that it ever occurred to me that there might have been problems. I know there were quite open liaisons, but if nobody pushed it, it was just a fact that we put up with or let slide. But no, I don't recall any culture of protection." The idea that anyone would have betrayed a comrade within the Tin Hats strikes Bill as senseless: "We certainly didn't want to break up

The Tin Hats. Many entertainment units included female impersonators. The army's Tin Hats had two: Bill Dunstan, "Trixie," and Johnny Haewood, "Trilby." Bill (left), who was not queer, remembers that everyone respected the range of relationships within the unit, many of which "didn't see the light of day." Courtesy of the National Archives of Canada/PA152148.

the show, which would have happened if a few people had been court-martialled." Like 24 Field Ambulance Company, the Tin Hats did not have to fear their officers, but they were rare within the military in allowing their homosexual interests to be expressed openly. In many units, homosexual men kept their sexual desires in check until they were a safe distance from their comrades.[48]

The 7th Field Security Section (7th FSS), a unit of the Intelligence Corps, made its way across northwest Europe with the Canadian Army in 1944 and 1945. Bert Sutcliffe remembers this small unit of thirteen people: "As we all had to work together, we were like one big family. We didn't have a sergeants' mess, we didn't have an officers' mess and we tended to work together and we tended to play together – not sexually – but we did things together. And everybody knew what everybody else was doing and where they came from. So it was really like a big family." In common with most units, the army had not included women in the establishment of the 7th FSS to perform the functions that Canadian society defined as feminine. The army did not provide for a division of labour within units based on sex.

However, the 7th FSS responded creatively to ensure that it could effectively accomplish its goals. In Caen, where the Canadian Army found itself stalled by intense German resistance, two thirty-year-old French women demonstrated their usefulness in various capacities and were unofficially seconded to the unit. Sutcliffe recalls: "We didn't have any cooks or anything and they did all of this type of work for us." The men in the unit paid them out of their own pockets and provided them with Canadian uniforms. Monique and Jeanette became integral members of the 7th FSS throughout its progress across northwest Europe. Their knowledge of the language, culture, and politics of wartime France made them invaluable to the unit. Moreover, their commitment to the cause of freeing Europe from Nazi domination grew out of four years of occupation. Bert describes the important military functions they came to perform: "We had no females in our unit and we were charged with picking females up and taking them back to our unit and processing them. In order to do that we had to search them. We had to have them take their clothes off and we had to have somebody around looking after them for six weeks ... we'd tell Jeanette to take them into the room and tell them to strip and search them for whatever they might find." As the 7th FSS came to depend upon Jeanette and Monique to perform such essential tasks, the two women became "a part of our unit." Eventually, Monique and the unit's driver fell in love with each other, as did Jeanette and an NCO. The affairs were open and became part of the social equation of the unit.

The 7th FSS remained a highly cohesive unit in operations throughout the campaign in northwest Europe. The inclusion of the women increased both the unit's effectiveness and morale. Their competence in 'women's' work relieved the men of some daily tasks. Meanwhile, simply because they were women, they were able to accomplish security tasks that would have been awkward for men. The evidence suggests that the introduction of romance and sexuality in the unit had only a positive effect on morale. However, it is possible that Sutcliffe may not have noticed jealousies or other complications that might have developed among his heterosexual comrades. Bonds of love were apparently powerful forces, adding to the overall cohesiveness of the 7th FSS. For his part, though, Sutcliffe found himself repressing his homosexuality unconditionally throughout the campaign. During the previous four years, he had fully come out in England's gay underground. At the front, his social world was limited to his unit. For Sutcliffe, a homosexual man, sex and romance required a safe environment, as socially remote from his unit as possible. So while he accepted the heterosexual relationships that grew within the 7th FSS as perfectly natural, the idea that he might carry on a homosexual affair within the unit was inconceivable: "It would never have crossed my mind. I would panic at the thought of it."[49]

While Sutcliffe assumed that restraint was the only viable option in adapting to his army company, this survey demonstrates that various military units improvised their own sexual standards. While some measure of invisibility was required in all cases, since all services prosecuted homosexual behaviour, the entertainment units reveal that, within formations, homosexual relationships could be pursued openly. The evidence available also suggests that it is a mistake to assume that homosexual behaviour belonged to any particular function of the military. Support, entertainment, medical, and fighting units could all harbour homosexual servicepeople. Under the discriminatory regulations and with fear of rejection by one's comrades, the difference among groups is not the existence of homosexual bonds, but their visibility.

PRISONERS OF WAR

For Canadians held in prisoner of war camps in Germany, bonds between pairs of soldiers became especially significant. Some saw that development as a threat to the looser, multidirectional bonds that, in principle, were thought to be the basis of unit cohesion. That homosexuality might have accompanied the emotional intimacy and commitment that developed between pairs of prisoners is a contested issue.

Few historical accounts of POW camps, either scholarly or autobiographical, address the issue of homosexuality in any depth. Kingsley Brown, a Canadian journalist who had spent several year in Stalag Luft III, addressed the subject in his 1989 memoir, *Bonds of Wire*: "Whenever sex is discussed in the context of prison life, there is inevitably a question asked about homosexuality. In a community of men without women, is the incidence of homosexuality likely to increase? Since there is a minimum of privacy in camp life, it was only to be expected that what deviation existed would be more than ordinarily conspicuous. There were instances of such relationships; we were aware but they were few." While Brown's account may be accurate, it is framed defensively, with the intention of assuring the reader that homosexuality was not widespread. That there were "few" homosexual relationships seems to speak well of the Allied soldiers held for years in all-male environments. If the absence of queer behaviour was simply a result of 'natural' human behaviour, there is a sense of relief that nature could control the sexual response. However, his account also suggests that not everyone was so sure that their morality could be controlled in the situation:

Most of us never gave the subject a thought, but Major Edward Monteuis, the camp medical officer, seems to have entertained a notion that new prisoners might feel some apprehension lest a prolonged separation from female company wreak havoc on their normal libido. He frequently took the occasion to reassure us. "Don't worry about it. If you were meant to be queer, it would have happened long before you got to this place. Sure, it may be a little more obvious here, but the percentage of deviation in a prison camp is no different than it is back home. All that stuff about prisons changing your sex life is just a lot of rot. Forget it!"

A more detailed study of the same camp asserts that orders issued by the ranking officer empowered certain prisoners to keep a watch on their comrades to make sure that they did not slide into degeneracy.[50]

Brown's assurance that "most of us never gave the subject a thought" is challenged not only by his own account of the medical officer and the incoming POWs, but also by some documentary evidence. A British soldier, Sapper Victor Croxford, for instance, published a weekly journal of life in Stalag VIIIB, which housed various Allied prisoners, including Canadians. Croxford distributed his broadsheet in order to provide "the sense of humour with which the prisoner spices his patient philosophy." By mischievously reporting the camp gossip, his chronicles provide rich insights into daily life in a prisoner of war camp. The early editions contain playful references to homosexual relationships in the camp. A short item in the 1 January 1942 edition of the *Daily Louse* reads: "Despite the climate being reverse to tropical certain people are getting some tanning now; whilst their relations are becoming 'browned-off.'" A June article in the *Weekly Wire* entitled "It's a Boy" reads: "A strong rumour to the affect [sic] that a comrade of a neighbouring lager [camp] has changed his sex was founded more upon circumstances than fact." One article provoked a charge of libel in 1942, and Croxford's weekly accounts of camp life came under the censorship of the ranking officer. Still, his paper continued to comment, albeit more warily, on camp sexuality.[51]

Croxford's allusions to homosexuality are often connected to his coverage of instances of cross-dressing. For instance, on 11 September 1942, he reported on a camp boxing event: "I stayed long enough to see the first four classic exhibitions of the masculin [sic] art and to observe the waitress work by two naval prisoners, dressed and bewigged as young ladies and bearing trays of tea (?) among the spectators about the ring. Price? per cup." The blurring of the masculine and feminine in camp society became increasingly apparent in his coverage. On 1 April 1944, in an article called "Hit and 'Miss,'" he reported: "A friend in E3 Boxing Club was much amused at telling us of Teddy (Matt) Morgan, featherweight. The hard-hitting 'all-rounder' goes straight from training-bouts into the next part of the hall, to rehearse his part as 'Yum Yum,' a demure songstress in 'The Mikado.'" Another performer involved in the camp's extravagant theatrical productions was reported to have been so committed to his female roles as "to grow his curly hair long enough to pass off his masculine frame without a wig." After a performance of "Cinderella," he reports that six chorus "'girls' ... trip daintily among the seats, to the satisfaction of the gents they caress." Reporting on a dancing competition in June 1943, he says that "[c]hampions, runners-up and in fact nearly all taking part seem to dance as either lady or gent with equal felicity."[52]

While Croxford jested about a camp society in which men played the roles of both sexes, the idea that comradely friendships might have been sexual or romantic in nature was a disturbing possibility to him. In February 1943 many prisoners were upset that their housing arrangements had to be altered because of the requirements of work parties. Croxford editorialized: "No true friendships are broken at partings, especially by such trivial distance. Any other kind of friendship must be unhealthy, if comradeship can be so easily killed." That POWs could become emotionally dependent on each other violated a standard of independence and self-sufficiency expected of men. Strong individual bonds, according to this perspective, interfered with the looser relationships that were transferable from comrade to comrade. However, memoirs suggest that such relationships did become increasingly significant as prisoners looked to their special mate for support. Prison argot developed words for intimate friends. One ex-prisoner provided a glossary of terms for Allied POWs held in Germany, including "winger," signifying a POW's "constant companion." In fact, the descriptions of POW life sometimes paint these relationships as male marriages, a fundamental military social unit according to Pierre Berton's analysis.[53]

When H. Wooley's plane was shot down over Germany, he became a prisoner in Stalag VIIIB, Croxford's camp. His memoir of his POW experience describes his maturing relationship with George, the British soldier with whom he messed. Wooley had hoped that George would prepare something special for his twenty-first birthday. When he realized that George had forgotten the date, he was deeply hurt: "I was beginning to feel like the young bride whose husband has failed to observe their first wedding anniversary." He describes the scene that evening when he became aware that George had forgotten his birthday: "I had no stomach for the food which we ate in silence. If George guessed the reason for my lack of interest he never gave any indication of it. Since I have never been one to mask my feelings, I'm quite sure he sensed my unhappiness. The subject was never raised again by me, and I never let him know how hurt I was." From his perspective of fifty years later back in Canada, Wooley sees the episode as "juvenile" and "trivial." However, he argues that, "like everything else in life, these matters must be considered in light of the circumstances in which they occurred."[54]

CONCLUSION

The development of male marriages among prisoners of war and many others who served in the Canadian forces suggests that intimate emotional and psychological bonds were not restricted to homosexual relationships. In fact, homosexual relationships did not necessarily entail emotional bonds. This discussion of social forms in the Canadian forces during the Second World War has largely sidestepped the terms of the current debate over the relationship between unit cohesion and military effectiveness. Whether intimate bonds inhibit or promote group cohesion is a contentious issue. Moreover, whether social cohesion in turn promotes task effectiveness is debatable. What should be clear, though, is that homosexual bonds, as such, were neither more nor less intimate than homosocial bonds.

Various forms of homosexual relationships developed among men and women throughout the Canadian forces during the Second World War. These relations found their place in the complex social arrangements of different units. Many queer comrades were heartily accepted within their units in all of the services. The military's pursuit and prosecution of individuals who were unfortunate enough to be discovered both affected the morale of the men targeted and disturbed the bonds they had forged with their unmarked comrades. In demonstrating that it was tough on the vice of homosexuality, the military also showed that it lacked compassion for men who were known to be contributing to ultimate victory. In contrast, non-queer men and women at all levels of command were far more flexible and considerate of their homosexual comrades.

CONCLUSION

During the Second World War, two contradictory processes evolved within the Canadian military regarding homosexuality. At the institutional level, homosexuals became increasingly vulnerable to prosecution and persecution. A panoply of intrusive policing and surveillance techniques meant that individual men were more vulnerable to exposure and harassment on the basis of their homosexual behaviour and desires. On the other hand, at the interpersonal level, individual queer men were increasingly accepted and appreciated within their military formations. In the early stages of unit formation, the sexual orientation of individual men was seldom known. As units matured militarily and socially, the queerness of some men became evident. Since such men had already been integrated into the units, their comrades most commonly chose to overlook their queer behaviour. Queer men, in turn, calibrated their openness according to their circumstances. Formations in different military environments evolved distinct ways of accommodating their homosexual members. In all cases, units needed to protect queer men from the institution, which remained resolutely opposed to homosexuality.

All official discussion of homosexuality in the Canadian military in the war years was based on the proposition that it was destructive to the individual, to relationships, to unit cohesion, to the military, and to the state. To medical services, queer men were "sexual psychopaths with abnormal sexual behaviour." As such, they were deemed military misfits and were thought to be universally harmful to the healthy functioning of units. Therefore, medical officers provided the administrative tools for their immediate discharge from the military. To the adjutant-general's and judge-advocate general's offices, queer men were assumed to disrupt good order and military discipline. Men accused of any behaviour considered to be homosexual

Back Home. Two soldiers from the Queen's Own Rifles of Canada return to Toronto after the war. They remind us of the bonds that soldiers
and sailors forged with each other throughout the war and the absence
of fear about being labelled homosexual on the basis of their physical
intimacy. Courtesy of the City of Toronto Archives, Fonds 1266, File
98478.

in nature appeared before martial courts and were sentenced to a wide range
of punishments. Military police were trained to investigate possible violators
and charge them under the Army, Air Force, or Naval Discipline Acts.
Meanwhile, postal and military censors were given unprecedented access to
knowledge of the private lives of soldiers in the course of their daily work.
Queer men who fell victim to these surveillance techniques were often severely punished.

While these official policies were left unchallenged by the institution,
more practical arrangements evolved among military personnel of all ranks.
Very few officers were willing to publicly challenge the notion that homosexuality was immoral and inimical to military pursuits, although most
knew that the application of anti-homosexual policies would have been ru-

inous to their own interests. Some were queer themselves, and others appreciated the diversity among their men. Commanding officers were aware that homosexuality was, in fact, not inimical to unit cohesion. Even those men brought before courts because of their pursuit of illicit pleasures were often praised by their comrades and superiors as effective and popular soldiers. When commanding officers did refer delinquent soldiers to medical services for disposal, it was because the men were unmanageable, not because they were homosexual. Competent queer soldiers who faced administrative or legal censure were usually outed by a third party – censors, police, or civilians.

Society's discomfort with homosexuality was often reflected it the attitudes of individuals. Some soldiers and officers accepted the ideological arguments regarding the evils of homosexuality and tried to eradicate it from their midst. Queer men were also challenged to accept their anti-social desires. Undisguised homosexuality could not be reconciled with any sanctioned male role in Canadian society. Typically, to be queer meant that one was morally degenerate or anti-social or had a woman's soul in a man's body. Homosexual men often chose to lead a double life; to varying degrees, they hid their queer pleasures from the world. Others chose to reject the standards of masculinity and to create their social and self-images according to their own imaginations. Many repressed their problematic sexualities, but such men were often the most vulnerable to police surveillance when, under the influence of alcohol, they recklessly acceded to their buried desires.

When a capable soldier became marked as queer in a hostile unit, the most practical response was to transfer him to a more friendly environment. This procedure was understood and sanctioned at all levels of command. While the administrative machinery existed to discharge homosexual men, there was no consensus over how to identify a true homosexual. In particular, personnel selection officers never asked recruits if they were homosexual and ignored the fact in cases where it was known. Medical officers, who claimed exclusive rights of diagnosis, saw homosexuality as a rare condition. Queer behaviour was not necessarily indicative of a homosexual character. In practice, doctors were unwilling to mark men as true homosexuals, a group that was cast by most medical models as degenerate and anti-social. It was impossible to reconcile that category with the healthy and productive homosexual men who were referred to them. However, since the majority of the men they were called upon to diagnose were sent to them because of behavioural problems, they were able to conceive of homosexuality, when they discovered it, as one element of a larger pathology.

The Canadian military tried to deter the expression of homosexuality at all ranks by punishing and humiliating the offenders. When evidence of homosexuality could not be contained within a unit, officers and other ranks faced court-martial boards. While officers were either acquitted or dismissed from the forces, most men in the ranks were sentenced to terms of detention or imprisonment. In this way, the forces tacitly accepted that those who behaved homosexually were nevertheless valuable to the war effort. Men who were disciplined for homosexual crimes continued to serve after their sentences had been completed, sometimes repeatedly.

In their own lives, most homosexual servicemen avoided the traps that would have exposed them as queer and left them vulnerable to punishment. Many remember the war years as formative in their sexual and social development. In stark contrast to wartime military assumptions, they interpreted the acceptance of their homosexual pleasures as part of their personal growth. The military, however, did not re-evaluate its received knowledge concerning homosexuality even in the face of such evidence. At the institutional level, it inflexibly applied its presumptions. Men who had sex with men were thought to have failed themselves, their comrades, the service, and their country. The power of that certainty forbade inquiries into the actual value of sexual and emotional attachments between men.

Historians Allan Bérubé and John D'Emilio have argued, in reference to the American case, that the Second World War laid the groundwork for the rise of the subsequent homophile and gay liberation movements. By collecting soldiers together in urban centres, the war promoted the development of gay communities. Bérubé and D'Emilio contend that American soldiers who had been persecuted during the war as homosexual subsequently organized themselves against the state on the basis of that identity. While my work has focused on the war years, both interviews and military records lead me to question their thesis. The Canadian military's attempt to marginalize soldiers and officers whom it marked as homosexual was largely successful. Most were deeply disturbed by the experience. In the postwar years, they chose to disavow the humiliation and bury the shame. During the war years, the state drew on a deep-seated aversion to homosexuality that had been diffused through religious, legal, medical, state, and social rhetoric and practices. The groundwork had been laid for the Canadian military, which mustered that revulsion and aimed it at individual queer men. Those men stood against the power of the state during a time of patriotic fervour. Most importantly, they felt that they stood alone and exposed. The Canadian state was thus largely successful in atomizing the 'sexually deviant' component within the military. Meanwhile, scholars have not found that the leaders of the postwar urban gay subcultures and homophile organizations were targeted as homosexual during the war. Neither have they described those communities as composed of demobilized soldiers. While repressive state policies have spawned resistance, we should be alert to the real ability of the state to isolate and discredit those who stand in opposition.

So what did happen to the subjects of this book? Through personnel records and interviews, I often gained knowledge of servicemen's postwar lives. Many did go on to explore the homoerotic desires they had felt during the war, often for the first time in their lives. Some made careers in the military and kept their homosexuality private. In time, they were either exposed as 'perverts' by the military or they retired to a social life more sympathetic to their sexual difference. Many married and raised families. In some cases, they pursued their homoerotic desires throughout their married lives, usually without their wives' knowledge. Most men interviewed saw their self-acceptance as gay as a lifetime process. They sought and found a variety of nurturing homosexual relationships. Some who had been persecuted by the services were bitter. One left Canada as a result; others tried to begin anew in communities where their shame was unknown. In some cases, their courts martial or discharges were used against them in later life.

Significant changes in public discourse have altered the military's relationship with homosexuals in the years since the Second World War. Gay men and lesbians have established a foothold in popular discourse from which to argue their equality and full right to citizenship. Both in Canada and the United States, they defend their right to defend their countries. By doing so, they challenge long-standing assumptions that continue to ground the category of soldier. Given the pervasiveness and depth of anti-homosexual attitudes documented here, it is not surprising that the concept of soldier has been so resistant to gay men's claims to inclusion. The reproduction of social categories occurs daily in countless ways. As demonstrated in these pages, common expletives embedded in the language, such as cocksucker, faggot, and bugger, (and gay), actively denigrate queer men below the policy radar. While militaries cannot control the complex production and reproduction of soldier as a social category, they can enable either tolerance or intolerance by official policy. Precisely because social categories such as soldier and queer are maintained in innumerable ways, their transformation is unpredictable and beyond the reach of any one person or organization.

APPENDICES

Appendix One

FIGURES

Figure 1
Homosexual Charges Laid against RCAF Personnal, 1940–1945 (partial data)

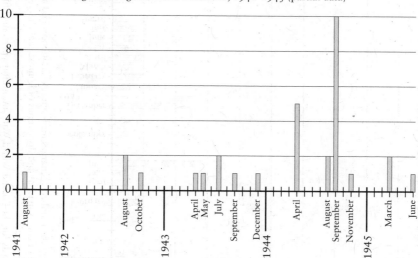

Note: This figure documents the trend in the number of charges for homosexual offences laid against RCAF personnel. It is based on an unknown (but probably small) percentage of the total charges laid.

Sources: RCAF *Routine Orders*, NA, RG 24, vols 22480–2; Archives of Ontario, RG 22-1391, boxes 3985–91, 225–33.

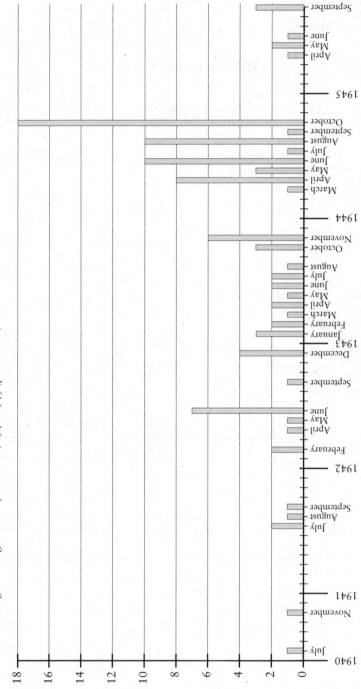

Figure 2
Homosexual Charges Laid against Army Personnel, 1940–1945 (partial data)

Note: This figure documents the trend in the number of charges for homosexual offences laid against army personnel for homosexuality. It is based on a survey of a substantial percentage of courts martial and discoveries of homosexual charges laid by civil courts mentionned in personnel files, CMHQ records, and Carleton County records.

Sources: NA, RG 24, court-martial records for the Second World War; NA, military personnel files; NA, RG 24, vols 12,712, 12,712, 12,724, 12,770, 18,712; Archives of Ontario, RG 22-1391, boxes 3985–91, 225–33.

Figure 3
Charges for Homosexual Offences, Carleton County, Ontario, 1939–1951

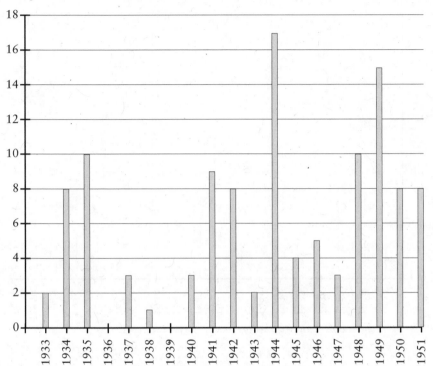

Sources: Archives of Ontario, RG 22-1391, boxes 3985–91, 225–33.

Figure 4
Homosexual Charges as a Percentage of Total Charges, Carleton County, 1933–1951

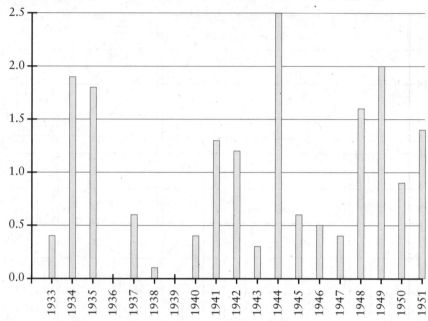

Sources: Archives of Ontario, RG 22-1391, boxes 3985–91, 225–33.

Figure 5
Homosexual Charges against Navy Personnel, 1942–1945 (partial data)

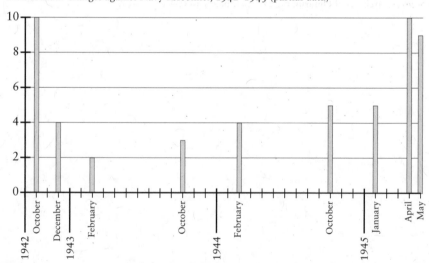

Note: This figure represents a probably small percentage of charges for homosexual offences laid against navy personnel.
Sources: DHH, file 82/401; Navy personnel files.

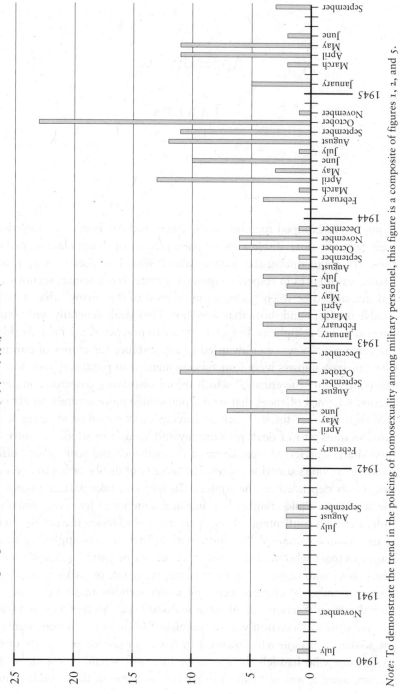

Figure 6
Total Homosexual Charges against Servicemen – All Theatres, 1940–1945 (partial data)

Note: To demonstrate the trend in the policing of homosexuality among military personnel, this figure is a composite of figures 1, 2, and 5.

Appendix Two

TABLES

Crimes were grouped together in the Army and Air Force Act according to their general nature. Table 1 shows the incidence of charges laid according to these groupings during the Second World War. Thus, sections 4, 5, and 6 named 27 offences in respect to military service. For instance, sections 4 and 5 distinguished between "offences in relation to the enemy" that were punishable by death and those that were not. They dealt generally with issues of cowardice and complicity. In fact, contrary to practice in the First World War, the death penalty was not awarded in any instance for crimes of cowardice. Nevertheless, soldiers were sometimes sentenced to penal servitude for "misbehaving before the enemy," which meant displaying cowardice under fire. Section 6 named offences that were "punishable more severely on active service than at other times," such as leaving one's patrol or sleeping at one's post. Sections 7 to 11 dealt with mutiny and insubordination. The most common charges preferred were those of disobedience and striking or "offering violence" to one's superior officer. The severity of disobedience to one's superior officer depended on the context. To refuse to take part in an attack on the front lines could commonly result in a sentence of five years penal servitude, although confirming officers were advised to lessen the penalty to three years. Section 10 named "insubordination," which was applied most commonly to those who resisted arrest or broke out of barracks. Section 11 punished those who neglected to obey camp, regiment, or garrison orders. The greatest number of charges were laid under sections 12 to 15, which dealt with desertion (Section 12), absence without leave (Section 15), and fraudulent enlistment. Desertion was distinguished from AWOL by the intention of the soldier: a person who intended to return to service was guilty of being AWOL; one who had left the service permanently would be convicted of desertion. Since it was difficult to prove the intention of the offender, most of those charged with desertion were actually convicted of the lesser offence of AWOL. Similarly, sections 20 to 22 addressed issues of servicepeople avoiding military duties by escaping arrest or confinement. Soldiers facing courts martial for desertion or AWOL were also frequently charged under section 24 with losing their military property. Meanwhile, stealing, embezzling, and fraudulently misapplying military property were all charged under section 17. Those offences were grouped together with sections 16 and 18, collectively called "Disgraceful Conduct," under which men were charged with homosexuality. Other sections dealt with a variety of administrative offences, such as falsifying official documents, refusing to cooperate with courts martial, or giving false evidence; there were also provisions against using traitorous words or disclosing military secrets. Unwanted behaviour which could not properly be framed by any other section was charged under section 40, which outlawed "any act, conduct, disorder, or neglect to the prejudice of good or/and military discipline."

Tables 1, 2, and 3 are based on the author's survey and analysis of a significant percentage (although not all) of army courts held in all theatres during the Second World War.

Table 1
Frequency of Charges Preferred by the Canadian Army by Type of Offence*

Army Act Sections	Offences	Charges	%
4, 5, 6	Offences in respect to military service	214	.9
7, 8, 9, 10, 11	Mutiny and insubordination	2046	8.8
12, 13, 14, 15	Desertion, fraudulent enlistment, and absence without leave	12,198	52.3
16, 17, 18	Disgraceful conduct	1,367	5.9
19	Drunkenness	385	1.7
20, 21, 22	Offences in relation to persons in custody	472	2
23, 24	Offences in relation to military property	2,545	10.9
25, 26, 27	Offences in relation to false documents and statements	44	.2
28, 29	Offences in relation to courts martial	28	.1
32, 33, 34	Offences in relation to enlistment	24	.1
35, 36, 37, 38, 39, 40	Miscellaneous military offences	3,235	13.9
41	Civil offences	771	3.3
Totals		23,329	100.1

* National Archives of Canada. This analysis is based on a survey of 23,329 charges preferred in the course of 14,275 courts martial called in Canada and all theatres of war abroad. It represents a significant, but unknown, portion of the entire number of charges laid. Alternative charges are not included in the statistics.

Table 2
Frequency of Charges Preferred by the Canadian Army by Army Act Section

Section	Offence	Charges	%
4	Offences in relation to the enemy punishable by death	2	.008
5 (total)	Offences in relation to the enemy not punishable by death	24	.102
5(1)	Without orders from his superior officer, leaving the ranks in order to secure prisoners or horses, or on pretence of taking wounded men to the rear	1	.004
5(5)	By word of mouth, or in writing, or by signals or otherwise, spreading reports calculated to create alarm or despondency	2	.008
5(7)	Misbehaving or inducing others to misbehave before the enemy in such manner as to show cowardice	20	.09
6 (total)	Offences punishable more severely on active service than at other times	188	.805
6(2)	(e) being a soldier acting as sentinel sleeping or being drunk on his post	119	0.5
6(3)	(c) impeding the provost marshal	24	0.10
6(1)	(b) without orders from his superior officer, leaving his guard, piquet, patrol, or post	5	0.02
7	Mutiny and insubordination	3	.013
8	Striking or threatening superior officer	679	2.91
9	Disobeying superior officer	815	3.49
10	Insubordination	244	1.046
11	Neglecting to obey orders	305	1.3
12	Desertion	4,060	17.4
13	Fraudulent enlistment	57	.24
14	Assisting desertion	1	.004
15	Absence without leave	8,080	34.6
16	Scandalous behaviour unbecoming the character of an officer and a gentleman	21	.1
17	Fraud by persons in charge of money or goods	75	.3
18 (total)	Disgraceful conduct	1,271	5.4
18(1)	Malingering, or feigning or producing disease or infirmity	13	.06
18(2)	Wilfully injuring oneself	140	0.6
18(3)	Wilfully disobeying any order thereby producing or aggravating disease or infirmity or delaying its cure	9	.04

Table 2 (*continued*)
Frequency of Charges Preferred by the Canadian Army by Army Act Section

Section	Offence	Charges	%
18(4)	Stealing property belonging to a person subject to military law	1016	4.36
18(5)	Fraud, or disgraceful conduct of an indecent, cruel, or unnatural kind	93	.399
19	Drunkenness	385	1.65
20	Permitting escape of person in custody	35	.15
21	Irregularly arresting or confining a person	7	.03
22	Escaping arrest or confinement	430	1.84
23	Dealing corruptly in respect of supplies to the forces	0	0
24	Injuring or being deficient in equipment	2,045	10.9
25	Falsifying official documents	42	.18
26	Signing documents relating to pay, arms, or stores but leaving any material portion blank	1	.004
27	Falsely accusing an officer or soldier	1	.004
28	Offences in relation to courts martial	4	.017
29	Giving false evidence	24	.103
32	Enlisting, having been discharged with ignominy or disgrace	2	.009
33	Giving false answers on enlistment	21	.090
34	Being concerned in irregular enlistment of recruits	1	.004
35	Using traitorous words	0	0
36	Injurious disclosure of military information	1	.004
37	Ill-treating a soldier	46	.197
38	Duelling and attempting to commit suicide	7	.03
40	Conduct to the prejudice of good order and military discipline	3,181	13.6
41	Committing a civil offence	771	3.3
Totals		23,329	100

* National Archives of Canada. This analysis is based on a survey of 23,329 charges preferred in the course of 14,275 courts martial called in Canada and all theatres of war abroad. It represents a significant, but unknown, portion of the entire number of charges laid. Alternative charges are not included in the statistics.

Table 3

Frequency of Charges Preferred Specifically Relating to the Character of Soldiers and Officers in the Canadian Army (Excluding Navy and Air Force)*

Army Act Section	Homosexual Charges	Non-homosexual Charges	% of Total Relating to Homosexual Activity
Scandalous behaviour unbecoming the character of an officer and a gentleman	10	10	50
Disgraceful conduct of an indecent, cruel, or unnatural kind	53	44	55

* National Archives of Canada. This analysis is based on a survey of 23,329 charges preferred in the course of 14,275 courts martial called in Canada and all theatres of war abroad. It represents a significant, but unknown, portion of the entire number of charges laid. Alternative charges are not included in the statistics.

Table 4

Courts Martial Listed in RCAF *Routine Orders*

Year	# of District Courts Martial	# of General Courts Martial	Total # of Courts	Queer Courts	% of General Courts Martial	% of Total
1945	257	20	277	1	5	.4
1944	344	50	394	10	20	.3
1943	271	54	325	6	11	.2
1942	139	19	158	1	5	.6
1941	33	2	35	1	50	3
Total	1,044	145	1,189	19	13	1.3

Source: NA, RG 24, vols 22480–2; RCAF *Routine Orders*.

Table 5
Neuropsychiatric Casualties for First Canadian Corps, 1 April 1944
to 20 June 1944, Including Battles of Gustaf and Hitler Lines

Diagnosis	Cases	%
Psychopathic personality; inadequate	378	55
Psychopathic personality; anti-social	1	.1
Chronic neurosis	63	9
Acute neurosis	56	8.1
Mental deficiency	31	4.5
Mental retardation with emotional instability	10	1.4
Hysteria	20	2.9
Exhaustion	15	2.2
Schizophrenia	17	2.5
Physical inferiority	15	2.2
NAD	50	7.2
Post-traumatic neurosis	5	.7
Reactive depression	5	.7
Latent homosexualism	1	.1
Hypertension	3	.4
Chronic alcoholism	1	.1
Petit epilepsy	1	.1
Post-traumatic syndrome	1	.1
Medical	19	2.7
Total	692	100

Source: NA, RG 24, CMHQ File Block 11, vol. 12, 631, file 11/Psychiatry/2/
2, "Report of 1 Cdn Corps Neuropsychiatrist, period 1 Apr–20 Jun 44,
including battle of Gustaf and Adolf Hitler Lines," Appendix 2.

Table 6
Psychopathic Personality Disorders, Canadian Military Headquarters,
1 January to 30 June 1944, Total Numbers

Diagnosis	S-3			S-4			S-5			Total
Psychopathic personality	M1	M2	M3	M1	M2	M3	M1	M2	M3	
Inadequate	149	78	0	743	409	16	408	162	162	2,127
Anti-social	3	0	0	16	8	0	180	54	25	286
With abnormal sexuality	0	0	0	1	0	0	14	1	1	17
Total	152	78	0	760	417	16	602	217	188	2,430

Source: NA, RG 24, CMHQ File Block 11, vol. 12, 631, file 11/Psychiatry/2/2, "Commentary on Morbidity and Military Loss from Neuropsychiatric Disorders Based on a Survey of Medical Boards (and Repatriation Certificates) for the Six Months Period 1 Jan–30 Jun 1944."

Table 7
Psychopathic Personality Disorders, Canadian Military Headquarters,
1 January to 30 June 1944, by Percentage

Diagnosis	S-3			S-4			S-5			Total
Psychopathic personality	M1	M2	M3	M1	M2	M3	M1	M2	M3	
Inadequate	7	3.7	0	35	19	.8	19	7.6	7.6	99.7
Anti-social	1	0	0	5.6	2.8	0	63	19	9	100.4
With abnormal sexuality	0	0	0	6	0	0	82	6	6	100

Source: NA, RG 24, CMHQ File Block 11, vol. 12, 631, file 11/Psychiatry/2/2, "Commentary on Morbidity and Military Loss from Neuropsychiatric Disorders Based on a Survey of Medical Boards (and Repatriation Certificates) for the Six Months Period 1 Jan–30 Jun 1944."

Table 8
Psychiatric Casualties in the Royal Canadian Navy

Diagnosis	Officers	Ratings	Total	%
Psychoneurosis	8	73	81	81
Anxiety state	5	55	60	
Hysterical type	3	14	1	
Reactive depression		3	3	
Neurasthenia		1	1	
Psychosis	1	5	6	6
Manic depressive		3	3	
Schizophrenia		2	2	
Psychoses undiagnosed	1		1	
Psychopathic personality		4	4	4
Simple adult maladjustment		2		2
Miscellaneous		7		7
Alcoholism		1		
Homosexual; hysteria		1		
Effort syndrome		1		
Enuresis		1		
Simple fear		1		
Undiagnosed		2		
Total	9	91	100	100

Source: Marvin Wellman, Surgeon Commander, R.C.N.V.R., and J.F. Simpson, Surgeon Lieutenant, R.C.N.V.R., "Psychiatric Casualties in the (RCN)," *American Journal of Psychiatry* 101 (1944–45): 625–8.

Appendix Three

Note on Sources

Canadian military historians have blessed and cursed the extensive collection of military documents at the National Archives. Allan English has compared working in RG 24 to "panning for gold; one has to go through a lot of gravel to get to the nuggets."[1] His analogy is particularly apt in relation to the study of homosexuality in the forces. There is much material, but finding it is a daunting task. Likewise, contacting veterans of the war who are willing to discuss homosexuality is challenging. Tracking both oral and textual evidence of homosexuality is itself a study in wartime attitudes. Only one military file dating from the war actually names homosexuality; controlling it was seen as inevitable and unremarkable. At the same time, military men preferred to keep it out of the records. While this may often have been the result of commanding officers' protecting their units' reputations, it could also result from friendly gestures. One gay navy captain (who does not appear in the list of interviewees) told me that when he discovered in the personnel file a report referring to the suspected homosexuality of a junior officer, he quietly removed it from the record and discarded it. While protecting his subordinate may have been a noble (and insubordinate) action, it made the work of the historian that much more difficult.

Vague references to courts martial for homosexual offences in the *Routine Orders* of the army and air force, as well as explicit naval citations, prompted my requests for access to those records at the National Archives. After months of debate over which arm of the state was responsible for the material and where, if it still existed, it was located, I was granted access.[2] The microfilm reels had been improperly stored for over thirty years in a federal records centre and needed to be refilmed before they could be viewed. A year from the initial request, I was granted access to more than three hundred microfilm reels. However, since they were unindexed, finding the relevant courts required long hours of tedious searches. That court-martial material became central to the construction of the book. Most of the navy courts-martial material had been accidentally destroyed over forty years ago, and the RCAF courts records were not available in time to be included. For those two services, other sources, such as *Routine Orders* and personnel files, helped me to reconstruct the courts. In the end, I surveyed approximately twenty thousand army court-martial proceedings. Since the courts are open, I could, in principle, identify the men prosecuted. I have chosen to use their first names only, however, except in the cases where men raised the issue of their homosexuality themselves.

Personnel files for the Second World War can contain much medical, administrative, and personnel documentation. Under Canada's Privacy Act, individuals have exclusive right to personal information until twenty years after their death. Under a research agreement with the National Archives, I was granted access to personnel files in order to become acquainted with the administration of homosexual cases. I have not used material that comes from those files in a manner that would allow any individual to be identified. Even in the cases of deceased servicemen whose history has entered the public domain, I have chosen to identify them in this work by first name only. Of course, I maintain the record of the files cited.

Personnel files were accessed according to different research criteria and are listed accordingly in the endnotes. First, files of servicemen in the army, air force, and navy who appeared before martial courts accused of homosexuality, or of being accomplices to acts, were consulted. Each was assigned an arbitrary number for identification and appears in the endnotes as simply "Army personnel file x," "RCAF personnel file x" and "Navy personnel file x." I viewed 121 army files, 30 navy files, and 33 RCAF files.

Since material in the personnel records relating to those who died during the war is open under privacy regulations, I was able to consult without difficulty the files of 162 servicemen and women who committed suicide. In a few cases, it appeared that homosexuality was a causal factor. In most cases, the deceased left the cause of their action a mystery. Citations referring to the suicide files cite the personnel file itself.

In 1944 RCAF policy directed that officers suspected of homosexuality be retired from the service. I accessed the files of thirty-one men of the hundreds who appeared before boards and were retired during that period. None of those I consulted were retired because of their sexual orientation. All were retired for other reasons, most commonly incompetence or unsuitability.

Forty personnel files of men who were convicted of sexual crimes by British courts were consulted.[3] Thirty-five per cent of the crimes (14) had been against female victims and 23 per cent (9) had related to sex with another male person. The personnel files were ambiguous concerning the gender of the partner in 35 per cent of the cases (14). One soldier had been convicted by two different British courts, once for sex with a man and once for bigamy. One case was for sex with an English setter (gender unspecified). Those are cited in the work as "SUS in UK," by number.

A further 109 personnel files of soldiers who underwent lengthy periods of detention were reviewed to test the response of the military doctors to men who contracted gonorrhea in prison. Those are cited as "SUS," by number.

The personnel files of thirty members of various entertainment units were accessed. They are listed as "Entertainment personnel file," by number.

Many veterans of the war offered me their time and recollections in valuable interviews. These individuals are listed below. A few men and women who were not veterans but were able to inform my research in some material way are also included in the list of interviewees. Most of the interviews are transcribed or recorded; in a few cases, notes were taken after the interview for subsequent reference. Many people to whom I spoke are not listed. In those cases, veterans had an anecdote about homosexuals in their units, but when asked if they would allow me to refer to it, they often declined. That material has not been used and the sources are not referenced here. (I have made one exception to that rule, in order to discuss, in principle, the problem of researching taboo subjects.) In September and October of 1998, I interviewed a number of German veterans who had been prisoners of war in Canada during the war. Since we discussed the Canadian Army's response to homosexual activity among the prisoners, they are included here. When a "+" sign appears next to the date of the interview, it means that I was in continuing contact with the person.

Interviewees

#	Name	Date of Initial Interview
1	Bob Grimson	1994+
2	Frances Hicks	June 1994
3	George Hislop	June 1994
4	Jack	June 1994+
5	John Gartshore	June 1994+
6	Russ Thomson	June 1994+
7	Tom Leon	June 1994+
8	Peter	June 1994
9	Bud	June 1994
10	Allan	June 1994
11	Hugh	July 1994+
12	Cliff	July 1994
13	Frank	July 1994
14	Jim Egan	July 1994
15	Bradbury (pseudonym)	July 1994
16	Tom	August 1994
17	Don	August 1994
18	Betty/Gordon (pseudonyms)	September 1994+
19	Bob Duncombe	June 1997+
20	Anonymous Ottawa Valley	June 1997+
21	Allin Hawkshaw	October 1997
22	Doctor Jack Griffin	October 1997
23	Byron (pseudonym)	October 1997+
24	John Ottawa	October 1997+
25	Gordon MacNamara	November 1997
26	Edward Toronto	November 1997
27	George Wilkes	July 1998+
28	Herb Little	July 1998
29	Anonymous British Columbia	September 1998
30	Kurt Vickert	September 1998

Interviewees (*continued*)

#	Name	Date of Initial Interview
31	Guenther Poppe	September 1998
32	Ernest Koeppler	September 1998
33	Gus Haase	September 1998
34	Alfred Weiss	September 1998
35	Margaret (pseudonym)	September 1998
36	Michael Babic	October 1998
37	Paul Mengelberg	October 1998
38	Viktor Freelandt	October 1998
39	Bob Schumacher	October 1998
40	Hermann Hutt	October 1998
41	Horst Thoman	October 1998
42	Max Weidauer	November 1998
43	Anonymous navy	July 2000
44	Henri Depierro	July 2000+
45	Anonymous Ottawa	August 2000
46	Aubyn (pseudonym)	August 2000+
47	Duty clerk	November 2000
48	Bert Sutcliffe	1994, November 2000+
49	Ralph Wormleighton	1994, November 2000+
50	Bill Dunstan	November 2000+
51	Anonymous British Columbia	December 2000+
52	Rudi Van Dantzig	March 2002+

NOTES

INTRODUCTION

1 Herman, *Rights of Passage*; Smith, *Lesbian and Gay Rights in Canada*; McLeod, *Lesbian and Gay Liberation in Canada*. On the term "gay," see Chauncey, *Gay New York*, 17.

2 Abelove, "Freud, Male Homosexuality and the Americans"; Lewes, *The Psychoanalytic Theory of Male Homosexuality*, chap. 7. For the origins of the word "homosexual," see Oosterhuis, *Stepchildren of Nature*, 44; Steakley, *The Homosexual Emancipation Movement in Germany*.

3 Halperin, *Saint Foucault*, 62, italics in original.

4 Trumbach, "London," in Higgs, ed., *Queer Sites*, 92.

5 The idea that Canadian myths are generated by the selective reporting of Canada's history is developed in Francis, *National Dreams*; Vance, *Death So Noble*.

6 Tobin, *Ernie Pyle's War*; Faludi, *Stiffed*, 16–30; Burstyn, *The Rites of Men*; Pronger, *The Arena of Masculinity*; Karst, "The Pursuit of Manhood and the Desegregation of the Armed Forces"; Bohls and Wangrin, "Athletes Revel in Being One of the Guys, Not One of the Gays."

7 Critiques of the male character-building hypothesis of sports are found in Sabo, "Sport Patriarchy and Male Identity"; Messner, "The Meaning of Success"; Townsend, "The Competitive Male as Loser"; Bohls and Wangrin, "Athletes Revel in Being One of the Guys, Not One of the Gays"; Gibson, *Warrior Dreams*. General Barrow is quoted in Thomas and Thomas, "Integration of Women in the Military," 70.

8 *Esprit de Corps* 4, no. 3 (1994); also see September 1993. Kinsman and Gentile, "*In the Interests of the State.*"

9 Herek, "Social Science, Sexual Orientation and Military Personnel Policy"; Park, "Opening the Canadian Forces to Gays and Lesbians"; Morton, *Canada*

and War; Russell, "The Political Purposes of the Canadian Charter of Rights and Freedoms," 33; Taylor and Nolan, *Tarnished Brass*.

10 "This is Mark Bingham," *The Advocate*, 22 January 2002.

11 "Banning Explosives Words," *Army Lines*, 26 November 2001; Michael Bronski, "Writing homophobic messages isn't okay, but bombing is?" 15 January 2002, <http://www.zmag.org/content/Gender/bronskibomb.cfm>.

12 McIntosh, "The Homosexual Role"; Foucault, *The History of Sexuality*, vol. 1; Weeks, *Coming Out*; Weeks, *Sex, Politics and Society*; D'Emilio, *Sexual Politics, Sexual Communities*; Altman, *The Homosexualization of America, The Americanization of the Homosexual*; Rubin, "Thinking Sex"; Rupp, "Toward a Global History of Same-Sex Sexuality"; Murray, *Homosexualities*; Greenberg, *The Construction of Homosexuality*.

13 Freedman and D'Emilio, *Intimate Matters*, 109–38; Chauncey, *Gay New York*, 26–27; Trumbach, *Sex and the Gender Revolution*; Bray, *Homosexuality in Renaissance England*; Sinfield, *The Wilde Century* (Sinfield argues that the Wilde trials marked same-sex sexuality as effeminate); D'Emilio, *Sexual Politics, Sexual Communities*, 9–22; Kinsman, *The Regulation of Desire*, chap. 9. The greater latitude of homosexual behaviour permissible between men in the Anglo-Saxon world before the end of the nineteenth century is discussed in Sedgwick, *Between Men*; Duberman, " 'Writhing Bedfellows' in Ante-Bellum South Carolina"; and between women, in Faderman, *Surpassing the Love of Men*.

14 Cott, "Passionlessness," 219–36, explains that sexual desire was indeed thought to flow from the male/masculine towards the female/feminine; Marshall, "Pansies, perverts and macho men," 142; Jagose, *Queer Theory*.

15 Sloan, *Oscar Wilde*; Cohen, *Talk on the Wilde Side* (although Cohen argues that Wilde was represented in the press as homosexual, his sources clearly describe that as an immoral category); Mort, *Dangerous Sexualities*.

16 Ihara, *The Great Mirror of Male Love*; Herdt, "Fetish and Fantasy in Sambian Initiation"; Ober, "The Evil Empire"; Halperin, *One Hundred Years of Homosexuality*, chap. 3; Dover, *Greek Homosexuality*, 191–4; Adam, "Anatomy of a Panic," 105.

17 Brown and Cook, *Canada 1986–1921*, chap. 15, analyses the effect of the First World War on the suffrage and labour movements and Prohibition; Newton, *The Feminist Challenge to the Canadian Left 1900–1918*, sees the war as undermining the growth of socialist-feminism; the Second World War again provided an impetus for working-class activism, as described by Webber, "The Malaise of Compulsory Conciliation"; the implementation of welfare policies are described in Granatstein, *Canada's War*, 249–93; the expansion of federal powers during the war are described in Owram, *The Government Generation*; the war also boosted First Nations activism, as described in Shewell, "Jules Sioui and Indian Political Radicalism in Canada, 1943–1944"; Keshen traces the impact of the Second

World War on women and juveniles in "Revisiting Canada's Civilian Women during World War II" and "Wartime Jitters over Juveniles"; Dean, *Imperial Brotherhood*; sexuality was explicitly controlled through legislation forbidding birth control or education explaining it – McLaren and McLaren, *The Bedroom and the State;* penalties were exacted on women who violated the code restricting sexual relations to marriage – Lévesque, "Deviants Anonymous," and Little, "Claiming a Unique Place"; Dubinsky, *Improper Advances*, 13–34, describes how decent women were expected to be above sexual interest; the channelling of sexuality into marriage is described in Dubinsky, *The Second Greatest Disappointment*, and the state's coercive tactics to keep it there in Snell, *In the Shadow of the Law.*

18 Granatstein and Neary, *The Veteran's Charter and Post–World War Two Canada*, describes state policies that encouraged a smooth transition to domestic life; Adams, *The Trouble with Normal*; Strong-Boag, "Home Dreams," describes women's isolation in postwar suburbia in Canada; Stacey and Wilson, *The Half-Million*, 136. During a gunner's court martial for absence without leave, a letter from his girlfriend was introduced containing the following plea: "There were patriots in 1837 in the province of Quebec there are still some in 1944 and it will be just too bad for them if the revolution starts ... I know how you feel but I am asking you, if you love me a little, not to let them get you to sign. They are going to make you nice promesses, you might pay them with your life ... They probably will try by all sorts of means to have you sign active, the French-Canadians ... say no, ..." (NA, RG 24, reel T-15, 563, file 55-B-1308).

19 Allin Hawkshaw correspondence.

20 Cohen, *Talk on the Wilde Side*; Chaytor, "Husbandry"; Maynard, " 'Horrible Temptations,' " discusses the limitations of narratology when using court records often short on evidence; Moran, " 'Oscar Wilde.' "

21 Bérubé, *Coming Out under Fire.*

22 Meyer, *Creating G.I. Jane*; Dean, *Imperial Brotherhood*, chap. 3.

CHAPTER ONE

1 See, for instance, Johnson, *Action with the Seaforths*; Collins, *The Long and the Short and the Tall*, 63; Berton, *Starting Out, 1920–1947*, 140, 246; Mowat, *And No Birds Sang*, 14; Brown, *Bonds of Wires*, 130; Ross, *Slow March to a Regiment*, 27–8, 45, 135; Pearce, *Journal of a War*, 28–9; Jones, *To the Green Fields Beyond*, 53. For an extensive meditation on contemporary Canadian sexual mores, see Ritchie, *An Appetite for Life, 1924–1927*, 19, 23, 32, 36, 45, 63–70, 74, 78, 138–9, 144, 149, 162, 166; *The Siren Years, 1937–45*, 71, 83, 125, 131, 199; and, *My Grandfather's House*, 74–6, 155.

2 Courts martial are a compendium of soldiers' marital difficulties and the incursion of their commanding officers and military administrative departments into

their private lives. Among the thousands of courts that could be cited, see NA, RG 24, reel T-15549, file, 55-A-477; reel T-15601, file 55-D-584; reel T-15601, file 55-D-585; reel T-15643, file 55-H-801; reel T-15601, file 55-D-596; reel T-15547, file 55-A-286; reel T-15550, file 55-A-581.

3 On the contemporary meanings of 'browned-off,' see interview John Ottawa; quotes from court-martial files NA, RG 24, reel T-15551, file 55-A-718; reel T-15635, file 55-G-1774; reel T-15661, file 55-L-176; reel T-15829, file XXX-139; reel T-15824, file 4F-93; reel T-15822, file XX-140; reel T-15845, file 4J-149; reel T-15845, file 4J-149; reel T-15846, file 5P-85; reel T-15845, file 10-R-64; reel T-15835, file 5E-19; reel T-15804, file 11-144; reel T-15851, file 50-107; reel T-15804, file BB-55; reel T-15804, file JJ-138; reel T-15804, file CC-41; reel T-15844, file OOO-17; reel T-15831, file DD-129.

4 Edward interview; Collins, *The Long and the Short and the Tall*, 17 (emphasis in original).

5 Herb Little interview.

6 Hannant, *The Infernal Machine*, 119–38; Bérubé, *Coming Out under Fire*, 12.

7 Feasby, *Official History of the Canadian Medical Services 1939–1945*, vol. 2, 101–4; Copp and McAndrew, *Battle Exhaustion*, chap. 2. It is difficult to determine the exact number of men discharged as homosexual, for they were categorized under code 0611, which represented psychopathic personalities. Since there were three subcategories of psychopathic personality (Inadequate, Antisocial, and With Abnormal Sexuality), numbers are unhelpful. Only a very small percentage of those discharged as psychopathic personality were diagnosed "with abnormal sexuality."

8 Copp and McAndrew, *Battle Exhaustion*, 33; Army personnel file 104; John interview; NA, RG 24, reel T-15815, file 106Q; Army personnel file 61.

9 Ralph Wormleighton interview; Army personnel file 114; Army personnel file 39.

10 Lucas, *Malta*, 268–71. Lucas relates the subsequent careers of the two men: "One was killed later in the war, leading a unit in the face of the enemy. He had notably enhanced his operational record in the interim. The other went on to achieve fighting commands – with decorations to match. He played out the innings, married well, raised a happy family and eventually became a distinguished figure in the professional and public life of his native country." Whether he was Canadian or from another corner of the Commonwealth (or the United States) is not specified.

11 Comeau, Beauregard, and Munn, *La Démocratie en Veilleuse*; NA, RG 2, series 14, vol. 5746, file 1, "Establishment of Canadian Postal Censorship," John Ross Stirrett to Norman McLarty and the committee on censorship; 04 June 1942, Wing Commander H.R. Stewart, director of intelligence, to F.E. Jolliffe, chief postal censor; 28 May 1942, Commissioner S.T. Wood to chief postal censor; 18

June 1942, Captain E.S. Brand, director of naval intelligence, to F.E. Jolliffe; 30 May 1942, Brand to Jolliffe; RG 2, series 14, vol. 5747, 13 October 1942, Major-General Montague, JAG Canadian Military Headquarters, to Rear Headquarters, First Canadian Corps.

12 Margaret interview.

13 At HMCS Cornwallis alone, four men censored between 1,200 and 1,600 letters per day: NA, RG 24, vol. 3885, file NSC 1029–18–1, vol. 1, Naval Monthly Order No. 981: "It is strictly forbidden ... to give a private letter, parcel, postcard or telegram to any person other than the ship's censor .... To post a private letter, parcel or postcard while ashore." For several punishments: NA, RG 24, vol. 8035, file NSC 1182–247, vol. 1, 7 August 1944, 28 August 1944; NA, RG 2, vol. 5476, 6 August 1943, Geo. Avery, acting superintendent of post office service to postmaster, Victoria: "A certain amount of mail, however, is still being posted ashore with the deliberate intent to avoid naval censorship"; NA, RG 24, vol. 8035, file NSC 1182–247, vol. 1, 18 August 1944; file NSC 1182–249 (RCAF Censorship – mails), 26 December 1941, H. Lannigan to Mrs Winard.

14 In the case of the RCAF, see RCAF personnel file 32; for the army and navy, see Navy personnel files 4 and 27; NA, RG 24, vol. 8035, file NSC 1182–247, vol. 1, 12 July 1944, A/Commander C.H. Little, RCNVR, director of naval intelligence, to security intelligence, officer, west coast.

15 Directorate of History and Heritage (hereinafter DHH) file 74/14.

16 Ibid.

17 Although an official information request had been submitted in September 1997 to access the RCAF courts martial, as of the spring of 2001, the microfilm reels had not been prepared for viewing. As a result, a comprehensive summary of RCAF courts martial was not possible. In the alternative, two sources that provided partial, albeit consistent, records of proceedings against RCAF personnel were used to calculate the effect of policing on air personnel. The RCAF routine orders listed, for deterrent purposes, the particulars of courts martial pertaining to especially abhorrent crimes. Meanwhile, the Carleton County police records provided the details of all charges laid in that jurisdiction, which includes Ottawa, a centre of RCAF activity during the war. As the Carleton County records provided the occupation of the accused, it was possible to determine the number of RCAF personnel who were passed to the civil authorities for prosecution. Since data for the entire war period was available for these two sources, it was possible to calculate the trend of charges preferred (DHH, file 74/10, 145–5–9).

18 Forbes, "Military Police at War"; Weaver, *Crimes, Constables and Courts*, 174. Personnel services attempted to place recruits in the most advantageous positions, so it is likely that many of the men cited by Weaver were assigned to the Canadian Provost Corps.

19 DHH, file 74/10, file 145-5-9.

20 Ibid., file 375-1-1, vol. 1; NA, RG 24, reel T-15657, file HQC 55-K-340; Archives of Ontario, RG 22-1391, Warrant Informations for Carleton County, boxes 3985-91, 225-33.

21 RCAF personnel file 5, 17 January 1945, report of Major Moorehouse. It is unclear what evidence led them to believe that there must have been a homosexual on the base.

22 NA, RG 24, reel T-15654, file HQC 55-K-121, and reel T-15775, file HQC 55-W-499.

23 Duty clerk interview; NA, RG 24, reel T-15775, file HQC 55-W-499, summary of evidence.

24 I suggest that Lieutenant W's frame-up was probably not explicitly discussed by the parties because, if it had been, it is much more likely that the duty clerk would have remembered his wartime testimony, if only to be consistent. For this reason, I speculate that it was a more "casual" (in his own words) meeting in which parties with a similar agenda agree on a truth.

25 Entertainment personnel file 26.

26 NA, RG 24, reel T-15815, file 271; Hannant, *The Infernal Machine*, 129.

27 NA, RG 24, reel T-15820, file 13P (In this case, the provost police in Britain entered the bedroom of a married woman to find her in bed with a Canadian soldier. He was court-martialled for absence without leave, and she was prosecuted in the civil courts for aiding and abetting a deserter); Army personnel file 65, 25 July 1941, commissioner of police of the metropolis, New Scotland Yard (special branch) London report; For instances of soldiers confessing to living with gay British men while AWOL: NA, RG 24, reel T-15647, file 55-H-1268; reel T-15671, file 55-L-1126; reel T-15587, file HQC 55-C-973; Army personnel file 101.

28 NA, RG 24, reel T-15649, file HQC 55-J-89; reel T-, file HQC 55-B-276, reel T-15554, file HQC 55-B-402; reel T-15823, file 4W-116; In one instance, a man who deliberately entrapped a homosexual career soldier, precipitating his court martial, was himself subsequently discharged as anti-social, deemed unfit for military service. The man whom he had targeted was sentenced to a period of detention and then continued in the service: Army personnel file 111; Re Italian campaign: NA, RG 24, file HQC 55-A-942; reel T-15804, file XXX-40; reel T-15635, file HQC 55-G-1817; reel T15808, file XXX-138.

29 NA, RG 24, reel T-15835, file 137L. Lieutenant Colonel Redman may have been suspicious that Lance Sergeant Kopanski had a grudge against the sergeant major. However, the fact that there were three witnesses suggests that Kopanski could not have been accused of fabricating the story.

30 NA, RG 24, reel T-15831, file CAOF-1-17.

31 Not all men were raised in an entirely anti-homosexual environment: NA, RG 24, reel T-15548, file HQC 55-A-385. There is a literature that explores how gay

men had internalized society's anti-homosexual attitudes. Such studies have been intended to raise cosciousness and thereby promote the gay liberation movement. See Hodges and Hutter, *With Downcast Gays*; NA, RG 24, reel T-15643, file HQC 55-H-731. The officer was court-martialled and dismissed; the driver continued in the army.

32 NA, RG 24, Acc. 1997–98/260, vol. 64, file C-37C-112, pt1, file 45–4–57, "Action Respecting Personnel Suspected of Homosexual Tendencies," 05 April 1944 CAS to All Commands.

33 English, *The Cream of the Crop*, 61–130; NA, RG 24, Acc. 1997–98/260, vol. 64, file C-37C-112, pt1, file 45–4–57. Special investigators worked in concert with the deputy assistant provost marshal in Scoudouc in July 1944, uncovering a group of homosexual airmen, and in Goose Bay in August 1944.

34 Ibid., 21 September 1944, Air Commodore Tice (the RCAF's top doctor) to director of personnel: "Despite any medical diagnosis of this type, punishment can be effected for conduct which contravenes normal social behaviour"; 23 December 1944 CAS to All Commands; 6 September 1944 S/L Kershman to director of personnel.

35 Katz, *Gay American History*, 159–75, cites electroshock, pharmacological shock, hormone medication, etc., in the 1930s and 1940s.

36 NA, RG 24, vol. 12,724, file 20/Review/1, 10 February 1944, Major Burton, Psychiatrist DMS Branch, to AMD 2; NA, RG 24, vol. 12,726, file 20/Det Bks/1, 31 January 1945, Colonel A.D. Cameron, deputy provost marshal, to AAG(Dis), Canadian Military Headquarters.

37 Ibid.: L.W. Fox, the chairman of the prison commission in England visited the field punishment camp and detention barracks of the Canadian Army and reported, "[T]he discipline appeared to us to be negative, mechanical and repressive. We were disturbed to find a 'silent system' in force which was abandoned in English prisons in the 19th century. We find it difficult to persuade ourselves that such a system can be necessary for any purpose that is not merely punitive and repressive, or that its effects can be other than pernicious." Also see, "Soldiers' Detention Barracks Run by Sadistic Guards," *Hush Free Press* 17 (23 March 1946), for accounts of several soldiers of their severe mistreatment by Canadian guards; NA, RG 24, reel T-15667, file HQC 55-L-746, for the court martial of a guard charged with twenty-four counts of "striking a soldier"; NA, RG 24, vol. 12,726, file 20/Sentence/1, 31 March 1944 Staff Sergeant Whidden complaint; NA, RG 24, reel T-15554, file HQC 55-B-402; reel T-15636, file HQC 55-G-1945; RCAF personnel file 9; Army personnel file of Lucien Graveline (deceased 1946), who served with 35 Canadian Provost Corps Company; RCAF personnel file 9, December 1942, Report from Service Police Force: "Speaks French and English. Experienced guard at a penal institution in Quebec. Should

make an efficient service police especially in a detention barracks" (he was later convicted of "Disgraceful conduct of an indecent kind upon the persons of Airmen in Barrack Blocks of this Unit"); similarly, Army personnel file 22, personnel report, reads: "A tall, well-built, powerful 38 year old single man (6'1½" tall, weighing 224 lbs)" (he served for five years and four months with the Canadian Provost Corps and was subsequently convicted of having sexual relations with a soldier at the Camp Borden Station Hospital); DHH, file 74/10, RCAF Provost and Security Services, 375–1–1, vol. 1.

38 Soldiers under Sentence personnel file 36; Army personnel file of Lucien Graveline (deceased 1946).

39 Cassell, *The Secret Plague*, covers venereal disease control in Canada up to the point of the Second World War.

40 NA, RG 24, vol. 6618, file HQC 8994–6, vol. 7, 10 June 1943, circular letter 238; In order to enforce strict adherence, soldiers were disciplined for their neglect of venereal disease regulations. For soldiers court-martialled, see NA, RG 24, reel T-15850, file 86T; reel T-15790, file QQ-146; reel T-15815, file XXX-103; reel T-15791, XXX-144. A brief discussion of the introduction of defence Regulation 33B in Britain in December 1943 is offered in Stacey and Wilson, *The Half-Million*, chap. 5. From that point, anyone named by two or more people as a possible source of venereal disease was required to present him- or herself for inspection and treatment, 152–3; NA, RG 24, vol. 6618, file HQ 8994–6, vol. 7, 28 March 1945, Major W. Sumner to DDGMS: "The Provincial Health Department and the Halifax City Health Commission are giving excellent co-operation in contact tracing ... 48.8% of contacts named were located"; vol. 6617, file HQ 8994–6, vol. 6, 20 September 1944, Lieutenant Colonel Williams to DDGMS asserts that, in New Brunswick, "a civilian hospital for the detention, treatment and rehabilitation of promiscuous infected girls is urgently needed" (New Brunswick's provincial legislation did not allow for the forced detention and treatment of venereal cases, as did other provinces); Pierson, "They're Still Women After All," 188–214; Stacey and Wilson, *The Half-Million*, 152–3.

41 NA, RG 24, vol. 15,948, "War Diary of No. 1 Canadian Disease Treatment Unit, Royal Canadian Army Medical Corps, vols 1–17; vol. 15,949, "1 Canadian Corps V.D. Centre, Royal Canadian Army Medical Corps"; NA, RG 24, vol. 6618, file HQC 8994–6, vol. 9, "History of Development and Progress Venereal Disease Control Programme Canadian Army Overseas"; ibid., vol. 7, 10 June 1943, Circular letter 236; ibid., vol. 10, "Precis of Lecture Protection against VD."

42 NA, RG 24, vol. 6618, file HQC8994-6, vol. 10. "Facts, *You* should know about V.D."; John interview; Chauncey, *Gay New York*, 186–92; Bérubé, *Coming Out under Fire*, 88, 90.

43 NA, RG 24, vol. 6617, file HQ 8996-4, vol. 2, 12 July 1943, G.B. Chisholm,
   DGMS, circular: "The Collection of Data Regarding Spread of Venereal Diseases" ibid., file HQ 8994-6, vol. 1, 19 April 1943, D. Cleveland (MD), Acting
   Director V.D. Control, B.C. Provincial Board of Health, to Col. Wallace Wetson,
   CMO Pacific Command; Army personnel 73, 19 June 1943, VD case sheet:
   "source of infection including all available particulars, address and name of
   town or location, etc.: not known – pick up on Water Street [St John's, New-
   foundland] – contact behind YMCA." This soldier was finally discharged for his
   homosexual activities. While he gave the location of his sexual encounter, he did
   not offer the gender of his partner; Pierson, "*They're Still Women After All*,"
   197.

44 NA, RG 24, vol. 6617, file HQS 8994-6, vol. 1, 3 May 1943, Lieutenant Colonel
   Hughes, DMO, MD 12 to DGMS; ibid., 3 May 1943, Private DeWolfe to prime
   minister; Psychiatric patients sometimes obsessed over the mistaken notion that
   they suffered from venereal infection. Private Norman Woods, twenty-four years
   old, committed suicide when he "became convinced that he had V.D. and was
   sure that his 'privates' were rotting away ... Nothing can convince him that his
   penis and testicles are not rotting off" (see Personnel file of Woods, 12 June
   1942, Captain McKercher and Major Richardson, Royal Canadian Army Medical Corps). Private Smith, twenty-nine years old, also committed suicide while
   under treatment at the Provincial Hospital in Saint John, New Brunswick. His
   medical history records: "first symptoms worry – inability to concentrate about
   2 mos. ago cohabited with a negress. Thought he contracted syphilis. Was told
   'nigger' syphilis could not be cured. Refused to believe a negative Wass. Report
   on blood." In other words, he did not actually have syphillis but could not be
   convinced of his health. See personnel file of Walter Smith.

45 Homosexual behaviour would be one factor in the case of discharges for misconduct. Men who had a string of absences without leave and other petty offences and had thus demonstrated an incorrigible unwillingness to soldier were
   discharged for misconduct; Ives, "The Veterans Charter," 87.

46 RCAF personnel file 25. In fact, several veterans discharged with ignominy re-
   enlisted in the military in the postwar years, which suggests that the forces were
   no longer tracking known homosexuals.

47 Entertainment personnel file 26, Board of Review decision November 1945.

48 Army personnel file 29 (The quote is from a form letter that was in use from
   1947); RCAF personnel file 7; Army personnel file 112; Army personnel file 118;
   RCAF personnel file 1, 14 November 1952, director of war service records to airman.

49 Evans, *John Grierson and the National Film Board*; Morris, *The National Film
   Board of Canada*; Nelson, *The Colonized Eye*.

50 *Soldiers All* (NFB, 1941). The analysis offered here is based on the final product as it was shown to Canadian audiences. The film was, of course, the creation of the director and editor: there is no way to know if what appears to be the audience's response to the drag scene is actually that or is instead footage constructed in the editing to suggest the audience reaction. By the Second World War, Arabia had a history as a mecca for British upper-class gay men.

51 *Globe and Mail*, 21 July 1941, 1; *Toronto Telegram*, 21 July 1941, 1.

52 NFB Archives, file, *Letter from Camp Borden*. The NFB documentary, *Open Secrets*, 2003, contains a short clip from, *Letter from Camp Borden* showing Ross Hamilton performing as Marjorie. Early in the film, he is the rather ample but dignified opera star in a white gown seen striding onto the stage and performing several bars to an appreciative audience of soldiers.

53 Personnel file of Ross Douglas Hamilton (died 29 September 1965). His misfortune in being discovered having homosexual sex at Camp Borden was communicated by Dr Jack Griffin, consultant psychiatrist in DMS during the war. The process by which men such as Hamilton who were discovered in homosexual encounters in the early years of the war were discharged can be understood through a study of the case of Gordon B, acting corporal in the Royal Canadian Army Medical Corps (NA, RG 24, reel T-15553, file HQC 55-B-276). After a summary of evidence was taken documenting his homosexual 'crimes,' the G.O.C.-in-chief of Pacific Command requested and received permission from the adjutant-general to discharge him for medical reasons under routine order 37(12). Thus, he was released from the army as unobtrusively as possible in November 1940. Also see personnel file 109 for a soldier also retired in 1940 "for other than medical reasons" who subsequently re-enlisted and was involved in court-martial proceedings as a participant in homosexual relations.

54 Jim Egan interview; Distribution of NFB films is discussed in Evans, *John Grierson and the National Film Board of Canada*.

55 Stacey, *Arms, Men and Government*, 48; Granatstein, *Conscription in the Second World War, 1939–1945*; Byers, "Mobilizing Canada" (There had been conscription for home service since 1940); Kinsey, *Sexual Behaviour in the Human Male*, 10, 76, 650.

56 NA, RG 24, reel T-15841, file VVV-129.

CHAPTER TWO

1 For an overview of military justice in Canada, see Madsen, *Another Kind of Justice*; Tooley, "Appearance or Reality?"; Rossignol, "National Defence Act"; Sherrill, *Military Justice Is to Justice as Military Music Is to Music*; Ulmer, *Military Justice and the Right to Counsel*; Costello, *Love, Sex and War*, 156; Bérubé,

Coming Out under Fire, 128–48; Shilts, *Conduct Unbecoming*; Weinberg and Williams, *Homosexuals and the Military*.

2 Army personnel file 56: Homosexuality was one part of this particular soldier's vulnerability to suicide; Army personnel file 95: This court, involving a soldier who had remained in the service, took place shortly after the war.

3 McDonald, "The Trail of Discipline"; Public General Statutes, p. 1051.

4 McDonald, "The Trail of Discipline," 19. The claim of the state to the body of its citizens is explored in Foucault, *Discipline and Punish*; Bourne, *Dismembering the Male*.

5 War Office, *Manual of Military Law* (hereinafter, MML), 442; ibid., 462.

6 MML, 445 n. 15.

7 After a search of 23,329 charges laid under the Army Act, not one referred to heterosexual indecent assault between servicepeople. The only such charge discovered to date was laid under the Air Force Act: RCAF personnel file 19. There was no minimum sentence stipulated, and the courts varied greatly in their sentences.

8 Margaret interview.

9 Pierson, "*They're Still Women After All*," 158, 219 (on public relations), 180–1 (on chivalry in the Canadian Army); Berton, *Starting Out 1920–1947*, states that he insisted his sister not join the CWAC: "God only knows what trouble she'd get into with these tough, hard-bitten lady soldiers. The odd thing is that I knew several CWACs, and none of them was tough or hard-bitten"; For studies of the chivalry of the courts, see Strange, "Wounded Womanhood and Dead Men," and Dubinsky, *Improper Advances*, 132.

10 NA, RG 24, file HQS 45-4-57, 12 April 1944, Air Commodore Tice to A.M.P. Recent work has shown that women in the American forces who do not respond to servicemen's sexual advances are vulnerable to charges of lesbianism. I have found no evidence to suggest that that occurred in the Canadian military during wartime. Since lesbians were not discharged or court-martialled, the motivation for such spurious charges may have been minimal.

11 MML, 460, 445, n. 14.

12 There were provisions for a 'special finding' under which minor alterations could be made to the particulars of a charge if the court found that the facts submitted in evidence were sufficient to prove the offence: MML, section 44(d), 648; NA, RG 24, reel T-15583, file 55-C-559.

13 NA, RG 24, reel T-15648, file 55-H-1381.

14 MML, chap. 7, "Offences Punishable by Ordinary Law," 115: "The offence of sodomy is committed when a male has carnal knowledge of an animal or of a human being 'per anima.' Penetration is required," and "It is an offence for a male person, either in public or private, to commit, or to be party to the

commission of, any act of gross indecency with another male person; or to pro-
cure the commission of any such act"; Gigeroff, *Sexual Deviations in the Criminal Law*; NA, RG 24, reel T-15583, file 55-C-560, p. 637; RG 24, reel T-15552,
file 55-A-942: In this case, the judge-advocate told the court that the act described in the evidence "would certainly be conduct of an unnatural or indecent
kind under Sec 18(5) AA." This judgment would seem to infringe upon the responsibility of the court to define "disgraceful conduct of an indecent kind."
However, the judge-advocate's advice was not questioned on review at the JAG
branch, suggesting that it was assumed to be beyond debate that oral homosexual acts were indecent and disgraceful.

15 The navy called general courts martial simply "courts martial," and district
courts martial, "disciplinary courts"; MML, chap. 5, "Courts-Martial," 45–6.

16 Herb Little interview; Some interviewees discussed the homosexual underworld
at Upper Canada College; Captain Bob Duncombe interview (Captain Duncombe retired in 1980 from his position commanding HMSC Carleton. He subsequently made his homosexuality public and is not outed by this passage).

17 Hannant, *The Infernal Machine*, 119–38; entries from RCAF personnel file 13,
RCAF retired 14.

18 See Stacey, *Six Years of War*, 236–7, for the establishment of the Canadian Officer Cadet Training Unit; Bert Sutcliffe and Ralph Wormleighton interviews.

19 Jones, *To the Green Fields Beyond*, 59; NA, RG 24, reel T-15839, file GCM-64.
The lieutenant was charged with "laying hands" on the corporal with aggressive, rather than sexual, intentions.

20 NA, RG 24, reel T-15817, file TTT-133; reel T-15830, file 111-39; reel T-15815,
file KKK-92.

21 NA, RG 24, reel T-15583, file 55-C-560, folio 563.

22 Bob Grimson interview. According to MML regulations, only an officer could
guard another officer.

23 See NA, RG 24, reel T-15657, file 55-K-340, inter alia, for a sense of appoint-
ments and functions; Green, "A Wartime Military Lawyer Reminisces"; Mc-
Donald, "The Legal Branch Law Firm of the Canadian Forces," 2; DHH file
111.601 3(D1): Transcripts of courts martial were reviewed and filed at the JAG
office; MML, 445, also "Rules of Evidence," 84.

24 I discovered these court-martial trials in various ways – searching through *Routine Orders* for most RCAF courts, reviewing hundreds of microfilm reels for the
army, and coming across references to a variety of courts maintained by the
navy. Servicemen convicted by civil courts in England and Canada were not included. None of these sources should have included a disproportionate number
of courts of officers or ranks.

25 *MML*, 115: "it is not necessary to prove that [sodomy] was committed against the consent of the person upon whom it was perpetrated; both agent and patient (if consenting) are equally guilty"; Russell, *Laws of Crimes*, vol. 3, 2282, cited by Major Dubeau, permanent president courts martial, MD 4 acting as judge-advocate, NA, RG 24, reel T-15657, file 55-K-340; NA, RG 24, reel T-15643, file 55-H-731; NA, RG 24, reel T-15657, file K-340 (Two soldiers had been pressured by the military police to testify against Major K, well respected in the highest social circles of Quebec society, a personal friend of Major-General Vanier and a decorated veteran of WWI. The court believed Major K's denials over the evidence of the two accomplices, even though they were clearly testifying against their own interests); *MML*, chap. 6, sections 95, 96, pp. 96, 97; NA, RG 24, reel T-15775, file 55-W-499.

26 *MML*, 106, quoted, inter alia, by the judge-advocate in NA, RG 24, reel T-15552, file 55-A-942; See *MML*, 25, for the uses of drunkenness as a factor in the mitigation of punishment.

27 NA, RG 24, reel T-15583, file 55-C-560, 19 June 1943, Brigadier Orde, JAG to deputy minister of justice; *MML*, "Rules of Procedure," 63, 661.

28 King's Regulations and Orders 530; NA, RG 24, reel T-15657, file 55-K-340; reel T-15583, file 55-C-560, Lieutenant Colonel J.E. McDermid, AD memo; 12 May 1943, Colonel Coch, director of administration to DAG(B); 19 June 1943 Brigadier Orde, JAG to deputy minister of justice.

29 Pierson, *"They're Still Women, After All,"* 183–4; NA, RG 24, vol. 22481, 30 April 1943, 23 February 1945.

30 No courts martial were published before 1941; sections 16 or 40 could also be referenced ambiguously; in the rare cases that the charge did refer to fraud, it was specified: see NA, RG 24, vol. 22480, 13 November 1942: William M. "was found guilty on a charge under section 18(5) air force act of cheating in a game, by using dice of fraudulent design."

31 Allin Hawkshaw correspondence.

32 NA, RG 24, reel T-15546, file 55-A-216; reel T-15552, file 55-A-942; reel T-15583, file 55-C-560, folio 597.

33 NA, RG 24, reel T-15548, file 55-A-365 (Courts often reduced charges for desertion to a finding of AWOL. Desertion entailed the intention to not return to the army, which was difficult to substantiate by evidence); Privacy regulations forbid me from discussing Anderson's fate in the army at this point.

34 The soldier would have been helping her out financially, since she would have been eligible for dependant's allowance during his service overseas. The Canadian forces tried to remain vigilant against the possibility of such abuse. See Stacey, *The Half-Million*, 136; While Anderson's defending officer suggested that a

psychiatrist would cure his homosexuality, Smith's defending officer
asserted that medicine could have no effect: NA, RG 24, reel T-15581,
file ZZ-102.

35 Smith's career up to the fall of 1945 is outlined in NA, RG 24, reel T-15581, file
ZZ-102, file 5D-59, and file 5N-61.

36 Tooley, "Appearance or Reality? Variations in Infantry courts Martial: 1st Canadian Infantry Division 1940–1945." Tooley considers the wide variation in
courts martial for AWOL and desertion among regiments and units in the first infantry division in Italy and concludes that the discrepancies result from the different use of courts by different regiments and individual commanding officers.
The same conclusion holds for homosexual charges. Subsequent chapters will
shed light on the differences among units.

37 MML, chap. 4, "Arrest." In the case of a soldier, the commanding officer could
impose summary punishment. With one exception, the only summary punishments I have found for homosexual offences were against German prisoners of
war in Canada. Based on a review of thousands of conduct sheets, which list
all infractions, I conclude that Canadian soldiers were invariably court-
martialled; district courts martial differed from general in the severity of sentence they could impose. A district court could sentence an accused to no more
than two years imprisonment with hard labour. Only general courts could try
officers. The minimum number of officers required to sit on a district court
was three, on a general court, five. General courts were meant to try serious
cases. Almost all homosexual offences were tried by general courts martial
(MML, 43–4, 48).

38 NA, RG 24, reel T-15583, file 55-C-560, 1943/05/13 Lieutenant-Colonel J.E.
MacDermid for file; 1943/05/12 Colonel H Coch to DAG(B). He was found
guilty of an alternative charge that specified, not any homosexual act, but "conduct to the prejudice of good order and military discipline," and was severely
reprimanded.

39 NA, RG 24, Acc 1997–98/260, vol. 64, file C-37c-112, pt 1, 28 January 1944,
A/V/M J.A. Sully, AMP to DPSS; 5 April 1944, S45-4-57 (D/D of P).

40 NA, RG 24, Acc 1997–98/260, pt 1, 12 April 1944, Air Commodore Tice to AMP.

41 Navy personnel file 27, 25 February 1944, Lieutenant Colonel L.R. MacDonald
AAG(Dis) Canadian Military Headquarters to DMS; NA, RG 24, reel T-15635,
file 55-G-1817.

42 NA, RG 24, reel T-15654, file 55-K-121; T-15808, file XXX-138; RCAF personnel
file 29; DHH file 82/401.

43 NA, RG 24, reel T-15695, file 55-M-1836.

44 RCAF personnel file 32, 23 May 1945, Case Sheet (specialist report) S/L J. Kershman, consultant in neuropsychiatry; Entertainment personnel file 26. There is a

suggestion that police used that evidence to elicit a confession of homosexual behaviour.

45 NA, RG 24, reel T-15793, file Y-62; reel T-15552, file 55-A-942; reel T-15832, file 4B-50.

46 See NA, RG 24, reel T-15546, file 55-A-216; reel T-15583, file 55-C-559; reel T-15564, file 55-K-121, for a defence of the right to call witnesses to demonstrate the homosexual inclination of the accused.

47 Russ Thomson interview; NA, RG 24, reel T-15701, file 55-M-2946, for instance. Section 8(2) named "Striking a superior officer" as an offence. By contrast, the defence that a soldier was gay was not mobilized by officers as a defence for section 37(1), "Striking a soldier."

48 NA, RG 24, reel T-15655, file HQC 55-K-193; reel T-15664, file HQC 55-L-507; reel T-15664, file HQC 55-L-508; reel T-15685, file HQC 55-M-832; reel T-15685, file HQC 55-M-831; reel T-15730, file HQC 55-R-328; reel T-15730, file HQC 55-R-327; reel T-15742, file HQC 55-S-570; reel T-15742, file HQC 55-S-569; reel T-15773, file 55-W-360.

CHAPTER THREE

1 Mort, *Dangerous Sexualities*; Weeks, *Sexuality and Its Discontents*; Dubinsky, *Improper Advances*; McLaren and McLaren, *The Bedroom and the State*; Weeks, *Sex, Politics and Society*; Rocke, *Forbidden Friendships*.

2 Weeks, *Sexuality and Its Discontents*; Brecher, *The Sex Researchers*; Lewes, *The Psychoanalytic Theory of Male Homosexuality*; Rowbotham and Weeks, *Socialism and the New Life*; Bland and Doan, *Sexology in Culture*; Bland and Doan, *Sexology Uncensored*; Thompson, *The Making of the English Working Class* (Thompson's famous formulation reminded scholars to study the agency of historical subjects); Oosterhuis, *Stepchildren of Nature*; Terry, *An American Obsession*; Maynard, "On the Case of the Case," 82.

3 Allin Hawkshaw correspondence.

4 Werlinder, *Psychopathy*; Archives of Canadian Psychiatry and Mental Health Services (hereinafter Archives of CP&MHS), file Walters 3.1, "Nomenclature of Mental Disorders."

5 Fisher, *An Introduction to Abnormal Psychology*, chaps 9–13, pp. 149–50, 192. Fisher's text, like that of the other contemporary works cited in this chapter, was in use in Canadian medical schools before the war. Fisher's was used at Queen's University.

6 English, *The Cream of the Crop*, 94; Copp and McAndrew, *Battle Exhaustion*.

7 NA, RG 24, Acc. 1997–98/26c, vol. 64, file C37C-112, pt 1, HQS 45-4-57, 1944/04/05, J.A. Sully directive.

8 Ibid., Air Commodore Tice to AMP, 12 April 1944; Katz, *Gay American History*, 162–73; NA, RG 24, Acc. 1997–98/26c, vol. 64, file C37C-112, pt 1, HQS 45-4-57, Air Commodore Tice to AMP, 12 April 1944.

9 NA, RG 24, HQS 45-4-57, Air Commodore Tice to AMP, 12 April 1944; J. Sully to air officer commanding-in-chief, RCAF overseas, 23 February 1945.

10 Henri DiPierro interview. The cases presented in this chapter involving homosexual men who were emotionally and psychologically maimed after putting their trust in the power of psychiatry are supported by published accounts. See Duberman, *Cures*.

11 RCAF personnel file 32.

12 Queen's University Archives. Calendars of the Faculty of Medicine list the following texts in service from 1931 to 1947, with some used from 1926 until the postwar years: Maurice Graig, ed., *Psychological Medicine, a Manual on Mental Diseases* (1912); V.E. Fisher, *An Introduction to Abnormal Psychology* (1937); D.K. Henderson and R.D. Gillepsie, *A Textbook of Psychiatry for Students and Practitioners* (1950); William McDougall, *Outlines of Abnormal Psychology* (1923); Aaron J. Rosanoff, ed., *Manual of Psychiatry* (1927); Edward A. Strecker, and Franklin G. Ebaugh, *Practical Clinical Psychiatry* (1940); William White, *Outlines of Psychiatry* (1907).

13 Terry, *An American Obsession*, chap. 2; Steakley, *The Writings of Dr. Magnus Hirschfeld*.

14 Oosterhuis, *Stepchildren of Nature* (Krafft-Ebing's argument was grounded in a Lamarkian concept of evolution in which acquired traits could be inherited); Rowbotham and Weeks, *Socialism and the New Life*, 156–9.

15 Gay, *Freud*, 548; Torgovnick, *Gone Primitive*, discusses Freud's class-based perspective; Lewes, *The Psychoanalytic Theory of Male Homosexuality*.

16 This sample was collected from cross-referring court-martial proceedings with service personnel files. Although I eventually discovered a greater number of cases of personnel engaging in homosexual acts, these men had been identified at the time that a privacy agreement with the National Archives provided access to the personnel records containing the psychiatric material. Not all personnel records could be found, and many did not include psychiatric case files; Navy personnel file 16.

17 NA, RG 24, Canadian Military Headquarters file block 11, vol. 12, 631, file 11/Psychiatry/2/2.

18 Wellman and Simpson, "Psychiatric Casualties in the (RCN)," 625–8.

19 Archives of CP & MHS, file Walters 3.1. These instructions were devised by Lieutenant Colonel Richardson, the senior neurologist at Basingstoke Neurological and Plastic Surgery Hospital.

20 NA, RG 24, vol. 12,630, 13 September 1943, E.A. McClusker DDMS First Canadian Corps to DDMS; "Psychiatric Reports and Medical Boards."

21 Army personnel files 29, 21, 12; RCAF personnel file 32; Army personnel files 120, 2.

22 NA, RG 24, reel T-15546, file HQS 55-A-216. Private A's health did not permit him to serve his prison sentence, which was remitted while he was in the military hospital with hypertension. However, he was discharged with ignominy and died in 1947.

23 Archives of CP & MHS, file Walters 3.37. Captain Fraser's notes read: "States he has never felt sexually attracted by other men in the army but has never had relations with other men." Since the two negations make the statement meaningless, I have changed it in the only way that it could make sense, and which, I presume, reflects the captain's intention.

24 Captain Ernest C. Armstrong had graduated from Queen's University in 1931 and worked as a neuropsychiatrist at Westminster Hospital in London, Ontario, from 1935 to 1941. Queen's Archives, file 3736.31, box 2; Archives of CP & MHS, file Walters 3.302 (The private was finally diagnosed as suffering from schizoid personality).

25 Army personnel file 2.

26 Army personnel file of Captain K.

27 Henri DiPierro interview.

28 Army personnel file 12, identity restricted. This soldier had served in the army since 1929, had landed in Sicily and fought through the Italian campaign. The court martial for homosexuality, however, and the psychiatric assessment occurred in 1949.

29 Army personnel file 23. Although the soldier had served during the war, this interview took place in the postwar period. In only one case of a recruit tabling his homosexuality did he actually not want to serve (NA, RG 24, reel T-15628, file HQC 55-G-728). In other cases where men acknowledged their homosexuality, they also asked to remain in the military.

30 Archives of CP & MHS, File Walters 3.240. Ulcers were dangerous for pilots, since they could perforate at high altitudes.

31 Navy personnel file 16; Army personnel file 21.

32 RCAF personnel files 1, 2, 3. Moorehouse helps us to understand the connection he was making between an airman's ethnicity and his motivation in RCAF personnel file 2: "This man is a French Canadian in the Service with poor motivation."

33 RCAF personnel file 25.

34 DHH, file 147.98009 (D4).

35 Army personnel file 94 (This homosexual charge occurred after the war); RCAF
   personnel file 6; RCAF personnel file 25; Army personnel file 12.
36 RCAF personnel file 20.
37 NA, RG 24, reel T-15643, file HQC 55-H-731 (Barraclough and Cathcart contributed their opinions to a very extensive petition filed by the accused in a fruitless
   attempt to have his dismissal quashed); for a similar case of exhaustion, see
   Pearce, *Journal of a War*, 165.
38 NA, RG 24, reel T-15793, file HQC 4L88. He was sentenced to two years imprisonment with hard labour and to discharge with ignomy, with a recommendation to mercy – an unusual addition to a court sentence.

CHAPTER FOUR

1 For instance, Chauncey, *Gay New York*; Kennedy and Davis, *Boots of Leather,
  Slippers of Gold*; Stein, *The City of Brotherly and Sisterly Love*; Stryker and van
  Buskirk, *Gay by the Bay*; Newton, *Cherry Grove, Fire Island*; Higgs, *Queer
  Sites*.
2 There is an extensive literature on the science of desire. Various scholars have
  addressed the value of looking for the causes of sexual orientation: Stein, *The
  Mismeasure of Desire*; Le Vay, *Queer Science*; Murphy, *Gay Science*.
3 Foucault, *The History of Sexuality*, 17–35; Don interview. In the foulcauldian
  sense, the knowledge that people have of homosexuality already includes fear
  and anxiety.
4 Clauncey, *Gay New York*, 2–6, challenges the myths of gay men's historic isolation, invisibility, and internalization of the dominant culture's view of homosexuality. While his corrective to those assumptions about the queer past was
  welcome in 1994, I tilt the sails back towards an appreciation of how those
  three factors also need to be understood in historical context.
5 Douglas, *Boys, Bombs and Brussels Sprouts*, 15.
6 Ralph Wormleighton interview.
7 Jim interview; Rich, "Compulsory Heterosexuality and Lesbian Existence,"
  631–60.
8 Hugh interview. His friend was killed in Europe before they could meet again.
  Hugh says, "I never found out if he felt the same way I did, but I'm sure he
  didn't."
9 Jim Egan interview.
10 Aubyn interview; Roberts, *The Classic Slum*, 55, describes how in the slums of
   Manchester, "[a]mong ignorant men, any interest in music, books or the arts in
   general, learning or even courtesy and intelligence could make one suspect. This
   linking of homosexuality with culture played some part, I think, in keeping the

lower working class as near illiterate as they were"; Fraser, *As for Me and My Body*, suggests that Philip's artistic nature was the false front meant to stand for his (and Sinclair Ross's) homosexuality in Ross's, *As for Me and My House*, published in 1941 as Ross enlisted in the Canadian Army.

11 Aubyn interview.

12 Brown, *When Freedom Was Lost*; *Le Droit*, 29 September 1933; *L'Autorité*, 23 September 1933. Also see "Miss Society of Women," *Vancouver Sun*, 24 February 1934, 22; "Not Soulless" (letter to the editor), *Vancouver Sun*, 27 February 1934; Broadfoot, *Ten Lost Years, 1929–1939*, 93–6; NA, RG 24, vol. 3184, HQ 1376-11-38.

13 D'Emilio, *Sexual Politics, Sexual Communities*, 38; Bérubé, *Coming Out under Fire*, 255. Bérubé also sees the screening of homosexuality during the Second World War as significant in the process of gay and lesbian community formation.

14 Edward interview; Goffman, *Asylums*, discusses the effects of "total institutions."

15 Bert Sutcliffe interview.

16 Aubyn interview; Russ Thomson interview; Bud interview.

17 Betty/Gordon interview; Coping with homosexuality in an anti-homosexual environment has been increasingly documented as a contributing factor to suicide since the Second World War. During the war, some psychiatrists were making the connection: O'Connor, "Some Notes on Suicide," 222–8; Lester, *Why People Kill Themselves*, 309–10; Saunders and Valente, "Suicide Risk among Gay Men and Lesbians," 1–23; Rich, "San Diego Suicide Study," 448–57; Bob Grimson interview.

18 Ralph Wormleighton interview.

19 Edward interview.

20 Bud interview.

21 Bob Grimson interview.

22 NA, RG 24, reel T-15668, file HQC 55-L-834 (Keith argued at the trial – incredibly – that he had spent the half hour resisting John. Nevertheless, he was not charged. John, in the wrong bed and older, was sentenced to 120 days imprisonment with hard labour and discharge with ignominy. Keith's damning testimony was probably the result of military police pressure. If he had said that nothing untoward had happened in bed, there would have been no case against either man); NA, RG 24, reel T-15546, file HQC 55-A-216.

23 NA, RG 24, reel T-15583, file HQC 55-C-559. They were given minor periods of detention and served effectively in the campaign in northwest Europe.

24 Jim interview.

25 George Wilkes interview.

26 Bob Grimson interview.

27 Betcherman, *The Swastika and the Maple Leaf*; Bob Grimson interview.

28 Ibid.

29 NA, RG 24, reel T-15546, file HQC 55-A-190.

30 John interview.

31 NA, RG 28, reel T-15775, file HQC 55-W-499.

32 Navy personnel file 27.

33 The court records corroborate the suggestion that fights were not uncommon. Also see Douglas, *Boys, Bombs and Brussels Sprouts*, 24–5.

34 Navy personnel file 27.

35 Byron interview.

36 Pearce, *Journal of a War*, 133–4.

37 RCAF personnel file 6. Quotation from psychiatrist's report.

38 Ibid.

39 His "feminine" characteristics were documented by the psychiatrist, Dr Moorehouse, in 1944.

40 RCAF personnel file 5. The quote is from Dr Moorehouse, who coincidentally was posted at both stations with Denis and lamented the fact that the RCAF had not been able to discharge him earlier.

41 RCAF personnel file 4. This description dates from June 1945 when he enlisted (against regulations) in the army, having served a term of detention and been discharged from the RCAF. His suggestible nature was also noted by the RCAF psychiatrist.

42 An even more detailed account of a similar situation in which a timid, "suggestible" young soldier was manipulated into providing oral sexual gratitification for a group of comrades is documented in NA, RG 24, reel T-15707, files 55-M-3488 and 55-M-3489. These soldiers were tried jointly with four others: files 55-B-3575, 55-C-2279, 55-L-2339, 55-O-366. This example dates, however, from 1948 and is therefore not included in this study of wartime sexuality.

43 All of the accused were sentenced to terms of imprisonment with hard labour and were discharged with ignominy.

44 Kinsey, *Sexual Behaviour in the Human Male*, 10, 76.

CHAPTER FIVE

1 NA, RG 24, reel T-15587, file HQC 55-C-1032.

2 On concealing identities, see Fitzherbert, *True to Both My Selves*; Velmans, *Edith's Story*; Opdyke, *In My Hands*; Aubrac, *Outwitting the Gestapo*; Begley, *Wartime Lies*.

3 Stanley, *Canada's Soldiers*; Stacey and Wilson, *The Half-Million*, xi; Dancocks, *The D-Day Dodgers*, 434; Bercuson, *Maple Leaf against the Axis*.

4 Stacey and Wilson, *The Half-Million*, 138.

5 Henri Dipierro interview; Maynard, "Through a Hole in the Lavatory Wall," discusses certain theatres in Toronto as sites of homosexual activity; Katz, *Love Stories*.

6 Canadian Lesbian and Gay Archives, Bert Sutcliffe autobiography, 33; Bert Sutcliffe interview. A "Saturday night soldier" refers to a reservist who trained regularly with his regiment but had a full-time civilian job.

7 Courts martial and cases of Canadians tried in the British criminal system reveal no military or civilian police presence in these bars. In Canada, at war's end, merely being present in a bar known as queer could bring one under the suspicion of military and civilian police. Henri DiPierro interview; Bert Sutcliffe interview; Costello, *Love, Sex and War*; Crisp, *How to Become a Virgin*, 152.

8 Ralph Wormleighton interview (Cars ran at night on parking lights only. Wartime traffic regulations forbade stopping on roadways at night, thereby inducing accidents). Also see Stacey, *The Half-Million*, chap. 2; Bert Sutcliffe interview; NA, RG 24, reel T-15850, file W-4.

9 Bob Grimson interview; Bert Sutcliffe autobiography, 33; Weeks, *Sex, Politics and Society*, 113–4 on the Cleveland Street Scandal; Walkowitz, *The City of Dreadful Delights*, 41, 128, on cross-class sexual liaisons in London; Forster, *Maurice*; Kennedy and Davis, *Boots of Leather, Slippers of Gold*, describes how a common lesbian sexual identity brought black and white lesbians into social contact in Buffalo, New York, in the postwar era; Bert Sutcliffe interview.

10 Bert Sutcliffe interview; Bert Sutcliffe autobiography, 34.

11 Bert Sutcliffe interview; Bob Grimson interview.

12 NA, RG 24, reel T-15654, file HQC 55-K-121.

13 LePan, *The Deserter*, 31; Round, "Douglas Valentine LePan."

14 Le Pan, *The Deserter*, 35; NA, RG 24, reel T-15647, file 55-H-1224, describes in detail how a Canadian soldier "with a fine physique" similarly picked up a British man and lived with him (and off of him) during his desertion. For a more explicit account of prostitution among His Majesty's Brigade of Guards, see Ackerly, *My Father and Myself*, especially 134–5, 193–203.

15 Spender, *The Temple*; Isherwood, *Mr Norris Changes Trains*; Crisp, *The Naked Civil Servant*.

16 NA, RG 24, reel T-15553, file HQC 55-B-316, personnel selection report from Canadian detention barracks, 16 March 1944: "Medical History of an Invalid," Lieutenant G. Blue, 25 March 1944 (The medical officer may have followed the personnel officer in his use of the phrase "preying" on perverts. It is less likely, I

think, that Private Robert used it in relation to his own activities. The form provided an entry for the patient's 'subjective' diagnosis. Few servicemen offered comments in their own words. Robert seems not to have been intimidated by the medical or administration officers); Major-General P. Montague, i/c administration, Canadian Military Headquarters, to the secretary, DND, 16 August 1944; Canada's unemployment policy during the Depression is detailed in Struthers, *No Fault of Their Own*.

17 NA, RG 24, reel T-15587, file HQC 55-C-973; reel T-15671, file 55-L-1126; Maynard, " 'Horrible Temptations.' "

18 See Moran, *The Homosexual(ity) of Law*, 51–6, on the issue of blackmail as discussed by the Wolfendon committee.

19 NA, RG 24, reel T-15647, file HQC 55-H-1268.

20 Bert Sutcliffe interview; Army personnel file 65, police reports.

21 NA, RG 24, reel T-15564, file HQC 55-K-121. This was a portion of Driver Hiebert's testimony at Captain K's court martial for "disgraceful conduct of an indecent kind."

22 Henri DiPierro interview; Bud interview.

23 NA, RG 24, reel T-15657, file HQC 55-K-340, André's testimony at the summary of evidence for the court martial of Major K. my translation: "He asked me to sit on his bed and unbutton my pants. He told me that he liked men and asked me to let him enjoy himself and that it would be a good time for me also. I unbuttoned my pants and took out my penis, and he sucked it. I didn't refuse, since he was a major and I worked for him. He didn't ask me to do anything to him and I didn't do anything."

24 Aubyn interview. In other British postings, Aubyn was also welcomed into local homes that had pianos for his practice.

25 NA, RG 24, reel T-15793, file Y-62. Sergeant Gordon C was found not guilty of the charge of "disgraceful conduct of an indecent kind."

26 Personnel file of James J. (Sergeant James J died shortly after the war); NA, RG 24, reel T-15649, file HQC 55-J-89 (James J was acting sergeant at the time of the offence discussed here); NA, RG 24, reel T-15823, file 4W-116, contains a more carefully planned case of entrapment of a queer soldier by his comrades, also in England.

27 NA, RG 24, reel T-15649, file HQC 55-J-89; reel T-15844, file D-69. Jeffrey said he took Smith's penis in his hand, while Smith said that he had taken it in his mouth. That is the only substantial difference in their testimony.

28 NA, RG 24, reel T-15800, file 281. My translations: "I have known Private [Paul] for a year. In October, at East Preston I started to go out with him. One pay night, we went to the Three Crowns and got drunk. On the way back, I asked [Paul], 'Do you give blow-jobs, yes or no?' He answered 'Yes.' We went on the

grass and he sucked me off and I did the same for him"; "Since the first of January, I haven't had intimate relations with him and I have rarely gone out with him, because I wanted to end this intimacy."

29 Ibid. My translations: "About 9 or 10 months ago, I was in London on a 7-day pass with Privates Belanger and Leo Beaudoin. I met a civilian who said his name was Bob, we were in a pub on Dean Street. We drank for awhile and I went back to his place. I was drunk. I spent the night there and the next morning, we met up with Belanger and Beaudoin at a Greek restaurant. Bob was wearing an engagement ring and I asked him if he would lend it to me. He lent it to me"; "it was a ring that was given to me by one of my 'tricks' in London." The bilingual military police translated *trousse* as "perverted friend" for the purposes of his court martial. Private Paul probably would have preferred a more playful translation.

30 Maynard, "'Horrible Temptations,'" 208.

31 Allan interview; Peter interview; Also see Bob Grimson interview for a similar recollection. Allan was an adolescent at the beginning of the war. His encounter with the soldier probably took place in 1939 or 1940.

32 SUS in U.K. personnel file 43; Lieutenant-General Murchie, chief of staff, Canadian Military Headquarters, to secretary DND, 1946/06/04. The sentences of seventy Canadians serving civil sentences in British prisons for various offences were remitted by the home secretary in June 1946.

33 NA, RG 24, reel T-15828, file OO-121.

34 SUS personnel file 43, Brig Ferguson, chair of War Service Gratuity Board of Review, to District Administration DVA, 15 October 1946. He was considered "exemplary" by the board, since, beyond his service in difficult battle conditions, he had no entries whatsoever on his conduct sheet after five years of service.

35 SUS personnel file 43, 19 February 1946, Lt-Col Graham AJAG to Canadian Military Headquarters (Lieutenant-Colonel Graham reviewed the case at the request of Arthur's family in Canada); 3 August 1945, Arthur to Mrs M; 10 August 1945, Arthur to Mrs M.

36 SUS personnel file 43, 29 June 1945, Capt. Green JAG Overseas to VJAG Canadian Military Headquarters. The Canadian Army sent representatives in all instances of Canadians charged in the British civil courts.

37 SUS personnel file 43. The doctor could not conclude that "some tenderness and slight excoriation" in the boy's anal region was the result of an "unnatural" offence. In the final instance, the soldier attempted to penetrate the boy. The pain of that attempt presumably outweighed the compensation he had been promised and he told a caretaker of the incident.

38 NA, RG 24, reel T-15795, file 4V-114. Private C was sentenced to 150 days detention.

39 Groth and Gary, "Heterosexuality, Homosexuality, and Pedophilia," documents that although most sexual molestations target girl victims, homosexual men continue to be scapegoated as the primary offenders; Personnel file of Private Donald Staley; *Lethbridge Herald*, 17 December 1948.

40 Personal correspondence with Rudi Van Dantzig. Those who refer to the film, also called, *For a Lost Soldier*, will be confused by the following discussion. Van Dantzig's book offers a much more complex account of the relationship. Jeroen's fears of Walt and his repulsion/attraction are not worked out on screen.

41 Van Dantzig, *For a Lost Soldier*, 101.

42 Ibid., 110–11, 124.

43 Ibid., 128.

44 Ibid., 127

45 Edward interview. The soldiers referred to by the other boys may well have been German, of course.

46 Edward interview; Army personnel file 21, 13 August 1943, Major-General Montague memorandum; 25 September 1943, Capt. Ruddy JAG review sheet.

47 NA, RG 24, vol. 16,674, War Diary, 7 August 1942; 1 February 1942; 13 April 1942; 10 April 1942: performing for an audience of 300 from Canadian reinforcement units and 14th Canadian General Hospital at Marlborough Lines Theatre.

48 Bill Dunstan interview; Bradbury interview (Bradbury, born in 1901, argued that he was not "technically" homosexual, since he was "attracted to the feminine in men").

49 Hugh interview; NA, RG 24, reel T-15833, file NNN-13. His conviction and sentence of three months detention was not confirmed by the confirming authority.

50 NA, RG 24, reel T-15552, file HQC 55-A-942 (Joseph was sentenced to ninety days detention. Also see reel T-15643, file HQC 55-H-731, for the case of a captain who gave in to previously restrained homosexual urges while suffering from battle exhaustion); reel T-15777, file HQC 55-W-649, for the case of a soldier whose advances in a pup tent in Italy were rejected.

51 NA, RG 24, reel T-15808 file XXX-138; reel T-15635, file HQC 55-G-1817; reel T-15804, file XXX-40.

52 Bert Sutcliffe interview; Edward interview; Trevelyan, *Rome '44*; Dancocks, *The D-Day Dodgers*; Clark, *A Keen Soldier*; Bob Grimson interview.

53 Burns, *The Gallery*, 133–52.

CHAPTER SIX

1 Marshall, *Men against Fire*; Kellett, *Combat Motivation*, summarizes competing theories regarding combat motivation; Manning, "Morale, Cohesion and Esprit de Corps."

2 Gade et al., "The Experience of Foreign Militaries"; Stanley and Scott, *Gays and Lesbians in the Military*, chaps 11–14; Meanwhile, MacCoun has articulated the various ways that a queer soldier could influence cohesion, arguing that, even in antagonistic units, cohesion could actually increase at his/her expense: MacCoun, "Sexual Orientation and Military Cohesion"; Sarbin, "The Deconstruction of Stereotypes."

3 Shilts, *Conduct Unbecoming*; Bérubé, *Coming Out under Fire*; Humphries, *My Country, My Right to Serve*; Belkin and McNichol, *Effects of the 1992 Lifting on Gay and Lesbian Service in the Canadian Forces*; Rowe, "Another Soldier's Story"; Kier, "Homosexuals in the U.S. Military," 5–39; Mullen and Copper, "The Relationship between Group Cohesiveness and Performance," 210–27; Ingraham, *The Boys in the Barracks*; Westbrook, "The Potential for Military Disintegration."

4 Herdt, *Guardians of the Flutes*, "Fetish and Fantasy in Sambia Initiation," and "Semen Transactions in Sambia Culture," 167. 'Sambia' is a pseudonym for the actual tribe studied by Herdt, xvi. Herdt argues that the issue of "who gives and receives semen is not one that much concerns Westerners today." While the significance of semen itself is different, he misjudges Western society, which has been obsessed with who gives semen to whom, when, and how. He overlooks the historical Christian concern in Western society over the 'spilling of seed' and the nineteenth-century medical warnings that masturbation would lead to insanity and other afflictions.

5 Willett, *A Heritage at Risk*; Bercuson, *Significant Incident*, chap. 5; Herdt, "Semen Transactions in Sambia Culture."

6 Ober, "The Evil Empire," 25.

7 Desbarats, *Somalia Cover-up*; Winslow, "Rites of Passage and Group Bonding in the Canadian Airborne," 429–57. The details of the initiation rituals are taken from Winslow's article and the Somalia Commission's proceedings. For a less critical defence of masculine rituals and warrior culture, see Bercuson, *Significant Incident*.

8 The masculinist foundation of military and paramilitary organizations is discussed in Gibson, *Warrior Dreams*; Winslow, "Rites of Passage and Group Bonding in the Canadian Airborne."

9 *MML*, 74.

10 NA, RG 24, reel T-15583, file 55-C-560. Colonel Milligan had signed the charge sheet that brought Lieutenant C to trial. The high regard evident in his testimony strongly suggests that he did so unwillingly. The real decision to prosecute was the result of discussions between NDHQ and Military District 2. The court "seemed impressed" in that Major Bristol asked the witness to repeat that testimony at the end of his questioning. Number 2 Engineer Service and Works Company had been 2 Detachment, Royal Canadian Engineers, prior to WWII. Lieutenant C had been with that unit since 1923.

11 NA, RG 24, reel T-15583, file 55-C-560.

12 Henderson, *Cohesion*, 4, 14, 19. Recent war movies reflect that proposition, such as, *Saving Private Ryan* (Steven Spielberg, 1999) and, *Black Hawk Down* (Ridley Scott, 2001), in which the soldier's bonds to his unit are seen to be more significant than any other, including family. Henderson's prescription for military cohesion recalls Goffman's study of the effect of institutional life on its inmates (Goffman, *Asylums*; 25, 76, 79). Henderson uses this assertion to argue for greater attention to be paid in American society to promoting a homogeneous view of the nation's history, values, and attitudes.

13 Marshall, *Men against Fire*; Kier, "Homosexuals in the U.S. Military"; Kellett, *Combat Motivation*; Watson, *When Soldiers Quit*; Mullen and Copper, "The Relationship between Group Cohesiveness and Performance," 211; Festinger, "Informal Social Communication," 274.

14 Archives of CP & MHS, file Walters 3.1, "Nomenclature of Mental Disorders."

15 NA, RG 24, reel T-15601, file 55-D-654; reel T-15609, file 55-B-1841; reel T-15669, file 55-L-934; reel T-15546, file 55-A-234; DHH 169.009 (D134).

16 NA, RG 24, reel T-15651, file 55-J-259; reel T-15646, file 55-H-1158. Clearly, the defending officer intended to say, "No one can deny that there is one."

17 NA, RG 24, reel T-15657, file 55-K-39.

18 Personnel file of Burwell Snyder.

19 NA, RG 24, reel T-15550, file 55-A-585.

20 NA, RG 24, reel T-15656, file 55-K-318. Courts of enquiry into the suicides of men who felt inadequate in basic training, and in service, sometimes interviewed the deceased man's 'buddy' or 'chum,' who had offered some measure of support. See personnel file of Samuel Desmond Taylor.

21 Russ Thomson interview. In fact, I have been able to find no court-martial proceedings relating to this incident. Either the charges were handled summarily or the authorities decided not to pursue the issue.

22 NA, RG 24, reel T-15653, file 55-J-485. Comrades constantly baited recruits to see if they had weaknesses. Ralph Wormleighton, an intellectual and a 'sissy,' remembers the men in his basic training trying to throw him off his food by vulgar talk. He ignored them. Ralph Wormleighton interview.

23 Most pacifists refused to wear the uniform and were court-martialled for "disobeying a lawful command" before they had the chance to experience training camp. For a study of pacifism in Canada, see Socknat, *Witness against War*; NA, reel T-15547, file 55-A-290; reel T-15549, file 55-A-532; reel T-15651, file 55-J-263; Byers, "Mobilizing Canada"; NA, RG 24, reel T-15563, file 55-B-1265.

24 Holmes, *Acts of War*, 311; Beevor, *Inside the British Army*; Kellett, *Combat Motivation*.

25 Berton, *Starting Out, 1920–1947*; Ross, *Slow March to a Regiment*, 45.

26 Personnel file of Desmond Samuel Taylor, court of enquiry into Taylor's death. See the testimony of Private H.S. Taylor, p. viii, and Private Spirnyak, p. ix. Private Villemaire said that Taylor's confession related to "sinful" actions. That the incident referred to homosexual actions follows from his admission to Spirnyak that the entries concerned "his past life and his sex life" and that "[h]e never spoke of women." Sergeant Paillefer, witness 25, who had known him for years, also testified that he "did not bother with girls." It is possible, but far less likely, that his sexual regrets concerned bestiality or some other practice not involving women.

27 NA, reel T-15609, file 55-D-1815; reel T-15653, file 55-J-610; Burstyn, *The Rites of Men*.

28 Wellman and Simpson, "Psychiatric Casualties in the (RCN)," 626.

29 Lamb, *The Corvette Navy*, 3; Macpherson and Milner, *Corvettes of the Royal Canadian Navy, 1939–1945*; Milner, *North Atlantic Run*.

30 Lamb, *The Corvette Navy*, 135.

31 Ibid., 50; Joe interview; Pugsley, *Saints, Devils and Ordinary Seamen*, 28, 45, 51, 54.

32 Lamb, *The Corvette Navy*, 49; Joe interview.

33 Margaret interview.

34 Morrison and Slaney, *The Breed of Manly Men*, 138, 150, 176.

35 Maynard, "Rough Work and Rugged Men," 159–69; Ramirez, *On the Move*, discusses a North Atlantic triangle in which Italian men were integrated into the Canadian economy in the late nineteenth and early twentieth centuries, moving back to Italy once they had amassed enough capital to establish a family. The normal patterns of sojourning and immigration were reversed during the war, and Canadian men eventually brought their wartime experiences back to Canada.

36 This analysis is based on NA, RG 24, reel T-15804, file XXX-40; reel T-15808, file XXX-138; reel T-15635, file 55-G-1817.

37 NA, RG 24, reel T-15808, file XXX-138.

38 Ibid.

39 NA, RG 24, reel T-15804, file XXX-40.

40 NA, RG 24, reel T-15636, file 55-G-1817.

41 Army personnel file 13.

42 NA, RG 24, reel T-15808, file XXX-138.

43 Army personnel files 14, 18, 19, 20.

44 For a sample of (often brutal) rape trials in Italy, see NA, RG 24, reel T-15838, file III-95; reel T-15824, file SSS-91; reel T-15846, file 4J-150; reel T-15797, file 4C-51; reel T-15795, file YYY-6; reel T-15558, file 55-B-822; reel T-15779, file 55-W-1028.

45 NA, RG 24, reel T-15635, file 55-G-1817.

46 NA, RG 24, reel T-15635, file 55-G-1817; reel T-15808, file XXX-138.

47 Ralph Wormleighton interview.

48 Bill Dunstan interview.

49 Bert Sutcliffe interview.

50 Vance, *Objects of Concern* (This otherwise comprehensive work contains no mention of homosexuality); Brown, *Bonds of Wire*, 130; Durand, *Stalag Luft III*, 219.

51 NA, RG 24, reel A-708, *Weekly Wire*, 10 July 1943, 13 September 1942, 8 January 1944.

52 NA, RG 24, reel A-708, *Weekly Wire*, 11 September 1942, 1 April 1944, 25 March 1944; *Daily Louse*, 1 January 1942; *Weekly Wire*, 2 June 1943.

53 NA, RG 24, reel A-708, *Weekly Wire*, 27 February 1943; NA, RG 30, E398, Harold Dothie, file 2; Australians named close friends "cobbers" : Grogan, *Dieppe and Beyond*, 35.

54 Wooley, *No Time Off for Good Behaviour*.

APPENDIX THREE

1 Allan English, *The Cream of the Crop*, 218.

2 However, once found, the court-martial records were judged to be in such delicate condition that the microfilm reels needed to be reproduced before they could be viewed. The first were ready a year after the initial request to view them. RG 24 national archivist Paul Marsden was most helpful in providing access to the material.

3 NA, RG 24, vol. 18,712 (file "Prison & Detention, Statements on Personnel in").

BIBLIOGRAPHY

Abelove, Henry. "Freud, Male Homosexuality and the Americans." In Henry Abelove et al., *The Lesbian and Gay Studies Reader*. New York: Routledge, 1993.

Ackerly, J.R. *My Father and Myself*. London: Bodley Head, 1968.

Adam, Barry. "Anatomy of a Panic: State Voyeurism, Gender Politics, and the Cult of
Americanism." In Wilbur Scott and Sandra Stanley, eds., *Gays and Lesbians in the
Military: Issues, Concerns and Contrasts*. New York: Aldine de Gruyter, 1994.

Adams, Mary Louise. *The Trouble with Normal: Postwar Youth and the Construction of Heterosexuality*. Toronto: University of Toronto Press, 1994.

Altman, Denis. *The Homosexualization of America, The Americanization of the
Homosexual*. New York: St Martin's Press, 1982.

Aubrac, Lucie. *Outwitting the Gestapo*. Lincoln: University of Nebraska Press,
1993.

Beevor, Anthony. *Inside the British Army*. London: Corgi Books, 1993.

Begley, Louis. *Wartime Lies*. New York: Ivy Books, 1991.

Belkin, Aaron, and Jason McNichol. *Effects of the 1992 Lifting on Gay and Lesbian Service in the Canadian Forces: Appraising the Evidence*. San Diego: Center
for the Study of Sexual Minorities in the Military, 2000.

Benecke, M., and K. Dodge. "Military Women in Non-traditional Job Fields: Casualties of the Armed Forces War on Homosexuals." *Harvard Women's Law Journal* 13 (1990).

Bercuson, David. *Maple Leaf against the Axis: Canada's Second World War*. Toronto: Stoddart, 1995.

– *Significant Incident: Canada's Army, the Airborne, and the Murder in Somalia*.
Toronto: McClelland and Stewart, 1996.

Berton, Pierre. *Starting Out, 1920–1947*. Toronto: McClelland and Stewart, 1987.

Bérubé, Allan. *Coming Out under Fire: The History of Gay Men and Women in
World War Two*. New York: Free Press, 1990.

Betcherman, Lita-Rose. *The Swastika and the Maple Leaf: Fascist Movements in Canada in the Thirties*. Toronto: Fitzhenry and Whiteside, 1975.

Bland, Lucy, and Laura Doan. *Sexology in Culture: Labelling Bodies and Desires*. Chicago: University of Chicago Press, 1998.

– *Sexology Uncensored*. Cambridge: Polity Press, 1998.

Blumenfeld, Warren, ed. *Homophobia: How We All Pay the Price*. Boston: Beacon Press, 1992.

Bohls, Kirk, and Mark Wangrin. "Athletes Revel in Being One of the Guys, Not One of the Gays." In Peter Donnelly, ed., *Taking Sport Seriously: Social Issues in Canadian Sport*. Toronto: Thompson Educational Publishing, 1997.

Bourne, Joanna. *Dismembering the Male*. Chicago: University of Chicago Press, 1996.

Bray, Alan. *Homosexuality in Renaissance England*. New York: Columbia University Press, 1995.

Brecher, Edward. *The Sex Researchers*. London: Deutsch, 1970.

Bridges, James Wilfred. *Psychology: Normal and Abnormal*. New York, London: D. Appleton and Company, 1930.

Broadfoot, Barry. *Ten Lost Years, 1929–1939*. Toronto: Doubleday, 1973.

Brod, Harry, ed. *The Making of Masculinities: The New Men's Studies*. New York: Routledge, 1987.

Brown, Kingsley. *Bonds of Wire*. Toronto: Collins Publishers, 1989.

Brown, Lorne. *When Freedom Was Lost: The Unemployed, the Agitator, and the State*. Montreal: Black Rose Books, 1987.

Brown, Robert Craig, and Ramsay Cook. *Canada 1986–1921: A Nation Transformed*. Toronto: McClelland and Stewart, 1974.

Burn, Shawn Meghan. "Heterosexuals' Use of 'Fag' and 'Queer' to Deride One Another: A Contributor to Heterosexism and Stigma." *Journal of Homosexuality* 40, no. 2 (2000).

Burns, John Horn. *The Gallery*. New York and London: Harper & Brothers Publishers, 1947.

Burstyn, Varda. *The Rites of Men: Manhood, Politics, and the Culture of Sport*. Toronto: University of Toronto Press, 1999.

Byers, Dan. "Mobilizing Canada: The National Resources Mobilisation Act, the Department of National Defence, and Compulsory Military Service in Canada, 1940–1945." Ph.D. thesis, McGill University, February 2001.

Cassell, Jay. *The Secret Plague*. Toronto: University of Toronto Press, 1990.

Chauncey, George. *Gay New York: Gender, Urban Culture and the Making of the Gay Male World, 1890–1940*. New York: Basic Books, 1994.

Chaytor, Miranda. "Husbandry: Narratives of Rape in the Seventeenth Century." *Gender and History* 7 (November 1995).

Clark, Andrew. *A Keen Soldier: The Execution of Second World War Private Harold Pringle*. Toronto: Alfred A. Knopf, 2002.

Cohen, Ed. *Talk on the Wilde Side: Towards a Geneology of a Discourse on Male Sexualities*. London: Routledge, 1993.

Collins, Robert. *The Long and the Short and the Tall: An Ordinary Airman's War*. Saskatoon: Western Producer Prairie Books, 1986.

Comeau, Paul-André; Claude Beauregard; and Edwidge Munn. *La Démocratie en Vuilleuse: Rapport des censeurs 1939–1945*. Montreal: Editions Québec, 1995.

Copp, Terry, and Bill McAndrew. *Battle Exhaustion: Soldiers and Psychiatrists in the Canadian Army, 1939–1945*. Montreal & Kingston: McGill-Queen's University Press, 1990.

Costello, John. *Love, Sex and War: Changing Values 1939–45*. London: Collins, 1985.

Cott, Nancy. "Passionlessness: An Interpretation of Victorian Sexual Ideology." *Signs* 4 (1978).

Crisp, Quentin. *How to Become a Virgin*. Glasgow: Fontana Paperbacks, 1981.

– *The Naked Civil Servant*. London: Jonathan Cape, 1968.

Dancocks, Daniel. *The D-Day Dodgers: The Canadians in Italy, 1943–1945*. Toronto: McClelland and Stewart, 1991.

Dean, Robert. *Imperial Brotherhood: Gender and the Making of Cold War Foreign Policy*. Amherst: University of Massachusetts Press, 2001.

D'Emilio, John. *Sexual Politics, Sexual Communities: The Making of a Homosexual Minority in the United States 1940 – 1970*. Chicago: University of Chicago Press, 1998.

Desbarats, Peter. *Somalia Cover-up: A Commissioner's Journal*. Toronto: McClelland and Stewart, 1997.

Douglas, J. Harvey. *Boys, Bombs and Brussels Sprouts: A Knees-Up, Wheels-Up Chronicle of WWII*. Toronto: McClelland and Stewart, 1982.

Dover, K.J. *Greek Homosexuality*. Cambridge: Harvard University Press, 1989.

Duberman, Martin. *Cures: A Gay Man's Odyssey*. New York: Dutto, 1991.

– " 'Writhing Bedfellows' in Ante-Bellum South Carolina: Historical Interpretation and the Politics of Evidence." In Martin Duberman et al., *Hidden from History: Reclaiming the Gay and Lesbian Past*. Markham: Penguin Books Canada, 1989.

Dubinsky, Karen. *Improper Advances: Rape and Heterosexual Conflict in Ontario, 1880–1929*. Chicago: University of Chicago Press, 1993.

– *The Second Greatest Disappointment*. Toronto: Between the Lines, 1998.

Durand, Arthur. *Stalag Luft III: The Secret Story*. Baton Rouge: Louisiana State University Press, 1988.

English, Allan. *The Cream of the Crop: Canadian Aircrew, 1939–1945*. Montreal & Kingston: McGill-Queen's University Press, 1996.

Esprit de Corps 4, no. 3 1994.

Evans, Gary. *John Grierson and the National Film Board: The Politics of Wartime Propaganda*. Toronto: University of Toronto Press, 1984.

Faderman, Lillian. *Surpassing the Love of Men: Romantic Friendship and Love between Women from the Renaissance to the Present*. New York: William Morrow, 1981.

Faludi, Susan. *Stiffed: The Betrayal of the American Male*. New York: William Morrow and Company, 1999.

Feasby, W.R., ed. *Official History of the Canadian Medical Services 1939–1945*. vol. 2: *Clinical Subjects*. Ottawa: Queen's Printer, 1953.

Feinman, Ilene Rose. *Citizenship Rights: Feminist Soldiers and Feminist Antimilitarists*. New York: New York University Press, 2000.

Festinger, L. "Informal Social Communication." *Psychological Review* 57 (1950).

Fisher, V.E. *An Introduction to Abnormal Psychology*. New York: MacMillan Company, 1937.

Fitzherbert, Katrin. *True to Both My Selves*. London: Virago, 1997.

Forbes, H.C. "Military Police at War: The No 2 Company Canadian Provost Corps in England and France, 1942–1945." *Quarterly, Royal Canadian Mounted Police*, no. 4 (1985).

Forster, E.M. *Maurice*. Scarborough, Ont.: New American Library of Canada, 1972.

Foucault, Michel. *Discipline and Punish*. Harmondsworth: Penquin, 1991.

– *The History of Sexuality: An Introduction*. New York: Random House, 1978; New York: Vintage Books, 1990.

Francis, Daniel. *National Dreams: Myth, Memory, and Canadian History*. Vancouver: Arsenal Pulp Press, 1997.

Fraser, Keith. *As for Me and My Body: Memoir of Sinclair Ross*. Toronto: ECW Press, 1997.

Freedman, Estelle, and John D'Emilio. *Intimate Matters: A History of Sexuality in America*. New York: Harper and Row, 1988.

Gade, Paul A., et al. "The Experience of Foreign Militaries." In Herek et al., *Out in Force: Sexual Orientation and the Military*. Chicago: University of Chicago Press, 1996.

Gay, Peter. *Freud: A Life for Our Time*. New York: W.W. Norton and Company, 1988.

Gibson, James William. *Warrior Dreams: Violence and Manhood in Post-Vietnam America*. New York: Hill and Wang, 1994.

Gigeroff, Alex. *Sexual Deviations in the Criminal Law: Homosexual, Exhibitionistic, and Pedophilic Offences in Canada*. Toronto: University of Toronto Press, 1968.

Goffman, Erving. *Asylums: Essays on the Social Situation of Mental Patients and Other Inmates*. New York: Doubleday, 1961.

Goldberg, Jonathan, ed. *Reclaiming Sodom*. London: Routledge, 1994.

Granatstein, Jack. *Canada's War: The Politics of the Mackenzie King Government 1939–1945*. Toronto: University of Toronto Press, 1990.

– *Conscription in the Second World War, 1939–1945*. Toronto: McGraw-Hill-Ryerson, 1969.

– and Peter Neary, eds. *The Veterans Charter and Post-World War II Canada*. Montreal & Kingston: McGill-Queen's University Press, 1998.

Green, L.C. "A Wartime Military Lawyer Reminisces." *Canadian Forces JAG Journal* 2 (1989).

Greenberg, David. *The Construction of Homosexuality*. Chicago: University of Chicago Press, 1988.

Grogan, John. *Dieppe and Beyond: For a Dollar and a Half a Day*. Renfrew: Juniper Books, 1982.

Groth, Nicholas A., and Thomas S. Gary. "Heterosexuality, Homosexuality, and Pedophilia: Sexual Offenses against Children and Adult Sexual Orientation." In Anthony M. Scacco, *Male Rape: A Casebook of Sexual Aggressions*. New York: AMS Press, 1982.

Halperin, David M. *One Hundred Years of Homosexuality*. New York: Routledge, 1990.

– *Saint Foucault: Towards a Gay Hagiography*. New York: Oxford University Press, 1995.

Hannant, Larry. *The Infernal Machine: Investigating the Loyalty of Canada's Citizens*. Toronto: University of Toronto Press, 1995.

Henderson, William Darryl. *Cohesion: The Human Element in Combat*. Washington: National Defense University Press, 1985.

Herdt, G.H. "Fetish and Fantasy in Sambian Initiation." In G.H. Herdt, ed., *Rituals of Manhood: Male Initiation in Papua New Guinea*. Berkeley: University of California Press, 1982.

– *Guardians of the Flutes: Idioms of Masculinity*. New York: McGraw-Hill, 1981.

– "Semen Transactions in Sambia Culture." In Gilbert H. Herdt, ed., *Ritualized Homosexuality in Melanesia*. Berkeley: University of California Press, 1984.

Herek, Gregory. "Beyond 'Homophobia'; A Social Psychological Perspective on Attitudes toward Lesbians and Gay Men." In John deCecco, ed., *Homophobia: An Overview*. New York: Haworth Press, 1984.

– "On Heterosexual Masculinity." *American Behavioral Scientist* 29 (1986): 563–77.

– "Social Science, Sexual Orientation and Military Personnel Policy." In Gregory Herek et al., *Out in Force: Sexual Orientation and the Military*. Chicago: University of Chicago Press, 1996.

Herman, Didi. *Rights of Passage: Struggles for Lesbian and Gay Legal Equality*. Toronto: University of Toronto Press, 1994.

Higgs, David, ed. *Queer Sites: Gay Urban Histories since 1600*. London: Routledge, 1999.

Hodges, Andrew, and David Hutter. *With Downcast Gays: Aspects of Homosexual Self-oppression*. Toronto: Pink Triangle Press, 1977.

Holmes, Richard. *Acts of War: The Behavior of Men in Battle*. New York: Free Press, 1985.

Humphries, Mary Ann. *My Country, My Right to Serve*. New York: HarperCollins, 1990.

Ihara, Saikuku. *The Great Mirror of Male Love*. Palo Alto: Stanford University, 1990.

Ingraham, L. *The Boys in the Barracks: Observations on American Military Life*. Philadelphia: ISHI, 1984.

Isherwood, Christopher. *Mr Norris Changes Trains*. London: Methuen, 1987.

Ives, Don. "The Compensation Principle and the Principle of Recognition for Service." In Peter M. Neary and J.L. Granatstein, eds, *The Veterans Charter and Post–World War II Canada*. Montreal & Kingston: McGill Queen's University Press, 1998.

Jagose, Annamarie. *Queer Theory: An Introduction*. New York: New York University Press, 1996.

Johnson, Charles Monroe. *Action with the Seaforths*. New York: Vantage Press, 1954.

Jones, Gwilym. *To the Green Fields Beyond: A Soldier's Story*. Burnstown, Ont.: General Store Publishing House, 1993.

Karst, K.L. "The Pursuit of Manhood and the Desegregation of the Armed Forces." *UCLA Law Review* 38 (1991): 499–581.

Katz, Jonathan Ned. *Gay American History: Lesbians and Gay Men in the U.S.A.* New York: Meridian, 1992.

– *The Invention of Heterosexuality*. New York: Dutton, 1995.

– *Love Stories: Sex between Men before Homosexuality*. Chicago: University of Chicago Press, 2002.

Kellett, Anthony. *Combat Motivation: The Behaviour of Soldiers in Battle*. Boston: Kluwer-Nijhoff, 1982.

Kennedy, Liz, and Madeline Davis. *Boots of Leather, Slippers of Gold: The History of a Lesbian Community*. New York: Routledge, 1993.

Keshen, Jeff. "Revisting Canada's Civilian Women during World War II." *Social History* 30, no. 60 (1997).

– "Wartime Jitters over Juveniles." In Jeff Keshen, ed., *Age of Contention: Readings in Canadian Social History, 1900–1945*. Toronto: Harcourt Brace and Company, 1997.

Kier, Elizabeth. "Homosexuals in the U.S. Military: Open Integration and Combat Effectiveness." *International Security* 23, no. 2 (1998).

Kinsey, Alfred. *Sexual Behaviour in the Human Male*. Philadelphia and London: W.B. Saunders Company, 1948.

Kinsman, Gary. " 'Character Weaknesses' and 'Fruit Machines': Towards an Analysis of the Anti-Homosexual Security Campaign in the Canadian Civil Service." *Labour/Le Travail* 35 (Spring 1995).

Kinsman, Gary. *The Regulation of Desire: Homo and Hetero Sexualities*. Montreal: Black Rose Books, 1996.

– and Patrizia Gentile. *'In the Interests of the State': The Anti-gay, Anti-lesbian National Security Campaign in Canada*. A Preliminary Research Report. Sudbury: Laurentian University, 1998.

Lamb, James B. *The Corvette Navy: True Stories from Canada's Atlantic War*. Toronto: Macmillan of Canada, 1977.

LePan, Douglas. *The Deserter*. Toronto: McClelland and Stewart, 1964.

Lester, David. *Why People Kill Themselves: A 1990s Summary of Research Findings on Suicidal Behavior*. Springfield, Ill.: Charles C. Thomas, 1992.

Le Vay, Simon. *Queer Science: The Use and Abuse of Research into Homosexuality*. Cambridge: MIT Press, 1996.

Lévesque, Andrée. "Deviants Anonymous: Single Mothers at the Hôpital de la Miséricorde in Montreal, 1929–1939." In Veronica Strong-Boag and Anita Fellman, eds, *Rethinking Canada: The Promise of Women's History*. Toronto: Oxford University Press, 1997.

Lewes, Kenneth. *The Psychoanalytic Theory of Male Homosexuality*. New York: Simon and Schuster, 1988.

Little, Margaret. "Claiming a Unique Place: The Introduction of Mothers' Pensions in British Columbia." In Veronica Strong-Boag and Anita Fellman, eds, *Rethinking Canada: The Promise of Women's History*. Toronto: Oxford University Press, 1997.

Lucas, Laddie. *Malta: The Thorn in Rommel's Side: Six Months That Turned the War*. London: Penguin Books, 1993.

MacCoun, Robert J. "Sexual Orientation and Military Cohesion: A Critical Review of the Evidence." In Gregory M. Herek et al., *Out in Force: Sexual Orientation and the Military*. Chicago: University of Chicago Press, 1996.

Macpherson, Ken, and Marc Milner. *Corvettes of the Royal Canadian Navy, 1939–1945*. St Catharines: Vanwell Publishing, 1993.

Maynard, Steven. " 'Horrible Temptations': Sex, Men, and Working-Class Male Youth in Urban Ontario, 1890–1935." *Canadian Historical Review* 78, no. 2 (June 1997).

- "On the Case of the Case: The Emergence of the Homosexual as a Case History in Early Twentieth-Century Ontario." In Franca Iacovetta and Wendy Mitchinson, eds, *On the Case: Explorations in Social History.* Toronto: University of Toronto Press, 1998.
- "Rough Work and Rugged Men: The Social Construction of Masculinity in Working-Class History." *Labour/Le Travail* 23 (1989).
- "Through a Hole in the Lavatory Wall: Homosexual Subcultures, Police Surveillance and the Dialectics of Discovery, Toronto, 1890–1930." *Journal of the History of Sexuality* 5, no. 2 (1994).

McDonald, LCol R.A. "The Legal Branch Law Firm of the Canadian Forces." *Canadian Forces JAG Journal* 2 (1987).
- "The Trail of Discipline: The Historical Roots of Canadian Military Law." *Canadian Forces JAG Journal* 1 (1985).

McIntosh, Mary. "The Homosexual Role." *Social Problems* 16, no. 2 (1968).

McLaren, Angus, and Arlene Tigar McLaren. *The Bedroom and the State: The Changing Practices and Politics of Contraception and Birth Control in Canada, 1880–1930.* Toronto: McClelland and Stewart, 1986.

McLeod, Donald. *Lesbian and Gay Liberation in Canada: A Selected Annotated Chronology, 1964–1975.* Toronto: ECW Press/Homewood Books, 1996.

Madsen, Chris. *Another Kind of Justice: Canadian Military Law from Confederation to Somalia.* Vancouver: University of British Columbia Press, 1999.

Manning, Frederick. "Morale, Cohesion and Esprit de Corps." In Reuven Gal and David Mangelsdorff, eds, *Handbook of Military Psychology.* New York: John Wiley and Sons, 1991.

Marshall, John. "Pansies, Perverts and Macho Men: Changing Conceptions of Male Homosexuality." In Kenneth Plummer, ed., *The Making of the Modern Homosexual.* New Jersey: Barnes & Noble Books, 1981.

Marshall, S.L.A. *Men against Fire: The Problem of Combat Command in Future War.* New York: William Morrow & Company, 1947.

Messner, Michael. "The Meaning of Success: The Athletic Development and the Meaning of Male Identity." In Harry Brod, ed., *The Making of Masculinities: The New Men's Studies.* New York: Routledge, 1987.

Meyer, Leisa D. *Creating G.I. Jane: Sexuality and Power in the Women's Army Corps during World War II.* New York: Columbia University Press, 1996.

Milner, Marc. *North Atlantic Run: The Royal Canadian Navy and the Battle for the Convoys.* Toronto: University of Toronto Press, 1985.

Mitchell, Brian. *Weak Link: The Feminization of the American Military.* Washington, D.C.: Regnery Gateway, 1989.

Moran, Leslie J. *The Homosexual(ity) of Law.* London: Routledge, 1996.

– " 'Oscar Wilde': Law, Power and the Proper Name." In Leslie Moran et al., eds, *Legal Queeries: Lesbian, Gay and Transgender Legal Studies*. London: Cassell, 1998.

Morris, Peter. *The National Film Board of Canada: The War Years*. Ottawa: Canadian Film Institute, 1965.

Morrison, Alex, and Ted Slaney. *The Breed of Manly Men: The History of the Cape Breton Highlanders*. Toronto: Canadian Institute of Strategic Studies, 1994.

Mort, Frank. *Dangerous Sexualities: Medico-Moral Politics in England since 1830*. London: Routledge and Kegan Paul, 1987.

Morton, Desmond. *Canada and War: A Military and Political History*. Toronto: Butterworths, 1981.

Mowat, Farley. *And No Birds Sang*. Toronto: McClelland-Bantam, 1979.

Mullen, Brian, and Carolyn Copper. "The Relationship between Group Cohesiveness and Performance: An Integration." *Psychological Bulletin* 115, no. 2 (1994): 210–27.

Murphy, Timothy. *Gay Science: The Ethics of Sexual Orientation Research*. New York: Columbia University Press, 1997.

Murray, Stephen O. *Homosexualities*. Chicago: University of Chicago Press, 2000.

National Defence Research Institute. *Sexual Orientation and U.S. Miltiary Presonnel Policy: Options and Assessment*. Santa Monica: RAND, 1993.

Nelson, Joyce. *The Colonized Eye: Rethinking the Grierson Legend*. Toronto: Between the Lines, 1988.

Newton, Esther. *Cherry Grove, Fire Island: Sixty Years in America's First Gay and Lesbian Town*. Boston: Beacon Press, 1993.

Newton, Janice. *The Feminist Challenge to the Canadian Left 1900–1918*. Montreal & Kingston: McGill-Queen's University Press, 1995.

Ober, Josiah. "The Evil Empire." *Quarterly Journal of Military History* 10, no. 4 (1998).

O'Connor, William. "Some Notes on Suicide." *British Journal of Medical Psychology* 21, no. 3 (1948).

Oosterhuis, Henry. *Stepchildren of Nature: Krafft-Ebing, Psychiatry, and the Making of Sexual Identity*. Chicago: University of Chicago Press, 2000.

Opdyke, Irene Gut. *In My Hands: Memories of a Holocaust Rescuer*. New York: Alfred A. Knopf, 1999.

Owram, Doug. *The Government Generation: Canadian Intellectuals and the State, 1900–1945*. Toronto: University of Toronto Press, 1986.

Park, Rosemary. "Opening the Canadian Forces to Gays and Lesbians: An Inevitable Decision but Improbable Reconfiguration." In Wilbur Scott and Sandra Stanley, eds, *Gays and Lesbians in the Military: Issues, Concerns and Contrasts*. New York: Aldine de Gruyter, 1994.

Pearce, Donald. *Journal of a War: Northwest Europe 1944–1945.* Toronto: Macmillan of Canada, 1965.

Pharr, Suzanne. *Homophobia: A Weapon of Sexism.* Inverness, Calif.: Chardon Press, 1988.

Pierson, Ruth Roach. *"They're still Women after all" : The Second World War and Canadian Womanhood.* Toronto: McClelland and Stewart, 1986.

Pronger, Brian. *The Arena of Masculinity: Sports, Homosexuality and the Meaning of Sex.* Toronto: Summerhill Press, 1990.

Public General Statutes. London: George Edward Eyre and William Spottiswoods, 1866.

Pugsley, William. *Saints, Devils and Ordinary Seamen: Life on the Royal Canadian Navy's Lower Deck.* Toronto: Collins, 1946.

Ramirez, Bruno. *On the Move: French-Canadian and Italian Migrants in the North Atlantic Economy, 1860–1914.* Toronto: University of Toronto Press, 1990.

Rich, Adrienne. "Compulsory Heterosexuality and Lesbian Existence." *Signs* 5, no. 4 (1980): 631-60.

Rich, Charles, et al. "San Diego Suicide Study: Comparison of Gay to Straight Males." *Suicide and Life-Threatening Behavior.* 16, no. 4 (1986).

Rimmerman, Craig A., ed. *Gay Rights, Military Wrongs: Political Perspectives on Lesbians and Gays in the Military.* New York and London: Garland Publishing, 1996.

Ritchie, Charles. *An Appetite for Life, 1924–1927.* Toronto: Macmillan of Canada, 1977.

– *My Grandfather's House.* Toronto: Macmillan of Canada, 1987.

– *The Siren Years, 1937–45.* Toronto: Macmillan of Canada, 1987.

Roberts, Robert. *The Classic Slum: Salford Life in the First Quarter of the Century.* London: Penguin Books, 1991.

Robinson, Daniel, and David Kimmel. "The Queer Career of Homosexual Vetting in Cold War Canada." *Canadian Historical Review.* 75, no. 3 (1994).

Rocke, M. *Forbidden Friendships: Homosexuality and Male Culture in Renaissance Florence.* New York: Oxford Unniversity Press, 1996.

Ross, Alexander. *Slow March to a Regiment.* St Catharines: Vanwell Publishing, 1992.

Rossignol, M. "National Defence Act: Reform of the Military Justice System." Research Branch, Library of Parliament.

Round, Jeffrey. "Douglas Valentine LePan." *Xtra*, 31 December 1998.

Rowbotham, Sheila, and Jeffrey Weeks. *Socialism and the New Life: The Personal and Sexual Politics of Havelock Ellis and Edward Carpenter.* London: Pluto Press, 1977.

Rowe, Michael. "Another Soldier's Story." *Fab* 9 (1998).

Rubin, Gayle. "Thinking Sex: Notes for a Radical Theory of the Politics of Sexuality." In Carole S. Vance, ed., *Pleasure and Danger: Exploring Female Sexuality.* London: Routledge and Kegan Paul, 1984.

Rupp, Leila J. "Toward a Global History of Same-Sex Sexuality." *Journal of the History of Sexuality* 10, no. 2 (2000).

Russell, Peter. "The Political Purposes of the Canadian Charter of Rights and Freedoms." *Canadian Bar Review* 61 (1983).

Sabo, D. "Sport Patriarchy and Male Identity: New Questions about Men and Sports." *Arena Review* 9, no. 2 (1985).

St Denis, Captain Thomas. "The Dangerous Appeal of the Warrior." *Canadian Military Journal,* Summer 2001.

Sarbin, Theodore. "The Deconstruction of Stereotypes: Homosexuals and Military Policy." In Gregory M. Herek et al., *Out in Force: Sexual Orientation and the Military.* Chicago: University of Chicago Press, 1996.

Saunders, Judith, and S. Valente. "Suicide Risk among Gay Men and Lesbians: A Review." *Death Studies* 11 (1983).

Sawatsky, John. *Men in the Shadows.* Toronto: Doubleday Canada, 1980.

Scott, Wilbur, and Sandra Stanley, eds, *Gays and Lesbians in the Military: Issues, Concerns and Contrasts.* New York: Aldine de Gruyter, 1994.

Sedgwick, Eve Kosofsky. *Between Men: English Literature and Male Homosexual Desire.* New York: Columbia University Press, 1985.

Sherrill, Robert. *Military Justice Is to Justice as Military Music Is to Music.* New York: Harper & Row, 1969.

Shewell, Hugh. "Jules Sioui and Indian Political Radicalism in Canada, 1943–1944." *Journal of Canadian Studies* 34, no. 3 (1999).

Shilts, Randy. *Conduct Unbecoming: Gays and Lesbians in the U.S. Military.* New York: St Martin's Press, 1993.

Sinfield, A. *The Wilde Century: Effeminacy, Oscar Wilde and the Queer Moment.* London: Cassell, 1994.

Sloan, John. *Oscar Wilde.* Oxford: Oxford University Press, 2003.

Smith, Miriam Catherine. *Lesbian and Gay Rights in Canada: Social Movements and Equality-Seeking, 1971–1995.* Toronto: University of Toronto Press, 1999.

Snell, James G. *In the Shadow of the Law: Divorce in Canada, 1900–1939.* Toronto: University of Toronto Press, 1991.

Socknat, Thomas. *Witness against War: Pacifism in Canada.* Toronto: University of Toronto Press, 1987.

Spender, Stephen. *The Temple.* London: Faber and Faber, 1981.

Stacey, C.P. *Arms, Men and Government: The War Policies of Canada 1939–1945.* Ottawa: Queen's Printer, 1970.

– *Six Years of War*. Ottawa: Edmond Cloutier, 1955.

– and Barbara Wilson. *The Half-Million: The Canadians in Britain, 1939–1946*. Toronto: University of Toronto Press, 1987.

Stanley, G.E.F. *Canada's Soldiers: The Military History of an Unmilitary People*. Toronto: Macmillan of Canada, 1960.

Steakley, James D. *The Homosexual Emancipation Movement in Germany*. New York: Arno, 1975.

– *The Writings of Dr. Magnus Hirschfeld: A Bibliography*. Toronto: Canadian Gay Archives, 1985.

Steihm, Judith. *Arms and the Enlisted Woman*. Philadelphia: Temple University Press, 1989.

Stein, Edward. *The Mismeasure of Desire: The Science, Theory, and Ethics of Sexual Orientation*. New York: Oxford University Press, 1999.

Stein, Mark. *The City of Brotherly and Sisterly Love: Lesbian and Gay Philadelphia*. Chicago: University of Chicago Press, 2000.

Strange, Carolyn. "Wounded Womanhood and Dead Men." In Franca Iacovetta and Mariana Valverde, eds, *Gender Conflicts: New Essays in Women's History*. Toronto: University of Toronto Press, 1992.

Strong-Boag, Veronica. "Home Dreams: Women and the Suburban Experiment in Canada, 1945–1960." *Canadian Historical Review* 72, no. 4 (1991).

Struthers, James. *No Fault of Their Own: Unemployment and the Canadian Welfare State, 1914–1941*. Toronto: University of Toronto Press, 1994.

Stryker, S., and J. van Buskirk. *Gay by the Bay: A History of Queer Culture in the San Francisco Bay Area*. San Francisco: Chronicle Books, 1996.

Stychin, Carl, and Didi Herman. *Sexuality in the Legal Arena*. London: Athlone Press, 2000.

Taylor, Scott, and Brian Nolan. *Tarnished Brass: Crime and Corruption in the Canadian Military*. Toronto: Lester Publishing, 1996.

Terry, Jennifer. *An American Obsession: Science, Medicine, and Homosexuality in Modern Society*. Chicago and London: University of Chicago Press, 1999.

Theodore, Peter, and Susan Basow. "Heterosexual Masculinity and Homophobia: A Reaction to the Self?" *Journal of Homosexuality* 40, no. 2 (2000).

Thomas, Patricia J., and Marie D. Thomas. "Integration of Women in the Military: Parallels to the Progress of Homosexuals?" In Gregory Herek et al., *Out in Force: Sexual Orientation and the Military*. Chicago: University of Chicago Press, 1996.

Thompson, E.P. *The Making of the English Working Class*. Harmondsworth: Pelican Books, 1968.

Tobin, James. *Ernie Pyle's War*. New York: Free Press, 1997.

Tooley, Robert. "Appearance or Reality? Variations in Infantry Courts Martial: 1st Canadian Infantry Division 1940–1945." *Canadian Defence Quarterly* 22, nos 2 and 3 (1992).

Torgovnick, Maianna. *Gone Primitive: Savage Intellects, Modern Lives.* Chicago: University of Chicago Press, 1990.

Townsend, R.C. "The Competitive Male as Loser." In D. Sabo and R. Runfola, eds, *Jock: Sports and Male Identity.* Englewood Cliffs, N.J.: Prentice-Hall, 1980.

Trevelyan, Raleigh. *Rome '44: The Battle for the Eternal City.* London: Hodder and Stoughton, 1983.

Trumbach, Randolf. "London." In David Higgs, ed., *Queer Sites: Gay Urban Histories since 1600.* London: Routledge, 1999.

– *Sex and the Gender Revolution: Heterosexuality and the Third Gender in Enlightenment England.* Chicago: University of Chicago Press, 1998.

Ulmer, Sidney. *Military Justice and the Right to Counsel.* Lexington: University Press of Kentucky, 1970.

Vance, Jonathan. *Death So Noble: Memory, Meaning and the First World War.* Vancouver: University of British Columbia Press, 1997.

– *Objects of Concern: Canadian Prisoners of War through the Twentieth Century.* Vancouver: University of British Columbia Press, 1994.

Van Dantzig, Rudi. *For a Lost Soldier.* London: Bodley Head, 1991.

Velmans, Edith. *Edith's Story: The True Story of a Young Girl's Courage and Survival during World War II.* New York: Bantam, 2001.

Walkowitz, Judith. *The City of Dreadful Delights.* Chicago: University of Chicago Press, 1992.

The War Office. *Manual of Military Law.* London: His Majesty's Stationery Office, 1939.

Warner, Michael, ed. *Fear of a Queer Planet: Queer Politics and Social Theory.* Minneapolis and London: University of Minnesota Press, 1993.

Watson, Bruce. *When Soldiers Quit: Studies in Military Disintegration.* Westport, Conn.: Greenwood Publishing Group, 1997.

Weaver, John C. *Crimes, Constables and Courts: Order and Transgression in a Canadian City, 1816–1970.* Montreal & Kingston: McGill-Queen's University Press, 1995.

Webber, Jeremy. "The Malaise of Compulsory Conciliation: Strike Prevention in Canada during World War II. In Bryan Palmer, ed., *The Character of Class Struggle: Essays in Canadian Working-Class History, 1850–1985.* Toronto: McClelland and Stewart, 1986.

Weeks, Jeffrey. *Coming Out: Homosexual Politics in Britain, from the Nineteenth Century to the Present.* London: Quartet Books, 1977.

– *Sex, Politics and Society: The Regulation of Sexuality since 1900*. London: Longman, 1981.

– *Sexuality and Its Discontents: Meanings, Myths and Modern Sexualities*. London: Routledge, 1985.

Weinberg, Martin, and Colin Williams. *Homosexuals and the Military: A Study of Less than Honorable Discharges*. New York: Harper & Row, 1971.

Wellman, Marvin, and J.F. Simpson. "Psychiatric Casualties in the (RCN)." *American Journal of Psychiatry* 101 (1944–45).

Werlinder, Henry. *Psychopathy: A History of the Concepts*. Stockholm: Uppsala, 1978.

Westbrook, Stephen. "The Potential for Military Disintegration." In Sam Sakesian, ed., *Combat Effectiveness: Cohesion, Stress and the Volunteer Military*. Beverly Hills: Sage Publications, 1980.

Willett, T.C. *A Heritage at Risk: The Canadian Militia as a Social Institution*. Boulder, Colo: Westview, 1989.

Winslow, Donna. "Rites of Passage and Group Bonding in the Canadian Airborne." *Armed Forces and Society* 25, no. 3 (1999).

Wolinsky, Marc, and Kenneth Sherrill, eds. *Gays and the Military: Joseph Steffan versus the United States*. Princeton: Princeton University Press, 1993.

Wooley, H. *No Time Off for Good Behaviour*. Burnstown, Ont: General Store Publishing House, 1990.

INDEX